Cosmopolitics

Cultural Politics

A series from the Social Text Collective

Aimed at a broad interdisciplinary audience, these volumes seek to intervene in debates about the political direction of current theory and practice by combining contemporary analysis with a more traditional sense of historical and socioeconomic evaluation.

Pheng Cheah

Bruce Robbins

editors

A Cultural

Politics Book

for the Social

Text Collective

Cosmopolitics

Thinking and
Feeling beyond
the Nation

Cultural Politics / Volume 14

University of Minnesota Press

Minneapolis ▸ London

Published by the University of Minnesota Press
111 Third Avenue South, Suite 290
Minneapolis, MN 55401-2520
http: //www.upress.umn.edu

Printed in the United States of America on acid-free paper

Library of Congress Cataloging-in-Publication Data

Cosmopolitics : thinking and feeling beyond the nation / Pheng Cheah
 and Bruce Robbins, editors.
    p.   cm. — (Cultural politics ; 14)
    "A cultural politics book for the Social Text Collective."
    Includes index.
    ISBN 0-8166-3067-4 (hc : alk. paper). — ISBN 0-8166-3068-2 (pb : alk. paper)
    1. Internationalism.   I. Cheah, Pheng.   II. Robbins, Bruce.
III. Social Text Collective.   IV. Series: Cultural politics
(Minneapolis, Minn.) ; v. 14.
JC362.C665   1998
327.1'7—dc21   97-43051

The University of Minnesota is an equal-opportunity educator and employer.

10 09 08 07 06 05 04 03 02 01 00 99 98   10 9 8 7 6 5 4 3 2 1

Contents

Part III. Toward a Cosmopolitan Cultural Studies

Part IV. Responses

Preface

The making of this book was itself a cosmopolitan enterprise. Like many of the contributors, we come from different nations as well as different disciplinary formations. We were constantly reminded that different vocabularies jostled for possession of our common object. Even the book's title remained in play right up to the end: Should we follow customary usage and refer to cosmopolitanism, or should we give up on that tarnished term and redirect attention instead to the field of the cosmopolitical? We would like to think that the resulting lack of a single unified position, along with the titular neologism that marks it, is more of an advantage for the book than not. In any case, rather than highlight our many common principles and concerns at the expense of the (perhaps no more interesting) differences between us, along with differences in our own developing ideas, we have elected to include two separate introductions as well as the earlier essays that initially brought us together in this project.

Introduction Part I:
Actually Existing Cosmopolitanism

Bruce Robbins

Something has happened to cosmopolitanism. It has a new cast of characters. In the past the term has been applied, often venomously, "to Christians, aristocrats, merchants, Jews, homosexuals, and intellectuals."[1] Now it
is attributed, more charitably, to North Atlantic merchant sailors, Caribbean
au pairs in the United States, Egyptian guest workers in Iraq, Japanese
women who take *gaijin* lovers.[2] James Clifford proposes that the "status of
travelers" should at long last be accorded to the "host of servants, helpers,
companions, guides, bearers, etc." who made Victorian travel possible, and
who had their own "specific cosmopolitan viewpoints."[3]

This change in personnel implies a change in definition. Understood as a
fundamental devotion to the interests of humanity as a whole, cosmopolitanism has often seemed to claim universality by virtue of its independence,
its detachment from the bonds, commitments, and affiliations that constrain
ordinary nation-bound lives. It has seemed to be a luxuriously free-floating
view from above. But many voices now insist, with Paul Rabinow, that the
term should be extended to transnational experiences that are particular
rather than universal and that are unprivileged—indeed, often coerced. Cosmopolitanism should be defined, Rabinow writes, as "an ethos of macro-interdependencies, with an acute consciousness (often forced upon people) of
the inescapabilities and particularities of places, characters, historical trajectories, and fates."[4] Following this lead, Arjun Appadurai calls for anthropology to "study the cosmopolitan (Rabinow 1986) cultural forms of the contemporary world without logically or chronologically presupposing either the
authority of the Western experience or the models derived from that experience."[5] Benita Parry agrees that "the 'global flows' of transnational cultural
traffic" have produced "an emergent *postcolonial* cosmopolitanism."[6] Arnold
Krupat places the culture of Native Americans within "the project of a cosmopolitan literature," which is "the projection of heterodoxy not to the level of
the universal, but, rather, to the level of the 'inter-national.'"[7] David Hollinger and Mitchell Cohen both describe their preferred form of cosmopolitanism as "rooted"; Homi Bhabha qualifies his as "vernacular."[8] The list could
include the specifically Asian cosmopolitanisms discussed in this volume by
Aihwa Ong and Louisa Schein as well as the specifically African cosmopolitanisms discussed by Kwame Anthony Appiah and Scott Malcomson.[9]

Usages like these mark a change the consequences of which seem both significant enough and ambiguous enough to warrant further inquiry. The "very old ideal of the cosmopolitan," in Martha Nussbaum's words, referred to "the person whose allegiance is to the worldwide community of human beings."[10] According to this ideal, there could be only one cosmopolitanism, for there is only one "worldwide community of human beings." Kant's dream of a cosmopolitan point of view leading to perpetual peace could thus be invoked only as a defiant reassertion of Greek or Enlightenment values, of (European) philosophical universalism. In this sense the term seemed to offer a clear-cut contrast to nationalism.

Now, to judge from the new usages, that commonsensical opposition is no longer self-evident. Like nations, cosmopolitanisms are now plural and particular. Like nations, they are both European and non-European, and they are weak and underdeveloped as well as strong and privileged. And again like the nation, cosmopolitanism is *there*—not merely an abstract ideal, like loving one's neighbor as oneself, but habits of thought and feeling that have already shaped and been shaped by particular collectivities, that are socially and geographically situated, hence both limited and empowered. Difficult as it may be to make a plural for "cosmos," it is now assumed more and more that worlds, like nations, come in different sizes and styles. Like nations, worlds too are "imagined."[11] For better or worse, there is a growing consensus that cosmopolitanism sometimes works together with nationalism rather than in opposition to it. It is thus less clear what cosmopolitanism *is* opposed to, or what its value is supposed to be.

Situating cosmopolitanism means taking a risk. Until now, only the enemies of cosmopolitanism have been eager to situate it. Cosmopolitanism's advocates, on the other hand, have most often felt obliged to keep it unlocated in order to preserve its sharp critical edge, as well as its privileges. Given what the clash of embodied interests has made of the world, there is always some seductiveness in calls for transnational altruism, however disembodied and unworldly they may sound. Recently, moreover, philosophical arguments in favor of universalism have returned with a vengeance, bringing with them renewed advocacy of cosmopolitanism in the older sense. But most of the voices gathered here take as their risky and perplexing occasion what contributor Scott Malcomson calls "actually existing" cosmopolitanism. They take off from a double assumption: first, that any cosmopolitanism's normative or idealizing power must acknowledge the actual historical and geographic contexts from which it emerges, and, second, that such an acknowledgment need not prove fatal. Or, to put it less enthusiastically, the authors of these essays concede that cosmopolitanism is located and embodied, and they go on to measure such critical, normative power as may remain to it. Exploring a range of diverse cosmopolitanisms, they participate in and comment on the term's scaling down, its pluralizing and particularizing. As Amanda Anderson notes, the result of this subphilosophical turn is both more modest and more worldly.

Another way to put the contrast is to say that instead of an ideal of detachment, actually existing cosmopolitanism is a reality of (re)attachment, multiple attachment, or attachment at a distance. In a discussion of Buddhist monks and merchants, the geographer Yi-Fu Tuan distinguishes in this way between cosmopolitans, "basically indifferent to where they lived," and cosmopolites, "habitants of a vast universe."[12] It is the latter, a sense of positive if complex and multiple belonging, that Tuan endorses. But perhaps there is nothing so simple as a choice here. Habitation that is complex and multiple is already shot through with unavoidable distances and indifferences, with comparison and critique; yet it does not thereby cease to be a mode of belonging.

To embrace this style of residence on earth (Pablo Neruda's phrase) means repudiating the romantic localism of a certain portion of the left, which feels it must counter capitalist globalization with a strongly rooted and exclusive sort of belonging. In a feature in *The Nation* devoted to "the dark side of globalization," we read, for example, "The myth of globalization is that we no longer need to be connected to a place on the earth."[13] The devastation covered over by complacent talk of globalization is of course very real. But precisely *because* it is real, we cannot be content to set against it only the childish reassurance of belonging to "a" place. The indefinite article is insufficient. Yes, we are connected to the earth—but not to "a" place on it, simple and self-evident as the surroundings we see when we open our eyes. We are connected to all sorts of places, causally if not always consciously, including many that we have never traveled to, that we have perhaps only seen on television—including the place where the television itself was manufactured. It is frightening to think how little progress has been made in turning invisibly determining and often exploitative connections into conscious and self-critical ones, how far we remain from mastering the sorts of allegiance, ethics, and action that might go with our complex and multiple belonging. But this is work that has to be done. We should not and perhaps cannot accept the old cosmopolitan ideal of transcending the distinction between strangers and friends. Still, we all depend on what Blanche DuBois calls the kindness of strangers. Less than kin or friendship but a good deal more than polite or innocent nonrelation, designating a field rather than an identity, this phrase is one way of describing the test and invitation offered by cosmopolitics.[14]

The most general form of the case against cosmopolitanism on the left is the assumption that to pass outside the borders of one's nation, whether by physical travel or merely by thoughts and feelings entertained while one stays at home, is to wallow in a privileged and irresponsible detachment. What is assumed is in fact a chain of successive detachments: from true feeling, hence from the responsibility that engages a whole person, not a sometime spectator; from responsibility, hence from the constituency to which one would be responsible; from constituency, hence from significant political action.[15] The cosmopolitan is held to be incapable of participating in the making of history, doomed to the mere aesthetic spectatorship that he or she is also held secretly to prefer. For a tradition that would include Gramsci and Fanon, though in each case with interesting complications, cosmopolitan identification with the human race serves as the thin, abstract, undesirable antithesis to a red-blooded, politically engaged nationalism.[16] The common premise is, as Gopal Balakrishnan remarks of Benedict Anderson, "that the springs of political action are ultimately rooted in the pathos of national membership."[17] Indeed, Anderson shows how the very concept of politics develops in relation to the nation-state. Can a primary concern with interests not defined by or restricted to the nation-state even count as political?

It is perhaps a coincidence that Anderson and Richard Rorty, both eloquent defenders of nationalism, have each represented the absence of genuine feeling or acting on a transnational scale as the absence of anything outside the nation that is worth dying for. The nation takes the place of religion, becoming "the most universally legitimate value in the political life of our time," Anderson says, because people are willing to die for it. But would anyone make the ultimate sacrifice on behalf of a supranational institution? "Who," he asks pointedly, "will willingly die for Comecon or the EEC?"[18] In a similar vein, Rorty argues that under the Nazis, those who risked their lives to save Jews did so less because they considered the Jews fellow human beings than because, together with the particular Jews involved, they belonged to some smaller social grouping, the same city or neighborhood or profession. The terms of rescue are always more parochial than "human being"; they work only within the bounds of "ethnocentrism." Common humanity is too weak a force to generate sufficient solidarity.[19]

It is not helpful simply to assert the contrary, as cosmopolitans of the older school do. Martha Nussbaum argues in *For Love of Country*, for example, that there is indeed powerful feeling at the philosophical level of humanity. For Norman Geras, those who rescued Jews from the Nazis, thereby putting their own lives in grave danger, did so precisely because they saw the Jews as fellow human beings. Maria Langthaler hid two Jewish escapees from nearby Mauthausen in February 1945 because, she said, "The Lord God is for the whole world, not only for the Germans."[20] The problem is the disparity between the few who did so and the many who did not. Why were there so few? When does the exception become a statistically significant rule? How do we get from few to many?

The abstract category of the human seems less pertinent to these questions than the messy, compromised particularity of Langthaler's specifically *Christian* cosmopolitanism or, to mention Europe's more recent genocide, the pan-Islamic cosmopolitanism that came to the aid of the Bosnians when the Christian or secular West turned its back and went about its business. Again, in recent California disputes about Proposition 187, which denies rights to undocumented immigrants, Linda S. Bosniak notes "the near-complete omission from the public debate of one particular opposing argument which might have seemed, in theory, an obvious one to make; this is the argument that Prop. 187 should be rejected on the grounds that its treatment of undocumented aliens is unjust" to the aliens themselves. The one major exception, Bosniak declares, was church-based organizations.[21] Adding to the usual racism argument (that "United States citizens or lawful permanent residents of color would be either maliciously or mistakenly ensnared by the initiative's provisions"),[22] aimed at "not the undocumented immigrants themselves but a class of nationals" who would be collaterally harmed, they and they alone refused to accept "the national community as the predominant community of normative concern."[23] Anyone familiar with solidarity movements on behalf of Latin American victims of U.S. Cold War policy will recognize the specific church-based cosmopolitanism at work here.

Geras argues more convincingly against the assumption that solidarity must somehow stop short at one's national borders:

> You either can identify, despite the size of this "community," with fellow Americans plus whoever; in which case you can identify with humanity also. Or else, for reasons of size, you cannot identify with humanity, and then nor can you with Americans plus whoever. It is just not credible that the significant threshold in this matter, where compassion and solicitude will go no further, lies somewhere beyond several hundred million people.[24]

This is both right and wrong. It is right in that if you can say yes to the nation, you can also say yes to units larger than the nation. If the problem is merely size, and not a difference in kind, then why not? If cosmopolitanism were really too big, then the nation would be too big as well.

But Geras is wrong, I think, in that the larger unit need not be "humanity" in the abstract.[25] The willingness to consider the well-being of people who do not belong to the same nation as you is not, in other words, something that is mysteriously pregiven by the simple fact of belonging to the human species. Larger loyalties can either be there or not be there. They have to be built up laboriously out of the imperfect historical materials—churches and mosques, commercial interests and immigrant diasporas, sentimentality about hungry children and technorapture over digitalized communication—that are already at hand. They do not stand outside history like an ultimate court of appeal. As Rorty argues in his contribution to this volume, "We cannot resolve conflicting loyalties by turning away from them all toward something categorically distinct from loyalty: the universal moral obligation to act justly." There is only a scale of loyalties, and a more or less well-founded hope that "what makes you loyal to a smaller group may give you reason to cooperate in constructing a larger group, a group to which you may in time become equally loyal, or perhaps even more loyal."

In short, Rorty's view of solidarity is not finally ethnocentric, though that is what he calls it. It is compatible with cosmopolitanism in the particular or actually existing sense. The same is true of Benedict Anderson's view of nationalism. For Anderson, too, there seems to be no legitimate feeling outside the nation. But this does not in fact follow from his premises. Feelings are produced within a bounded administrative unit on a national scale, but in Anderson's argument it is not the bounds themselves that do the producing. And the technologies and institutions that do produce national feeling now exist massively and increasingly on a transnational scale. Anderson's linking of nationalism to "print-capitalism" in general and to the newspaper in particular invites comparison with the description of the press that ends Ferdinand Tönnies's famous *Gemeinschaft und Gesellschaft* (1887). Tönnies describes the press as the "real instrument" of "public opinion," possessing a "universal power" that

> is comparable and, in some respects, superior to the material power that the
> states possess through their armies, their treasuries, and their bureaucratic
> civil service. Unlike those, the press is not confined within natural borders,
> but, in its tendencies and potentialities, it is definitely international, thus
> comparable to the power of a temporary or permanent alliance of states. It
> can, therefore, be conceived as its ultimate aim to abolish the multiplicity of
> states and substitute for it a single world republic, coextensive with the

world market, and which would be ruled by thinkers, scholars, and writers who could dispense with means of coercion other than those of a psychological nature.[26]

If Anderson sees the press as quintessentially nationalist, Tönnies sees it as quintessentially—if also nightmarishly—cosmopolitan. The same excess of human relations beyond "face-to-face contact" is described by one as the very essence of the nation, by the other as the threat of its attenuation and collapse. One writer's warm, emotional nationalism is the other's chilly, individualistic cosmopolitanism. But as their common attention to the press suggests, the chill that Tönnies feels outside the nation could as well be recognized within it, and the warmth that Anderson feels inside the nation can just as well be extended beyond it. Anderson "splits off the nationalizing effect of the print technology," Richard Maxwell observes, "from the capitalist structure in which it arose and to which it has been tied ever since." As a result, "we are left to fend for ourselves if we want to understand more about the tension inherent in a technology that at once invites communicative action to be national while its owners are searching for ways to make it international."[27] If people can get as emotional as Anderson says they do about relations with fellow nationals they never see face-to-face, then now that print-capitalism has become electronic- and digital-capitalism, and now that this system is so clearly transnational, it would be strange if people did *not* get emotional in much the same way, if not necessarily to the same degree, about others who are *not* fellow nationals, people bound to them by some transnational sort of fellowship. One need go no farther in search of evidence, as Balakrishnan remarks, than Anderson's own example, religion—certainly considered worth dying for by many, yet also at least as cosmopolitan as it is national.[28]

This is why, according to Arjun Appadurai, "it may be time to rethink monopatriotism, patriotism directed exclusively to the hyphen between nation and state, and to allow the material problems we face—the deficit, the environment, abortion, race, drugs, and jobs—to define those social groups and ideas for which we would be willing to live, and die. . . . Some of us may still want to live—and die—for the United States. But many of these new sovereignties are inherently postnational."[29]

Anderson's "print-capitalism" helps explain the less-than-ideal, not entirely enlightened historical process by which loyalties are in fact stretched both within the nation *and* beyond it, thus eliciting emotional solidarities outside the nation that are continuous with the emotions elicited in the process of nation building. It also helps explain why, though cosmopolitanism is clearly an outgrowth or ideological reflection of global capitalism, it remains possible to speak (in Rabinow's phrase) of "*critical* cosmopolitanism."[30] Anticosmopolitans frequently assume that capitalism is simply a destroyer of collectivities, yet nothing could be more counterintuitive. After all, why shouldn't the profit motive lead corporations to distinguish and nourish collective identities that they can then target and sell to, even identities that the buyers may go on to feel worthy of the ultimate sacrifice? This is one of the implications of Anderson's account of nationalism. "Instead of capitalism, the great profaner of all that is sacred," Balakrishnan comments, Anderson's argument turns the compound "print-capitalism" into "the matrix and crucible of its secular reconstitution." Just as it produced the nation (and the proletariat), so capitalism nurtures what Balakrishnan calls "vernacular sociabilit[ies]" that, like nationalism itself, have the potential to inflect, constrain, or even oppose it.[31] Capital may be cosmopolitan, but that does not make cosmopolitanism into an apology for capitalism.

Instead of assuming that capitalism's insatiable drive to occupy every corner of the globe has led to the imminent collapse of the nation-state, we should consider how tied to particular places capitalism remains and how strong (if unequal) an interest it has in propping up the nation-state. According to Michael Mann, the theory of "breathless transnationalism" simply does not square with the facts: "It is doubtful whether, in many respects, capitalism is more transnational than it was before 1914, except for the special case of the increasing integration of the European Union. This is hardly an economic base on which to ground any grand generalizing theories of the end of the nation-state."[32] Under many circumstances capitalism *needs* the stabilizing powers of the nation-state and will work to build the state up, not tear it down.

This means that there is no simple relation between cosmopolitanism and the state. For one thing, the two are historically intertwined. For better or worse, as Louisa Schein shows in her contribution to this volume, the state has "a dialectical relation to the production of the transnational"; it is "crystallized in part through its engagement with that which breaches its border control, its putative sovereignty." Thus cosmopolitics is by no means necessarily postnational politics. It is true that what we have learned to recognize as politics remains formed by experience at the scale of the nation-state, as Benedict Anderson and Jonathan Rée argue in their chapters. And it is true that, as Etienne Balibar observes, "borders have stopped marking the limits where politics ends because the community ends." Thus there must be a stretching of political theory if we are to re-form "public opinion" and habits of citizenship to work on a larger-than-national scale. Politics must be forced to include the variable power of sympathetic imagination to define collectivities of belonging and responsibility in the absence of that long history of face-to-face interaction that Dewey thought was necessary to community. But if the nation-state is not the one political unit capable of doing something to control the world market, nor (therefore) the inevitable focus of our best political energies, neither is it cosmopolitanism's proper and inevitable antagonist. Struggles for social justice that simply begin at home, within a given nation-state, do not demand to be described as nationalist or to be dismissed as parochial. Even if delinking from global capitalism were a feasible option, which it does not appear to be,[33] it could certainly be imagined in nonnationalist terms. Samir Amin himself has written movingly in favor of the cosmopolitan ideal.[34] Indeed, as Alejandro Colás argues, "cosmopolitanism will have to shed some of its inherent distrust of state-centric approaches to political action, and adopt a more *realist* attitude toward both the force of the state and the international system, and its capacity to fulfil many of the political and social rights defended by cosmopolitans."[35]

It also follows that cosmopolitanism cannot simply gape in admiration before the brave new world of international civil society. It is not just that this world remains dominated by sinister supranational units like the International Monetary Fund and the World Bank. Even the most humanitarian of the nongovernmental organizations (NGOs) require strict supervision, and they are less likely to receive it because the transnational domain they inhabit is not fitted with the usual well-tried domestic alarms. "Coinciding with a new eagerness to enforce the writ of the Security Council with troops, the early Nineties marked the clearest opportunity," Alex de Waal notes, for what he calls "the humanitarian international" of NGOs, which has managed to induce military intervention in situations where the political and economic consequences are extremely unpredictable. "If war is too important to be left to the generals," he concludes, "humanitarianism is too important to be left to the relief agencies."[36] The neologism *cosmopolitics* is also intended to underline the need to introduce intellectual order and accountability into this newly dynamic space of gushingly unrestrained sentiments, pieties, and urgencies for which no adequately discriminating lexicon has had time to develop.

Politics has always been a matter of timing. A long or evolutionary perspective, which in the past often claimed cosmopolitanism as its ultimate goal, can also serve on the contrary to delay its arrival on the agenda. In the debates over Prop. 187, for example, progressives could find little or no room for the interests of the undocumented aliens themselves, for "the fact that the normative world which preoccupies progressives is a national world is apparently so obvious, so much a given, as to require no specific assertion at all."[37] To accept what Bosniak calls "normative nationalism" is to tell noncitizens precisely what was said to women at earlier moments of dramatic political movement: "Your cause may well be just, but it is unfortunately premature. Wait a bit longer. Let us go first." If history does not teach that this was ever good advice, history also provides concrete reasons for thinking that this collection is well-timed. The opportunities for turning distant economic interdependence into conscious political cooperation have never been so promising. The time for cosmopolitics is now.

This is so in part because of transnational conflicts of loyalty that have already arisen, because discrepant cosmopolitanisms are colliding with each other much as different cultures and nations are, though perhaps not in quite the same ways.[38] Recent metropolitan attention to Third World sweatshops offers an illustration. It is capitalism itself that, by turning the "TV personality" Kathie Lee Gifford into a newsworthy commodity, made possible the dramatic exposure of conditions in the Honduran *maquiladoras* where Gifford's Wal-Mart clothing line is produced.[39] But now that the Honduran apparel workers have emerged from their convenient invisibility, it is unclear *how* they should be factored into calculations of global well-being. U.S. unions have been hurt by the flight of capital to places like Honduras. Their cosmopolitan interest in enforcing universal human rights standards around the world is not always easy to distinguish from a competitive interest in making the *maquiladoras* less profitable, even at the cost of Honduran jobs. How can union and consumer outrage against U.S. retailers be mobilized so as to protect those jobs? Meanwhile, some Honduran unions, while fighting to improve the lot of their workers, also defend a level of child labor that by U.S. standards would constitute abuse. Like the U.S. unions, they argue by comparison; they are both national and (increasingly, necessarily) cosmopolitan. Perhaps there is a single fragile collectivity that might provisionally embrace them both. But in a world of such desperate inequality, even cosmopolitanisms must learn to negotiate.

Conflicts like this have become familiar to the feminist and ecology movements, among others. Internationalism may well be, in Peter Waterman's phrase, "an unimagined and unimaginable community. . . . Yet if the old internationalism is dead, the internationalisms of the new social movements (women, ecology, peace, human rights) are alive and kicking."[40] They are also kicking each other, of course. Linking the global and the grassroots is on everyone's agenda, but there are no guarantees that one link will not block or sever another. Still, some such efforts have been extremely impressive, as for example when Randall Robinson's TransAfrica Forum, which spearheaded the boycott of South Africa under apartheid, organized public support for sanctions against the government of Nigeria.[41] Since women's rights were defined as human rights in the NGO-dominated Vienna conference of 1993, it has been possible for transnational activists to hold states accountable without pretending that the state itself is the sole or prime source of human rights abuses.[42] Referring to human rights has become a way of addressing matters once held to be "private." Hopefully, activists will now turn their attention to such "private" economic matters as the workers' right to organize—rights that unsurprisingly are not made much of by governments clamoring loudly about the right to development.

In the meantime, there is cause to worry, as Benedict Anderson does, about the consequences of proliferating ethnic identities, offered on the cheap, that have been cut loose from the structured accountability and the sacrifices that accompany old-fashioned citizenship. For Anderson, "the impending crisis of the hyphen that for two hundred years yoked nation and state" means that "portable nationality, read under the sign of 'identity,' is on the rapid rise as people everywhere are on the move."[43] One example of the result would be the highly orchestrated mob violence at the Ayodhya mosque, an operation paid for in large part by Hindus living in the United States and Canada. Anderson describes this as "long-distance nationalism": "a rapidly spreading phenomenon whereby well-off immigrants to the rich, advanced countries (and their children) are becoming key sources of money, guns, and extremist propaganda in their distant, putative countries of origin—in perfect safety and without any form of accountability."[44]

Anyone tempted to use the word *cosmopolitan* as a simple honorific must deal with the fact that these long-distance nationalisms could just as easily be called cosmopolitanisms. (Appadurai, who calls them "trojan nationalisms," notes that they "actually contain transnational, subnational links and, more generally, nonnational identities and aspirations.")[45] To what extent do they deserve such honor as might still cling to the term *cosmopolitanism*? Clearly, there is no inherent virtue in transnationality. Is there then, as Anderson suggests, inherent vice: the dangerous license to meddle that comes of feeling passionately engaged in a given state's affairs without accepting the duties of a citizen or being physically present on its territory? Is it distance itself that produces effects like Ayodhya, or does the distance of the supporters merely exaggerate our own sense of powerlessness before ethnic and religious violence that is more often produced entirely *within* the state, violence that citizenship itself is equally incapable of handling? Is it premature to detect, in "human rights culture" and the vocabulary slowly growing up around transnational NGOs, emergent forms of accountability-at-a-distance that, without mimicking the established domestic forms of citizenship, nevertheless tend to soften rather than intensify the furies of ethnic nationalism?

Khachig Tölölyan asks much the same questions about the related term *diaspora*. That concept has been seductive because it could be played off against the nation-state. But Tölölyan warns against an "inadvertent discursive complicity between diasporists and the transnational project of disabling the nation and its state": "For all too many theorists of diaspora . . . the project of re-articulating the nation-state seems also to require the option of dis-articulating it." Lobbying the state and dependent on it, genuine diasporas, Tölölyan argues, are not merely ethnic identities; they are quasi-political units that "act in consistently organized ways to develop an agenda for self-representation in the political or cultural realm, either in the hostland or across national boundaries."[46] Like citizenship, diaspora has to entail a cost, a sacrifice.[47] And like citizenship, it therefore has to include some very unsavory examples: Cuban Americans dedicated to the downfall of Castro, Jewish Americans supporting an extension of armed Jewish settlements on the West Bank. Crucial to the concept's success, Tölölyan writes, was "the emergence of the Israeli state as a figure of diasporan achievement."[48]

Like diaspora, cosmopolitanism offers something other than a gallery of virtuous, eligible identities. It points instead to a domain of contested politics—hence our title. Thinking of cosmopolitics not as universal reason in disguise, but as one on a series of scales, as an area both within and beyond the nation (and yet falling short of "humanity") that is inhabited by a variety of cosmopolitanisms, we will not perhaps be tempted to offer the final word on the dilemmas above.[49] But it is something merely to expose them in their full multivoiced complexity, thereby making it clear at least what justice on a global scale would have to resolve. It is something to bring to light the thousand gross and subtle ways in which we are told every day that people outside our borders are too distant to matter. And it is something else to explore the equally varied ways in which they already do or can perhaps be made to matter.

There are of course local reasons for the existence of a book on cosmopolitanism here and now. One reason is the state of the debate over U.S. multiculturalism, which has been misperceived (and, to a lesser extent, has misperceived itself) as merely particularistic, a celebration of difference for its own sake. Our elaboration of the term *cosmopolitics* represents one effort to describe, from within multiculturalism, a name for the genuine striving toward common norms and mutual translatability that is also part of multi-culturalism.

Another, equally peremptory, reason is the resurgence of nationalism since the end of the Cold War, including the new and dangerously reinvigorated U.S. nationalism. Theorists of nationalism seem drawn to such manifest absurdities as Elie Kedourie's remark that "nationalism is unknown" in the United States.[50] What we have here is a nationalism that does not know itself as such—a nationalism that sees itself as civic rather than ethnic, hence not really nationalism at all, or else as aligned righteously against the corporate globalism of Wall Street, as if Wall Street and its globalism were not as American as subsidies to agribusiness. Scholarly opinion in the United States is sometimes characterized as predominantly and comfortably globalist, antinationalist, cosmopolitan. This characterization misses the large extent to which multinational and transnational corporations remain rooted in their nations of origin. It misses the extent to which, for that reason, American policy remains a version of realpolitik, dedicated to a defense of the national interest—a national interest that gives much to the rich and little to the poor, of course, but that still favors the national poor over the nonnational poor and has some real success in exporting social problems beyond our national borders. Thus it also misses the way the national imagination even of progressives remains in thrall to those borders, routinely unwilling or unable to register the moral and political weight of noncitizens.[51]

In "For a New Nationalism," John Judis and Michael Lind issue a "challenge to the globalism of the American establishment."[52] In practice, this takes the form of Lind's crusade for drastic cuts in immigration. And it entails a certain provocation for those of us who—like all of the contributors to this book—are professionally concerned with culture, for it highlights the special culpability of culture in naturalizing the national interest.

Blaming immigration for U.S. poverty, Lind notes, as if in an afterthought, that "immigration restriction should . . . be accompanied by checks upon the expatriation of American industry."[53] But why not just *start* with the "checks," with stopping capital flight? Surely that would address the economic problem more directly. It appears that Lind, like Patrick Buchanan, needs culture—here, a cultural distaste for immigrants—to cover his equivocation over the amorality of capitalism and the U.S. national interest.[54] His "new nationalism" systematically confuses an affirmation of U.S. cultural identity, which is innocuous enough, with an affirmation of U.S. economic advantage and military strength, both of which entail shameless superiority over unnamed others. A natural appreciation for the "language and culture" that define the American nation slowly becomes an "economic nationalism," an imperative to defend "the relative status of [one's] nation in the world economy."[55]

Given the current distribution of the world's resources and the way the relative prosperity of the United States depends on its active impoverishment of so many citizens of so many other countries, for a U.S. citizen to make such an argument is nothing less than obscene. Pride is certainly one mark of attachment to one's country—but so is shame. It is as an American that I feel shamed by sentiments like these—shame at belonging to a culture and writing in a public sphere that accept them as normal. This book was assembled largely in the hope of making such sentiments seem more exceptional and more exceptionable.

Notes

1. Paul Rabinow, "Representations Are Social Facts," in James Clifford and George E. Marcus, eds., *Writing Culture: The Poetics and Politics of Ethnography* (Berkeley: University of California Press, 1986), 258.
2. Marcus Rediker, *Between the Devil and the Deep Blue Sea: Merchant Seamen, Pirates, and the Anglo-American Maritime World, 1700–1750* (Cambridge: Cambridge University Press, 1987); Bruce Robbins, "Upward Mobility in the Postcolonial Era: Kincaid, Mukherjee, and the Cosmopolitan Au Pair," *Modernism/Modernity* 1, no. 2 (1994): 133–51; Amitav Ghosh, *In an Antique Land* (New York: Alfred A. Knopf, 1993); Karen Kelsky, "Flirting with the Foreign: Interracial Sex in Japan's 'International' Age," in Rob Wilson and Wimal Dissanayake, eds., *Global/Local: Cultural Production and the Transnational Imaginary* (Durham, N.C.: Duke University Press, 1996).
3. James Clifford, "Traveling Cultures," in Lawrence Grossberg, Cary Nelson, and Paula A. Treichler, eds., *Cultural Studies* (New York: Routledge, 1992), 106–7.
4. Rabinow, "Representations," 258.
5. Arjun Appadurai, "Global Ethnoscapes: Notes and Queries for a Transnational Anthropology," in Richard G. Fox, ed., *Recapturing Anthropology: Working in the Present* (Santa Fe, N.M.: School of American Research Press, 1991), 192.
6. Benita Parry, "The Contradictions of Cultural Studies," *Transition* 53 (1991): 41.
7. Arnold Krupat, *The Voice in the Margin: Native American Literature and the Canon* (Berkeley: University of California Press, 1989), 198.
8. David A. Hollinger, *Postethnic America: Beyond Multiculturalism* (New York: Basic Books, 1995); Mitchell Cohen, "Rooted Cosmopolitanism," *Dissent* 39, no. 4 (1992); Homi Bhabha, "Unsatisfied Notes on Vernacular Cosmopolitanism," in Peter C. Pfeiffer and Laura García-Moreno, eds., *Text and Narration* (Columbia, S.C.: Camden House, 1996), 191–207.
9. On Asian cosmopolitanism, the reader may wish to consult the forthcoming work of Naoki Sakai, whose superb analysis of Japanese imperial cosmopolitanism in the 1930s is unfortunately too long to be included in the present collection.

10. Martha C. Nussbaum, "Patriotism and Cosmopolitanism," in *For Love of Country: Debating the Limits of Patriotism* (Boston: Beacon, 1996), 4.

11. The reference is to Benedict Anderson's *Imagined Communities: Reflections on the Origin and Spread of Nationalism*, rev. ed. (London: Verso, 1991 [1983]). As an example of the world conceived as one term on a sliding scale, rather than as an ultimate philosophical horizon, take Joseph Levenson's account of two stages of Chinese cosmopolitanism: "When Confucianism was vital . . . it was cosmopolitan: it did not simply correspond to 'day-to-day life in rural China.' But when China ceased to be a world and became a nation, or struggled to become one, Confucianism was provincial in that larger world that contained the Chinese nation. The intellectuals left it then, for a new cosmopolitanism." Joseph R. Levenson, *Revolution and Cosmopolitanism: The Western Stages and the Chinese Stages* (Berkeley: University of California Press, 1971), 5.

12. Yi-Fu Tuan, *Cosmos and Hearth: A Cosmopolite's Viewpoint* (Minneapolis: University of Minnesota Press, 1996), 159–60.

13. Helena Norberg-Hodge, "Break Up the Monoculture," *The Nation*, July 15–22, 1996, 20.

14. For the relevance of Tennessee Williams's famous formula, see Bonnie Honig, *"No Place Like Home": Democracy and Foreignness* (Princeton, N.J.: Princeton University Press, forthcoming) chap. 1. For an argument that, unlike Honig's, uses the impossibility of overcoming the friend/stranger distinction to argue against cosmopolitanism as such, see Michael J. Sandel, *Democracy's Discontent: America in Search of a Public Philosophy* (Cambridge: Harvard University Press, 1996), 342–43. Sandel makes his argument easier by assuming that cosmopolitans hold that "the more universal communities we inhabit must *always* take precedence over more particular ones" (343; emphasis added)

15. In "The Weird Heights: Cosmopolitanism, Feeling, and Power," *differences* 7, no. 1 (1995): 165–87, I make a similar argument about cosmopolitanism in Etienne Balibar.

16. For Gramsci, "the central fact" about Italian intellectuals is their "international or cosmopolitan function," which is "both cause and effect of the state of disintegration in which the peninsula remained from the fall of the Roman Empire up to 1870." "A kind of vague 'cosmopolitanism,'" emerging from "the cosmopolitanism and universalism of the Catholic Middle Ages," signals the thinness of Italian national consciousness. Antonio Gramsci, *Selections from the Prison Notebooks*, ed. and trans. Quintin Hoare and Geoffrey Nowell Smith (New York: International, 1971), 17–18, 274. Note that for Gramsci this cosmopolitanism does not contradict the "particular form of Italian chauvinism" (274). And see "La Lingua Unica È l'Esperanto," in Antonio Gramsci, *La Città Futura*, ed. S. Capriogli (Turin: Einaudi, 1982) for further complications. John Patrick Diggins, "Il Cosmopolitanismo e la Ricerca dell' 'Intellectuale Organico': il Fardello di Antonio Grasmci," in W. Tega, ed., *Gramsci e l'Occidente* (Bologna: Cappelli Editore, 1990) offers a critique in the name of universalism.

For Fanon, the "profoundly cosmopolitan mold" imprinted on the mind of the national middle class in Europe's colonies belongs with "intellectual laziness" and "spiritual penury" as a sign that it has not fulfilled its national vocation: "to make the totality of the nation a reality to each citizen." Frantz Fanon, *The Wretched of the Earth*, trans. Constance Farington (New York: Grove Weidenfeld, 1963), 149, 200.

Alejandro Colás suggests that, along with their "optimistic belief in evolution," Marx and Engels "grasped the historical import of supporting certain nationalist movements (Irish, Polish, Italian) insofar as they represented the toppling of the *ancien régime*." These two factors explain "why socialists have preferred to talk of internationalism, as opposed to the more blatantly anti-nationalist *cosmopolitanism*." Alejandro Colás, "Putting Cosmopolitanism into Practice: The Case of Socialist Internationalism," *Millenium: Journal of International Studies*, 23, no. 3 (1994): 519.

17. Gopal Balakrishnan, "The National Imagination," *New Left Review* 211 (May/June 1995): 58.

18. Anderson, *Imagined Communities*, 3, 53.

19. See Richard Rorty, "Solidarity or Objectivity?" in John Rajchman and Cornel West, eds., *Post-Analytic Philosophy* (New York: Columbia University Press, 1985), 3–19.

20. In addition to *For Love of Country*, see Nussbaum's *Poetic Justice: The Literary Imagination and Public Life* (Boston: Beacon, 1996) on the status of feeling. Langthaler is quoted in Norman Geras, *Solidarity in the Conversation of Mankind: The Ungroundable Liberalism of Richard Rorty* (London: Verso, 1995), 8.

21. Linda S. Bosniak, "Opposing Prop. 187: Undocumented Immigrants and the National Imagination," *Connecticut Law Review* 28, no. 3 (1996): 567–68. Bosniak writes: "Undocumented immigrants present a terribly confounding case for progressives: for these immigrants suffer the same kind of social exclusion progressives routinely deplore, yet at the same time, their exclusion from territory and membership quite often seems a necessary, if unfortunate, condition of political life as we have both known and imagined it" (597).

22. Ibid., 569.

23. Ibid., 559.

24. Geras, *Solidarity in the Conversation*, 78.

25. Geras writes: "Starting, for instance, from fellow Americans, you might begin to extend your sense of 'we' to Mexicans, Brazilians, Chileans and so forth, and thence to the peoples of Europe. Or starting from fellow Catholics, you might move on to every kind of Christian, then to Jews and Muslims. But this process either stops short somewhere within humankind, on account of the needed contrast-effects, or it does not. If it does, then some people, the people of Africa perhaps, or Hindus and atheists, get to be excluded from moral concern and they can go hungry or be massacred for all you care." Ibid., 77.

26. Ferdinand Tönnies, *Community and Society (Gemeinschaft und Gesellschaft)*, trans. and ed. Charles P. Loomis (East Lansing: Michigan State University Press, 1957 [1887]), 221. The passage continues: "Such tendencies and intentions will perhaps never find a clear expression, let alone realization, but their recognition serves to assist in the . . . realization of the fact that the existence of natural states is but a temporary limitation of the boundaryless Gesellschaft. In this context it must be pointed out that the most modern and Gesellschaft-like state, the United States of America, can or will least of all claim a truly national character."

27. Richard Maxwell, "Technologies of National Desire," in Michael J. Shapiro and Hayward R. Alker, eds., *Challenging Boundaries: Global Flows, Territorial Identities* (Minneapolis: University of Minnesota Press, 1996), 348.

28. Balakrishnan, "The National Imagination," 63. Balakrishnan notes that the religion/kinship analogy on which Anderson's view of nationalism depends (What are you willing to die for?), hence also the life-and-death line separating nationalism from cosmopolitanism, assumes an implicit state of war (67). It is only under threat of war that people are willing to die for their nation. Thus what undermines nationalism most is peace.

29. Arjun Appadurai, *Modernity at Large: Cultural Dimensions of Globalization* (Minneapolis: University of Minnesota Press, 1996), 176.

30. See also Benjamin Lee, "Critical Internationalism," *Public Culture* 7 (1995), 559–92.

31. Balakrishnan, "The National Imagination," 61, 66.

32. Michael Mann, "As the Twentieth Century Ages," *New Left Review* 214 (Novem-

ber/December 1995): 117–18. Transnationalism is much more pronounced in finance than in trade and industry, Mann argues. "The national bases of production and trade seem undiminished. Ninety per cent of global production remains for the domestic market. . . . Furthermore, almost all the so-called 'multinational corporations' are still owned overwhelmingly by nationals in their home-base country, and their headquarters and research and development activities are still concentrated there" (117). True, financial transnationalism cuts down the ability of nation-state to control interest rates and currency valuation (118), but this was in any case a rather unused power. Mann argues that the social welfare state is in retreat for other reasons, especially economic stagnation and its impact on state finances. Similar doubts are expressed by Simon Bromley in "Globalization?" *Radical Philosophy* 80 (November/December 1996): 2–5.

33. Fredric Jameson recently remarked on "the impossibility for any national or regional area to achieve its own autonomy and subsistence or to delink or uncouple itself from the world market." Fredric Jameson, "Five Theses on Actually Existing Marxism," *Monthly Review* 47, no. 11 (1996): 10. If nationalism is primarily or properly defensive, a response to external threat, then what do we make of a situation in which everyone in the world, including the Afrikaners and the Bosnian Serbs, can claim to feel threatened from outside, and to some extent *is* threatened?

34. Samir Amin, *Eurocentrism*, trans. Russell Moore (New York: Monthly Review Press, 1989), 105.

35. Colás, "Putting Cosmopolitanism into Practice," 533. Some would argue, with Michael Ignatieff, that "cosmopolitanism is the privilege of those who can take a secure nation-state for granted." Michael Ignatieff, *Blood and Belonging: Journeys into the New Nationalism* (New York: Farrar, Straus & Giroux, 1993), 13.

36. Alex de Waal, "Humanitarian Juggernaut," *London Review of Books*, June 22, 1995, 10.

37. Bosniak, "Opposing Prop. 187," 581.

38. In the past, cosmopolitanism was associated with a prophetic, totalizing teleology. Liberal cosmopolitans of the nineteenth century could support nationalism as well as free trade because they saw the nation as a necessary step on the evolutionary path toward ultimate world peace and understanding. Bigger was better, in politics as in economics. It remains tempting to think of the movement from smaller to larger loyalties as a translation of what was once called rationality. But if larger loyalties seem better matched to the larger depredations that global capitalism has wrought, size cannot claim to signify virtue, synthesis, or resolution on the left any more than on the right.

39. Larry Rohter, "Hondurans in 'Sweatshops' See Opportunity," *New York Times*, July 18, 1996, A1, A14. For a scathing critique of the Rohter article, consult the National Labor Committee, 275 Seventh Avenue, New York, NY 10001, (212) 242–3002; and Andrew Ross, ed., *Fashion Victims: Sweatshops, Celebrities, and the Rights of Labor* (London: Verso, 1997).

40. Peter Waterman, "Internationalism Is Dead! Long Live Global Solidarity!" in Jeremy Brecher, John Brown Childs, and Jill Cutler, eds., *Global Visions: Beyond the New World Order* (Boston: South End, 1993), 257. See also Christina Gabriel and Laura Macdonald, "NAFTA, Women and Organizing in Canada and Mexico: Forging a 'Feminist Internationality,'" *Millenium: Journal of International Studies* 23, no. 3 (1994): 535–62.

41. Steven A. Holmes, "U.S. Blacks Battle Nigeria over Rights Issue," *New York Times*, June 15, 1995, A6.

42. See, for example, Bruce Robbins, "Sad Stories in the International Public Sphere: Richard Rorty on Culture and Human Rights," *Public Culture* 9, no. 2 (1997): 209–32.

43. Benedict Anderson, "Introduction," in Gopal Balakrishnan, ed., *Mapping the Nation* (London: Verso, 1996), 8–9.

44. Benedict Anderson, "Ice Empire and Ice Hockey: Two Fin de Siècle Dreams," *New Left Review* 214 (November/December 1995): 150. Anderson makes much the same case in "Exodus," *Critical Inquiry* 20, no. 2 (1994): 314–27.

45. Arjun Appadurai, "Patriotism and Its Futures," *Public Culture* 5, no. 3 (1993): 417.

46. Khachig Tölölyan, "Rethinking Diaspora(s): Stateless Power in the Transnational Moment," *Diaspora* 5, no. 1 (1996): 5, 16–17.

47. Ibid., 15.

48. Ibid., 24.

49. For the geographer Neil Smith, body, home, community, urban space, region, nation, and globe are all specific and distinct scales that are never simply homologous with each other. There is a family resemblance here to the evolutionary politics of scale that Hobsbawm's Marxism shares with nineteenth-century liberalism: a rising sequence of more and more inclusive stages. For Smith, as for this cosmopolitan tradition, political failure may be defined as a failure to "jump scales"—he gives the example of Stalin's failure to move beyond "socialism in one country." The difference is that if there are moments when it is politically necessary to move from a "lower" to a "higher" scale, Smith insists that the reverse is also true; the most politically urgent task can also require moving from a larger to a smaller scale—from a politics of the nation, say, to a politics of the body, or a politics of the body-on-the-level-of-the-nation. Hierarchy has only a contingent, not an "ontological," status. "These different scales are better seen as nested rather than hierarchical, the hierarchical ordering of scales being a certain candidate for abolition in a revolutionized social geography." The benefit of the cosmopolitanism to be derived from Smith on scale, then, is that it measures both the effort or struggle necessary to "jump scales" and the possibly injurious or regressive consequences of so doing—without assuming, in other words, that there is anything "natural" about movement in either direction. Neil Smith, "Contours of a Spatialized Politics: Homeless Vehicles and the Production of Geographical Scale," *Social Text* 33 (1992): 66.

50. Elie Kedourie, *Nationalism*, 4th ed. (Oxford: Basil Blackwell, 1993 [1960]), 143.

51. A good example is Benjamin Barber's *Jihad vs. McWorld: How Globalism and Tribalism Are Reshaping the World* (New York: Ballantine, 1995), which tries to reclaim American nationalism by claiming for it the vast area between the book's polemically polarized titular terms. Consider Barber's treatment of cosmopolitanism. The first sentence of his first chapter is a quotation from the chairman of Gillette: "I do not find foreign countries foreign." "Welcome to McWorld," Barber announces grandly (23). It is an astounding moment of nonillumination. If the head of a multinational firm fails to recognize an essential difference between U.S. citizens and the citizens of foreign nations, then what follows? Perhaps that those of us who abhor the results of unrestrained multinational capital *should* find foreigners foreign?

52. John B. Judis and Michael Lind, "For a New Nationalism," *New Republic*, March 27, 1995, 19–27. Judis, writing earlier in *In These Times*, declared: "The left should reclaim from the right the cause of nationalism—nationalism as opposed to sectionalism and individualism. The left should stand for policies and programs that put the national interest before that of private corporations or Washington interest groups. The left should be at the forefront of those urging the economic revitalization of the country, and it should be vigilant about protecting America's interests against those of foreign governments and corporations and the new globalists of Wall Street and Washington." John Judis, "Looking Left and Right: The Evolution of Political Direction," *In These Times*, June 12–25, 1991, 12–13.

53. Michael Lind, *The Next American Nation: The New Nationalism and the Fourth American Revolution* (New York: Free Press, 1995), 322.

54. For an astute commentary on the place of culture in debates over immigration, see Jürgen Habermas, "Citizenship and National Identity: Some Reflections on the Future of Europe," in Omar Dahbour and Micheline Ishay, eds., *The Nationalism Reader* (Atlantic Highlands, N.J.: Humanities Press, 1995), 333–43.

55. See Lind, *The Next American Nation*, 8, 371, 375.

Introduction Part II:
The Cosmopolitical—Today

Pheng Cheah

Seluruh dunia kini dapat megawasi tingkah-laku seseorang. Dan orang dapat megawasi tingkah-laku seluruh dunia.

[The entire world can now observe the actions of any person. And people can observe the actions of the entire world.]
► *Pramoedya Ananta Toer*[1]

We live in an era where nationalism seems to be out of favor in some sections of academia and for some journalists spanning the entire political spectrum. The catchwords of the moment are *globalization, transnationalism,* even *postnationalism*. Many argue that the accelerated pace of economic globalization—the intensification of international trade, fiscal and technology transfers, and labor migration, and the consolidation of a genuinely global mode of production through subcontracting—in "advanced post-Fordist" or "late capitalism," the transnationalization of military command structures through NATO, and the rise of global hybrid cultures from modern mass migration, consumerism, and mass communications in the past two decades have combined to create an interdependent world in which the nation-state faces imminent obsolescence as a viable economic unit, a politically sovereign territory, and a bounded cultural sphere. Even official U.S. nationalism feels the need to put on nonnational costume now and then, either as the champion of world trade liberalization or as the protector of international human rights.

Indeed, the unprecedented growth of academic research on nationalism in recent years predominantly takes the tone of an officiation at a wake foretold. Scholars of both liberal and leftist persuasions in the humanities and the social sciences have tried to hasten the demise of nationalism by pointing to its pathological nature. Nationalism has been linked to the right-wing racist ideologies of the Axis powers of the Second World War, the rise of new right-wing movements and xenophobia in Western Europe, and genocidal wars in Eastern Europe. Third World statist ideologies justifying the oppression of religious and ethnic minorities and, more recently, Islamic patriarchal fundamentalism and oppressive identity politics in the postcolonial

South have also been described as nationalist. It is argued that these nationalist discourses give the lie to the promise of freedom made by national liberation movements during decolonization. To narrow focus for a moment, the subfield of postcolonial cultural studies emerges from this general disenchantment with nationalism, more specifically exemplified by the argument of the subaltern studies scholars of India that nationalism is an ideological humanism engendered from colonialist discourse.[2]

Yet, if nationalism as a mode of consciousness and the nation-state as an institution are both undesirable and outmoded, it is not entirely clear what the alternatives are and whether these alternatives actually exist or are capable of being realized. Because contemporary critics of nationalism regard it as a particularistic mode of consciousness or even a privative ethnic identity that disguises itself as a universalism, cosmopolitanism is the obvious choice as an intellectual ethic or political project that can better express or embody genuine universalism. The main purpose of this book is to explore the feasibility of cosmopolitanism as an alternative to nationalism in our contemporary era, and the essays in this collection take up this debate from various disciplinary perspectives ranging across the humanities and the social sciences.

In their philosophically oriented contributions, Allen Wood, Kwame Anthony Appiah, and Jonathan Rée make erudite and forceful arguments for cosmopolitanism as an ideal project and a style of practical consciousness that overcomes nationalist particularism. The chapters by Louisa Schein, Bonnie Honig, Bruce Robbins, Scott Malcomson, and Amanda Anderson focus on transcultural encounters, mass migration, and population transfers between East and West, First and Third Worlds, North and South. These authors variously suggest that by rearticulating the boundaries of regional and national consciousness and local ethnic identities, past and present globalizing processes objectively embody different forms of normative, nonethnocentric cosmopolitanism. In comparison with the more philosophical approaches to cosmopolitanism, some of these authors take James Clifford's phrase "discrepant cosmopolitanisms" as a point of reference, arguing that cosmopolitanism is no longer merely an ideal project but a variety of actually existing practical stances. Whatever reservations they have about contemporary transnationalism, they see it as providing the material conditions for new radical cosmopolitanisms from below.

Other contributors are more skeptical about the emancipatory nature of cosmopolitanisms based in contemporary globalization. In her essay, Aihwa Ong points to the entrepreneur business migrant riding the crest of capital flows unrestrained by citizenship ties as an important type in contemporary

Chinese cosmopolitanism. Benedict Anderson, probably the most well-known defender of nationalism among contemporary scholars, rejects the dominant tendency to equate ethnicity with nationalism and universalism with cosmopolitanism. He makes the striking argument that nationalism operates according to a universalistic logic of unbounded seriality and that it is the cosmopolitan migrant who obeys the logic of a bounded essentialized ethnicity that remains unchanged in exile and leads to fundamentalist identity politics. The feasibility of cosmopolitanism as an alternative to nationalism in our contemporary era thus remains an open question. In the following section, I want to speculate a little on why this is so.

The Unstable Opposition between Cosmopolitanism and Nationalism from Historical and Intellectual-Historical Perspectives

One fundamental theoretical reason why the choice between cosmopolitanism and nationalism as alternative vehicles of universalism remains so contentious is that the putative thematic opposition between these terms has always been unstable. In the next section, I suggest that this opposition is even more volatile today with the loosening of the hyphen between nation and state in globalization. But in the first place, it is anachronistic from both historical and intellectual-historical perspectives to regard cosmopolitanism *qua* institutional project or intellectual ethic as something that comes after and seeks to transcend an anterior mass-based nationalism. As a central concept of the eighteenth-century French philosophes, *cosmopolitanism* is derived from *kosmo-polites*, a composite of the Greek words for "world" and "citizen," by way of the *esprit cosmopolite* of Renaissance humanism. It primarily designates an intellectual ethic, a universal humanism that transcends regional particularism. The regional particularism that is opposed here may be defined territorially, culturally, linguistically, or even racially, but it is not defined *nationally* as we now understand the term, because in a Europe made up of absolutist dynastic states, the popular national state did not yet exist. Nor, indeed, had the doctrine of nationalism been fully articulated. Cosmopolitanism thus precedes the popular nation-state in history and nationalism in the history of ideas.

A second look at Immanuel Kant's moral-political project for perpetual peace is instructive, for it reveals that cosmopolitanism is not identical to "internationalism" and that its antonym is not *nationalism* but *statism*. As Allen Wood points out in his contribution to this volume, Kant's vision of institutional cosmopolitanism involves a shift from a merely voluntary ethical community of intellectuals to a world political community grounded in right.

What Kant calls "a universal *cosmopolitan existence*" refers to nothing less than the regulative idea of "a perfect civil union of mankind."[3] This constitutional global federation of all existing states "based on *cosmopolitan right*" (*ius cosmopoliticum*) is articulated around the idea that "individuals and states, co-existing in an external relationship of mutual influences, may be regarded as citizens of a universal state of mankind."[4] It is a legitimately institutionalized world community that falls somewhere between the political community of the state in its lawful relations with other states (*ius gentium*) and a world-state. At times more ambitiously described as "a universal federal state" (*allgemeiner Völkerstaat*),[5] this world political community would be able to assert cosmopolitan right—make rightful claims on its constituent states with respect to their treatment of individuals and other states in the name of humanity—even though it does not possess the coercive means of enforcement available to a world-state. Kant argued that the material conditions for fostering such a community already existed in international commerce and an emerging universal culture comprising the fine arts and sciences.

Kant's cosmopolitanism signifies a turning point where moral politics or political morality needs to be formulated beyond the polis or state form, the point at which "the political" becomes, by moral necessity, "cosmopolitical." His vision remains the single most important philosophical source for contemporary normative theories of international relations, including accounts of global civil society and the international public sphere. For present purposes, however, what is striking is the historical timing of Kant's vision.

Writing at the cusp between feudal and capitalist modes of production, Kant argued that international commerce was a historical condition of the cosmopolitical community because commerce was incompatible with war and the self-interest of states. We can, however, situate Kant's cosmopolitanism even more exactly as a vision essentially formulated prior to the spread of nationalism in Europe. Written in 1795, Kant's "Perpetual Peace" clearly precedes what Lord Acton disparagingly names as the age of "the modern theory of nationality"—the period between 1825 and 1831 when nationality, in search of statehood, emerges for the first time, as the primary basis of revolution.[6] This era of the nationality principle saw the rise of Greek, Belgian, and Polish nationalist movements, first aroused by the Napoleonic invasion, and now rebelling against their Ottoman, Dutch, and Russian governments for the primary reason that these were foreign regimes. Because Kant's idea of the cosmopolitical is formulated too early to take into account the role of nationalism in the transition between the age of absolutism and the age of liberalism, it is more a philosophical republicanism and federalism designed to reform the absolutist dynastic state than a theory opposing the modern theory of nationality. (Wood points out that "Perpetual Peace" was written after the Treaty of Basel in March 1795, which ended the War of the First Coalition between the monarchical states of Europe and France and can be read as an implicit defense of republican France as the potential leader of a peaceful cosmopolitan federation.) Indeed, because Kant writes at a time when the phenomenon and concept of "the nation" is still at an embryonic stage, he points out that the Right of Nations is a misnomer, because it actually refers to the lawful relation of states to one another, *ius publicum civitatum*.[7]

The original antagonist of Kant's cosmopolitanism is therefore absolutist statism and its appropriate historical context is not the age of nationalism but the interstate system of anarchy established by the Treaty of Westphalia after the breakup of the vast religious political communities of the medieval period. This interstate system, which arguably prevails in the twentieth century, is anarchic in at least two senses.[8] First, because the states within the system are not subject to an overarching universal sovereign authority, they are sovereign actors who claim absolute authority over the territories they govern. Second, much like corporations in a market, these states relate to each other and to individuals according to utlitarian principles of self-help and self-interest, without any cohering normative principles or moral purposes to regulate their actions. Kant's vision of cosmopolitical right asserted in the name of a common humanity attempts to provide an ideal institutional framework for regulating the anarchic behavior of states.

It follows that cosmopolitanism in the narrow sense of noncommitment and unfeeling detachment from particular affective and concrete ties deviates from the spirit of cosmopolitanism in its original articulations. Kant's notion of cosmopolitan right is not anti- or postnationalist. A prenationalist attempt to reform absolutist statism, it is not in the least an ideal of detachment opposed to national attachment. It is instead a form of right based on existing attachments that bind us into a collectivity larger than the state; it can be claimed against states because "individuals and states, co-existing in an external relationship of mutual influences, may be regarded as citizens of a universal state of mankind" (PP, 98–99n). This collectivity also includes states because international commerce is a form of sociability that brings states and individuals into relation, connecting all of us into a larger whole.

However, Kant could not possibly predict that capitalism or, more specifically, print-capitalism, to use Benedict Anderson's felicitous phrase, was also the material condition of possibility of a different type of collective glue with similar humanizing aims. I am, of course, speaking of nationalism, which, like cosmopolitanism, also sought to provide rightful regulation for the behavior of absolutist states toward their individual subjects. In the initial moment of its historical emergence, nationalism is a *popular* movement distinct from the state it seeks to transform in its own image. Thus, before the nation finds its state, before the tightening of the hyphen between nation and state that official nationalism consummates, the ideals of cosmopolitanism and European nationalism in its early stirrings are almost indistinguishable. As late as 1861, Giuseppe Mazzini would emphasize that the nation is the only historically effective threshold to humanity:

> Your first Duties . . . are . . . to Humanity. You are *men* before you are *citizens* or *fathers*. . . . But what can *each* of you, with his isolated powers, *do* for the moral improvement, for the progress of Humanity? . . . The *individual* is too weak and Humanity is too vast. . . . But God gave you this means when he gave you a country, when, like a wise overseer of labour, who distributes the different parts of work according to the capacity of workmen, he divided Humanity into distinct groups upon the face of our globe, and thus planted the seeds of nations. . . . Without Country you have neither name, token, voice, nor rights, no admission as brothers into the fellowship of Peoples. You are the bastards of Humanity. . . . Do not beguile yourselves with the hope of emancipation from unjust social conditions if you do not first conquer a Country for yourselves. . . . Do not be led away by the idea of improving your material conditions without first solving the national question. . . . In labouring according to the true principles for our Country we are labouring for Humanity; our Country is the fulcrum of the lever which we have to wield for the common good. If we give up this fulcrum we run the risk of becoming useless to our Country and to Humanity. Before *associating* ourselves with the Nations which compose Humanity we must exist as a Nation.[9]

Indeed, even when cosmopolitanism is diluted in its usage to designate a universally normative concept of culture identified with the culture of a certain ethnolinguistic people, such as in Fichte's *Addresses to the German Nation* (1808), it is still compatible with nationalism because the national culture in question is not yet bonded to the territorial state and can be accorded world historical importance without being imperialistic. The crucial point here is that prior to its annexation of the territorial state, nationalism is not antithetical to cosmopolitanism. Thus in his classical study *Cosmopolitanism and the National State*, the German social historian Friedrich Meinecke argues that in its initial phase, German spiritual or ethical national feeling was also cosmopolitan in nature and that cosmopolitanism was superseded by nationalism only with the birth of a genuinely national state.[10] This unbounded and cosmopolitical extensiveness of prestatized nationalism may further indicate that nationalism is not reducible to ethnicity and that nationalist politics is not necessarily a form of identity politics. (The contrasting essays in this volume by Rée and Benedict Anderson take up this question.)

The secondary understanding of cosmopolitanism that opposes it to nationalism and sometimes equates it with exilic migrancy only makes sense after the nation has been bonded to the territorial state, which then naturalizes its boundaries through official nationalism. In the history of ideas, the notorious tensions between nationalism and cosmopolitanism and the derisive connotations associated with the latter become more apparent from Marx onward. Whereas cosmopolitanism in idealist philosophy had designated a normative horizon of world history, for Marx, cosmopolitanism is realized as exploitation on a world scale through international commerce and the establishment of a global mode of production.

> The need of a constantly expanding market for its products chases the bourgeoisie over the whole surface of the globe. It must nestle everywhere, settle everywhere, establish connections everywhere.
>
> The bourgeoisie has through its exploitation of the world market given a *cosmopolitan* character to production and consumption in every country. To the great chagrin of reactionists, it has drawn from under the feet of industry the national ground on which it stood. All old-established national industries have been destroyed or are daily being destroyed. . . . In place of the old local and national seclusion and self-sufficiency, we have intercourse in every direction, universal interdependence of nations. And as in material, so also in intellectual production. The intellectual creations of individual nations become common property. National one-sidedness and narrow-mindedness become more and more impossible, and from numerous national and local literatures, there arises a world literature.[11]

This passage documents the two crucial developments that occur between the cosmopolitanisms of Kant and Marx. For Marx, cosmopolitanism is no longer just a normative horizon or a matter of right growing out of international commerce. It is an existing and necessary condition resulting from the development of forces of production on a global scale. But more important, in the intervening years between Kant's "Perpetual Peace" and the *Manifesto of the Communist Party* (1848) a significant sense of national belonging had obviously developed. Nationality was not even an issue in Kant's vision of the cosmopolitical. It is therefore a little startling to see Marx characterizing the nation and its appendages—national economy, industry, and culture—in naturalistic and primordial terms only fifty-three years later. Indeed, by then the nation is sufficiently annexed to the state for it to be characterized as a particularity to be opposed and eroded by (capitalist and proletarian) cosmopolitanism. For Marx, nationality belonged to an initial phase of capitalist production, the natural or immediate stage of the appearance of the capitalist form of capital. Even though this natural/national phase of capitalism was antiquated and in the process of being sublated (*aufgehoben*) into the higher and truer phase of cosmopolitan capitalism, it still existed, and its passing had to be hastened by ideology-critique.

Marx's ambivalence toward capitalist cosmopolitanism is well-known. As the unfolding of the true nature of capital as a concrete universality, the monstrous global totality that cosmopolitan bourgeois capital builds in its own image is both the necessary and positive condition of a worldwide proletarian revolution and also that which proletarian cosmopolitanism has to destroy. But Marx is also ambivalent about the nation. In his early writings, he unmistakably depicts the sundering of natural local ties by liberated cosmopolitan capital as a violent dehumanizing process of upheaval that deprives labor of the last vestiges of "an *apparently* social meaning, the meaning of genuine community" it still has under feudal forms of agriculture and urban crafts, guilds, and corporations.[12] It is this ameliorative dimension of feudal ties that Marx likens to nationality:

> In feudal landownership we already find the domination of the earth as of an alien power over men. . . . But . . . the lord at least *appears* to be king of the land. . . . there is still the appearance of a relationship between owner and land which is based on something more intimate than mere *material* wealth. The land is individualized with the lord, it acquires his status, it is baronial or ducal with him, has his privileges, his jurisdiction, his political position etc. It appears as the inorganic body of its lord. . . . In the same way the rule of landed property does not appear directly as the rule of mere capital. Its relationship to those dependent on it is more like that of a fatherland. It is a sort of narrow nationality. (EPM, 318)

Thus, although Marx regards nationality in similar terms to religion—as a false form of consciousness obstructing the genuine development of universal human nature—there is still a weak compensatory dimension to it insofar as it provides the appearance of a natural collective psychological or affective barrier against the dehumanizing, atomizing effects of capital. But at the same time, the nation turns out to be a false natural community, an ideological construction: the appeal to nationality in Listian exhortations to protect the national economy and industry mystifies the class interests of less developed bourgeois states.[13]

Marx's anti- and postnationalist cosmopolitanism is thus different from Kant's prenationalist cosmopolitanism. Kant missed the potential of popular nationalism as an emancipatory force against statism because he could not predict that the material interconnectedness brought about by capitalism would engender the bounded political community of the nation. Marx summarily dismissed nationalism although he witnessed its rise. Identifying the nation too hastily with the bourgeois state, Marx reduced the nation to an ideological instrument of the state and saw nationalism as a tendentious invocation of anachronistic quasi-feudal forms of belonging in modernity. The antagonistic relation between socialist cosmopolitanism and nationalism is premised on this collapsing of the nation into the state. Marx's cosmopolitanism presupposes a historical scenario in which the masses are able to recognize the nation as a tool of oppression because the hyphen between nation and bourgeois state has been rendered so tight that it has completely disappeared. The aphorism "The working men have no country" (*MCP*, 84) refers to the inevitable inability of bourgeois nations to command the loyalty of their proletariat in global exploitation and pauperization. Indeed, Marx was more concerned about abolishing the state-apparatus than its epiphenomenon, the nation-form. Because nationality was already becoming obsolete, its dismantling would not require much effort, and the proletariat should direct their efforts at seizing state power instead: "The supremacy of the proletariat will cause [national differences] . . . to vanish still faster. . . . In proportion as the antagonism between classes within the nation vanishes, the hostility of one nation to another will come to an end" (*MCP*, 85).

Marx's teleological argument about socialist cosmopolitanism is often dismissed for ignoring the continuing disparity between the working classes of different countries, a fact illustrated by the breakup of the Second International. But the more important reason Marx missed the tenacity of nationalism so badly may be that he deduced the ideological nature of nationality too hastily from the economic and cultural nationalism of European states, and so foreclosed its popular dimension and its potential as an ally of Marxist cosmopolitanism. Furthermore, the father of historical materialism works with an entirely ahistorical premise. He takes it for granted that the hyphen welding the nation to the state is immutable. Capitalism is certainly the progenitor of the European territorial national state. But in different historical situations, the global interconnectedness brought about by capitalism can also mutate to loosen the stranglehold of the bourgeois state over the nation so that the state can undergo a popular renationalization. Marx seems to make a similar point in his unelaborated notion of the proletarian nation that occupies the interregnum between the bourgeois nation-state and the proletarian world-community: "Since the proletariat . . . must constitute itself as the nation, it is, so far, itself national, though not in the bourgeois sense of the word" (*MCP*, 84).

Not surprisingly, the most notable revaluation of the national question in socialism so far has occurred in response to anticolonialist struggles.[14] Using national liberation movements in Asia as his example, Lenin argued in 1914 for a strategic alliance between the proletarian struggle and the right of nations to political self-determination based on the principle that the former would be served by supporting the bourgeoisie of an oppressed nation to the extent that it fights against imperialism:

> *If* the bourgeoisie of the oppressed nation fights against the oppressing one, we are always, in every case, and more resolutely than anyone else, *in favour*. . . . But if the bourgeoisie of the oppressed nation stands for *its own* bourgeois nationalism, we are opposed. We fight against the privileges and violence of the oppressing nation, but we do not condone the strivings for privileges on the part of the oppressed nation. . . . The bourgeois nationalism of *every* oppressed nation has a general democratic content which is directed *against* oppression, and it is this content that we support *unconditionally*, while strictly distinguishing it from the tendency towards national exceptionalism.[15]

Lenin's argument widens the small foothold opened by Marx's tentative acknowledgment that as a form of collective solidarity that shelters the worker against capital's atomizing effects, nationality has a compensatory dimension. Decolonizing nationalisms flourish in this opening, seizing this precarious foothold and filling Lenin's abstract notion of nationality with positive cultural content.

In the colonial situation, global capitalism has enslaved African and Asian territories either by establishing colonial administrative states (colonial India, Africa, or Malaya) or by the indirect colonization of traditional dynastic states through extraterritorial demands (China, Siam, Ethiopia). At the same time, it leads to the birth of nations with interests diverging from those of existing colonial or colonized states. No longer just an ideological tool of the state, the decolonizing nation can now serve as an agent of socialist cosmopolitanism to the extent that it attempts to save the state from the clutches of cosmopolitan capital. By bringing to the fore again the similar aims of cosmopolitanism and nationalism that Marx obscured, and by distinguishing these progressive goals from those of an imperializing cosmopolitanism, decolonizing nationalism destabilizes Marx's rigid antithesis between the two terms.[16] Thus, in words that seem to adapt Mazzini's position to decolonizing Asia, Sun Yat-sen, the father of modern China, argues that nationalism is the necessary basis of genuine cosmopolitanism:

> [Western colonial powers] are now advocating cosmopolitanism to inflame us, declaring that, as the civilization of the world advances and as mankind's vision enlarges, nationalism becomes too narrow, unsuited to the present age, and hence, that we should espouse cosmopolitanism. In recent years some of China's youths, devotees of the new culture, have been opposing nationalism, led astray by this doctrine. But it is not a doctrine which wronged races should talk about. We . . . must first recover our position of national freedom and equality before we are fit to discuss cosmopolitanism. . . . We must understand that cosmopolitanism grows out of nationalism; if we want to extend cosmopolitanism we must first establish strongly our own nationalism. If nationalism cannot become strong, cosmopolitanism certainly cannot prosper.[17]

But it is not only progressive nationalism that can ally itself with genuine cosmopolitanism. Reactionary (bourgeois) nationalism can also be the accomplice of capitalist cosmopolitanism. Thus Frantz Fanon suggests that the retrograde national consciousness of underdeveloped countries is "the result of the intellectual laziness of the national middle class, of its spiritual penury, and of the profoundly cosmopolitan mold that its mind is set in."[18] Similarly, Naoki Sakai has argued that in the Second World War, Japanese imperial nationalism actively modulated into a violent institutional cosmopolitanism: the Greater East Asian Co-Prosperity Sphere that stretched from Southeast Asia through Korea and China to conquered Russian territory.

The Cosmopolitical in Contemporary Globalization

From a historical perspective, it is evident that the relationship between cosmopolitanism and nationalism has fluctuated between varying degrees of alliance and opposition and that both discourses have progressive as well as reactionary dimensions. This shifting relationship between cosmopolitanism and nationalism and the unpredictable content and consequences of both practical discourses imply several things. First, it is precipitous to consider nationalism as an outmoded form of consciousness. An existing global condition ought not to be mistaken for an existing mass-based feeling of belonging to a world community (cosmopolitanism) because the globality of the everyday does not necessarily engender an existing popular global political consciousness. Ipso facto, neither cosmopolitanism nor nationalism can be seen as the teleologically necessary and desired normative outcome of past and present globalizing processes. Popular nationalist movements contain exclusionary moments that can easily develop into oppressive official nationalist ideologies when these movements achieve statehood. Conversely, the staging of an international civil society of elite nongovernmental organizations (NGOs) at U.N. World Conferences can become an alibi for economic transnationalism, which is often U.S. economic nationalism in global guise. Through strings-attached funding to elite NGOs that take over some social services from the public sector in developing states, international aid agencies can erode the ability of these already weakened states to implement genuine social redistribution. In the latter case, the point is to look at the consequences of cosmopolitanist claims in a given historical situation, just as in the first case, the point is not to demonize the state as the corrupter of the nation-people but to account for the necessary link between decolonizing nation and state in the current conjuncture and the built-in dangers of official nationalism.

In other words, the ethico-political work that nationalism and cosmopolitanism can do at any given moment depends on how either formation emerges from or is inscribed within the shifting material linkages and interconnections created by global capitalism at a particular historical conjuncture. The corollary to this is that although capitalism is the condition of possibility of both nationalism and cosmopolitanism, neither discourse can be reduced to its ideological instrument or regarded as its simple reflection. The tightness or laxity of the hyphen between nation and state is an important historical factor in the evaluation of the aims of nationalism and their compatibility with normative cosmopolitanism. Hence, instead of indulging in the complacent demystification of nationalism as "a derivative discourse" or moralistically condemning cosmopolitanism as uncommitted bourgeois detachment, we ought to turn our critical focus to the mutating global field of political, economic, and cultural forces in which nationalism and cosmopolitanism are invoked as practical discourses.

The cosmopolitical is an apposite term for this global force field of the political. To return to the theme of this collection of essays, the question is whether the cosmopolitical today is conducive to the rise of new normative cosmopolitanisms, mass-based emancipatory forms of global consciousness, or actually existing imagined political world communities.

In contemporary cultural studies, postnationalism has become an increasingly popular trend. Adopting the modes-of-production narrative that Fredric Jameson borrowed from Ernest Mandel, some argue that the deterritorialization of space in transnational, flexible, disorganized, or late capitalism erodes the naturalized borders of the nation, pointing to its imminent demise or, at least, to the eventual development of an alternative spatialization of politics. For instance, Arjun Appadurai suggests that contemporary transnational cultural flows create a zone in which emergent global forms of cosmopolitanism are brought into a conflictual relationship with nationalist forms of culture. Appadurai claims that the cosmopolitanization of cultural consumption—the widening of its horizons by greater frequency of travel and improved media communications—has political repercussions because national culture is the site where oppressive politics and culture are conjoined.[19] He suggests that insofar as the state attempts to tether the masses to it by deploying ideologies of "national belonging" and "national culture," subnational/local uses of transnational cultural messages and deterritorialized ideas of nationhood formed from population flows challenge the nation-state's cultural hegemony and contribute to its crisis.[20] For Appadurai, these are signs of the dawning of a postnational, poststatist age, and they require a theoretical vocabulary that can express "complex, non-territorial, postnational forms of allegiance" and "capture the collective interests of many groups in translocal solidarities, cross-border mobilisations and postnational identities."[21] Otherwise, "the incapacity of many de-territorialised groups to think their way out of the nation-state is itself a cause of much global violence since many movements of emancipation and identity are forced, in their struggle against existing nation-states, to embrace the very imaginary they seek to escape" (PF, 418).

Appadurai's argument is a useful example of postnationalism in cultural studies because it details its three fundamental presuppositions. First, like Marx, the postnationalist relies on a restrictive definition of the nation as "the ideological alibi of the territorial state" (PF, 412). In this definition, popular nationalism involves masses who are duped by state ideology. Second, the postnationalist subscribes to the teleological argument that flexible capitalist accumulation tends toward a postnational age. Appadurai, for instance, suggests that a global economy constituted by disjunctive flows offers greater resources for undermining the oppressive nation-state. Thus, where intellectuals participating in anticolonial liberation movements had considered the loose hyphen between emerging nation and state in colonialism as an opportunity for a popular renationalization of the state, the postnationalist takes the distending of the hyphen in contemporary globalization as a sign of the disintegration of both nation and state. Finally, the postnationalist suggests that the constraining discourse of nationalism/statism can be transcended through acts of thought and imagination that find sustenance in a large variety of existing transnational movements. Grouping transnational NGOs and philanthropic movements, diasporic communities, refugees, and religious movements under the rubric of actually existing "postnational social formations," Appadurai suggests that these organizational forms are "both instances and incubators of a postnational global order" (PF, 421) because they challenge the nation-state and provide nonviolent institutional grounding for larger-scale political loyalties, allegiances, and group identities.

There are, however, more cogent reasons to be more cautionary about the virtues of contemporary transnationalism and less dimissive of the future of the nation-state and nationalism. In the first place, transnationalism is not only a contemporary phenomenon; it has always coexisted with the state. Michael Mann points out that European capitalism "was especially transnational in its early industrial phase, with virtually free mobility of capital and labor and with most of its growth zones located in border or cross-border areas, like the Low Countries, Bohemia and Catalonia."[22] Nor does the intensification of transnational capitalism today undermine the utility of states. Instead, "the increasing density of global society gives states new geopolitical roles," notably in negotiations over tariffs, communications, and environmental issues (138). Indeed, even though capitalism erodes state sovereignty, it also needs the agency of states. Capitalism, Mann suggests, "seems to be near its state-subverting limits" and "will not further reduce the nation-state": "Capitalist profit-taking has resulted in not quite Fredric Jameson's 'postmodern hyperspace.' Though capitalism has reduced the social citizenship powers of the nation-state, and in association with military and geopolitical trends it has also reduced the military sovereignty of most states, it still depends on continuous negotiations between sovereign states in a variety of ad hoc agencies" (138–39).

The necessity of popular nationalism as an agent of ethico-political transformation in transnationalism becomes clearer once we observe that, notwithstanding increased transnational labor migration in the contemporary era, the deterritorialization of peoples remains limited for reasons that are structural to the global political economy. Samir Amin suggests that popular nationalism in the periphery is a necessary step toward socialist cosmopolitanism because we live in an uneven capitalist world-system that largely confines the most deprived masses of humanity to national-peripheral space. He points out that the globalization of production—liberalization of trade and capital flows—involves the global integration of commodities and capital but stops short of an unlimited integration of labor—the unrestricted opening of the centers to labor migration from less or nonindustrialized peripheries where the bulk of capital's reserve army is located.[23] Consequently, "the mobility of commodities and capital leaves national space to embrace the whole world while the labour force [largely] remains enclosed within the national framework" (*RPP*, 74).

As long as there is no free movement of workers worldwide, the globality of capital remains truncated. Contrary to the neoliberal sermon that the global spread of free market mechanisms will lead to generalized development and global democratization, neocolonial globalization only exacerbates world polarization and leads to the formation of comprador states. Resource-intensive and wasteful macropolicies of economic development and market economy-led linear models espoused by international development agencies and financial institutions like the World Bank and IMF mortgage the state to transnational capital, and state adjustment to global restructuring loosens the hyphen between nation and state. Because the compradorized state cannot actively shape its own society and political morality, democratic national projects for social welfare in the periphery are either killed off or handicapped from the start. For social redistribution to occur, the state must resist structural adjustment. But resistance is possible only if the state is made to serve the people's interests. Thus, instead of producing large groups of deterritorialized migrant peoples who prefigure the nation-state's demise and point to a postnational global order, *uneven* globalization makes popular nationalist movements in the periphery the first step on the long road to social redistribution.

The contrast between Amin's argument for the sociopolitical necessity of popular nationalism in the South and postnationalism in cultural studies is even more striking because of Amin's Marxist-internationalist bent. For Amin, the new phase of globalization beginning in the 1970s intensifies global crisis. The negative impact of the former phase was mainly felt as the failure of national development and the stillbirth of genuine social democracy in the South. Contemporary globalization, however, clashes with national interests in the center. The rise of an autonomous global economy through heightened forms of financial and technological transnationalization is not matched by the emergence of supranational social and political mechanisms for regulating accumulation.[24] Even as the historic role of the nation-state as a framework for economic management is eroded in the new phase of globalization, existing forms of social and political power remain based on national realities. Amin points out that

> the US and Japan are not merely geographical areas of a world economy that is under construction. They are and will remain national economies, with a state that ensures the continuance of national structures while grabbing the lion's share of world trade. . . . These national options remain decisive at such levels as: spending on research, development, and labour force retraining; de facto protection of agriculture; mineral and oil resource development; and even manufacturing and financial management. (*EC*, 46)

Consequently, the increasing interpenetration of national productive systems at the center "destroys the effectiveness of traditional national policies and delivers the overall system to the dictates and errors of the constraint of the world market, which cannot be regulated as there are no genuinely supranational political institutions, or even a political and social consciousness that really accepts this new demand of capitalism" (*RPP*, 211).

Amin's internationalist solution to global crisis is emphatically not postnationalist because it begins from and revolves around the success of popular nationalist movements in the periphery. Only an international political and social consciousness can equitably regulate the uneven global economy. But in the initial instance, popular nationalisms, whatever their shortcomings, are needed to save the state from capitulation to the demands of transnationalization. They alone can renationalize the state and allow it to gain control over accumulation: "The system of real existing capitalism being first and foremost a system condemned to perpetuate, reproduce and deepen world polarization, the revolt of the peoples of the periphery against the fate that had been ordained for them constitutes the central axis of the recomposition of the internationalism of the peoples" (SM, 137). As was the case with decolonizing nationalisms, this proposed alliance between nationalism and cosmopolitanism also grows out of a situation where the hyphen between nation and state needs to be strengthened because global neocolonialism has unmoored the state from its nation. Amin's example is the comprador state in Africa, but his general argument can be extended to describe people's diplomacy in the Philippines, the popular mobilization in support of Sukarnoputri in Indonesia, and so on.

However, these arguments about the structural necessity of the nation-state in the global political economy do not exactly answer the question of whether the cosmopolitical today is conducive to the rise of new normative cosmopolitanisms. They certainly show us the untenability of postnationalism. But then cosmopolitanism need not be postnationalist. As we have seen, cosmopolitanism and nationalism are not logical antagonists, and some of the new cosmopolitanisms articulated in this volume stress the importance of a strategic alliance with the nation-state. Proponents of new cosmopolitanisms and postnationalists do, however, share one assumption. They both suggest that existing transnational movements translate into actually existing popular cosmopolitanisms understood as pluralized forms of popular global political consciousness comparable to the national imagining of political community. The question is whether this claim is premature.

The necessity and even urgency of a cosmopolitical frame of analysis is not in question here. The problem is not whether there is material interconnection on a global scale, whether more women and men of discrepant class and cultural backgrounds are transnationally mobile and inhabit competing worlds. The world is undoubtedly interconnected, and transnational mobility is clearly on the rise. However, one should not automatically take this to imply that popular forms of cosmopolitanism already exist. Whether this mobility and interconnectedness give rise to meaningful cosmopolitanisms in the robust sense of pluralized world-political communities is an entirely separate issue. Anthony Smith, for instance, suggests that a mass-based global loyalty is anthropologically impossible:

> A timeless global culture answers to no living needs and conjures no memories. If memory is central to identity, we can discern no global identity-in-the-making, nor aspirations for one, nor any collective amnesia to replace existing "deep" cultures with a cosmopolitan "flat" culture. The latter remains a dream confined to some intellectuals. It strikes no chord among the vast masses of peoples divided into their habitual communities of class, gender, region, religion and culture. Images, identities, cultures, all express the plurality and particularism of histories and their remoteness from . . . any vision of a cosmopolitan global order.[25]

But even if a popular global consciousness exists, is it or can it be sufficiently institutionalized to be a feasible political alternative to the nation-state form? Or is it merely a cultural consciousness without political effectivity?

The uneven force field of the cosmopolitical has produced and will continue to produce inspiring examples of politically oriented cosmopolitanisms: Amnesty International, Médecins sans Frontières, the Asian Pacific People's Environmental Network based in Penang, Malaysia, for example. Mainly articulated by intellectuals and activists in both North and South, these cosmopolitanisms deserve support and admiration. However, it is questionable whether these cosmopolitanisms are mass based, even though they initiate or participate in grassroots activities. Even grassroots feminist NGOs do not represent "all women." Moreover, it is unclear how these cosmopolitan activities are related to transnational underclass migrant communities. For instance, over and above interventions on behalf of underprivileged migrant minority groups on an ad hoc basis, to what extent can activist cosmopolitanisms take root in the latter in a consistent manner to generate a genuinely pluralized mass-based global political community within the Northern constitutional nation-state as distinguished from the defensive identity politics of ethnic, religious, or hybrid minority constituencies? Can these cosmopolitanisms be embedded in a global community in the South forged from transnational media networks? This leads to the most difficult question of all: In an uneven neocolonial world, how can struggles for multicultural recognition in constitutional-democratic states in the North be brought into a global alliance with postcolonial activism in the periphery? The realizability of a global civil society or an international public sphere capable of representing/mediating the needs and desires of humanity's radically different constituencies through cross-identifications stands or falls here.

Transnational mobility notwithstanding, it is doubtful whether transnational migrant communities can be characterized as examples of cosmopolitanism in the robust normative sense even after we have acknowledged that this normative dimension is necessarily diluted or compromised by historical contextualization. It is unclear how many of these migrants feel that they belong to a world. Nor has it been ascertained whether this purported feeling of belonging to a world is analytically distinguishable from long-distance, absentee national feeling.[26] Second, the argument that transnational print and media networks extend a world community beyond transnational migrancy to include peoples dwelling in the South has to reckon with the banal fact that many in the South are illiterate and/or do not have access to televisions or other hardware capable of receiving CNN and Rupert Murdoch's Asia-based Star TV. Finally, if we recall that the nation is a *mass-based* imagined *political* community, it is unclear whether in the current interstate system, the so-called international public sphere or global civil society (names for mass-based global political communities) formed by transnational networks can achieve social redistribution on a global scale if it does not go through the institutional agency of the nation-state.[27]

Especially in the postcolonial South, relying on the state as an agent for social development involves changing its political morality, more often than not by a counterofficial popular nationalism and electoral education. As long as the state is mortgaged to global capital and unmoored from its nation-people, talk of social democracy in the South is meaningless. If transnational networks can be politically effective only by working through popular nationalism, then it may be more appropriate to describe such activity as nationalisms operating in a cosmopolitical force field rather than mass-based cosmopolitanisms (see my contribution to this volume). This would also allow us to exercise due caution toward the World Bank's cosmopolitan rhetoric: its utilization of the concept of international civil society to bypass the beleaguered sovereignty of Southern states and dictate adjustment according to the imperatives of global restructuring. In her essay in this volume, Gayatri Spivak calls the non-Eurocentric ecological movement and the women's movement against population control and reproductive engineering "globe-girdling movements" and emphatically distinguishes them from both the international civil society of elite NGOs and the postnationalism of "Northern radical chic." The point is that in the cosmopolitical today, even activist cosmopolitanisms are in a conflictual embrace with the popular nationalisms that are imperative in the postcolonial South. These popular nationalisms cannot afford to refuse the resources and gifts of aid offered by transnational networks. However, given their irreducible inscription within the material linkages of global capital, these giving cosmopolitanisms can also unintentionally undermine popular attempts to renationalize the compradorized state. Global justice involves an interminable navigation through the uneven and shifting force field of the cosmopolitical that engenders and circumscribes nationalisms and activist cosmpolitanisms alike.

As the vigorous and sometimes heated debates in this collection indicate, the tension between nationalism and cosmopolitanism is far from being resolved. The contributors cannot pretend to possess the key to cosmopolitical transformation, to know the way out of uneven neocolonial globalization. However, their individual essays at least begin to broach the most pressing political topic of our time with the intellectual rigor and theoretical clarity that it requires and deserves. These interdisciplinary essays exemplify in themselves the extensive reach of the topic. They bear witness to the fact that nationalism, cosmopolitanism, and the cosmopolitical are formed from the complicated intertwinings of culture, politics, and economics, and that we can conceptualize these phenomena adequately only by working in the volatile zone where ethical philosophy, political theory, cultural anthropology, social theory, critical theory, and cultural studies intersect.

Notes

1. Pramoedya Ananta Toer, *Bumi Manusia* (Kuala Lumpur: Wira Karya, 1983), 316; my translation. The first volume of the Buru quartet has been translated as *This Earth of Mankind*, in Pramoedya Ananta Toer, *Awakenings*, trans. Max Lane (Melbourne: Penguin, 1991).
2. See Partha Chatterjee, *Nationalist Thought and the Colonial World: A Derivative Discourse?* (London: Zed, 1986); Ranajit Guha, *A Construction of Humanism in Colonial India* (Amsterdam: Centre for Asian Studies, 1993).
3. Immanuel Kant, "Idea for a Universal History with a Cosmopolitan Purpose," in *Political Writings*, ed. Hans Reiss (Cambridge: Cambridge University Press, 1991), 51.
4. Immanuel Kant, "Perpetual Peace: A Philosophical Sketch," in *Political Writings*, ed. Hans Reiss (Cambridge: Cambridge University Press, 1991), 98–99 n (hereafter cited in text as PP). See Kant's discussion of cosmopolitan right, in *The Doctrine of Right*, §62, in *The Metaphysics of Morals* (Cambridge: Cambridge University Press, 1991), 158–59.
5. Immanuel Kant, "On the Common Saying: 'This May Be True in Theory, but It Does Not Apply in Practice,'" in *Political Writings*, ed. Hans Reiss (Cambridge: Cambridge University Press, 1991), 92.
6. See Lord Acton, "Nationality," in *The Nationalism Reader*, ed. Omar Dahbour and Micheline R. Ishay (Atlantic Highlands, N.J.: Humanities Press, 1995), 108–18.
7. Kant, *The Doctrine of Right*, §53, 150. *The Doctrine of Right* was first published in January 1797.
8. For a succinct account of the Westphalian system as international anarchy and an alternative account of global civil society, see Ronnie Lipschutz, "Reconstructing World Politics. The Emergence of Global Civil Society," *Millennium: Journal of International Studies* 21, no. 3 (1992): 389–420.
9. Giuseppe Mazzini, *The Duties of Man*, extracted in *The Nationalism Reader*, ed. Omar Dahbour and Micheline R. Ishay (Atlantic Highlands, N.J.: Humanities Press, 1995), 91–94.
10. Friedrich Meinecke, *Cosmopolitanism and the National State*, trans. Robert B. Kimber (Princeton, N.J.: Princeton University Press, 1970). "Cosmopolitanism and nationalism stood side by side in a close, living relationship for a long time. And even if the idea of the genuine national state did not come into full bloom within such a relationship, the meeting of these two intellectual forces was by no means unfruitful for the national idea" (94).
11. Karl Marx, *Manifesto of the Communist Party, The Revolutions of 1848: Political Writings*, vol. 1, (Harmondsworth: Penguin, 1973), 71; emphasis added (hereafter cited in text as *MCP*).
12. Karl Marx, "Economic and Philosophical Manuscripts," in *Early Writings* (Harmondsworth: Penguin, 1975), 337. (hereafter cited in text as EPM).
13. See Karl Marx, "Draft of an Article on Friedrich List's Book, *Das nationale System der politischen Ökonomie*," in Karl Marx and Friedrich Engels, *Collected Works*, vol. 4 (New York: International, 1975), 265–93, especially 280–81. For a more extended discussion, see Roman Szporluk, *Communism and Nationalism: Karl Marx versus Friedrich List* (New York: Oxford University Press, 1988).
14. For a concise summary of the national question in socialist cosmopolitanism, see Alejandro Colás, "Putting Cosmopolitanism into Practice: The Case of Socialist Internationalism," *Millennium: Journal of International Studies* 23, no. 3 (1994): 513–34.
15. Vladimir Ilyich Lenin, *The Right of Nations to Self-Determination* (New York: International, 1951), 24–25.

16. In his concise and detailed account of cosmopolitanism and nationalism in Latin America, however, Noël Salomon distinguishes cosmopolitanism from internationalism, arguing that the former is supranational and has a negative meaning, whereas the latter affirms nationalism. See his "Cosmopolitism and Internationalism in the History of Ideas in Latin America," *Cultures* 6 (1979): 83–108.

17. Sun Yat-sen, *San Min Chu I: The Three Principles of the People*, trans. Frank Price (Shanghai: China Committee, Institute of Pacific Relations, 1927), 89.

18. Frantz Fanon, *The Wretched of the Earth*, trans. Constance Farrington (New York: Grove Weidenfeld, 1963), 149.

19. See Arjun Appadurai and Carol Breckenridge, "Why Public Culture?" *Public Culture* 1, no. 1 (1988): 5–9. "The world of the late twentieth is increasingly a cosmopolitan world. More people are widely travelled, are catholic in their tastes, are more inclusive in the range of cuisines they consume, are attentive to world-wide news, are exposed to global media-covered events and are influenced by universal trends in fashion" (5).

20. See Arjun Appadurai, "Disjuncture and Difference in the Global Cultural Economy," *Public Culture* 2, no. 2 (1990): 14–15.

21. Arjun Appadurai, "Patriotism and Its Futures," *Public Culture* 5, no. 3 (1993): 418 (hereafter cited in text as PF).

22. Michael Mann, "Nation-States in Europe and Other Continents: Diversifying, Developing, Not Dying," *Daedalus* 122, no. 3 (1993): 119. Further citations appear in text.

23. The analytic distinction is between Marx's theory of the capitalist mode of production on a world scale (presupposing a truly generalized world market that integrates commodities, capital, and labor and results in global homogenization) and capitalism as an existing world-system (leaving labor unintegrated and leading to polarization). See Samir Amin, *Re-reading the Postwar Period: An Intellectual Itinerary*, trans. Michael Wolfers (New York: Monthly Review Press, 1994), 74. (hereafter cited in text as RPP). See also Samir Amin, "The Social Movements in the Periphery: An End to National Liberation?" in *Transforming the Revolution: Social Movements and the World-System*, ed. Samir Amin, Giovanni Arrighi, Andre Gunder Frank, and Immanuel Wallerstein (New York: Monthly Review Press, 1990), 96–138 (hereafter cited in text as SM).

24. Samir Amin, *Empire of Chaos* (New York: Monthly Review Press, 1992): "The new stage [of globalization] marks the emergence of a 'world economy,' i.e., a much deeper degree of integration. The consequences of this change are major. Accumulation in the central nations was formerly regulated by national political and social conflicts that structured the hegemonic alliances. But there exists today no analogous mechanism that could structure such alliances on the grand scale of the economic decisions being made—not even for the United States-Japan-EC tri-polar cluster." (10) (hereafter cited in text as EC).

25. Anthony D. Smith, *Nations and Nationalism in a Global Era* (Cambridge: Polity, 1995), 24.

26. Long-distance nationalism in postcoloniality is the flip side of minority ethnic politics in the North. As Benedict Anderson notes, "That same metropole which marginalizes and stigmatizes [the ethnic minority] simultaneously enables him to play, in a flash, on the other side of the planet, national hero." Benedict Anderson, "Exodus," *Critical Inquiry* 20, no. 2 (1994): 327.

27. For critiques of the concept of global civil society in international relations theory, see M. J. Peterson, "Transnational Activity, International Society and World Politics," *Millennium: Journal of International Studies* 21, no. 3 (1992): 371–88; Martin Shaw, "Civil Society and Global Politics: Beyond a Social Movements Approach," *Millennium: Journal of International Studies* 23, no. 3 (1994): 647–67. Peterson cautions

against regarding international society as a larger version of civil society because it operates in a decentralized political system where loyalty to the world as a whole is insignificant. Shaw points out that civil society institutions are largely defined in terms of national bases and that social movements have little impact on interstate relations because they rely on cultural impact instead of connections within the political system. He suggests that global civil society is more potential than actual and that, at best, social movements with global networks make national civil societies more globally aware.

Part I ► Cosmopolitanism and Nationalism: Some Philosophical Arguments

Justice as a Larger Loyalty

Richard Rorty

All of us would expect help if, pursued by the police, we asked a family member to hide us. Most of us would extend such help even if we knew the child, sibling, or parent asking for help to be guilty of a sordid crime. Many of us would be willing to perjure ourselves in order to supply this family member with a false alibi. But if an innocent person were wrongly convicted as a result of our perjury, most of us would be torn by a conflict between loyalty and justice.

We would feel such a conflict, however, only to the extent to which we could identify with the innocent person whom we have harmed. If the person is a neighbor, the conflict would probably be intense. If a stranger, especially one of a different race, class, or nation, it may be considerably weaker. There has to be *some* sense that he or she is "one of us" before we start being tormented by the question of whether we did the right thing when we committed perjury. So it may be equally appropriate to describe us as torn between conflicting loyalties—loyalty to our family and loyalty to a group large enough to include the victim of our perjury—rather than between loyalty and justice.

Our loyalty to such larger groups will, however, weaken, or even vanish altogether, when things get really tough. Then people whom we once thought of as like ourselves will be excluded. Sharing food with impoverished people down the street is natural and right in normal times, but perhaps not in a famine, when doing so amounts to disloyalty to one's family. The tougher things get, the more ties of loyalty to those near at hand tighten, and the more those to everyone else slacken.

Consider another example of expanding and contracting loyalties: our attitudes toward other species. Most of us nowadays are at least half convinced that the vegetarians have a point, and that animals do have some sort of rights. But suppose that the cows, or the kangaroos, turn out to be carriers of a newly mutated virus that, though harmless to them, is invariably fatal to humans. I suspect that we would then shrug off accusations of "speciesism" and participate in the necessary massacre. The idea of justice between species would suddenly become irrelevant, because things have gotten very tough indeed, and our loyalty to our own species must come first. Loyalty to a larger community—that of all living creatures on our home planet—would, under such circumstances, quickly fade away.

As a final example, consider the tough situation created by the accelerating export of jobs from the First World to the Third. There is likely to be a continuing decline in the average real income of most American families. Much of this decline can plausibly be attributed to the fact that you can hire a factory worker in Thailand for a tenth of what you would have to pay in Ohio. It has become the conventional wisdom of the rich that U.S. and European labor is overpriced on the world market. When American businesspeople are told that they are being disloyal to the United States by leaving whole cities in our Rust Belt without work or hope, they sometimes reply that they place justice over loyalty.[1] They argue that the needs of humanity as a whole take moral precedence over those of their fellow citizens, and override national loyalties. Justice requires that they act as citizens of the world.

Consider now the plausible hypothesis that democratic institutions and freedoms are viable only when supported by an economic affluence that is achievable regionally but impossible globally. If this hypothesis is correct, democracy and freedom in the First World will not be able to survive a thoroughgoing globalization of the labor market. So the rich democracies face a choice between perpetuating their own democratic institutions and traditions and dealing justly with the Third World. Doing justice to the Third World would require exporting capital and jobs until everything is leveled out—until an honest day's work, in a ditch or at a computer, earns no higher a wage in Cincinnati or Paris than in a small town in Botswana. But then, it can plausibly be argued, there will be no money to support free public libraries, competing newspapers and networks, widely available liberal arts education, and all the other institutions that are necessary to produce enlightened public opinion, and thus to keep governments more or less democratic.

What, given this hypothesis, is the right thing for the rich democracies to do? Be loyal to themselves and each other? Keep free societies going for a third of humankind at the expense of the remaining two-thirds? Or sacrifice the blessings of political liberty for the sake of egalitarian economic justice?

These questions parallel those confronted by the parents of a large family after a nuclear holocaust. Do they share the food supply they have stored in the basement with their neighbors, even though the stores will then only last a day or two? Or do they fend those neighbors off with guns? Both moral dilemmas bring up the same question: Should we contract the circle for the sake of loyalty, or expand it for the sake of justice?

I have no idea of the right answers to these questions, neither about the right thing for the parents to do nor about the right thing for the First World to do. I have posed these questions simply to bring a more abstract, and merely philosophical, question into focus: Should we describe such moral dilemmas as conflicts between loyalty and justice, or rather, as I have suggested we might, as conflicts between loyalties to smaller groups and loyalties to larger groups?

This amounts to asking, Would it be a good idea to treat "justice" as the name for loyalty to a certain very large group, the name for our largest current loyalty, rather than the name of something distinct from loyalty? Could we replace the notion of "justice" with that of loyalty to that group—for example, one's fellow citizens, or the human species, or all living things? Would anything be lost by this replacement?

Moral philosophers who remain loyal to Kant are likely to think that a *lot* would be lost. Kantians typically insist that justice springs from reason and loyalty from sentiment. Only reason, they say, can impose universal and unconditional moral obligations, and our obligation to be just is of this sort. It is on another level from the sort of affectional relations that create loyalty. Jürgen Habermas is the most prominent contemporary philosopher to insist on this Kantian way of looking at things—the thinker least willing to blur either the line between reason and sentiment or the line between universal validity and historical consensus. But contemporary philosophers who depart from Kant, either in the direction of Hume (like Annette Baier) or in the direction of Hegel (like Charles Taylor) or in that of Aristotle (like Alasdair MacIntyre) are not so sure.

Michael Walzer is at the other extreme from Habermas. He is wary of such terms as *reason* and *universal moral obligation*. The heart of his recent book *Thick and Thin* is the claim that we should reject the intuition that Kant took as central: the intuition that "men and women everywhere begin with some common idea or principle or set of ideas and principles, which they then work up in many different ways." Walzer thinks that this picture of morality "starting thin" and "thickening with age" should be inverted. He says that "morality is thick from the beginning, culturally integrated, fully resonant, and it reveals itself thinly only on special occasions, when moral language is turned to special purposes."[2]

Walzer's inversion suggests, though it does not entail, the neo-Humean picture of morality sketched by Annette Baier in her book *Moral Prejudices*. In Baier's account, morality starts out not as an obligation, but as a relation of reciprocal trust among a close-knit group, such as a family or clan. To behave morally is to do what comes naturally in your dealings with your parents and children, or your fellow clan members. It amounts to respecting the trust they place in you. Obligation, as opposed to trust, enters the picture only when your loyalty to a smaller group conflicts with your loyalty to a larger group.[3]

When, for example, the families confederate into tribes, or the tribes into nations, you may feel obliged to do what does not come naturally: to leave your parents in the lurch by going off to fight in the wars, or to rule against your own village in your capacity as a federal administrator or judge. What Kant would describe as the resulting conflict between moral obligation and sentiment, or between reason and sentiment, is, in a non-Kantian account of the matter, a conflict between one set of loyalties and another set of loyalties. The idea of a *universal* moral obligation to respect human dignity gets replaced by the idea of loyalty to a very large group—the human species. The idea that moral obligation extends beyond that species to an even larger group becomes the idea of loyalty to all those who, like yourself, can experience pain—even the cows and the kangaroos—or perhaps even to all living things, even the trees.

This non-Kantian view of morality can be rephrased as the claim that one's moral identity is determined by the group or groups with which one identifies—the group or groups to which one cannot be disloyal and still like oneself. Moral dilemmas are, in this view, the result not of conflict between reason and sentiment but of conflict between alternative selves, alternative self-descriptions, alternative ways of giving a meaning to one's life. Non-Kantians do not think that we have a central, true, self by virtue of our membership in the human species—a self that responds to the call of reason. They can, instead, agree with Daniel Dennett that a self is a center of narrative gravity. In nontraditional societies, most people have several such narratives at their disposal, and thus several different moral identities. It is this plurality of identities that accounts for the number and variety of moral dilemmas, moral philosophers, and psychological novels in such societies.

Walzer's contrast between thick and thin morality is, among other things, a contrast between the detailed and concrete stories you can tell about yourself as a member of a smaller group and the relatively abstract and sketchy story you can tell about yourself as a citizen of the world. You know more about your family than about your village, more about your village than about your nation, more about your nation than about humanity as a whole, more about being human than about simply being a living creature. You are in a better position to decide what differences between individuals are morally relevant when dealing with those whom you can describe thickly, and in a worse position when dealing with those whom you can describe only thinly. This is why, as groups get larger, law has to replace custom and abstract principles have to replace *phronesis*. So Kantians are wrong to see *phronesis* as a thickening up of thin abstract principles. Plato and Kant were misled by the fact that abstract principles are designed to trump parochial loyalties into thinking that the principles are somehow prior to the loyalties—that the thin is somehow prior to the thick.

Walzer's thick/thin distinction can be aligned with Rawls's contrast between a shared *concept* of justice and various conflicting *conceptions* of justice. Rawls sets out that contrast as follows:

> The concept of justice, applied to an institution, means, say, that the institution makes no arbitrary distinctions between persons in assigning basic rights and duties, and that its rules establish a proper balance between competing claims. . . . [A] conception includes, besides this, principles and criteria for deciding which distinctions are arbitrary and when a balance between competing claims is proper. People can agree on the meaning of justice and still be at odds, since they affirm different principles and standards for deciding these matters.[4]

Phrased in Rawls's terms, Walzer's point is that thick, "fully resonant" *conceptions* of justice, complete with distinctions between the people who matter most and the people who matter less, come first. The thin concept, and its maxim "Do not make arbitrary distinctions between moral subjects," is articulated only on special occasions. On those occasions, the thin concept can often be turned against any of the thick conceptions from which it emerged, in the form of critical questions about whether it may not be merely arbitrary to think that certain people matter more than others.

Neither Rawls nor Walzer thinks, however, that unpacking the thin concept of justice will, by itself, resolve such critical questions by supplying a criterion of arbitrariness. They do not think that we can do what Kant hoped to do—derive solutions to moral dilemmas from the analysis of moral concepts. To state the point in the terminology I am suggesting: we cannot resolve conflicting loyalties by turning away from them all toward something categorically distinct from loyalty—the universal moral obligation to act justly. So we have to drop the Kantian idea that the moral law starts off pure but is always in danger of being contaminated by irrational feelings, which introduce arbitrary discriminations among persons. We have to substitute the Hegelian-Marxist idea that the so-called moral law is, at best, a handy abbreviation for a concrete web of social practices. This means dropping Habermas's claim that his "discourse ethics" articulates a transcendental presupposition of the use of language, and accepting his critics' claim that it articulates only the customs of contemporary liberal societies.[5]

Now I want to raise in more concrete form the question of whether to describe the various moral dilemmas with which I began as conflicts between loyalty and justice or rather as conflicting loyalties to particular groups. Consider the question of whether the demands for reform made on the rest of the world by Western liberal societies are made in the name of something not merely Western—something like morality, or humanity, or rationality—or are simply expressions of loyalty to local, Western, conceptions of justice.

Habermas would say that they are the former. I would say that they are the latter, but are none the worse for that. I think it is better not to say that the liberal West is better informed about rationality and justice, and instead to say that, in making demands on nonliberal societies, it is simply being true to itself.

In a recent paper titled "The Law of Peoples," Rawls discusses the question of whether the conception of justice that he has developed in his books is something peculiarly Western and liberal or rather something universal. He would like to be able to claim universality. He says that it is important to avoid "historicism," and believes that he can do this if he can show that the conception of justice suited to a liberal society can be extended beyond such societies through formulating what he calls "the law of peoples."[6] He outlines in that paper an extension of the constructivist procedure proposed in his book *A Theory of Justice*—an extension that, by continuing to separate the right from the good, lets us encompass liberal and nonliberal societies under the same law.

As Rawls develops this constructivist proposal, however, it emerges that this law applies only to "reasonable" peoples, in a quite specific sense of the term *reasonable*. The conditions that nonliberal societies must honor in order to be "accepted by liberal societies as members in good standing of a society of peoples" include the following: "Its system of law must be guided by a common good conception of justice . . . that takes impartially into account what it sees not unreasonably as the fundamental interests of all members of society."[7]

Rawls takes the fulfillment of that condition to rule out violation of basic human rights, which include "at least certain minimum rights to means of subsistence and security (the right to life), to liberty (freedom from slavery, serfdom, and forced occupations) and (personal) property, as well as to formal equality as expressed by the rules of natural justice (for example, that similar cases be treated similarly)."[8] When Rawls spells out what he means by saying that the admissible nonliberal societies must not have unreasonable philosophical or religious doctrines, he glosses "unreasonable" by saying that these societies must "admit a measure of liberty of conscience and freedom of thought, even if these freedoms are not in general equal for all members of society."[9] Rawls's notion of what is reasonable, in short, confines membership of the society of peoples to societies whose institutions encompass most of the hard-won achievements of the West in the two centuries since the Enlightenment.

It seems to me that Rawls cannot both reject historicism and invoke this notion of reasonableness, for the effect of that invocation is to build most of the West's recent decisions about which distinctions between persons are arbitrary into the conception of justice that is implicit in the law of peoples. The differences among varying *conceptions* of justice, remember, are differences among the features of people that are seen as relevant to the adjudication of their competing claims. There is obviously enough wriggle room in phrases like "similar cases should be treated similarly" to allow for arguments that believers and infidels, men and women, blacks and whites, gays and straights should be treated as relevantly *dis*similar. So there is room to argue that discrimination on the basis of such differences is *not* arbitrary. If we are going to exclude from the society of peoples societies in which infidel homosexuals are not permitted to engage in certain occupations, those societies can quite reasonably say that we are, in excluding them, appealing not to something universal, but to very recent developments in Europe and the United States.

I agree with Habermas when he says that "what Rawls in fact prejudges with the concept of an 'overlapping consensus' is the distinction between modern and premodern forms of consciousness, between 'reasonable' and 'dogmatic' world interpretations." But I disagree with Habermas, as I think Walzer also would, when he goes on to say that Rawls

> can defend the primacy of the right over the good with the concept of an overlapping consensus only if it is true that postmetaphysical worldviews that have become reflexive under modern conditions are epistemically superior to dogmatically fixed, fundamentalistic worldviews—indeed, only if such a distinction can be made with absolute clarity.

Habermas's point is that Rawls needs an argument from transculturally valid premises for the superiority of the liberal West. Without such an argument, he says, "the disqualification of 'unreasonable' doctrines that cannot be brought into harmony with the proposed 'political' concept of justice is inadmissible."[10]

Such passages make clear why Habermas and Walzer are at opposite poles. Walzer is taking for granted that there can be no such thing as a non-question-begging demonstration of the epistemic superiority of the Western idea of reasonableness. There is, for Walzer, no tribunal of transcultural reason before which to try the question of superiority. Walzer is presupposing what Habermas calls "a strong contextualism for which there is no single 'rationality.'" In this conception, Habermas continues, "individual 'rationalities' are correlated with different cultures, worldviews, traditions, or forms of life. Each of them is viewed as internally interwoven with a particular understanding of the world."[11]

I think that Rawls's constructivist approach to the law of peoples can work if he adopts what Habermas calls a "strong contextualism." Doing so would mean giving up the attempt to escape historicism, as well as the attempt to supply a universalistic argument for the West's most recent views about which differences between persons are arbitrary. The strength of Walzer's argument in *Thick and Thin* seems to me to be his explicitness about the need to do this. The weakness of Rawls's account of what he is doing lies in an ambiguity between two senses of universalism. When Rawls says that "a constructivist liberal doctrine is universal in its reach, once it is extended to . . . a law of peoples,"[12] he is not saying that it is universal in its validity. Universal reach is a notion that sits well with constructivism, but universal validity is not. It is the latter that Habermas requires. That is why Habermas thinks that we need really heavy philosophical weaponry, modeled on Kant's—why he insists that only transcendental presuppositions of any possible communicative practice will do the job.[13] To be faithful to his own constructivism, I think, Rawls has to agree with Walzer that this job does not need to be done.

Rawls and Habermas often invoke, and Walzer almost never invokes, the notion of "reason." In Habermas, this notion is always bound up with that of context-free validity. In Rawls, things are more complicated. Rawls distinguishes the reasonable from the rational, using the latter to mean simply the sort of means-end rationality that is employed in engineering, or in working out a Hobbesian modus vivendi. But he often invokes a third notion, that of "practical reason," as when he says that the authority of a constructivist liberal doctrine "rests on the principles and conceptions of practical reason."[14] Rawls's use of this Kantian term may make it sound as if he agrees with Kant and Habermas that there is a universally distributed human faculty called practical reason (existing prior to, and working quite independent of, the recent history of the West)—a faculty that tells us what counts as an arbitrary distinction between persons and what does not. Such a faculty would do the job Habermas thinks needs doing: detecting transcultural moral validity.

But this cannot, I think, be what Rawls intends, for he also says that his own constructivism differs from all philosophical views that appeal to a source of authority, and in which "the universality of the doctrine is the direct consequence of its source of authority." As examples of sources of authority, he cites "(human) reason, or an independent realm of moral values, or some other proposed basis of universal validity."[15] So I think we have to construe his phrase "the principles and conceptions of practical reason" as referring to *whatever* principles and conceptions are in fact arrived at in the course of creating a community.

Rawls emphasizes that creating a community is not the same thing as working out a modus vivendi—a task that requires only means-end rationality, not practical reason. A principle or conception belongs to practical reason, in Rawls's sense, if it emerged in the course of people starting thick and getting thin, thereby developing an overlapping consensus and setting up a more inclusive moral community. It would not so belong if it had emerged under the threat of force. Practical reason for Rawls is, so to speak, a matter of procedure rather than of substance—of how we agree on what to do rather than of what we agree on.

This definition of practical reason suggests that there may be only a verbal difference between Rawls's and Habermas's positions. Habermas's own attempt to substitute "communicative reason" for "subject-centered reason" is itself a move toward substituting "how" for "what." The first sort of reason is a source of truth, truth somehow coeval with the human mind. The second sort of reason is not a source of anything, but simply the activity of justifying claims by offering arguments rather than threats. Like Rawls, Habermas focuses on the difference between persuasion and force, rather than, as Plato and Kant did, on the difference between two parts of the human person—the good rational part and the dubious passionate or sensual part. Both would like to de-emphasize the notion of the *authority* of reason—the idea of reason as a faculty that issues decrees—and substitute the notion of rationality as what is present whenever people communicate, whenever they try to justify their claims to one another rather than threaten one another.

The similarities between Rawls and Habermas seem even greater in the light of Rawls's endorsement of Thomas Scanlon's answer to the "fundamental question why anyone should care about morality at all," namely, that "we have a basic desire to be able to justify our actions to others on grounds that they could not reasonably reject—reasonably, that is, given the desire to find principles that others similarly motivated could not reasonably reject."[16] This suggests that the two philosophers might agree on the following claim: the only notion of rationality we need, at least in moral and social philosophy, is that of a situation in which people do not say, "Your own current interests dictate that you agree to our proposal," but rather, "Your own central beliefs, the ones that are central to your own moral identity, suggest that you should agree to our proposal."

This notion of rationality can be delimited using Walzer's terminology by saying that rationality is found wherever people envisage the possibility of getting from different thicks to the same thin. To appeal to interests rather than beliefs is to urge a modus vivendi. Such an appeal is exemplified by the speech of the Athenian ambassadors to the unfortunate Melians, as reported by Thucydides. To appeal to your enduring beliefs as well as to your current interests is to suggest that what gives you your *present* moral identity—your thick and resonant complex of beliefs—may make it possible for you to develop a new, supplementary, moral identity.[17] It is to suggest that what makes you loyal to a smaller group may give you reason to cooperate in constructing a larger group, a group to which you may in time become equally loyal, or perhaps even more loyal. The difference between the absence and the presence of rationality, on this account, is the difference between a threat and an offer—the offer of a new moral identity and thus a new and larger loyalty, a loyalty to a group formed by an unforced agreement among smaller groups.

In the hope of minimizing the contrast between Habermas and Rawls still further, and of rapprochement between both and Walzer, I want to suggest a way of thinking of rationality that might help to resolve the problem I posed earlier: the problem of whether justice and loyalty are different sorts of things, or whether the demands of justice are simply the demands of a larger loyalty. I said that question seemed to boil down to the question of whether justice and loyalty had different sources—reason and sentiment, respectively. If the latter distinction disappears, the former one will not seem particularly useful. But if by rationality we mean simply the sort of activity that Walzer thinks of as a thinning-out process—the sort that, with luck, achieves the formulation and utilization of an overlapping consensus, then the idea that justice has a different source than loyalty no longer seems plausible.[18]

In this account of rationality, being rational and acquiring a larger loyalty are two descriptions of the same activity. This is because *any* unforced agreement between individuals and groups about what to do creates a form of community, and will, with luck, be the initial stage in expanding the circles of those whom each party to the agreement had previously taken to be "people like ourselves." The opposition between rational argument and fellow feeling thus begins to dissolve, for fellow feeling may, and often does, arise from the realization that the people whom one thought one might have to go to war with, use force on, are, in Rawls's sense, "reasonable." They are, it turns out, enough like us to see the point of compromising differences in order to live in peace, and of abiding by the agreement that has been hammered out. They are, to some degree at least, trustworthy.

From this point of view, Habermas's distinction between a strategic use of language and a genuinely communicative use of language begins to look like a difference between positions on a spectrum—a spectrum of degrees of trust. Baier's suggestion that we take trust rather than obligation to be our fundamental moral concept would thus produce a blurring of the line between rhetorical manipulation and genuine validity-seeking argument—a line that I think Habermas draws too sharply. If we cease to think of reason as a source of authority, and think of it simply as the process of reaching agreement by persuasion, then the standard Platonic and Kantian dichotomy of reason and feeling begins to fade away. That dichotomy can be replaced by a continuum of degrees of overlap of beliefs and desires.[19] When people whose beliefs and desires do not overlap very much disagree, they tend to think of each other as crazy or, more politely, as irrational. When there is considerable overlap, on the other hand, they may agree to differ and regard each other as the sort of people one can live with—and eventually, perhaps, the sort one can be friends with, intermarry with, and so on.[20]

To advise people to be rational is, in the view I am offering, simply to suggest that somewhere among their shared beliefs and desires there may be enough resources to permit agreement on how to coexist without violence. To conclude that somebody is irredeemably *ir*rational is not to realize that she is not making proper use of her God-given faculties. It is rather to realize that she does not seem to share enough relevant beliefs and desires with us to make possible fruitful conversation about the issue in dispute. So, we reluctantly conclude, we have to give up on the attempt to get her to enlarge her moral identity, and settle for working out a modus vivendi—one that may involve the threat, or even the use, of force.

A stronger, more Kantian, notion of rationality would be invoked if one said that being rational guarantees a peaceful resolution of conflicts—that if people are willing to reason together long enough, what Habermas calls "the force of the better argument" will lead them to concur.[21] This stronger notion strikes me as pretty useless. I see no point in saying that it is more rational to prefer one's neighbors to one's family in the event of a nuclear holocaust, or more rational to prefer leveling off incomes around the world to preserving the institutions of liberal Western societies. To use the word *rational* to commend one's chosen solution to such dilemmas, or to characterize one's way of making up one's mind as "yielding to the force of the better argument," is to pay oneself an empty compliment.

More generally, the idea of "the better argument" makes sense only if one can identify a natural, transcultural relation of relevance that connected propositions with one another so as to form something like Descartes's "natural order of reasons." Without such a natural order, one can evaluate arguments only according to their efficacy in producing agreement among particular persons or groups. But the required notion of natural, intrinsic relevance—relevance dictated not by the needs of any given community, but by human reason as such—seems no more plausible or useful than that of a God whose will can be appealed to in order to resolve conflicts between communities. It is, I think, merely a secularized version of that earlier notion.

Non-Western societies in the past were rightly skeptical of Western conquerors who explained that they were invading in obedience to divine commands. More recently, they have been skeptical of Westerners who suggest that they should adopt Western ways in order to become more rational. (This suggestion has been abbreviated by Ian Hacking as "Me rational, you Jane.") In the account of rationality I am recommending, both forms of skepticism are equally justified. But this is not to deny that these societies *should* adopt recent Western ways by, for example, abandoning slavery, practicing religious toleration, educating women, permitting mixed marriages, tolerating homosexuality and conscientious objection to war, and so on. As a loyal Westerner, I think they should indeed do all these things. I agree with Rawls about what it takes to count as reasonable, and about what kind of societies we Westerners should accept as members of a global moral community.

But I think that the rhetoric we Westerners use in trying to get everybody to be more like us would be improved if we were more frankly ethnocentric and less professedly universalist. It would be better to say: "Here is what we in the West look like as a result of ceasing to hold slaves, beginning to educate women, separating church and state, and so on. Here is what happened after we started treating certain distinctions between people as arbitrary rather than fraught with moral significance. If you would try treating them that way, you might like the results." Saying that sort of thing seems preferable to saying: "Look at how much better we are at knowing what differences between persons or arbitrary and which not—how much more *rational* we are."

If we Westerners could get rid of the notion of universal moral obligations created by membership in the species, and substitute the idea of building a community of trust between ourselves and others, we might be in a better position to persuade non-Westerners of the advantages of joining in that community. We might be better able to construct the sort of global moral community that Rawls describes in "The Law of Peoples."In making this suggestion, I am urging, as I have on earlier occasions, that we peel apart Enlightenment liberalism from Enlightenment rationalism.

I think that discarding the residual rationalism that we inherit from the Enlightenment is advisable for many reasons. Some of these are theoretical and of interest only to philosophy professors, such as the apparent incompatibility of the correspondence theory of truth with a naturalistic account of the origin of human minds.[22] Others are more practical. One practical reason is that getting rid of rationalistic rhetoric would permit the West to approach the non-West in the role of someone with an instructive story to tell, rather than in the role of someone purporting to be making better use of a universal human capacity.

Notes

A slightly different version of this essay was read at the Seventh East-West Philosophers' Conference (held January 9–20, 1995, in Honolulu), and will appear in the proceedings of that conference, to be published by the University of Hawaii Press.

1. Donald Fites, CEO of the Caterpillar tractor company, explained his company's policy of relocation abroad by saying, "As a human being, I think what is going on is positive. I don't think it is realistic for 250 Americans to control so much of the world's GNP." Quoted in Edward Luttwack, *The Endangered American Dream* (New York: Simon & Schuster, 1993), 184.

2. Michael Walzer, *Thick and Thin: Moral Argument at Home and Abroad* (Notre Dame, Ind.: Notre Dame University Press, 1994), 4.

3. Baier's picture is quite close to that sketched by Wilfrid Sellars and Robert Brandom in their quasi-Hegelian accounts of moral progress as the expansion of the circle of beings who count as "us."

4. John Rawls, *Political Liberalism* (New York: Columbia University Press, 1993), 14 n.

5. This sort of debate runs through a lot of contemporary philosophy. Compare, for example, Walzer's contrast between starting thin and starting thick with that between the Platonic-Chomskian notion that we start with meanings and descend to use, and the Wittgensteinian-Davidsonian notion that we start with use and then skim off meaning as needed for lexicographical or philosophical purposes.

6. John Rawls, "The Law of Peoples," in *On Human Rights: The Oxford Amnesty Lectures, 1993*, ed. Stephen Shute and Susan Hurley (New York: Basic Books, 1993), 44. I am not sure why Rawls thinks historicism undesirable, and there are passages, both early and recent, in which he seems to throw in his lot with the historicists. (See the passage quoted in note 10, below, from his recent "Reply to Habermas.") Some years ago, I argued for the plausibility of a historicist interpretation of the metaphilosophy of Rawls's *A Theory of Justice* (Cambridge, Mass.: Belknap, 1971) in my "The Priority of Democracy to Philosophy," which has been reprinted in Richard Rorty, *Objectivity, Relativism and Truth* (Cambridge: Cambridge University Press, 1991).

7. Rawls, "The Law of Peoples," 81, 61.

8. Ibid., 62.
9. Ibid.
10. All quotations in this paragraph are from Jürgen Habermas, *Justification and Application: Remarks on Discourse Ethics* (Cambridge: MIT Press, 1993), 95. Habermas is here commenting on Rawls's use of "reasonable" in writings earlier than "The Law of Peoples." The latter appeared subsequent to Habermas's book.

When I wrote the present essay, the exchange between Rawls and Habermas published in the *Journal of Philosophy* 92, no. 3 (March 1995) had not yet appeared. This exchange rarely touches on the question of historicism versus universalism, but one passage in which this question emerges explicitly is in Rawls's "Reply to Habermas": "Justice as fairness is substantive . . . in the sense that it springs from and belongs to the tradition of liberal thought and the larger community of political culture of democratic societies. It fails then to be properly formal and truly universal, and thus to be part of the quasi-transcendental presuppositions (as Habermas sometimes says) established by the theory of communicative action" (179).
11. Habermas, *Justification and Application*, 95.
12. Rawls, "The Law of Peoples," 46.
13. My own view is that we do not need, either in epistemology or in moral philosophy, the notion of universal validity. I argue for this in "Sind Aussagen Universelle Geltungsansprueche?" *Deutsche Zeitschrift fuer Philosophie* 42, no. 6 (1994): 975–88. Habermas and Apel find my view paradoxical, and likely to produce performative self-contradiction.
14. Rawls, "The Law of Peoples," 46.
15. Ibid., 45.
16. I quote here from Rawls's summary of Scanlon's view in *Political Liberalism*, 49 n.
17. Walzer thinks it is a good idea for people to have lots of different moral identities: "Thick, divided selves are the characteristic products of, and in turn require, a thick, differentiated, and pluralistic society." *Thick and Thin*, 101.
18. Note that in Rawls's semitechnical sense an overlapping consensus is not the result of discovering that various comprehensive views already share common doctrines, but rather something that might never have emerged had the proponents of these views not started trying to cooperate.
19. Davidson has demonstrated that any two beings that use language to communicate with each other necessarily share an enormous number of beliefs and desires. He has thereby shown the incoherence of the idea that people can live in separate worlds created by differences in culture or status or fortune. There is always an immense overlap—an immense reserve army of common beliefs and desires to be drawn on at need. But this immense overlap does not, of course, prevent accusations of craziness or diabolical wickedness, for only a tiny amount of nonoverlap about certain particularly touchy subjects (the border between two territories, the name of the One True God) may lead to such accusations, and eventually to violence.
20. I owe this line of thought about how to reconcile Habermas and Baier to Mary Rorty.
21. This notion of "the better argument" is central to Habermas' and Apel's understanding of rationality. I criticize it in "Sind Aussagen Universelle Geltungsansprueche?"
22. For a claim that such a theory of truth is essential to "the Western rationalist tradition," see John Searle, "Rationality and Realism: What Difference Does It Make?" *Daedalus* 122, no. 4 (1992): 55–84. See also my reply to Searle in "Does Academic Freedom Have Philosophical Presuppositions?" *Academe* 80, no. 6 (1994): 52–63. I argue there that we should be better off without the notion of "getting something right," and that writers such as Dewey and Davidson have shown us how to keep the benefits of Western rationalism without the philosophical hang-ups caused by the attempt to explicate this notion.

Kant's Project for Perpetual Peace

Allen W. Wood

It has been a little more than two hundred years since the publication of Kant's essay *Zum ewigen Frieden: Ein philosophischer Entwurf* (Toward perpetual peace: A philosophical project).[1] As the twentieth century nears its end, it is a good time to reflect on that essay, to consider its background, the reason for its past and continuing popularity, and how far we have come on the road of history Kant projected in it. It is high time too, for the philosophically inquisitive, to ponder some of the interpretive problems it presents, and also to try out an approach to Kant's philosophy that would give *Perpetual Peace* a more central place in his system than it has usually been accorded.

Probably the immediate occasion for Kant to write an essay on the subject of peace between nations in that year was the Treaty of Basel, concluded between France and Prussia in March of 1795. It effectively ended the War of the First Coalition between the monarchical states of Europe and the French Republic. *Perpetual Peace* may be read as an expression of support for the Republic itself and for the Prussian policy of peace with France. The cause of the Republic is endorsed both in the First Definitive Article, which says that the constitution of every state should be republican, and in Kant's remark in the Second Definitive Article that peace might come about if, through good fortune, "one powerful and enlightened nation can educate itself up to the form of a republic" and then make itself into the "focal point for a federative union of other states" (AK 8:356). The monarchical states, in other words, should not merely tolerate revolutionary France, but even view it as the potential leader of a peaceful cosmopolitan federation.

Of course Kant could not write with any expectation that such views would be shared by those in power. Less than a year had passed since King Friedrich Wilhelm II, through his education minister J. C. Wöllner, had reprimanded Kant for the Socratic offenses of misleading the youth and showing disrespect for the Christian religion and the Holy Scriptures. The letter of reproof had elicited Kant's promise to his sovereign neither to lecture nor to write on religious topics—a promise he kept faithfully until after the king's death in July 1797. *Perpetual Peace* may be read as Kant's assertion that he had no intention of keeping silent on *other* matters of general public concern.

Kant was far from the first to subscribe to the idea that peace between states should be achieved under a system of international law. The notion of a "right of nations" (*ius gentium*) was present even in the ancient world, and Kant alludes to its treatment by early modern theorists such as Hugo Grotius and Samuel Pufendorf (AK 8:355). Nor was Kant the first to advocate an international federation of states. In the late seventeenth century, both the young Leibniz and William Penn had advanced proposals for an international authority in Europe that was to guarantee a lasting peace between Christian peoples.[2] Kant's immediate models, however, were the *Projet pour rendre la paix perpetuelle en Europe* (Project to render peace perpetual in Europe) by Charles-Irénée Castel, Abbé de Saint-Pierre, and an extract from this work written by Jean-Jacques Rousseau.[3] Kant had cited both precursors by name in his 1784 essay *Idea toward a Universal History in a Cosmopolitan Respect*, arguing that the human race must seek perpetual peace between nations through a free federation of states (AK 8:24; see also 8:313). Even before 1780, Kant's lectures on moral philosophy had made the Abbé de Saint-Pierre's project the focus of their conception of humanity's final end in history (AK 27:470–71). *Perpetual Peace* itself conspicuously alludes to the Abbé de Saint-Pierre's *Projet* by setting forth "articles" of peace, arranged under distinct headings, just as the Abbé had done.[4]

The Abbé de Saint-Pierre wrote his *Projet* in 1713, on the occasion of the Congress of Utrecht, which successfully resolved several dynastic and religious disputes among the ruling families of England, France, and Spain. The Abbé's peace project was only one of many ambitious proposals for political improvement that he put forward during his career. Like most of them, it was almost universally regarded—even by Leibniz, for example—as a well-intentioned but naive scheme devised by an overly optimistic visionary. In the 1720s, the Abbé de Saint-Pierre was further discredited when his criticism of Louis XIV's policies led to his expulsion from the Collège de France. It may have been precisely this reputation—as high-minded, impractical, also slightly subversive—that attracted Rousseau to the Abbé's writings. In 1761, he took up the task of editing them, completing the extract of the *Projet* based on the Abbé's own 1729 abridgment, but never finishing the larger task owing to the turmoil into which his own political writings were soon to plunge him.

Rousseau's approach to the topic of peace between nations is not quite the same as the Abbé's. The Abbé de Saint-Pierre assumes the legitimacy of the existing European states and the system of dynastic absolutism; he seeks to persuade the monarchs that submitting international disputes to a league of states is conducive to their own enlightened self-interest. Rousseau, however, is openly skeptical of the idea that the interest of the rulers tends to coincide with the public good. He doubts that absolute monarchs are even capable of pursuing their own rational self-interest when it threatens to conflict with their unjust caprices and despotic delusions.

To an extent, Kant's *Perpetual Peace* may be seen as mediating between the approaches of these two predecessors. Like the Abbé de Saint-Pierre, Kant earnestly addresses heads of state, urging that they take the advice of philosophers and arguing that there is some degree of natural harmony between the commands of moral reason and reasons of state (AK 8:343, 368–69). Yet Kant's articles of peace are presented as principles of *right*, not of political expediency. Kant concedes it is sometimes uncertain whether it would be politically prudent to ignore the articles, but insists it is always certainly wrong and dishonorable to violate them (AK 8:373, 377–78).

Kant postulates that power corrupts the will of those who have it, and infers, with Rousseau, that the policies of absolute rulers are often opposed both to right and to the public good (AK 8:345, 369, 373–74). He argues that the constitution of every state should be republican not only in order that it may accord with the idea of right, but also because decisions about war and peace ought to be made by representatives accountable to the people (AK 8:349–53). Throughout *Perpetual Peace*, Kant casts himself—with a mixture of dignified self-assertion and self-deprecating good humor—in the role of the idealistic philosophical moralist whose distance from practical affairs makes him all the more qualified to give advice to cynical politicians where the final ends of humanity are concerned (AK 8:343, 370–86). At the same time, however, he is concerned to rebut any accusation that he is naive or excessively optimistic about human nature. Again and again he alludes to his own doctrine of the innate human propensity to evil, emphasizing that radical evil will always make peace difficult to achieve even between justly constituted states under politically favorable conditions (AK 8:345, 355, 375 n, 379, 380, 381).

Kant's aim in *Perpetual Peace*, however, significantly diverges both from the Abbé de Saint-Pierre's and from Rousseau's. Unlike the former, he is not giving counsel to heads of state from their own standpoint. Nor, like the latter, is he merely remonstrating with them and exposing their habits of duplicity and injustice. The primary audience of *Perpetual Peace* is humanity in general; it sets forth principles of international right that are binding on all human beings collectively, and only for this reason pertinent especially to those who hold power over states. Kant regards perpetual peace between nations as both a demand of right and a final end of the human race, which must therefore be of interest to its morally disposed members. As he later expressed it in the Doctrine of Right, "perpetual peace [is] the ultimate goal of the entire right of nations" (AK 6:350).

Unlike the Abbé de Saint-Pierre's project, which was proposed to a definite congress of states at a given time and place as an opportune extension of the terms of a particular treaty, Kant's project is purely *philosophical*; its articles have an unrestrictedly cosmopolitan intent and are presented as commands of each individual's own reason. Yet it would also be a serious error to see them as merely a set of timeless moral principles, for Kant conceives his philosophical project in light of a definite philosophy of history, addressing himself to a determinate historical situation and articulating the specific historical task of the coming age.

It is not difficult to explain why *Perpetual Peace* is the most popular of all Kant's writings. It is the best-known piece of writing by any major philosopher on the topic of peace between nations. In our century, this topic has become literally a matter of life and death for the entire planet. Kant's project also anticipates our century's most forward-looking practical projects in the field of international relations—the League of Nations after the First World War and the United Nations since the Second.[5] It is a measure of the hopes we still place in the United Nations that we submit some of the world's most intractable problems to its care—such as civil wars and ethnic conflicts in Cambodia, Somalia, Rwanda, and the former Yugoslavia—and criticize it for failing to solve them, even with the restricted mandates and resources imposed on it by the powerful nations of the world as long as they are too timid to assume these same responsibilities. We read *Perpetual Peace* as both a philosophical articulation and an important historical declaration of these vast and still-unfulfilled hopes.

Perpetual Peace is startlingly prophetic of twentieth-century realities in other ways that set it apart from any earlier project of a similar kind. The peaceful federations proposed by Kant's predecessors were all restricted to the Christian states of Europe. The Abbé de Saint-Pierre, for example, proposed an international army not only in order to enforce a ban on states that refuse to comply with rulings of the court of arbitration, but even more with a view to protecting the European Union itself from threats to the East. Kant's philosophical project, however, is truly cosmopolitan in its intent, not limited by any geographic or cultural borders. Its articles are meant not merely as precepts of a *ius gentium*, applying to the relations between sovereign states, but beyond this also as principles of a *ius cosmopoliticum*, which regards *all* peoples of the earth as a "single universal community" or "universal state of humankind" founded on a "universal right of humanity" (AK 8:349 n, 360; compare AK 6:352–53).

If Kant's project is not limited to the European states, still less does it privilege the rights of European peoples in relation to non-Europeans. In his discussion of the Third Definitive Article of perpetual peace, pertaining to the "right of hospitality," Kant bluntly condemns the practices of the European peoples whose "discovery" and "visitation" of other parts of the world have been equivalent to conquest, and who looked upon all other parts of the world as "mere ownerless territories; for the native inhabitants were counted as nothing." He therefore commends the policies of the Chinese and Japanese, who have restricted the movements and enterprises of European explorers and exploiters. These restrictions, he says, are necessary if independent nations are to escape the terrible injustices suffered by native Americans, Africans, spice islanders, and other peoples of the world who have been victimized by European colonization (AK 8:358–59; compare AK 6:265–66, 353–54).

Kant is not proposing a single all-embracing world-state. To him that would be a "soulless despotism" or "graveyard of freedom" that would "crush the germ of goodness" in human beings and, as the bonds of public law became thinner, eventually "lapse into anarchy" (AK 8:367). He regards the separation of peoples from one another in independent states as a necessary protection both of individual liberty and the tendencies to social progress. He even regards war itself as a useful device of nature insofar as it has preserved the independence of peoples (AK 8:119–20).[6] But Kant holds that human history is now reaching a critical point: the positive effects war has had on the development of human faculties are being overtaken by the destructive effects of a system of states whose security is based on military power (AK 8:367–68; compare AK 6:344). If the historical development of our species-capacities is to continue, a system of mutually independent states must gradually grow toward a federal union, naturally grounded on ties of commerce and mutual self-interest, and effected by an increasing unity of principles based on ever-expanding communication and the consequent emergence of a single enlightened world culture.

Kant's argument for the conclusion that a peaceful cosmopolitan federation of states is historically indispensable for humanity's future arises out of his uncannily prescient reflections on the *economic* significance of the fact that modern states view their security as based on a perpetual readiness to go to war. He sees this as a *recent* historical development and the greatest threat to the final aims of our species yet encountered in human history (AK 8:22–24, 310). Kant distinguishes three powers within a state on which its military power depends: the power of the army, the power of alliance, and the power of money. He singles out the last of these as the most reliable instrument of war, noting especially the significance of the novel practice of contracting national debt to finance not only wars themselves, but even more significantly, the readiness for war on which states found their external security even in (what is called) "peacetime" (AK 8:345; compare AK 8:28). Kant insists that the capacity of a nation to make war is far more dependent on the strength of its economy than on the valor of its soldiers or the strategic ability of its statesmen and generals. In this way, Kant has begun to see how modern warfare is becoming less a clash between two armies than a conflict between two economies.

The strength of modern states, in Kant's view, rests on the "spirit of commerce," which is ultimately incompatible with war (AK 8:368). A nation that must give first priority to being fully armed not only deprives its people of well-being, but also impoverishes its scientific, cultural, and moral development. "The necessity of holding [ourselves] in constant readiness for war," Kant says, involves a wastefulness of human capacities that "stunts the full development of human nature" (AK 8:26; compare 8:24, 121, 312, 345). For this reason, Kant regards the economic effects of a perpetual arms race as the chief threat to humanity—even more dangerous in the long run to the destiny of our species than the actual devastation and bloodshed of wars themselves.

Perpetual Peace thus represents not only war but even the idea of national security based on military defense as something human beings should increasingly regard as historically obsolete. Kant utterly condemns the conventional wisdom thrust at us in the brazen paradox "If you wish peace, prepare for war." He denies that genuine peace between nations can ever be obtained through a system of mutual military deterrence. As for a system of alliances designed to preserve a balance of power, Kant compares this derisively to the house in Jonathan Swift's story that was so perfectly built that it collapsed as soon as a sparrow alit on the roof (AK 8:312). The perpetual peace required by the final ends of humanity must rather be a condition in which the collective influence of a federation of states renders war such a remote and unpromising course of action that it also makes a state of readiness for it both unnecessary and impossible (AK 8:343, 345–46).

In Kant's view, however, the increasing dependence of military power on economic power also tends to work subtly in favor of this moral aim (AK 8:360–68), for it suggests that the policy of sacrificing the development of science and commerce to military preparedness will in the end be counterproductive (AK 8:28; compare AK 8:313, 368). Nations whose economies are geared for war will tend to lose out *economically* to those oriented to the well-being and progress of their people, and hence over time they will also tend to lose out *militarily* as well. Further, the states that are freer and more just—whose constitutions are republican rather than military-despotic—will be the economically more powerful states; and as more states become republican, decisions about war and peace will be made less often by those who benefit from giving priority to military power and more often by those who will have to bear the costs of such policies. In this way, states will be compelled to renounce the strategy of achieving external security through independent military might, and people will come to realize that the only true national security lies in joining other states in a peaceful federation.

No doubt twentieth-century experience of the republican state founded on a spirit of commerce has acquainted us with a whole barrage of powerful social interests that work directly contrary to these optimistic tendencies. We know that serious threats to peace and progress can arise not only from the political institutions of early modern feudal despotism, but also directly from those of the liberal representative republic in which Kant placed his hopes. He would surely have been disheartened to know that two centuries after he wrote, the world's leading modern republic would also be one of the world's chief suppliers of armaments and the nation whose economy is most profoundly and conspicuously dependent on military technology and production. Yet the historical trends and forces Kant describes are evidently still at work as well. Republics are wary of going to war, and it is doubtful that the position of a superpower grounded in a military economy is indefinitely sustainable. For this reason, the wiser republics have already chosen economic over military power as a basis of international influence. We are involved in a historical process beset with conflicts and crosscurrents, whose eventual outcome nobody can claim to predict.

Our predicament in this respect remains fundamentally the one described by Kant's philosophy of history. Kant declares that philosophy too has its "chiliasm," which is not utopian because it is based on a practical idea toward which we can strive (AK 8:27). Nevertheless, he clearly has no expectation that the millennium of peace, justice, freedom, and enlightenment will arrive any time soon. Moreover, as Kant holds that the burden of fulfilling the human race's historical vocation must always rest on human beings as free agents, he never claims that the victory of reason in history will be easy or inevitable. The historical task of philosophy, therefore, is not to foment violent revolutions to bring the world to an end, but only to keep alive the spirit of enlightenment, as the single necessary condition for humanity to continue its slow and painful movement in a progressive direction.

It is not surprising that *Perpetual Peace* should be Kant's most popular work. What is more difficult to explain is its relative neglect by rigorous scholarship. *Perpetual Peace* has not received the same intense treatment given to Kant's more systematic writings on the foundations of knowledge or morality, or even to his thinking on mathematics, physics, aesthetics, politics, or religion.[7] This cannot be explained by saying that as a piece of popular writing, *Perpetual Peace* is simple and unproblematic, its argument so plain and straightforward that it needs no exegesis or critical discussion. On the contrary, the text bristles with problems that have scarcely been noticed, let alone solved.

To what literary genre does *Perpetual Peace* belong? Kant describes it as an *Entwurf*, a "project" or "outline." This, along with the reference to "articles," is no doubt an allusion to the Abbé de Saint-Pierre's *Projet*, but Kant's essay is not a draft of a treaty in any but a very metaphorical sense. It is clearly not a philosophical treatise of any ordinary kind either. If it contains a connected argument at all, then it is one that the reader must reconstruct. It is as if Kant (writing in an age of enlightenment, for readers who must think for themselves) wants to underline, through the very form of his essay, the tentativeness and open-endedness of his questioning, and also to challenge his readers to work out on their own—to carry further, or even to correct—the path of thinking on which he has invited them.

Accordingly, the structure of the essay is also anomalous and enigmatic. After a brief, ironical preamble, Kant begins with an enumeration of "articles," first "preliminary," then "definitive," for a condition of peace between states. Where does Kant get these articles? How does he propose to argue for them? How are the two sets of articles related to one another? The articles are then followed by two curious "additions," the first dealing with the philosophy of history, the second with the role of philosophers as advisers to political leaders on issues of war and peace. *Perpetual Peace* concludes with two "appendices" on the relation between morality and politics. How do these "additions" and "appendices" relate to each other and to the two sets of articles?

Nearly forty years ago, in an unassuming introduction to an English translation of *Perpetual Peace*, Lewis White Beck proposed a terse answer to these questions. According to Beck, Kant's argument starts with the anthropological-historical account presented in the First Addition's "guarantee of perpetual peace." This account legitimates a second, moral-philosophical phase of the argument, by demonstrating the practicability of the moral-political principles found in the Second Addition and the two appendices. The principle of respect for human beings as ends in themselves and the derivative moral criterion of publicity in regard to political maxims justify in turn the Definitive Articles, which (according to Beck) are nothing but moral laws translated into the language of right and politics, establishing the moral foundation for an idea of peaceful relations between states. Finally, the Definitive Articles ground the Preliminary Articles (with which the essay began), the Preliminary Articles merely specifying in pragmatic or technical terms how states should behave toward one another with a view to actualizing the idea represented in the Definitive Articles.[8]

Beck's reading of *Perpetual Peace* has much to recommend it. Yet even a brief description of it serves to indicate how opaque and problematic this text is, hence how indirect, speculative, and controversial any interpretation of its overall argument will have to be. If Beck is right, then *Perpetual Peace* is grounded in Kant's anthropology and philosophy of history—an aspect of his philosophy that is also neglected and not well understood. What is the basis of the guarded historical optimism from which Kant derives his so-called guarantee of a perpetual peace? Is its basis empirical and theoretical? Or is it merely a practical postulate or article of moral faith like immortality and the existence of God, which we are to accept for practical purposes, but has no theoretical support? If the latter, then what sort of guarantee could Kant expect this to provide the cynical politicians he hopes to convince? But then again, how strong a "guarantee" does Kant really claim for perpetual peace? Does he hold that eventual peace between nations is an *inevitable* result of nature's purposiveness in history? If not, how can he hope to persuade the rulers of nations that their only hope for security lies in a peaceful federation? But if so, then what role would be left for free human effort in actualizing the idea of perpetual peace?[9]

On any reading of *Perpetual Peace*, there are also troubling questions about the nature of the international federation Kant is proposing. He implies that the federation of states will be voluntary, and yet he also projects the hope that this federation will progress toward something stronger, a "universal state of nations" (*allgemeiner Völkerstaat*) (AK 8:313). Clearly, neither the federation nor the state of nations is to be an all-embracing world-state, for the members are themselves sovereign states, united under common principles of right.[10] Yet unlike the Abbé de Saint-Pierre, whose project included a court of arbitration and an international army to enforce a ban on states that do not comply with its judgments, Kant proposes no specific mechanisms for determining or enforcing international rights. In his earlier lectures on ethics, Kant appears to hold that the Abbé de Saint-Pierre's hopes will not be realized by political means but only through a *moral* community created solely by education (AK 27:470–71). By the time he wrote *Perpetual Peace*, however, Kant drew a clear distinction between a political community grounded in right and a wholly voluntary ethical community (modeled on a church) (AK 6:95–100). In *Perpetual Peace* the international federation is quite evidently grounded in right rather than in morality. This implies that it requires coercive power, but Kant's account lacks not only the practical mechanisms but even the theoretical foundations for the system of right that would apply to such an organization.

The solutions to all these perplexities may, of course, lie hidden in the text of *Perpetual Peace*, needing only to be extracted through patient and perceptive scholarship. But most Kant scholars have tended to overlook all these problems, and I think the reason for this is that *Perpetual Peace* is not usually seen as addressing the chief concerns of Kant's philosophy, according to the architectonic suggestions Kant himself worked out in the three Critiques. If we are to take *Perpetual Peace* seriously as an important part of Kant's philosophy, then, what we most need is a new way of looking at the unity of that philosophy that enables us to locate the issues of *Perpetual Peace* more centrally. What follows is my own project or outline of such a new approach.

My proposal is that Kant regards not only *Perpetual Peace* but even the critical philosophy as a whole historically—as addressing a specific situation within the universal process of human history. We can see *Perpetual Peace* as central to the critical philosophy by viewing the unity of that philosophy in terms of its own self-definition of its historical task.

Human history for Kant is a purposive natural process. As with all species of living things, nature's end regarding the human species is the complete development of its predispositions and faculties (AK 8:18). Because human beings have what Rousseau calls "perfectibility"—a capacity for developing, inventing, and even choosing their modes of life in relation to nature—the powers of the human species belong to humanity collectively more than they do to individuals, and to the entire historical succession of human generations more than to human beings in any single time or place (AK 8:18–20). Nature's means for the development of these faculties is correspondingly unique. It consists in establishing relationships among human beings, making them simultaneously interdependent yet fundamentally antagonistic to one another—a relationship to which Kant gives the suitably paradoxical name "unsociable sociability" (AK 8:20–22). This relationship is grounded on the propensity in human nature Kant calls "self-conceit" (AK 5:73). It is the desire to have, and to be recognized by others as having, a greater self-worth than our fellow human beings. Self-conceit grounds our irrational belief that we have a superior claim to happiness, and hence the prerogative of using others as mere means to our ends and of exempting ourselves from the rules we would will rational beings in general to obey (AK 4:424).

According to nature's plan, self-conceit provokes an unsociably sociable state of discontented competitiveness among human beings, and this competition, in turn, while making us both evil and unhappy, promotes the collective development of our species-capacities. Unsociable sociability flourishes most abundantly in a "civilized" condition—an urban society of highly diversified crafts and industries grounded on an agricultural economy.[11] Civilization leads to an endless variety of different life activities and the competitive development of all human faculties. As we have seen, war itself plays a positive role in this process, by separating different peoples, compelling them to live in every habitable region of the earth, distinguishing their material modes of life, and thus developing the manifold faculties of human nature (AK 8:364–65).

The most fundamental human faculty, at the same time the highest and most independent, is *reason*. Viewed negatively, reason provides the freedom from instinct that enables human beings to develop and perfect their nature generally. Yet reason also has a positively liberating side, as the capacity to give laws and set ends that are independent of—and even in certain ways diametrically opposed to—the ends set for human beings by their instincts and natural propensities (AK 8:111–15).

"In the course of things human," Kant says, "almost everything, considered in the large, is paradoxical" (AK 8:41). The basic paradox of human history is that when reason liberates itself from nature, it comes to recognize a self-worth in human beings that directly conflicts with the propensity to self-conceit. The law given by reason is universally binding on all rational beings without privilege or exception because it is based on the dignity, the absolute and incomparable worth, of every rational being as an end in itself. This law commands human beings to see themselves as members of an ideal realm in which the ends of rational beings would no longer be mutually antagonistic but would form an organic whole or "realm of ends" (AK 4:421–37). The civilized condition has thus far been characterized by wide differences in social status and extremes of wealth and poverty that systematically violate the principles of right and morality autonomously prescribed by reason (AK 8:116–18). Accordingly, our natural inclinations, grounded in self-preference and competitiveness, necessarily experience the laws of reason as a burdensome constraint. This is why for us those laws must be imperatives, and the best human will can never do more than submit itself reluctantly to duty.

Viewed historically, therefore, our species suffers the paradoxical fate that in acting freely we must struggle against those very propensities of our nature—our self-conceit and unsociable sociability—to whose operations we owe our freedom. In fact, for Kant human nature itself is characterized fundamentally by this paradoxical and peculiarly *historical* trait—of having to transform our unsociable sociability into a systematic harmony based on reason, or, in short, of having to turn a state of war into one of peace: "What is characteristic of the human race in comparison with the idea of possible rational beings on earth is in general this: that nature has placed in it the seed of *discord* and willed that its own reason should produce *concord*" (AK 7:322).

The history that fundamentally characterizes human nature also has a critical turning point. This comes when reason has matured far enough that it is able to break free of nature and give its law explicitly to itself. At this stage, which Kant describes as the "adolescence" of the human species (AK 6:121–22), human beings must emerge from their tutelage to nature and to human authority. Because reason itself exists only through human communication (KrV A738/B766), it becomes the task not only of human individuals but of an entire public to throw off the leading-strings of both nature and tradition. Kant's name for this emergence from tutelage is "enlightenment," and the principle of enlightenment is "Think for yourself" (AK 8:35, 146–47 n). Kant regards his own age not as enlightened, but as in the process of becoming enlightened. The specific historical task of such an age, and especially of its philosophers, is to articulate the principles of a reason that is coming to think for itself, or, in other words, to become *self-legislative*.

Another name Kant gives to this turning point in history, especially in a theoretical context, is "critique." The preface to the first edition of *Critique of Pure Reason* describes this critique itself as a metaphorical court of justice in which reason applies its own self-given laws to separate the legitimate claims of theoretical cognition from illegitimate ones, which are grounded in reason's self-conceited pretensions and often devised to support traditional religious superstitions (KrV Axi–xii). The same preface declares the present age to be an "age of critique," in which all claims—not only those of science but also those of religious faith and political authority—must submit themselves to the free and open examination of public, rational inquiry (KrV Axi n).

In practical philosophy, the age of enlightenment or critique goes by the name "autonomy." A moral philosophy for an age of enlightenment must be grounded in the recognition that rational beings can be obligated by no laws except those they give themselves through their own reason (AK 4:432–33). In articulating a moral philosophy founded on autonomy, Kant is not merely solving an old philosophical problem about moral obligation; more important, he is addressing a new philosophical task that truly arises only at the turning point of human history.

Kant's anthropology represents the human condition as one of conflict—both externally, in unsociable sociability, social inequality, and war between nations, and internally, in the antagonism between self-conceit and human dignity and the consequent tension between natural inclination and reason. But in human history, nature and reason cooperate as well as conflict. The unsociable sociability of human nature is the means by which nature drives us into the civil condition, in which our lawless freedom is curbed through the rational coercion of right (AK 8:21, 310, 365–66). Then when the state of war between nations threatens the full development of our natural faculties, nature supplies a guarantee of perpetual peace, using human passions themselves to compel nations toward a peaceful federation (AK 8:310–11, 368).

The cooperation between nature and reason must work in the other direction as well. At the earlier stages of human culture, social antagonism promotes the development of human faculties and predispositions, but only if conflict is kept within acceptable limits by the coercive enforcement of a system of right. At the stage of history we have now reached, this same development can continue only if human beings freely progress toward the idea of a perfect civil constitution. Thus the problem of devising such a constitution—which Kant calls the "last and greatest problem for the human species"—is thus one human reason must solve for the sake of *nature's* end (AK 8:22–23, 366). And because a political state organized around preparations for war must pervert human culture and undermine humanity's progress toward justice, this last and most difficult problem can be solved only if the human race also achieves just and peaceful external relations between states (AK 8:24–26). In human history, therefore, the paths of nature and reason ultimately converge; neither reason nor nature can make progress without the other's aid (AK 8:27–28). Nature's ends themselves regarding the human species can be achieved only through enlightenment, through the project of critical philosophy in theory and autonomy in practice.

The unity of Kant's philosophy may thus be viewed as the unity of the *historical* task of enlightenment. Looking at it in this way, the project of perpetual peace emerges as the central focus of Kant's critical or enlightenment philosophy. As distinct from the progress of morality in each individual, of knowledge in particular sciences, of justice in independent states, perpetual peace is the global or cosmopolitan project in which the human race must unite if it is to advance in its historical vocation, and hence preserve its nature as a species destined to turn natural discord into rational concord. The three Critiques, and the system of philosophy which is to be built upon them, aim at a rational system of thought whose historical actuality as human activity is vitally bound to the project of perpetual peace, for this project is the condition of the historical possibility of every other end of both nature and reason regarding the human species.

Kant's time, of course, is no longer ours. In the past two centuries, his Enlightenment project has been developed and expanded, meeting with both victories and defeats. Right now it is under attack from many sides. Its confidence in reason is assailed both by corrosive forms of skepticism and by enthusiasms new and old. Its cosmopolitanism is rejected equally by communitarians and cultural relativists. Its radical historical optimism is ridiculed by those who react to the failures of twentieth-century socialism with either bitter disillusionment or trimphant glee. Even we philosophers can no longer entertain the wish, expressed in the Second ("Secret") Article to *Perpetual Peace*, that we might influence the course of things by having our rational projects gain the favor of benevolent despots.[12] The fact is that we no longer believe in benevolent despots, and our current despots, who are our representatives in a far from ideal republic, have in any case often been elected precisely on the basis of their open *malevolence* toward anything advertised as a humanitarian scheme of an enlightenment philosopher with cosmopolitan aims.

Yet Kant himself also wrote *Perpetual Peace* under a regime about which he had no illusions, addressing it to those very authorities who had recently rebuked him for his Enlightenment ideas. If Kant placed his hopes on the French Revolution, he also rejected revolution in principle as a means of political progress, and even admitted about the French experiment that it "may be so filled with misery and atrocities that no right thinking human being would ever decide to make the experiment again at such costs, even if he could hope to carry it out with good fortune in the second attempt" (AK 7:85). He warns us that nature's "guarantee" of perpetual peace is "not sufficient to *prophesy* it (theoretically) but still suffices in a practical respect and makes it into a duty to work toward this (not merely chimerical) end" (AK 8:368). Even Kant's defense of historical progress was always qualified by the acknowledgment that "it may at times be *interrupted*, though never finally *broken off*" (AK 8:309).

Some have seen in these qualifications an unattractive complacency, or even a fundamentally conservative spirit.[13] I see something quite different, and something badly needed in our time: a wise insistence that the chiliasm of philosophy must never become an enthusiasm, and its historical hopes must never be entertained in any spirit of urgency or impatience, as though we could not devote ourselves to final ends of humanity philosophers are still learning to articulate unless we see clear signs that humanity is on the brink of fulfilling them. Conversely, we must not permit these hopes to be turned to despair by the failure of any single social movement or political experiment, nor may we abandon them simply because we have the misfortune to be living at a time when humanity's progress has been interrupted and the engines of history have fallen into the hands of those who would throw the mechanism into reverse. Still less should we permit our disillusionment to turn us against the very ideas of enlightenment, reason, humanity, and progress—as was to happen to many of the romantics in the early nineteenth century, and again to similarly confused and restless minds at the end of the twentieth.

In its own century, the Abbé de Saint-Pierre's project, which he named the European Union, was scoffed at or condescended to by all but a few impractical dreamers and cloistered philosophers. Yet today there is a European Union that has not only achieved, but even utterly surpassed, all the Abbé's hopes that were dismissed as fantastic by his contemporaries. Do we really know that it will not someday be the same with other dreams and projects, such as Kant's own projects of an ideally just republican constitution and the necessary condition for it, a society free of the threat of war and the stifling burden of armaments? Or the idea of enlightenment itself—of an entire public constituted by people who think for themselves instead of having their thoughts enslaved to traditional prejudices or selectively manipulated by the system of mass communication? Or again, still other, more radical aims and projects arising from the Enlightenment tradition: The idea of democracy, which to Kant was an object of fear rather than hope, and which has never existed anywhere in a genuine form on a large scale? Or the projects of abolishing racial, religious, and ethnic hate and oppression, or of dismantling the prison walls, both internal and external, of patriarchy and homophobia, or of ending the exploitation of those who labor by those who own, and with it the terrible gulf between rich and poor, both within society and between societies?

None of these projects now seems feasible in any of our lifetimes. Today many such goals even appear to be rapidly receding from us—just as the Abbé de Saint-Pierre's dream of a European Union surely must have seemed farther than ever from being realized during the two monstrous wars that ravaged Europe during the first half of this century. From a Kantian standpoint, however, the only question to be asked about such grand historical aims is whether it is the collective duty of the human race to work toward them. If it is, then it is also reasonable to shape our view of ourselves and our history by the postulate that they can someday be achieved, and then to search for natural and social mechanisms cooperating with our efforts to achieve them.

The twentieth century has not been the century of enlightenment, but the century of disillusionment. At its end, the timeliest (if also the most unfashionable) message of *Perpetual Peace* is surely its cautious hopefulness in relation to history—and regarding the finite reasonableness of our corrupt, fallible species, which is its only guide in history. It is this stubborn, sober, principled hopefulness alone in which Kant finally grounded the argument of his uniquely popular and uniquely timely historical "project."

Notes

This essay has benefited from comments by and discussions with B. Sharon Byrd, Paul Guyer, Renate Knoll, John Rawls, and Rega Wood.

1. Immanuel Kant, *Zum ewigen Frieden: Ein philosophischer Entwurf. Kants Gesammelte Schriften.* Ausgabe der königlich preussischen Akademie der Wissenschaften (AK) 8:341–86. The revised and expanded edition now known to us, including the Second Addition or "Secret Article," was not published until January 1796. Kant's writings are cited in notes and in text according to AK by volume:page number. The only exception is the *Critique of Pure Reason*, which is abbreviated "KrV" and cited according to A/B pagination. All translations are my own. Kant's earliest published project for perpetual peace came ten years earlier, and was occasioned by the offhand remark of a follower. In the February 1784 issue of the *Gothaischen Gelehrte Zeitungen*, Kant's colleague Johann Schulze wrote an article in which appears the following rather cryptic remark: "A favorite idea of Professor Kant is that the final end of the human race is the attainment of the most perfect political constitution, and he wishes that a philosophical historian would undertake to provide us in this respect with a history of humanity, and to show how far humanity in different ages has approached this final end or distanced itself from it, and what is still to be done to attain it" (AK 8:468). Kant himself developed Schulze's hint in the essay *Idea toward a Universal History in a Cosmopolitan Respect*, published in November of the same year. In it, Kant sets forth both the methodology and the basic substance of his philosophy of history.

2. Gottfried Wilhelm Leibniz, "Securitas publica interna et externa" (1670), in *Gottfried Wilhelm Leibniz: Sämtliche Schriften und Briefe*, ed. Paul Ritter (Darmstadt: Preussischen Akademie der Wissenschaften, 1923), 1:4, 131–68. See R. W. Meyer, *Leibnitz and the Seventeenth Century Revolution* (Glasgow: Bowes & Bowes, 1952), 129–32. In later life, Leibniz moved away from his early espousal of the idea of a Christian republic. In 1715, he commented on the Abbé de Saint-Pierre's *Project*, which he regarded as utopian and unworkable; see *Leibniz: Political Writings*, 2d ed., ed. Patrick Riley (Cambridge: Cambridge University Press, 1988), 176–84. But Kant's allusion to the sign of the Dutch innkeeper, with which *Perpetual Peace* begins, seems to have been drawn from Leibniz's *Codex Iuris Gentium* (1693); see *Leibniz: Political Writings*, 166: and Patrick Riley, *Kant's Political Philosophy* (Totowa, N.J.: Rowman & Littlefield, 1983), 122.

   William Penn, *An Essay on the Present and Future Peace of Europe by the Establish-*

ment of a European Diet, Parliament or Estates (1693). As Leibniz's memorandum was not widely circulated, this is generally considered the first well-known proposal for a European peace through an international federation. Other precursors of the Abbé de Saint-Pierre and Kant are discussed in Miriam Eliav-Feldon, "Grand Designs: The Peace Plans of the Late Renaissance," *Vivarium* 27 (1989): 51–76.

3. Charles-Irénée Castel, Abbé de Saint-Pierre (1658–1743), *Projet pour rendre la paix perpetuelle en Europe* (Cologne: J. le Pacifique, 1712; Utrecht: Antoine Shouten, 1713); the first English translation was *A Project for Settling on Everlasting Peace in Europe*, by the Abbot St. Pierre of the French Academy (London: J. Watts, 1714). Jean-Jacques Rousseau, in *Extrait du projet de paix perpetuelle* (1761), in *Oeuvres complètes* (Paris: Pleiade, 1964), 3:561–89. Rousseau also wrote *Jugement sur la paix perpetuelle*, published posthumously (1782) in *Oeuvres complètes* 3:590–600.

4. Kant lists six "preliminary" and three "definitive" articles. The Abbé de Saint-Pierre lists eight "fundamental" articles, seven "necessary" articles, and six "useful" articles. For a discussion of their contents, see Carl Joachim Friedrich, *Inevitable Peace* (Cambridge: Harvard University Press, 1948), 163–69: Riley, *Kant's Political Philosophy*, 125–26. Following the Abbé's own 1729 abridgment, Rousseau reduced the twenty-one articles to five: (1) providing for a European Union, (2) assessing revenues for the support of an international army to support it, (3) subjecting its members to binding mediation and a court of arbitration, (4) providing for a ban and enforcement mechanisms for the court's judgments, and (5) allowing for a modification of the terms of the articles (Rousseau, *Oeuvres complètes* 3:575–76). These evident allusions give us sufficient reason to translate Kant's essay into English under the title *Perpetual Peace: A Philosophical Project*. In writing *Perpetual Peace*, Kant may also have been influenced by Voltaire's criticisms of the Abbé de Saint-Pierre in *De la paix perpetuelle* (1769), written under the pseudonym of Dr. Goodheart. See Riley, *Kant's Political Philosophy*, 129–31.

5. This was very much in the minds of Max Adler, Paul Natorp, and Julius Ebbinghaus, who wrote about *Perpetual Peace* in the 1920s, and of Karl Jaspers and Carl Friedrich, who wrote about it after World War II. Max Adler, "Kant und der ewige Friede" (1924), in *Immanuel Kant zu ehren*, ed. Wolfgang Kopper and Rudolf Malter (Frankfurt, 1974), 269–89; Paul Natorp, *Kant über Krieg und Frieden: Ein geschichtsphilosophischer Essay* (Erlangen, 1924); Julius Ebbinghaus, "Kants Lehre vom ewigen Frieden und die Kriegsschuldfrage" (1929), in *Gesammelte Aufsätze, Vorträge und Reden* (Hildesheim: Olms, 1968), 24–57; Friedrich, *Inevitable Peace*; Karl Jaspers, "Zum ewigen Frieden" (1957), in *Aneignung und Polemik. Gesammelte Reden und Aufsätze zur Geschichte der Philosophie*, ed. H. Saner (Munich, 1968), 205–32.

6. On this point Kant's views are not as distant as many think from the views of Hegel, with which they are often contrasted. In the *Critique of Judgment*, Kant writes: "Even war has something sublime about it if it is carried on in an orderly way and with respect for the sanctity of the rights of citizens. At the same time it makes the way of thinking of the nation that carries it on in this way all the more sublime in proportion to the number of dangers in the face of which it courageously stands its ground. A prolonged peace, on the other hand, tends to promote a mere spirit of commerce, and along with it a base selfishness, cowardice and softness, and to debase that nation's way of thinking" (AK 5:263). Compare Georg W. F. Hegel, *Elements of the Philosophy of Right* (Cambridge: Cambridge University Press, 1991), §324. Kant and Hegel are largely in agreement about the *past* role of war in human affairs. Where they differ is that Hegel thinks war will continue to play this same role, whereas Kant thinks that it cannot continue to do so because of the economic effect of the international arms race as a historical *novum*. On this point, then, Hegel has the more ahistorical view.

7. There are few recent book-length studies of the peace essay (but see Georg Cavaller, *Pax Kantiana* [Vienna: Böhlau, 1992].) *The Cambridge Companion to Kant*, a recent comprehensive presentation of state-of-the-art scholarship on Kant's philosophy, includes essays dealing in some detail with each of the topics just mentioned, but its discussion of *Perpetual Peace* (in the article on Kant's political philosophy) is less than two pages in length.

8. Lewis White Beck, "Introduction," in Immanuel Kant, *Perpetual Peace*, ed. Lewis White Beck (New York: Bobbs-Merrill, 1957), ix–xiv.

9. Beck's reading further implies that not only Kant's theory of international right but also his conception of political morality depends on anthropological considerations. This is in apparent contradiction to Kant's own insistence that moral principles must be applied to anthropology but never based on it (AK 4:387–88, 6:216–17). It also implies that at least in international relations, principles of right are grounded on principles of morality, in contrast to the independence of the realm of right as Kant presented it only a couple of years later (AK 6:218–19, 229–31, 396-98).

10. As Patrick Riley has noted, Kant is proposing something more than a treaty among states, but also something less than a world government. *Kant's Political Philosophy*, 118.

11. In "Conjectural Beginning of Human History" (1786), Kant provides a conjectural narrative of the history through which civilization came to be (AK 8:109–23).

12. This relationship between philosophers and benevolent despots has been stated even more explicitly from the other side of the relation, by Frederick the Great: "It pertains to philosophers to be the teachers of the world and the leaders of princes; they must think consequently, and it pertains to us to act consequently; they must discover, we must carry it out." Quoted by Friedrich Paulsen, "Aufklärung und Aufklärungspädagogik" (1903), in *Aufklärung, Absolutismus und Bürgertum in Deutschland*, ed. F. Kopitsch (Munich, 1976), 280. I am grateful to Arthur Strum for bringing this quotation to my attention.

13. See Frederick C. Beiser, *Enlightenment, Revolution, Romanticism* (Cambridge: Harvard University Press, 1992), chap. 2.

Cosmopolitanism and the Experience of Nationality

Jonathan Rée

Nationalism is not overcome through mere internationalism; it is rather expanded and elevated thereby into a system.
▶ *Martin Heidegger*[1]

The twentieth century is slipping into the past tense, but few will regret its departure. It began with high hopes, and dreams of peace and plenty. It proceeded with ambitious schemes for political and cultural reform, and using science to eliminate want from the world. But as the century ends, its achievements—whether in education, wealth, health, or political emancipation—appear compromised, to say the least, while its failures—wars, genocides, disaffections, inequality, fear, political murders, misbegotten revolutions, and ecological disasters—look absolutely catastrophic.

Moralists like to think that the century demonstrates a collapse of ethical values. We have sunk, they say, to uncharted depths of bestial depravity. We have positively relished the sufferings of the rest of the world, as long as our own interests were safe, and then we have enjoyed them even more when our own luck has run out. In politics, we have entrusted state power to moral monsters; in morality, compassion and selflessness have deserted us.

But is the moralistic diagnosis convincing? If anything, surely, the century presents a heartbreaking record of altruism, of people in the millions giving up their private happiness for the sake of some public good. What makes the century disconcerting is the battery of calamities brought about not by greed, irresponsibility, and malevolence, but by active sacrifices on behalf of others and of future generations. What is unsettling is not that generous and enlightened motives have been overwhelmed by destructive malice, but that they have led in practice to disaster. Righteous fervor has turned out to be a source of corrosive evil. Consciences have been clear enough; it is intelligence that has been clouded. We have suffered not so much from guilty minds as from confused ones.

The highest hopes of the century rode on the brave ideal of international peace and cooperation, based on a kind of world citizenship that would transcend the narrow boundaries of patriotism and put a final end to war and colonial plunder. The idea has a long history, of course. It goes back, particularly, to Kant's essay on the "cosmopolitan point of view," with its projection of a "universal *cosmopolitan existence*" as the only form in which the capacities of the human race could ever be fully developed and expressed.[2] The essay was written in 1784, and over the following decade Kant turned the idea of cosmopolitanism into the *Project for a Perpetual Peace*, with its proposal for a "Federation of nations" all freely uniting with each other under a self-imposed collective "law of nations."[3]

But there was a fateful slippage in Kant's transition over the years from the idea of cosmopolitanism to that of perpetual peace. In the process, the shining ideal of world citizenship was reduced to a grudging concession that we ought always to allow foreigners to travel among us unmolested, provided they do not stay around too long—an obligation that Kant derived from a "right all men have, . . . founded upon common possession of the surface of the earth, whose spherical form obliges them to suffer others to subsist contiguous to them." Apart from this depressing reflection on human sociability, *Perpetual Peace* allows cosmopolitan rights to be swallowed up again by the old patriotisms they were originally meant to supplant. In Kant's scheme, individuals were subsumed, by virtue of shared language and religion, in their nation, and each nation was matched, ideally, with the constitutional arrangements of a particular political state—states being not only administrative units, for Kant, but treelike "communities" or "societies," each its "own roots" in a native soil. States so defined are "moral persons," Kant says, and "nations, as states, like individuals, if they live in a state of nature and without laws, by their vicinity alone commit an act of lesion."[4] Kant's cosmopolitanism, in short, transformed itself into internationalism, without anyone noticing the difference.

Kant did not express his analysis in terms of *internationalism*, however; nor was there any trace of the word in the English translation of *Perpetual Peace*, which appeared in 1796 (a year after the original version) and from which I have been quoting. The term was still very new, in fact, having been invented by Bentham in 1780, to name the part of legal theory traditionally known as the "law of nations." The word was, perhaps, as Bentham hoped, self-explanatory, but it had the effect of emphasizing the paradox involved in the idea of a code that might control the relations between "nations," in the same way that national legal codes control the relations between individual citizens. What authority could legitimate such a law, and what sovereign power enforce it? If an "international" body intervened in a dispute between nations, would it not be acting as just another national power, disguised in the trappings of supranational right?

The 1824 supplement to the *Encyclopaedia Britannica* elaborated the Kantian version of cosmopolitanism in some detail, using the newfangled vocabulary of internationalism. The author of the piece—identified only as F.F.—argued for an "international code" of "international law," to be interpreted by an authoritative "international tribunal," but he had to admit that, unlike national legislators, international ones had few punishments at their disposal. They could appeal only to purely *moral* sanctions, that is to say, the forces of popular approval or disapproval. This was a very feeble resource, of course, as long as state power was controlled by monarchs and aristocrats, because they could always surround themselves with courtly flatterers to protect them from the shafts of public opinion. It followed that international legality could not become an effective force without the spread of democracy: "It is only in those countries, the rulers of which are drawn from the mass of the people, in other words, in democratical countries, that the sanction of the laws of nations can be expected to operate with any considerable effect."

International law should therefore be taught in all schools, so as to diffuse a "moral sentiment" among the citizens, and in due course the feeling would grow so strong that national leaders could no longer ignore it. Citizens would require their governments to conduct international affairs in such a way that the country's "justice, generosity, and magnanimity" would become "the theme of general applause" throughout the world. Because no one could wish his or her own nation to be spoken of by others "with disgust and indignation," public sentiment in democracies would give "a wonderful efficacy to the international jurisdiction."[5]

Now it is easy to see, with hindsight, that F.F. was mistaken about the connection between popular democracy and international lawlessness. He thought that under democratic government, self-interested national rapaciousness would be reined in by the moral force of popular national pride. But two centuries of historical experience seem to prove the exact opposite: that national pride exults in national difference and national strength, and that nations are more likely to despise each other's good opinion than to struggle to deserve it. Killing foreigners is a well-known recourse for governments in democratic states facing difficult electoral contests. National pride, one might conclude, is a terrible engine of international injustice, rather than a solid bulwark against it.

Still, there is some insight behind F.F.'s ingenuous non sequitur. Nationalistic sentiments are indeed connected with the rise of democracy, and, far from being thwarted or frustrated by the modern framework of "international relations," they may in fact presuppose them. Internationalism and nationalism, in other words, are inseparable partners, two aspects of a single historical phenomenon—the phenomenon of "internationality," as it may be called.[6] But what kind of a phenomenon might that be?

Political philosophers and international relations theorists can make short work of internationality by insisting on the proper observance of analytic distinctions between state and nation, nation-state and state-nation, nationality and nationalism, or ethnic and civic nationalisms. They can swiftly show, too, that "international law" is a misnomer for interstate law, or that Britain and the United States, despite the rhetoric of their politicians, are states rather than nations. Given the terminological confusions that infect internationality as a whole, the theorists will shed few tears for the verbal difficulties experienced by Kant, or for the unfortunate translators who have tried to help him out by translating *Völkerrecht* either as "public right" or "right of Nations," *Völkerstaat* as "peoples . . . forming one and the same state" or "international state," and *Staaten* as "nation states."[7]

Edward Said has dismissed the terminological squeamishness of the theorists as the worst kind of pedantry. Nationalism, he reminds us, is not a theoretical conjecture but a "historical fact," and "it is no more useful to oppose that than to oppose Newton's discovery of gravity."[8] But whereas Said's impatience is understandable, his objection is rather blunt. Of course he is right that nationalisms are not just sets of theoretical concepts that we can accept or reject or refine in a philosophical seminar. They are indeed forces at work in the world. But unlike gravity, they owe their power to the fact that they are forms of human experience. They are ways in which people interpret their worlds and try to make sense of their lives. As such, they presuppose complex networks of concepts and doctrines, images and sentiments. In addition, they may teem with contradictions, fictions, and confusions—indeed, they might be unable to function at all without them. Remove the ambiguities, and there would not be much left of nationalism as a "historical fact."

It could be more than a coincidence, therefore, that the classic theorist of cosmopolitanism and international peace was also the classic analyst of the fictions inherent in our experience of the world. In the *Critique of Pure Reason*, Kant distinguishes three different kinds of illusion that our cognitive apparatus is liable to. First of all, there are purely empirical illusions, like optical illusions, which, with care, we can avoid being deceived by. Second, there are conceptual illusions, or illusions of the understanding, which we can never correct, though we may neutralize them through insight into their logical behavior. And finally there are dialectical illusions, or illusions of reason, which will never cease to make fools of us, even after we have grasped how they work. Coincidentally or not, internationality would seem to comprise illusions that fall into three similar groups: empirical, conceptual, and dialectical.

Among the empirical illusions of internationality, the most obvious is the idea that nations are as old as the hills, and that one's own, in particular, stems from time immemorial, or even that it goes back to the first creation.[9] Case by case, however, it turns out that most national traditions are inventions of the past two hundred years—indeed, it seems to be widely accepted among historians and social theorists that the principle of nationality, despite its trappings of misty antiquity, is a defining feature of "modernity" as such.[10]

A nation's claim to antiquity will also, nearly always, involve the affirmation of a continuous chain of racial inheritance going back to a biologically pure past, whose contamination will be thought of as an ever-present danger. But, case by case again, it turns out that the idea of pure racial origins is an unhistorical fantasy. And from a scientific point of view it is clear that such genetic isolation and interbreeding would be a biological disaster anyway.

A third empirical illusion involved in national self-consciousness is a reference to a territory—a territory that, originally, is supposed to have belonged exclusively and naturally to one's nation. But again and again, images of virgin territories, self-evident boundaries, and datable original occupation turn out to be mere mirages: territorial claims become more obscure, not clearer, the further you dig into their past.

The fourth empirical illusion of internationality concerns language and culture. There was a time, before the rise of internationality, when travelers took linguistic differences in their stride. Of course, communication is difficult between people who do not share a language. But because any language can be learned by anyone who wants to do so, the difficulty can always be overcome. In general, traditional travelers expected to rediscover familiar habits when they visited foreign lands, and would be puzzled or annoyed if they encountered anything absolutely baffling or strange. But today's tourists approach their experiences with the opposite expectations: they treat linguistic differences as insuperable barriers, and expect members of foreign nations to be entirely inscrutable. They are then horrified to discover all the ways in which abroad is quite like home, feeling cheated of an absolute exoticism they assumed they had a right to expect.

The empirical illusions of internationality can be corrected by reference to facts of history, biology, geography, culture, and language. But behind them there is a set of *conceptual* illusions that are rather more difficult to pin down. Illusions of this order concern the principle of nationality itself, and its imagined nature and origin. They can be seen at work not only in simple-minded nationalists, but also in would-be sophisticated cosmopolitans—such, for example, as Bertrand Russell. Rather like Edward Said, Russell considered it worthwhile to emphasize, as he put it in an essay written during the first World War, that "national sentiment is a fact," and one that "should be taken account of by institutions."

> What constitutes a nation is a sentiment and an instinct, a sentiment of similarity and an instinct of belonging to the same group or herd. The instinct is an extension of the instinct which constitutes a flock of sheep, or any other group of gregarious animals. The sentiment which goes with this is like a milder and more extended form of family feeling. When we return to England after being on the Continent, we feel something friendly in the familiar ways, and it is easy to believe that Englishmen on the whole are virtuous, while many foreigners are full of designing wickedness.[11]

Ironically enough, these patrician statements on behalf of "we Englishmen" were written for delivery to a meeting of Scottish workingmen. The lecture was banned, however, by the British War Office, and was not published in the United Kingdom until 1963, thus presenting a nice emblem of the notorious nonidentity of England, Britain, and the United Kingdom. Nevertheless, Russell managed to incorporate all the essential patterning of national thinking into his own would-be cosmopolitanism.

His main claim was that national experience is basically a matter of rootedness in local conditions, and of respect and affection for them. Such attachments to places and people, probably the places and people of one's childhood, are of course real enough. But by what right are they annexed to the principle of nationality? It is worth remembering, for a start, that part of the meaning of nationality is the obliteration of local particularity in favor of national uniformity; indeed, Dr. Johnson's dictionary defined *national* as meaning "publick; general; not private; not particular." And as soon as you begin to analyze the substance of local sentiments—memories of songs, poems, or stories, or of honey for tea, or getting your shoes yellow with buttercup pollen, smelling the smoke of Gauloises, or hearing the crackling flames as you fall asleep in front of a fire—it becomes evident that they all define different localities, different communities, different networks of social sympathy. It is fantastic to suppose that they could all extend precisely to the edges of a single nation and there come abruptly to a halt—that, as Hume once put it in a heroic victory over his customary skepticism, "the same national character follows the authority of government to a precise boundary."[12] It is in the nature of our local loyalties, on the contrary, that they will be plural and out of alignment with each other, and indeed that they will change over a lifetime, as different local pasts acquire different saliences for us. But nationalities are categorically different: as a rule, you only have one of them and, normally, you have to keep it for life. It may be essential to the principle of nationality that it present itself as the embodiment of intimate local feelings—it would lose most of its popular attraction otherwise—but the claim is essentially false, nevertheless.[13]

The second rogue element in Russell's attempt at an unillusioned description of the "fact" of nationality is the idea of national sentiment as spontaneous or self-originating. Russell assumes that you begin by loving yourself, and that self-love then spreads itself outward in widening circles of sympathy to embrace first your family, then your friends, and then—in "a milder and more extended form of family feeling," as he puts it—your entire kith and kin, your nation.

Apart from its inherent implausibility as a description of the moral experiences of selfhood, narcissism, and family life, Russell's analogy between family feeling and national feeling overlooks the fact that you cannot have a sense of belonging to the same nation as your neighbors unless you are aware of it as one nation among others and of an imagined totality of nations forming, eventually, a kind of world system, perhaps arranged in some order of seniority. People can never experience themselves as British, for instance, unless they have an idea of France, or as Irish unless they have a sense of England and then Britain. Nations exist only in the plural, in other words, and if every nation but one were supposed destroyed, then the last one would cease to be a nation as well. Local sentiments acquire national significance only in the light of an imagined international order. It is essential to the principle of nationality that it presuppose internationality, but perhaps it is equally essential that it should cover this presupposition up, by presenting the nation as an extended family.

As you can see, I am constructing a kind of pyramid of internationality. At its base are the four empirical illusions of national experience—historical, biological, geographic, and cultural-linguistic. On the next level are the two conceptual illusions associated with the principle of nationality—one confounding locality with nationality, the other pretending that nationality is a spontaneous sentiment that precedes internationality. This leaves, at the apex of the pyramid, the dialectical illusion of internationality—the illusion from which it is most difficult, if not impossible, to escape.

This supreme fiction of internationality is the idea that our life is nothing apart from our nation, and that if our nation were to perish, then we might as well be dead too. Internationality binds people to each other, in other words, by making them think of themselves as members one of another within the transcendent unity of their nation. And it thereby acquires a unique and terrible social power: people will gladly kill for their nation, and gladly die for it, because they somehow manage to identify its life with their own.

The imaginary world of internationality functions by bringing together three dimensions of human experience that would usually be thought of as metaphysically quite separate: the natural, the political, and the subjective. Nations would count for nothing, that is, if they were not imagined as originally ordained by nature, and as having a life of their own, or even as superhuman personality. (The etymological connections with nativity and naturalness remain a good guide to some of the latent meanings of *nationality*.) But nations would not be nations unless they were also thought of as aspiring to self-realization in a political form, as national states: it is against nature, surely, for a nation to lack independence. Indeed, it is often supposed that political power cannot be legitimate except as the expression of a "national" will. But a national will is not to be equated with an arithmetical summation of the opinions or interests that members of the nation happen to have. National feeling is imagined as welling up from the depths of all our subjectivities: our truest self, according to the principle of nationality, is the same as our nation, and our nation indistinguishable from our truest self.

It may be thought that these imagined links among subjectivity, politics, and nature—however fantasmatic they may be in theory—amount in practice to an affirmation of the virtues of collectivism in human affairs, as distinct from the vices of atomistic and egotistical individualism. If you want people to look out for each other, and to care for shared amenities like peace or a good physical and cultural environment, then you should be in favor of the principle of nationality. Nations, it will be said, are the institutions best suited to protecting the disadvantaged and to providing all those goods that are essentially shared.

But, even though the principle of nationality walks part of the road toward recognizing collective needs, it soon veers off in a different direction. In the first place, while it acknowledges the bonds among members of the same nation, it diminishes the claims of everyone else. And second, it imagines its collective life as a historical reality, though one that may now be under mortal threat. Nationalist collectivism lives defensively for its past, rather than hopefully for the future.

The imaginary principles of internationality do not confine themselves to suggesting empirical links among nature, politics, and subjectivity. Their logic is one not of linkage, but of substitution. By a kind of dialectical conjuring trick, they make it seem as if nature, politics, and subjectivity could all be translated into each other without remainder. They enable you to imagine that every action carried out by your nation, and everything that happens to it, is your own personal concern, and that leaders and members are interchangeable, one for all, all for one.[14] And this system of mutual deputization is underwritten or guaranteed or stabilized by the assurance that your sense of unity with the rest of your nation has been authorized by nature itself.

The naturalized interchangeability of public politics and personal subjectivity within the imaginary world of internationality is attested by the ease with which the same words get applied to individuals as to nations, and not by way of metaphorical extension but by way of literal, natural application. Persons and nations become conceptually interchangeable in the easy swings from personal to national character, personal to national culture, personal to national guilt, personal to national self-determination, personal to national rights, personal to national survival, personal to national interest—and then back from the national to the personal once more. Personality and nationality are united in a single dialectical blur.

But in recent years the preferred expression of this dialectical hypnosis has been the word *identity*. Originally, of course, it designated a technical concept in philosophical Latin: identity was the element of permanent continuity beneath apparent change. Locke's discussion of the special difficulties of defining identity in the case of human beings—what he called the question of "personal identity"—was so influential that during the eighteenth century the word *identity* came to be used, elliptically, to mean personality, or the distinctive, enduring subjective core, if there was one, of an individual person. The habit was reinforced in Kant's arguments to the effect that the identity-over-time of the subject of experience was not an empirical matter at all, because we could not even begin to have a coherent experience unless our subjectivity endured from one moment to the next, linking our perceptions, past, present, and future, in a single temporal sequence. You could not be aware of change, he pointed out—not even change in your own subjective states—unless you could compare successive experiences; and this means that however much you might think you had changed, you would still have to presuppose that your basic identity as an experiencer endured.

Freud complicated the language of identity by speaking of the unconscious acts of "identification"—especially with parents—through which the structures of the personality are formed. After he died, however, his concept of identification was all but swamped by a neo-Freudian weakness for the word *identity*, which, unlike *identification*, was no part of Freud's own conceptual vocabulary. The practice was popularized, if not invented, by Erik Erikson, who, from 1950 onward, tried to develop an ego-psychology for which "psychosocial functioning" depended upon having a "mature identity" or a "strong identity." This proposal was revisionist, to say the least, given that it collapsed not only Kant's ontological distinction (between the identical ego that is presupposed by experience and the empirical ego that is subject to change) but also Freud's psychological distinction between the real foundations of personality, which are unconscious, and the conscious representations and misrepresentations of them in the ego. Eriksonian identity, in other words, together with subsequent popularizations in the theory of "identity politics," identified identity with self-image or self-definition, thus denying the sad, unruly, and unfathomable ambiguities that were the objects of Freudian analysis. After Erikson, we could misunderstand ourselves no longer—how could we if there was nothing to our selfhood except our conscious, even consciously chosen, self-images?[15]

The Eriksonian idea of identity is perfectly adapted to articulating the dialectical illusions of internationality. Under its influence, the phrase *national identity* came to complement *personal identity*, giving a new twist to the old duality of national and personal character. National identity ceased to mean the enduring and possibly buried elements that supposedly bind together a national group, and started to mean its collective self-image, and by further extension it was also applied to individuals insofar as they shared that self-image: each of them had an individual "national identity," but in each of them it was exactly the same. With the help of this small measure of verbal intoxication, nations magically appeared as individuals, and individuals as nations; by a semantic trick, politics became immediately psychological, and personal life immediately political. Through the language of "identity," the illusions of internationality gained an even stronger hold on our imaginations.

But, it may be objected, the idea that the imaginary world of internationality is delusional is as abstract and irrelevant as the most academic formulations of political philosophy or international relations theory. Nations are still "facts," as Russell or Said would say, even if dialectical self-hypnosis has been built into their brickwork. That being so, what on earth is the *political* point of the philosophical critique of internationality?

Perhaps, however, the objection begs the entire question, for the category of politics is itself bound up with the experiences and principles of nationality. What exactly constitutes politics, when all is said and done? Politics as opposed to what? What is special about the political dimension of our lives, and why is it that it has been endowed with a foundational philosophical dignity, from Plato and Aristotle to Russell and Rorty and Stalin and Mao? What, in short, is political *form*?

It is clear that every social grouping—a family, a firm, or an army, for instance—needs collectively recognized means of facing up to collective dilemmas and enforcing and administering decisions about them. However, it is only when the unit is a "society" as a whole that these collective processes are called political, and then they take the specific form of *politics* only when they are referred to an agency that lays claim to a monopoly of decision-making power—namely, the sovereign political state. Politics, in other words, is the form that certain social issues take in particular historical contexts; and it plays quite diverse kinds of roles, and has very variable degrees of influence, within different social formations. But these variations will inevitably be hidden from any social theory that makes a fetish of politics and assumes in advance that it is the master phenomenon of human existence. It is this failure to relativize the phenomenon of politics, I suspect, that has prevented all kinds of political theory from providing a rounded account of the experience of nationality, or even from wishing to do so.[16]

The defining feature of political form is that it presupposes a single center of legitimate collective self-knowledge and self-control, capable of reaching into every corner of society. It defines, in other words, a unitary realm of public decisions, and implies that they must be gathered together under a central institution—the state—minimally defined, as Weber noted, by its monopoly of legitimate force.[17] But this means that political form is the other face of internationality as a whole. "Political mindedness" and "patriotism" are basically the same thing, as Hegel remarked.[18] And internationality then serves to isolate the social units in which political power is exercised, differentiating them from each other within a global system of nations while unifying each of them in themselves through sentiments of national character or national identity. The fundamental units of politics are nations, in rather the same sense that organisms are the fundamental units in biology. It belongs to the concepts of nation and politics, respectively, that political power is exercised primarily over nations and that each nation ought to be a political entity in itself. The historical evolution of internationality and the development of political form are two aspects of the same process; therefore, to restrict one's analysis of internationality to political terms is to condemn oneself to a kind of cloistered circularity, in which we will be able to conceive of no alternative to the transcendentalization of both nationality and political form.

When people look for ways of summing up the twentieth century—the century of genocides, or of world wars waged in the name of world peace—

they tend to favor such descriptions as "psychopathic," or "violent," or "evil." But perhaps it would be best to call it simply the century of *politics*. It is the century in which people have sought political solutions to all their problems, and in which, consequently, they have been obliged to take the nation as the basic unit of social existence.

But it has not always been so. Before the establishment of international-ity as a world system, politics presented itself as the somewhat abstruse con-cern of a small political class, rather than the supreme form of human associ-ation, and it is only in the twentieth century that it has become compulsory for everyone to have a nationality, an "identity" that is supposed to assign them to the jurisdiction of a particular political power.

You can get a glimpse of a premodern experience of cultural and geo-graphic difference—an experience innocent of any ideas of national charac-ter or identity—from the beautiful reconstruction of the life of a twelfth-century Jewish merchant called Ben Jiju, in Amitav Ghosh's book *In an Antique Land*. Ben Jiju certainly had no national roots, as he moved from Aden up to Mangalore, and set up a household there with an Indian woman whom he first bought as a slave and then manumitted. Nor did his Indian slave, Bomma—who was also his business partner—who went back to Aden and traded for him there. They both ended up in Egypt, Ben Jiju's half-Indian daughter having gone off to marry her Jewish cousin in Palermo. This was a well-traveled and versatile family, without a doubt; however, it was neither national nor international, but simply cosmopolitan. The paradox is that as world travel has become more common, our responsiveness to the in-dividuality of different lives around the world has become severely attenu-ated, as cosmopolitanism has yielded ground to the prejudices of identity and internationality.[19]

Is it possible to hope for a new cosmopolitanism, after internationality? The system of national states that grew up with capitalism certainly seems less appropriate, now that financial and technical conditions pay decreasing regard to state boundaries, and the old divisions between the industrialized West and its colonies are, if not destroyed, at least under reconstruction. So perhaps we may look forward to a future in which people could interpret themselves without any reference to the idea that their nation is their self, in fact without any essential reference to nationality at all. We can perhaps imagine a world where local peculiarities are no longer subsumed under na-tional types; a postnational and postinternational world, which would no longer make a fetish of political form; a new cosmopolitan world, which could put the illusions of internationality behind it, for good.

Notes

1. Martin Heidegger, *Brief über den "Humanismus,"* translated by Frank A. Capuzzi and J. Glenn Gray as "Letter on Humanism," in David Farrell Krell, ed., *Martin Heidegger: Basic Writings*, 2d ed. (London: Routledge, 1993), 244.
2. Immanuel Kant, *Idee zu einer allgemeinen Geschichte in weltbürgerlicher Absicht* (1784), translated by H. B. Nisbet as "Idea for a Universal History with a Cosmopolitan Purpose," in Hans Reiss, ed., *Kant: Political Writings*, 2d ed. (Cambridge: Cambridge University Press, 1991), 51.
3. Immanuel Kant, *Zum ewigen Frieden* (1795), translated as *Project for a Perpetual Peace: A Philosophical Essay* (London, 1796), 21; see also "Perpetual Peace," translated by H. B. Nisbet in *Kant: Political Writings*, 2d ed. (Cambridge: Cambridge University Press, 1991), 102.
4. Kant, *Project for a Perpetual Peace*, 28, 21; "Perpetual Peace," 106, 102.
5. F.F. (?), "Nations, Law of" in supplement to *Encyclopaedia Britannica*, 4th, 5th, and 6th eds., vol. 6, 11, 22.
6. For an attempted justification of this term, see Jonathan Rée, "Internationality," *Radical Philosophy* 60 (Spring 1992): 3–11.
7. I have listed eighteenth-century translations first, then the ones from the twentieth century; see Kant, *Project for a Perpetual Peace*, 21; "Perpetual Peace," 102.
8. Edward W. Said, *Culture and Imperialism* (London: Chatto & Windus, 1993), 263.
9. Where this is manifestly not the case, as in Australia or the United States, the problem is solved by an invocation of "exceptionalism."
10. The national groups in Europe that have the best claims to many centuries of continuous existence are, significantly, those with no securely held collective territory to call their own—Romanies and Jews.
11. Bertrand Russell, *Political Ideals* (1917) (London: Unwin, 1963), 78–79.
12. David Hume, "Of National Characters," in *Essays Moral, Political and Literary* (London: Oxford University Press, 1963), 209.
13. The function of the identification of nationalism with localism is illustrated in English debates over the powers of the European Union. The regions of a large centralized state such as the United Kingdom have every reason to see the Union as an opportunity to break away from interfering powers in London. But anti-European politicians, by identifying the Ukanian state with a nation and hence a locality, are able to claim, on the contrary, that the local particularity of Britain is threatened by the European superstate.
14. "In a kind of democratic dispersal of monarchical hubris, each national subject can proclaim, *La nation, c'est moi.*" See Jonathan Rée, "National Passions," *Common Knowledge* 2, no. 3 (1993): 51.
15. See Erik H. Erikson, *Childhood and Society* (New York: W. W. Norton, 1950).
16. The specificity of politics is a fundamental tenet of classical Marxism, and its vital importance for understanding interstate relations (and hence criticizing international relations theory) has received an exemplary demonstration in Justin Rosenberg, *The Empire of Civil Society: A Critique of the Realist Theory of International Relations* (London: Verso, 1994). "What if the autonomy of the political is itself a contingent historical development?" Rosenberg asks. "Would this not mean that a crucial dimension of the modern system was opaque to realism?" (61–62). See also Rosenberg's "Isaac Deutscher and the Lost History of International Relations," *New Left Review* 215 (January–February 1996): 3–15.
17. "What is a state? . . . Today, we have to say that a state is a human community that (successfully) claims the monopoly of the legitimate use of force within a given terri-

tory." See Max Weber, "Politik als Beruf" (written and delivered in the midst of the Revolutionary Winter of 1917–18), in *Gesammelte Politische Schriften* (Tübingen: Mohr, 1971), 505–6; translated in Max Weber, *From Max Weber: Essays in Sociology*, trans. Hans H. Gerth and C. Wright Mills (New York: Oxford University Press, 1958), 77–78.

18. The words in question are "politischer Geist" and "Vaterlandsliebe." See G. W. F. Hegel, *System der Philosophie*, pt. 3, sec. 394, *Zusatz*, in *Sämtliche Werke* (Jubiläumsausgabe), ed. by Hermann Glockner (Stuttgart: Fromann, 1932), vol. 10, 87; *Encyclopedia*, *Philosophy of Mind*, translated by William Wallace and A. V. Miller (Oxford: Oxford University Press, 1971), 51.

19. See Amitav Ghosh, *In an Antique Land* (London: Granta, 1992).

Cosmopolitan Patriots

Kwame Anthony Appiah

My father was a Ghanaian patriot. He once published a column in the *Pioneer*, our local newspaper in Kumasi, under the headline "Is Ghana Worth Dying For?" and I know that his heart's answer was yes.[1] But he also loved Asante, the region of Ghana where he and I both grew up, a kingdom absorbed within a British colony and then a region of a new multiethnic republic, a once-kingdom that he and his father also both loved and served. And, like so many African nationalists of his class and generation, he always loved an enchanting abstraction they called Africa.

When he died, my sisters and I found a note he had drafted and never quite finished, last words of love and wisdom for his children. After a summary reminder of our double ancestry—in Ghana and in England—he wrote, "Remember that you are citizens of the world." He went on to tell us that this meant that wherever we chose to live—and, as citizens of the world, we could surely choose to live anywhere—we should make sure we left that place "better than [we] found it." "Deep inside of me," he wrote, "is a great love for mankind and an abiding desire to see mankind, under God, fulfil its highest destiny."

The favorite slander of the narrow nationalist against us cosmopolitans is that we are rootless; what my father believed in, however, was a rooted cosmopolitanism, or, if you like, a cosmopolitan patriotism. Like Gertrude Stein, he thought there was no point in roots if you couldn't take them with you. "America is my country and Paris is my hometown," Stein said.[2] My father would have understood her.

We cosmopolitans face a familiar litany of objections. Some, for example, have complained that our cosmopolitanism must be parasitic: Where, they ask, could Stein have gotten her roots in a fully cosmopolitan world? Where, in other words, would all the diversity we cosmopolitans celebrate come from in a world where there were only cosmopolitans?

The answer is straightforward: the cosmopolitan patriot can entertain the possibility of a world in which *everyone* is a rooted cosmopolitan, attached to a home of his or her own, with its own cultural particularities, but taking pleasure from the presence of other, different, places that are home to other, different, people. The cosmopolitan also imagines that in such a world not everyone will find it best to stay in a natal patria, so that the circulation of people among different localities will involve not only cultural tourism (which the cosmopolitan admits to enjoying) but migration, nomadism, diaspora. (In the past, these processes have too often been the result of forces we should deplore; the old migrants were often refugees, and older diasporas often began in involuntary exile. But what can be hateful if coerced can be celebrated when it flows from the free decisions of individuals or of groups.)

In a world of cosmopolitan patriots, people would accept the citizens' responsibility to nurture the culture and the politics of their homes. Many would, no doubt, spend their lives in the places that shaped them, and that is one of the reasons local cultural practices would be sustained and transmitted. But many would move, and that would mean that cultural practices would travel also (as they have always traveled). The result would be a world in which each local form of human life is the result of long-term and persistent processes of cultural hybridization—a world, in that respect, much like the world we live in now.

Behind the objection that cosmopolitanism is parasitic there is, in any case, an anxiety we should dispel, an uneasiness caused by an exaggerated estimate of the rate of disappearance of cultural heterogeneity. In the global system of cultural exchanges there are, indeed, somewhat asymmetrical processes of homogenization going on, and there are forms of human life disappearing. Neither of these phenomena is particularly new, but the range and speed they now exhibit probably are. Nevertheless, as forms of culture disappear, new forms are created, and they are created locally, which means they have exactly the regional inflections that the cosmopolitan celebrates. The disappearance of old cultural forms is consistent with a rich variety of forms of human life, because new cultural forms that differ from each other are being created all the time as well.

Liberalism versus Patriotism?

Cosmopolitanism and patriotism, unlike nationalism, are both sentiments more than ideologies. Different political ideologies can be made consistent with both of them. Some cosmopolitan patriots are conservative and religious; others are secularizers of a socialist bent. Christian cosmopolitanism is as old as the merger with the Roman Empire, through which stoicism came to be a dominant shaping force in Christian ethics. (On my father's bedside were Cicero and the Bible. Only someone ignorant of the history of the church would see this as an expression of divided loyalties.) But I am a liberal, and both cosmopolitanism and patriotism, as sentiments, can seem to be hard to accommodate to liberal principles.

Patriotism often challenges liberalism. Liberals who propose a state that does not take sides in the debates among its citizens' various conceptions of the good life are held to be unable to value a state that celebrates itself, and modern self-described patriots, here in the United States, at least, often desire a public education and a public culture that stoke the fires of the national ego. Patriots also seem especially sensitive these days to slights to the national honor, to skepticism about a celebratory nationalist historiography—in short, to the critical reflection on the state that we liberals, with our instrumental conception of it, are bound to engage in. No liberal should say, "My country, right or wrong," because liberalism involves a set of political principles that a state can fail to realize; and the liberal will have no special loyalty to an illiberal state, not least because liberals value people over collectivities.

This patriotic objection to liberalism can also be made, however, to Catholicism, to Islam, to almost any religious view—indeed, to any view, including humanism, that claims a higher moral authority than one's own particular political community. And the answer to it is to affirm, first, that someone who loves principle can also love country, family, friends; and second, that a true patriot holds the state and the community within which he or she lives to certain standards, has moral aspirations for them, and that those aspirations may be liberal.

Liberalism versus Cosmopolitanism?

The cosmopolitan challenge to liberalism begins with the claim that liberals have been too preoccupied with morality *within* the nation-state. John Rawls's *Theory of Justice*, which began the modern reformulation of philosophical liberalism, left the questions of international morality to be dealt with later; how to develop the Rawlsian picture in an international direction is a current preoccupation of professional political philosophy. The cosmopolitan is likely to argue that this order of priorities is all wrong.[3]

It is all very well to argue for, fight for, liberalism in one country—your own—but if that country, in its international operations, supports (or even tolerates) illiberal regimes elsewhere, then it fails, the cosmopolitan will argue, because it does not sufficiently weigh the lives of human beings as such. Liberals take it to be self-evident that we are all "created equal" and that we each bear certain "inalienable rights," and then seem almost immediately to become preoccupied with looking after the rights of the local branch of the species, forgetting—this is a cosmopolitan critique—that their rights matter as human rights, and thus matter only if the rights of foreign humans matter too.[4]

This is surely more of an objection to the practice of liberalism than to its theory (and, as I shall argue later, cosmopolitans have a reason for caring about states, too). At the heart of the liberal picture of humanity is the idea of the equal dignity of all persons; liberalism grows with an increasing appreciation of the inadequacy of an older picture in which dignity is the possession of an elite. Not every premodern society made its elite hereditary, as the eunuchs who ran the Ottoman Empire would have attested. But it is only in the modern age that the idea has grown that every one of us begins life with an equal entitlement to respect, an entitlement that we may, perhaps, lose through misbehavior, but that remains with us otherwise for all our lives.

This idea of the equal dignity of all persons can be cashed out in different ways, but it is what undergirds the attachment to a democracy of unlimited franchise; the renunciation of sexism and racism and heterosexism; the respect for the autonomy of individuals, which resists the state's desire to fit us to someone else's conception of what is good for us; and the notion of human rights—rights possessed by human beings as such—that is at the heart of liberal theory.

It would be wrong, however, to conflate cosmopolitanism and humanism, because cosmopolitanism is not just the feeling that everybody matters. The cosmopolitan celebrates the fact that there are *different* local human ways of being, whereas humanism is consistent with the desire for global homogeneity. Humanism can be made compatible with cosmopolitan sentiments, but it can also live with a deadening urge to uniformity.

A liberal cosmopolitanism, of the sort I am defending, might put its point like this: we value the variety of human forms of social and cultural life; we do not want everybody to become part of a homogeneous global culture; and we know that this means that there will be local differences (both within and between states) in moral climate as well. So long as these differences meet certain general ethical constraints—so long, in particular, as political institutions respect basic human rights—we are happy to let them be.

Part of what the equal dignity of all persons means for liberals is that we respect people's autonomous decisions for themselves, even when they make decisions we judge mistaken—or simply choices we would not make for ourselves. This is a liberal principle that fits well with the cosmopolitan feeling that human cultural difference is actively desirable. The requirement that the state respect basic human rights is, as a result, very demanding. It rules out states that aim to constrain people beyond what is necessary to enable a common life. Voluntary associations that are the products of autonomous affiliations may demand a great deal of people as long as those people retain the right of exit (a right that it is one of the state's proper purposes to sustain). Thus I can bind myself with a vow of obedience so long as I retain my autonomy—that is, if I finally decide that I can no longer obey, whoever I have bound myself to is obliged to release me. Broad freedom of contract—and the state's enforcement of contracts freely made—is rightly seen as a liberal practice, giving force to the autonomous decisions of free individuals. But not every contract can be enforced by a state that respects autonomy—in particular, a contract to give up one's autonomy.[5]

In short, where the state's actions enable the exercise of autonomous decision, my sort of liberal will cheer it on. Cosmopolitanism can also live happily with this liberal individualism. The cosmopolitan ideal—take your roots with you—is one in which people are free to elect the local forms of human life within which they will live.

Patriotism versus Cosmopolitanism?

Patriotism, as communitarians have spent much time reminding us recently, is about the responsibilities as well as the privileges of citizenship. But it is also and above all, as I have been suggesting, not so much a matter of action—of practical morality—as of sentiment. If there is one emotion that the very word brings to mind, it is surely pride. When the national anthem plays, when the national team wins, when the national army prevails, there is that shiver down the spine, the electric excitement, the thrill of being on the winning side. But the patriot is surely also the first to suffer his or her country's shame: it is the patriot who suffers when the country elects the wrong leaders, or when those leaders prevaricate, bluster, pantomime, betray "our" principles. Patriotism is about what the nineteenth-century Liberian scholar-diplomat Edward Blyden once so memorably called "the poetry of politics," which is the feeling of "people with whom we are connected."[6] It is the connection and the sentiment that matter, and there is no reason to suppose that everybody in this complex, ever-mutating world will find their affinities and their passions focused on a single place.

My father's example demonstrates for me, more clearly than any abstract argument, the possibilities that the enemies of cosmopolitanism deny. We cosmopolitans *can* be patriots, loving our homelands (not only the states where we were born but the states where we grew up, the states where we live); our loyalty to humankind—so vast, so abstract, a unity—does *not* deprive us of the capacity to care for lives nearer by.

My father's example makes me suspicious, however, of the purportedly cosmopolitan argument against patriotism (my father's Ghanaian patriotism, which I want to defend) that alleges that nationality is, in the words of a fine essay of Martha Nussbaum's, "a morally irrelevant characteristic." Nussbaum argues that in "conceding that a morally arbitrary boundary such as the boundary of the nation has a deep and formative role in our deliberations, we seem to be depriving ourselves of any principled way of arguing to citizens that they should in fact join hands" across the "boundaries of ethnicity and class and gender and race."[7]

I can only say what I think is wrong here if I insist on the distinction between state and nation.[8] Their conflation is a perfectly natural one for a modern person—even after Rwanda, Sri Lanka, Amritsar, Bosnia, Azerbaijan. But the yoking of nation-state in the Enlightenment was intended to bring the arbitrary boundaries of states into conformity with the "natural" boundaries of nations. The idea that the boundaries of one could be arbitrary while the boundaries of the other were not is easy enough to grasp, once we are reminded of it.

Not that I want to endorse this essentially Herderian way of thinking; nations never preexist states.[9] A nation—here is a loose and unphilosophical definition—is an "imagined community" of culture or ancestry running beyond the scale of the face-to-face and seeking political expression for itself.[10] But all the nations I can think of that are not coterminous with states are the legacy of older state arrangements, as Asante is in what has become Ghana, and as are the Serbian and Croatian nations in what used to be Yugoslavia.

I want, in fact, to distinguish the nation and the state to make a point entirely opposite to Herder's—namely that, if anything is morally arbitrary, it is not the state but the nation. Because human beings live in political orders narrower than the species, and because it is within those political orders that questions of public right and wrong are largely argued out and decided, the fact of my being a fellow citizen of yours—someone who is a member of the same order—is not morally arbitrary at all. That is why the cosmopolitan critique of liberalism's focus on the state is overstated: it is exactly because the cultural variability that cosmopolitanism celebrates has come to depend on the existence of a plurality of states that we need to take states seriously.

The nation, on the other hand, *is* arbitrary, but not in a sense that means we can discard it in our moral reflections. It is arbitrary in the root sense of that term, because it is, in the *Oxford English Dictionary*'s lapidary formulation, "dependent upon will or pleasure." Nations often matter more to people than do states: monoethnic Serbia makes more sense to some than multicultural Bosnia; a Hutu (or a Tutsi) Rwanda makes more sense to others than a peaceful shared citizenship of Tutsi and Hutu; only when Britain and France became nations as well as states did ordinary citizens come to care much about being British or French.[11] But notice that the reason nations matter is that they matter *to people*. Nations matter morally, when they do, in other words, for the same reason that football and opera matter: as things desired by autonomous agents, whose autonomous desires we ought to acknowledge and take account of, even if we cannot always accede to them.

States, on the other hand, matter morally intrinsically; they matter not because people care about them, but because they regulate our lives through forms of coercion that will always require moral justification. State institutions matter both because they are necessary to so many modern human purposes and because they have such great potential for abuse. As Hobbes famously saw, the state, to do its job, has to have a monopoly of certain forms of authorized coercion, and the exercise of that authority cries out for (but often does not deserve) justification even in places, like so many postcolonial societies, where many people have no positive feeling for the state at all.

There is, then, no need for the cosmopolitan to claim that the state is morally arbitrary, in the way that I have suggested the nation is. There are many reasons to think that living in political communities narrower than the species is better for us than would be our engulfment in a single world-state, a cosmopolis of which we cosmopolitans would be not figurative but literal citizens. It is, in fact, precisely this celebration of cultural variety—within states as well as between them—that distinguishes the cosmopolitan from some of the other heirs of Enlightenment humanism.

It is because humans live best on a smaller scale that we should defend not just the state, but the county, the town, the street, the business, the craft, the profession, the family, *as* communities, as circles among the many circles narrower than the human horizon, that are appropriate spheres of moral concern. We should, in short, as cosmopolitans, defend the right of others to live in democratic states, with rich possibilities of association within and across their borders, states of which they can be patriotic citizens. And, as cosmopolitans, we can claim that right for ourselves.

Cosmopolitanism as Liberalism

The fundamental thought of the cosmopolitanism I defend is that the freedom to create oneself—the freedom that liberalism celebrates—requires a range of socially transmitted options from which to invent what we have come to call our identities. Our families and schools, our churches and temples, our professional associations and clubs, provide two essential elements in the tool kit of self-creation: first, they provide ready-made identities—son, lover, husband, doctor, teacher, Methodist, worker, Muslim, Yankee fan, *mensch*—whose shapes are constituted by norms and expectations, stereotypes and demands, rights and obligations; second, they give us a language in which to think about these identities and with which we may shape new ones.

Let me offer an example to give concreteness to these abstractions. Seventeenth-century England endowed English people with gender identities as men and as women; beginning with these ready-made identities, and drawing on a host of ideas about sex, gender, and social life, the urban men who created the Molly culture of London—which is one ancestor of modern Western European gay identities—shaped a new identity as a Molly, which interpreted sexual desire for men in a man as evidence that he was, in certain respects, a kind of woman.[12] This is, of course, much too simple a story; what actually happened is that the Molly identity shaped a new gender option for people who were morphologically male, an option that led them to express their sexual desire for other men by feminizing themselves, cross-dressing, and giving each other women's names.

But, as this case should make absolutely clear, it is social life that endows us with the full richness of resources available for self-creation, for even when we are constructing new and counternormative identities, it is the old and the normative that provide the language and the background. A new identity is always post-some-old-identity (in the now familiar sense of *post* in which "postmodernism" is enabled by the very modernism it challenges).[13] If, like some of our fellow mammals, we lived with a parent only long enough to become *physically* independent, we would have a hugely impoverished range of such conceptual implements and institutional frameworks for exploring our autonomy.

These conceptual and institutional contributions are hugely important, but it would be a philosopher's mistake not to mention that it is social life, shaped (but not determined) by the state—particularly in the form of the modern market economy—that has provided the material conditions that have enabled this exploration for a larger and larger proportion of people, especially in the industrialized world.

Among the resources thus made available in our contemporary form of social life is something that we can call a national identity, a form of identity that is central to the possibility of a modern patriotism. I want to ask now how we are to understand national identity, and more particularly what, for a cosmopolitan patriot, the role of a national culture might be in it.

National Culture and Common Culture

Here is one model of the role of the national culture, a model that we might call the *tribal fantasy*. There is an ideal—which is to say imaginary—type of a small-scale, technologically uncomplicated, face-to-face society, in which one conducts most interactions with people one knows, that we usually call *traditional*. In such a society, all adults who are not mentally disabled speak the same language. All share a vocabulary and a grammar and an accent. Although there are some words in the language that are not known by everybody—the names of medicinal herbs, the language of some religious rituals—most are known to all normal adults. To share a language is to participate in a complex set of mutual expectations and understandings, but in such a society it is not only linguistic behavior that is coordinated through universally known expectations and understandings. People in this society share an understanding of many practices—marriages, funerals, other rites of passage—and largely share their views about the general workings not only of the social but also of the natural world. Even those who are skeptical about particular elements of belief nevertheless know what everyone is supposed to believe, and they know it in enough detail to behave very often as if they believe it too.

A similar point applies to many of the values of such a society. It may well be that some people, even some groups, do not share the values that are enunciated in public and taught to children. But, once more, the standard values are universally known, and even those who do not share them know what it is to act in conformity with them and probably do so much of the time.

In such a traditional society, we may speak of the shared beliefs, values, signs, and symbols as the *common culture*—not, to insist on a crucial point, in the sense that everyone in the group actually holds the beliefs and values, but in the sense that everybody knows what they are and everybody knows that they are widely held in the society.

There is a second crucial feature of the common culture in the tribal fantasy: it is that the common culture is, in a certain sense, at the *heart* of the culture of every individual and every family.[14] By this I mean not just that, for each individual, the common culture encompasses a significant proportion of his or her culture—the socially transmitted beliefs, values, signs, and symbols that populate the individual's mental life and shape his or her behavior—but that, whatever other socially transmitted skills or beliefs or values or understandings the individual has, the common culture provides a majority of those that are most important to him or her.[15] Where the common culture of a group is also, in this way, at the heart of an individual's culture, I shall say that individual is "centered on the common culture"; and I want to make it part of the definition of being centered on a common culture that those who are centered on it think of themselves as a collectivity, and think of the collectivity as consisting of people for whom a common culture is central.[16]

Now the citizens of one of those large "imagined communities" of modernity we call nations are not likely to be centered on a common culture of this sort. There is no single shared body of ideas and practices in India that sits at the heart of the lives of most Hindus and most Muslims, that engages all Sikhs and excites every Kashmiri, that animates every untouchable in Delhi and organizes the ambitions of every Brahmin in Bombay. And I am inclined to say that there is not now and never has been a centering common culture in the United States, either. The reason is simple: the United States has always been multilingual, and has always had minorities who did not speak or understand English. It has always had a plurality of religious traditions, beginning with American Indian religions and Iberian Catholics and Jews and British and Dutch Puritans, and including now many varieties of Christianity, Judaism, Islam, Buddhism, Jainism, Taoism, Baha'i, and so on. And many of these religious traditions have been quite unknown to each other. More than this, Americans have also always differed significantly even among those who do speak English, from North to South and East to West, and from country to city, in customs of greeting, notions of civility, and a whole host of other ways. The notion that what has held the United States together historically over its great geographic range is a citizenry centered on a common culture is—to put it politely—not sociologically plausible.

The observation that Americans are not centered on a national culture does not answer the question of whether there *is* an American national culture; comments about American culture, taken as a whole, are routine, and it would be taking on a fairly substantial consensus to deny them all. American culture is, for example, held to be individualist, litigious, and race obsessed. I think each of these claims is actually true, because what I mean when I say that Americans are not centered on a common culture of the United States is not what is denied by someone who says that there is an American culture; such a person is describing large-scale tendencies within American life that are not invariably participated in by—and are certainly not equally important to—all Americans. I do not mean to deny that these exist. But for such tendencies to be part of what I am calling the *common culture*, they would have to derive from beliefs and values and practices (almost) universally shared and known to be so. For it to center the lives of

Americans, such a common culture would then have to be at the core of the individual cultures of most Americans. I want to deny that there is any common culture that *centers* most Americans in this way.

At the same time, it has always been true that there was a dominant culture in these United States. It was Protestant, it spoke English, and it identified with the high cultural traditions of Europe and, more particularly, of England. This dominant culture included much of the common culture that centered most members of the dominant classes—the government and business and cultural elites—but it was familiar to many others who were subordinate to them. And it was not merely an effect but also an instrument of their domination.

American Patriotism

The United States of America, then, has always been a society in which people have been centered on a variety of common cultures. Recognizing that we in the United States are not centered on a national common culture is, as I have said, consistent with recognizing that (with, no doubt, a few exceptions) American citizens do have a common culture; what is interesting and important about it is that for many Americans that American core—and, in particular, the attachment to the constitutional order and the rights it conveys—is not what centers their lives. They support and favor those institutions; many people have come here precisely because they exist. But still, these values are not instrumental in their lives. What they desire centrally, what shapes their lives, is what the American freedoms make possible—your experience in a temple or mosque or church; my life with my family and the cultural riches of New York City or Boston that surround us; his search for philosophical understanding; their existence in a lesbian commune. Americans need America—they will defend it, especially, against foreigners who deplore its materialism or its vulgarity—but it is not at the heart of their dreams.

We have come to a crux: If this is the situation, shouldn't the cosmopolitan who is an American patriot resent these fellow citizens for whom their country is a mere instrument, a means, not an end? My answer is no. The French and American Revolutions invented a form of patriotism that allows us to love our country as the embodiment of principles, as a means to the attainment of moral ends. It is true that the patriot values always more than what the state makes possible for me and mine, but if among the ideals we honor in the United States is that it aims to enable a certain kind of human freedom, then we cannot, in consistency, enforce attachment either to the state or to the principles. In valuing the autonomous choices of free people, we value what they have chosen *because they have chosen it*. A forced attachment to a fine principle does not diminish the principle, but the force makes the attachment unworthy.

But if force is not the answer, there is, of course, another possibility. Why not argue out democratically a common culture on which to center our national life?

My first answer is, Because we do not have to do so. The question presupposes that what we *really* need is shared core values, a centering common culture. I think this is a mistake. What I think we really need is not citizens centered on a common culture, but citizens committed to common institutions, to the conditions necessary for a common life.

To live together in a nation, what is required is that we all share a commitment to the organization of the state—the institutions that provide the overarching order of our common life. But this does not require that we have the *same* commitment to those institutions, in the sense that the institutions must carry the same meaning for all of us.

We live already with examples of this situation so familiar that they are easily forgotten. The First Amendment, for example, separates church and state. Some of us are committed to this because we are religious; we see it as the institutionalization of a Protestant insistence on freedom of conscience. Some of us are committed to it because we are Catholics or Jews or Muslims, and do not want to be pressed into conformity by a Protestant majority. Some of us are atheists who want to be left alone. We can live together with this arrangement provided we all are committed to it for our different reasons.

There is a useful analogy here with much mass culture and other mass-produced goods. People in London and in Lagos, in New York and New Delhi, listen to Michael Jackson and drink Coca-Cola. The people exist, in part, as an audience for his work, as consumers of that drink. But nobody thinks that what either of these products means in one place must be identical with what it means in every site of its consumption. Similarly, the institutions of democracy—the election, the public debate, the protection of minority rights—have different meanings to different people and groups. Once more, there is no reason to require that we all value them in the same way, for the same reasons. All that is required is that everybody is willing to "play the game."

A shared political life in a great modern nation is not like the life of the tribal fantasy. It can encompass a great diversity of meanings. When we teach children democratic habits, what we are creating is a shared commitment to certain forms of social behavior. We can call this a political culture if we like, but the meanings citizens give to their lives and to the political within their lives in particular, will be shaped not only (through the public schools) by the state, but also by family and church, reading and television, and in individuals' professional and recreational associations. If American political culture is what Americans have in common, it is pretty thin gruel—and, so I am arguing, none the worse for that.

A Patriot's Objection

This sanguine conclusion will cause many patriots to object. "In a world of changing challenges, shared institutions (shared laws, for example) need interpreting to fit new situations (new cases). And in thinking about these new cases, doesn't appeal have to be made to shared values, to substantial principles, even, in the end, to deep metaphysical convictions?"[17] If we are to decide, say, whether to permit abortions, this argument suggests, we must decide first whether our shared commitment to the preservation of innocent human life—a commitment some derive from the thought that we are all children of a loving God—applies to the fetus in its first three months. Many—though certainly not for all—Americans would oppose abortion rights if it were uncontroversially clear that abortion constitutes the killing of an innocent human being.[18] Don't our difficulties in discussing this question flow, in part, from precisely the lack of shared values that I am arguing we must accept?

I am not sure that the answer to this last question is yes. I suspect that the difficulties about abortion have at least as much to do with the refusal of those who oppose it to acknowledge how large a part views about the control of women's sexuality—indeed, of sexuality in general—play in shaping the intensity of some of their responses. But this, too, may turn in the end on deep differences about metaphysical and moral questions; so, in the end, I agree that these will sometimes have to be faced.

It is here that the political values of the American republic have to come to have some weight of their own; our democratic traditions require us to engage respectfully with our fellow citizens who disagree with us. In this sense, a political culture—the shared commitment to the political institutions of the republic, the content of a common citizenship—is more than an agreement to abide by the Constitution and the laws, by the judgments of courts, by the decisions of democratically elected lawmakers. It also involves a shared—and *evolving*—sense of the customary practices of political engagement in the public sphere.

Now, I admit that there are circumstances in which such a sense of common citizenship is unavailable to some. While Jim Crow laws held in the American South, it is hard to see why African Americans should have felt a commitment to the customary practices of the American republic (even if they could and did feel attachment to most of the principles expressed in the Constitution, precisely because they were at odds with the practice of Jim Crow). It is, of course, *because* citizens are entitled to participation in the political culture of their state that the effective exclusion of blacks from voting was inconsistent with democratic political morality. It follows, I concede, that if the state's actions so repudiate you, and if, as a result, you are unable to accept and participate in the political culture in this sense, your fellow citizens cannot expect you to conform to the law.

Here then is a point where a defender of a centering national culture might find a new starting point. Why not admit, she might say, that you must guarantee at least this much—that citizens are trained in (and immigrants taught and required to assent to) the essentials of the political culture? And if that is desirable, will it not be best achieved by centering Americans on a broader common culture, by centering every American on shared values, shared literary references, shared narratives of the American nation?

Once more, to the first question I answer yes, sure. And to the second I say no. If the political culture carries some weight for us, we will accept the laws and the terms of debate that it entails, and we will struggle within that framework for justice, as each of us understands it. If, as some claim is true of abortion, there are central debates that we cannot resolve within this framework, this is certainly a problem we would not face if every American were brought up with the same metaphysical convictions. But constraining a quarter of a billion American citizens into a life centered on a common culture—cultural Americanism, let us call it—would be too high a price to pay for the dissolution of this conflict. If, after all, the disputes about abortion seem contentious, think how bitter would be the argument if we insisted— as the Bill of Rights wisely insists we should not—on a single religion (or even, more modestly, a single view of family life) to teach all our children.

American citizenship, in other words, does require us to accept the political culture, and, as the case of African Americans shows, it is important that that culture has built into it the possibility of change. But if, as a result of the processes of democracy, laws are passed that are deeply repugnant to you—as is perfectly possible in a society not centered on a strong common culture—you may well reach the point where you consider that you have been, in the phrase I used earlier, repudiated by the state. The price of having no common culture to center our society is that possibility, but the cosmopolitan patriot believes that the creation of a common culture rich enough to exclude this possibility would exact a higher price. This is something that many in the world—Catholic bishops in Ireland, Buddhist politicians in Sri Lanka, ayatollahs in Iran, Communist Party members in China—do not believe. They want to live in societies where every political dispute can be resolved because everyone has been constrained to accept a common sense of the meaning of life, where everyone has a common cultural center. The political culture of the American state excludes this vision, because it is (in the understanding of a term long forgotten in our public debates) a liberal political culture, one that values individuals and celebrates, with cosmopolitanism, the great variety of what individuals will choose when given freedom.

There must be some who believe the rhetoric about the murder of infants that (in my judgment) pollutes the debate about abortion. For them, perhaps, religious duty transcends the demands of citizenship. But I do not see that we can resolve a disagreement with them by finding a common metaphysics of the person on which to center the next generation of Americans; it is precisely our disagreements about *that* that account for some of the intensity of the debate.

Surely, however, most of those who believe abortion should not be legal do not really think that the abortion of a first-trimester fetus is really *exactly the same* as the killing of a living child. If they did believe that, they would surely not even contemplate exemptions for rape and incest, for even those of us who favor laws allowing choice would not favor a rape exception for infanticide. Like many who favor choice, I believe, as I say, that some of the intensity of the debate about abortion has to do with attitudes toward sexuality and toward women that the feminism of the past few decades and the practical successes of the women's movement have challenged. I think this is a fair thing to argue in the debates about choice. But I also think the political culture we have inherited in the United States requires us to take on the arguments of those who oppose choice on their merits; and, where the disagreement flows from fundamentally different visions of the human good, I do not see that it profits us to deny or ignore this fact.

So, unlike many who favor the liberalism of our Constitution and the political culture that surrounds it, I do not favor silence in the public sphere about the religious views that underlie some of our deepest disagreements. Our laws and customs require us not to impose religious ideas on each other, but they also encourage us to debate among equals.

The Dangers of National Culture

A final reason for skepticism about the creation of a national common culture to center our lives is historical; for us to center ourselves on a national culture, the state would have to take up the cudgels in defining both the content of that culture and the means of its dissemination. I have already argued that this would create deep schisms in our national life, but history suggests an even deeper difficulty. Collective identities have a tendency, if I may coin a phrase, to "go imperial," dominating not only people of other identities, but the other identities, whose shape is exactly what makes each of us what we individually and distinctively are.

In policing this imperialism of identity—an imperialism as visible in national identities as anywhere else—it is crucial to remember always that we are not simply Americans or Ghanaians or Indians or Germans, but that we are gay or straight or bisexual; Jewish, Christian, Muslim, Buddhist, Confucian; brothers and sisters, parents and children; liberals, conservatives, and leftists; teachers, lawyers, autoworkers, and gardeners; fans of the Padres and the Bruins; amateurs of grunge rock and lovers of Wagner; movie buffs, MTV-holics, and mystery readers; surfers and singers; poets and pet lovers; students and teachers; friends and lovers. The state makes much possible for all of us, and we owe it at least the consistent support to which it is entitled in virtue of those possibilities; it would be a grand irony if the price we pay for the freedom the state creates were to allow it to subject us to new tyrannies.

This is an especially powerful thought here in the United States, for so many have loved America, in part, exactly because it has enabled them to choose who they are, and to decide, too, how central America is in their chosen identity. Those of us who are Americans not by birth but by election, and who love this country precisely for *that* freedom of self-invention, should not seek to compel others to an identity we ourselves celebrate because it was freely chosen.

Cosmopolitanism, Liberalism, Patriotism: Together at Last

I have been arguing, in essence, that you can be cosmopolitan—celebrating the variety of human cultures; rooted—loyal to one local society (or a few) that you count as home; liberal—convinced of the value of the individual; and patriotic—celebrating the institutions of the state (or states) within which you live. The cosmopolitanism flows from the same sources that nourish the liberalism, for it is the variety of human forms of life that provides the vocabulary of the language of individual choice. And the patriotism flows from the liberalism, because the state carves out the space within which we explore the possibilities of freedom. For rooted cosmopolitans, all this is of a single piece.

But I have also been arguing that we do not need to insist that all of our fellow citizens be cosmopolitans, or patriots, or loyal to the nation; we need them only to share the political culture of the state. And sharing that political culture does not require them to be centered on it, and certainly does not require them to be centered on a culture wider than the political.[19] What *is* essential is only—though this is, in fact, a great deal—that all of us share respect for the political culture of liberalism and the constitutional order it entails.

This formula courts misunderstanding, for the word *liberal* has been both divested of its original content and denied a solid new meaning. So let me remind you again that, for me, the essence of this liberal culture lies in respect for the dignity and autonomy of individual persons.[20] There is much to be said about the meaning of autonomy and of dignity; much too, about how, in practice, they are to live with other values, political and not, that we cherish. This is not the place for that exploration. But let me say one thing: because I believe that the state can be an instrument for autonomy, I do not share the current distaste for the state that drives much of what in the United States is now called conservatism, and so I am often a liberal in the more colloquial sense as well.

The point, in sum, is this: it is important that citizens should share a political culture; it is not important (in the United States, without massive coercion, it is not even possible) that the political culture be important to all citizens, let alone that it matter to all of them in the same way. (Indeed, one of the great freedoms that a civilized society provides is the freedom *not* to preoccupy oneself with the political.) Only politicians and political theorists are likely to think the best state is one where every citizen is a politician (and when Western theorists think this, it may be because they are overly influenced by the view of politics taken by some in the small, self-governing town of Athens in the fifth century BCE).

Not being political is not the same as being unsociable (though that is something we should be legally free to be also!); many people express concern for their communities by acting through churches and charities, and, as observers since Tocqueville have pointed out, this is a distinctively American tradition. Part of what makes this tradition attractive is that it reflects elective affinities rather than state-imposed obligation.

You will notice, now, that I have been arguing for a form of state and of society that is pretty close to the model of a multicultural liberal democracy, and you may ask, Where now is your much-vaunted cosmopolitanism? After all, the world is full of people—Chinese party leaders, Hindu nationalists, British Tories—who insist precisely on centering all citizens on a single culture that extends beyond the narrowly political. Do I not want there to be this option, too?

When I first thought about this question, I was tempted to bite the bullet and say yes. But I didn't believe it, and I now understand why I must answer no. It is because cosmopolitanism values human variety for what it makes possible for free individuals, and some kinds of cultural variety constrain more than they enable. In other words, the cosmopolitan's high appraisal of variety flows from the human choices it enables, but variety is not something we value no matter what.[21] There are other values. There can be an enormous amount of diversity among societies, even if they are all, in some sense, democratic.[22] But the fundamental idea that every society should respect human dignity and personal autonomy is more basic than the cosmopolitan love of variety; indeed, as I say, it is the autonomy that variety enables that is the fundamental argument for cosmopolitanism.

A society could in theory come to be centered on a single set of values without coercion. I might be skeptical about the virtues of such a homogenized society as a place for myself to live (even if the culture it is centered on is in some sense mine); I would think it might require in the end a kind of closing oneself off from the rest of the world that would have many cultural, economic, and moral perils. But those in such a society would no doubt have things to say in response—or might refuse to discuss the matter with me at all—and, in the end, they might well find their considerations more weighty than mine. Freely chosen homogeneity, then, raises no problems for me; in the end, I would say, "Good luck to them." But what British Tories and Hindu chauvinists and Maoist party bosses want is not a society that chooses to be uniform, but the imposition of uniformity. That the cosmopolitan patriot must oppose.

One final corollary of the grounding of cosmopolitanism in individual freedom is worth insisting on. Cosmopolitans value cultural variety, but we do not ask other people to maintain the diversity of the species at the price of their individual autonomy. We cannot require others to provide us with a cultural museum to tour through or to visit on satellite television's endless virtual safari, or an assortment of Shangri-las to enlarge the range of our own options for identity. But, as I said at the start, there is no ground for thinking that people are rushing toward homogeneity; in fact, in a world more respectful of human dignity and personal autonomy, such movement toward homogeneity as there is would probably slow down.

Asante Liberalism

Skepticism about the genuinely cosmopolitan character of the view I have been defending may flow in part from the thought that it seems so much a creature of Europe and its Enlightenment.[23] So it may be as well to insist in closing, as I did at the start, that my own attachment to these ideas comes, as much as anything, from my father, who grew up in Asante, at a time when the independence of its moral climate from that of European Enlightenment was extremely obvious. Of course, he also went on to live in London for many years, and acquired there the training of an English lawyer; and, of course, the school he went to in Ghana was a Methodist school, a colonial variant of the English boys' public school, where he was taught to think morally through Cicero and Caesar as much as the New Testament. It would be preposterous to claim, in short, that he came to his cosmopolitanism or his patriotism or his faith in human rights and the rule of law unaffected by European cultural traditions.

But it would be equally fatuous to deny that the view he arrived at had roots in Asante (indeed, as one travels the world, reviewing the liberal nationalisms of South Asia and Africa in the midcentury, one is struck not only by their similarities but also by their local inflections). Two things, in particular, strike me about the local character of the source of my father's increasing commitment to individual rights: first, that it grew out of experience of illiberal government; second, that it depended on a sense of his own dignity and the dignity of his fellow citizens that was almost entirely the product of Asante conceptions.

The first point—about experience—is crucial to the case for liberalism. It is the historical experience of the dangers of intolerance—religious intolerance in Europe in the seventeenth century, for example, for Locke; racial intolerance in the colonial context, for Gandhi (or for my father)—that often lies behind the skepticism about the state's interventions in the lives of individuals that itself underlies much liberal sentiment. My father saw the colonial state's abuses of his fellows and, in particular, the refusal to pay them the respect that was their due; he was imprisoned, later, by Kwame Nkrumah, without trial (and then released after a year and a half in detention with as little explanation as when he was arrested). As a lawyer and a member of the opposition, he traveled Ghana in the years after independence, defending people whose rights were being abused by the postcolonial state.

The political tradition of liberalism is rooted in these experiences of il-liberal government, and that liberal restraint on government recommends it-self to people rooted in so many different traditions is a reflection of its grasp of a truth about human beings and about modern politics.

Just as the centrality of murderous religious warfare in the period lead-ing up to Locke's *Treatises* placed religious toleration at the core of Locke's understanding of the liberalism he defended, so the prime place of the per-secution of political dissenters in the postcolonial experience of tyranny made protection of political dissent central to my father's liberalism.[24] (My father worried little about the state's entanglement with religion. Once, I re-member, as the national television broadcast day came to an end, my father sang along with the national hymn that was played; this hymn, played on some evenings, was the religious twin of the more secular national anthem played on others. "This would be a much better national anthem," he said to me. And I replied, ever the good liberal, "But the anthem has the advantage that you don't have to believe in God to sing it sincerely." "No one in Ghana is silly enough not to believe in God," my father replied.[25] And, now, I think he was right not to be worried about the entanglement: there is no history of religious intolerance in Ghana of the sort that makes necessary the separa-tion of church and state; a genial ecumenism has been the norm—at least until the arrival of American TV evangelism.)

But more important yet, I think, to my father's concern with individual human dignity were its roots in the preoccupation of free Asante citizens— both men and women—with notions of personal dignity, with respect and self-respect. Treating others with the respect that is their due is a central preoccupation of Asante social life, as is a reciprocal anxiety about loss of re-spect, shame, disgrace.[26] Just as European liberalism—and democratic senti-ment—grew by extending to every man and (then) woman the dignity that feudal society offered only to the aristocracy, and thus presupposes, in some sense, aspects of that feudal understanding of dignity, so Ghanaian liberal-ism—at least in my father's form—depends on the prior grasp of concepts such as *animuonyam* (respect). It is clear from well-known Akan proverbs that respect is something that in the past did not belong to everybody:

Agya Kra ne Agya Kwakyerɛmɛ, emu biara mu nni animuonyam.

[Father Soul and Father Slave Kyerɛmɛ, neither of them has any respect.]

That is, whatever you call him, a slave is still a slave.

But just as *dignitas*, which was once by definition the property of an elite, has grown into human dignity, which is the property of every man and woman, so *animuonyam* can be the basis of the respect for all others that lies at the heart of liberalism.[27] Indeed, *dignitas* and *animuonyam* have a great deal in common. *Dignitas*, as understood by Cicero, reflects much that was similar between republican Roman ideology and the views of the nineteenth-century Asante elite; it was, I think, as an Asante that my father recognized and admired Cicero, not as a British subject.

Envoi

"In the course of my life I have seen Frenchmen, Italians, Russians etc.; I even know, thanks to Montesquieu, that one can be Persian; but as for *man*, I declare I have never met one in my life."[28] So wrote Joseph de Maistre—no friend to liberalism—in his *Considérations sur la France*. It is a thought that can, ironically, be made consistent with a liberal cosmopolitanism, a thought that may even lead us to the view that cosmopolitanism is, in certain ways, inconsistent with one form of humanism. A certain sort of humanist says that she finds nothing human alien, and we could gloss this as saying that she respects each other human being as a human being. Maistre is suggesting that we never really come to terms with anybody as a human, because each actual person we meet, we meet as a French person, or as a Persian—in short, as a person with an identity far more specific than "fellow human."[29] Exactly, the cosmopolitan says. And a good thing too. But we do not have to deal decently with people from other cultures and traditions *in spite of* our differences; we can treat others decently, humanely, *through* our differences. The humanist requires us to put our differences aside; the cosmopolitan insists that sometimes it is the differences we bring to the table that make it rewarding to interact at all. That is, of course, to concede that what we share can be important, too, though the cosmopolitan will remind us that what we share with others is not always an ethnonational culture; sometimes it will just be that you and I—a Peruvian and a Slovak—both like to fish, or have read and admired Goethe in translation, or responded with the same sense of wonder to a postcard of the Parthenon, or believe, as lawyers with very different trainings, in the ideal of the rule of law.

That is, so to speak, the anglophone voice of cosmopolitanism. But, in the cosmopolitan spirit, let me end with a similar thought from my father's, no doubt less familiar, tradition. Kuro kɔrɔ mu nni nyansa, our proverb says: In a single πὸλις there is no wisdom.[30]

Notes

My thinking on the topics discussed in this essay has evolved out of discussions of multiculturalism over the past few years and was stimulated profoundly by an invitation to read and respond to Martha Nussbaum's essay "Patriotism and Cosmopolitanism" in the October/November 1994 issue of *Boston Review*. I am particularly grateful to Homi Bhabha, Lawrence Blum, Richard T. Ford, Jorge Garcia, Henry Louis Gates Jr., Amy Gutmann, Martha Minow, Maneesha Sinha, Charles Taylor, David Wilkins, and David Wong, and to those participants in two conferences—"Text and Nation" at Georgetown University in April 1995, and the Annual Conference of the Association of University Teachers of English in South Africa at the University of Natal, Pietermaritzburg, in July 1995—who commented on earlier versions of these thoughts.

1. This question was first put to him by J. B. Danquah, leader of the major opposition party in Nkrumah's Ghana, in 1962. See Joseph Appiah, *Joe Appiah: The Autobiography of an African Patriot* (New York: Praeger, 1990), 266. My father's column is reprinted in Joseph Appiah, *Antiochus Lives Again: Political Essays of Joe Appiah*, ed. Ivor Agyeman-Duah (Kumasi, Ghana: I. Agyeman-Duah, 1992).
2. Gertrude Stein, *An American and France* (1936), in *What Are Masterpieces?* (Los Angeles: Conference, 1940), 61.
3. Like most philosophers who have thought about justice recently, I have learned a very great deal from reading Rawls. This essay obviously draws sustenance from his work and the discussions it has generated; indeed, his *Theory of Justice* was the most important book I read during the summer I was deciding whether or not to be a philosopher. I find it hard, however, to relate the position I am taking here explicitly to what I understand of Rawls's current views, and so, much as I would have liked to do so, I have found it best not to take them on.
4. We liberals do *not* all agree on where the rights come from. I favor an "antirealist" view in which human rights are embodied in legal arrangements within and between states, rather than one in which they somehow antecedently exist or are grounded in human nature or divine ordinance.
5. A (lifetime) vow of obedience—even if, because I receive something in return for my vow, it may look like a legal contract—should be enforced only if enforcing it is consistent with respecting the autonomy of the person who made the vow. There are difficult issues. On the one hand, moral persons are historically extended in time, and treating someone as a single moral person requires holding later "stages" of him or her responsible for the commitments of earlier "stages." On the other hand, there are moral limits on what people can bind their later selves to do, and one relevant limit is that we may not bind our later selves to abstain from rational ethical reflection. (An enforceable lifetime vow of obedience looks awfully like a contract to enslave oneself, which would presumably be unconstitutional in the United States. But it turns out to be quite hard to say what is wrong with offering "freely" to be a slave in return for some benefit, if you believe in freedom of contract.)
6. Quoted in Howard Brotz, *Negro Social and Political Thought* (New York: Basic Books, 1966), 197.
7. Martha Nussbaum, "Patriotism and Cosmopolitanism," *Boston Review* 19, no. 5 (1994): 3.
8. The tendency in the anglophone world to sentimentalize the state by calling it *the nation* is so consistent that if earlier I had referred to the "state team" and the "state anthem," this would have made them seem cold, hard, and alien.
9. For discussion of Herder's views, see Kwame Anthony Appiah, *In My Father's House: Africa in the Philosophy of Culture* (New York: Oxford University Press, 1992), chap. 1.

10. The expression "imagined community" was given currency by Benedict Anderson's *Imagined Communities: Reflections on the Origin and Spread of Nationalism* (London: Verso, 1983).

11. See, for example, Linda Colley, *Britons: Forging the Nation, 1707–1837* (New Haven, Conn.: Yale University Press, 1992).

12. Rictor Norton, *Mother Clap's Molly House: The Gay Subculture in England, 1700–1830* (London: GMP, 1992).

13. See my "Is the 'Post' in 'Postcolonial' the 'Post' in 'Postmodern'?" *Critical Inquiry* 17 (Winter 1991), 336–57.

14. I should hasten to add that it would be preposterous to claim that most of the societies that have been called traditional fit anything like this pattern, though we might suppose that, for example, congeries of related hunter-gatherer groups, speaking closely related dialects, might have fit such a pattern.

15. The *American Heritage Dictionary III for DOS* (Novato, Calif.: Wordstar International Incorporated, 1993) defines culture (in part) as "the totality of socially transmitted behavior patterns, arts, beliefs, institutions, and all other products of human work and thought." The focus on social transmission in defining culture is extremely important.

16. I don't think we should require that people cannot be mistaken about exactly who is in the group or exactly what is in the common culture, but I think that the less they are right about either of these things, the less it makes sense to speak of the group as really centered on a common culture.

17. This is an objection Charles Taylor proposed in discussion.

18. *Innocent* here should presumably be understood, as it is in discussions of just killing in warfare, to mean "posing no harm," and not "guiltless." It seems pretty clear that we cannot blame the fetus, even if its existence threatens the life or well-being of the woman who bears it.

19. I think that in the United States, having a grasp of the political culture probably requires knowing (some) English. But, because English, like the rest of the political culture, need not center an individual's life, understanding the political culture is consistent with speaking other languages as well, and, indeed, with loving other languages more than English.

20. Despite recent communitarian arguments to the contrary, I do not think that the liberal respect for autonomy is inconsistent with recognizing the role of society in creating the options over which free individuals exercise their freedom. As Charles Taylor has argued so powerfully, it is in dialogue with other people's understandings of who I am that I develop a conception of my own identity, and my identity is crucially constituted through concepts and practices made available to me by religion, society, school, and state, and mediated to varying degrees by the family. But all of this can, in my view, be accepted by someone who sees autonomy as a central value. See my "Identity, Authenticity, Survival: Multicultural Societies and Social Reproduction," in Charles Taylor, *Multiculturalism: Examining The Politics of Recognition* (Princeton, N.J.: Princeton University Press, 1994), 149–64.

21. This is one reason I think it is not helpful to see cosmopolitanism as expressing an aesthetic ideal.

22. There is no reason to think that every society needs to implement the idea of popular choice in the same way, so that different democratic institutions in different societies are consistent with the basic respect for autonomy, too.

23. I should explicitly record my opposition to the view that this origin in any way discredits these ideas, either for non-Europeans or, for that matter, for Europeans. The issues I want to explore have to do with the ways in which these views can be rooted in different traditions; I am not interested in the nativist project of arguing for these

principles in the name of authentically Asante (or African) roots. The issues raised in the following paragraphs are thus historical, not normative.

24. Such historical context is important, I think, because, as Michael Oakeshott has observed, political education should instill in us "a knowledge as profound as we can make it, of our tradition of political behaviour." Michael Oakeshott, "Political Education," in *Rationalism in Politics and Other Essays* (Indianapolis: Liberty Fund, 1991), 61. We might say that liberal institutions are to be recommended, in part, as a practical response to the circumstances of modern political life.

25. My father's thought clearly was not so much that there are no atheists in Ghana, but that their views do not matter. Locke, of course, agreed: "Those are not at all to be tolerated who deny the being of a God. Promises, covenants, and oaths, which are the bonds of human society, can have no hold upon an atheist. The taking away of God, though but even in thought, dissolves all." John Locke, "A Letter Concerning Toleration," in *Political Writings of John Locke*, ed. David Wootton (New York: Mentor, 1993), 426.

26. There are scores of adages on this theme in *Bu Me Bɛ: The Proverbs of the Akan*, a volume of more than seven thousand Akan proverbs that my mother, Peggy Appiah, will be publishing with my assistance soon.

27. The European history is taken up in Charles Taylor, *Sources of the Self: The Making of the Modern Identity* (Cambridge: Harvard University Press, 1989).

28. Joseph de Maistre, *Considérations sur la France*, 2d ed. (London: Bâle, 1797), 102; my translation. "J'ai vu, dans ma vie, des Français, des Italiens, des Russes, etc.; je sais même, graces à Montesquieu, qu'on peut être Persan: mais quant à l'homme, je déclare ne l'avoir recontré de ma vie."

29. If you communicate on the Internet, think about how difficult it is not to imagine your e-mail correspondents (who present, after all, only strings of unspoken words) as having, for example, specific race, gender, and age.

30. *Kuro* is usually translated as "town," but towns were relatively self-governing in the Asante past, so πòλις seems a translation that gets the right sense.

Part II ▶ Belonging to a World:
Actually Existing Cosmopolitanism?

Nationalism, Identity, and the World-in-Motion:
On the Logics of Seriality

Benedict Anderson

Wenn die Tiger trinkend sich im Wasser erblicken werden sie oft gefährlich.
► *Bertolt Brecht*

The purposes of this essay are essentially three. The first, and most important, is to reframe the problem of the formation of collective subjectivities in the modern world by consideration of the material, institutional, and discursive bases that necessarily generate two profoundly contrasting types of seriality, which I will call *unbound* and *bound*. Unbound seriality, which has its origins in the print market, especially in newspapers, and in the representations of popular performance, is exemplified by such open-to-the-world plurals as nationalists, anarchists, bureaucrats, and workers. It is, for example, the seriality that makes the United Nations a normal, wholly unparadoxical institution. Bound seriality, which has its origins in governmentality, especially in such institutions as the census and elections, is exemplified by finite series like Asian Americans, *beurs*, and Tutsis. It is the seriality that makes a United Ethnicities or a United Identities unthinkable. The second purpose is to draw as clear an analytic line as feasible between nationalism and ethnicity and, in related, indirect fashion, between universality and "cosmopolitan" hybridity. The third is to dispose of such bogeys as "derivative discourses," and "imitation" in understanding the remarkable planetary spread not merely of nationalism, but of a profoundly standardized conception of politics, in part by reflecting on the everyday practices, rooted in industrial material civilization, that have displaced the cosmos to make way for "the world." I will draw a good deal of my illustrative material from the *ci-devant* Third World, where the speed and scale of change experienced over the past century has been so rapid as to throw the rise of the two serialities into the highest relief.

Seriality Unbound

On February 29, 1920, in the little Central Java town of Delanggu, surrounded on all sides by gigantic colonial and local-royal sugar plantations, the first-ever open-air public rally in the region took place. Among the speakers who addressed the probably bewildered but excited assembly of peasants and sugar factory workers, none seems today, and perhaps was even then, more strangely striking than Haji Misbach, pious returned pilgrim from Mecca and ardent Communist, with his dark face positioned between a gleaming white pith helmet and a smartly tailored, Dutch-style white jacket. In the course of his speech, he bellowed the following:

> The present age can rightly be called the *djaman balik boeono* [an ancient Javanese folk expression meaning "age of the world-turned-upside-down"]— for what used to be above is now certainly under. It is said that in the country of Oostenrijk [Dutch for "Austria-Hungary"], which used to be headed by a Radja [Indonesian for "monarch"], there has now been a *balik boeono*. It is now headed by a Republic, and many *ambtenaar* [Dutch for "government official"] have been killed by the Republic. A former *ambtenaar* has only to show his nose for his throat to be cut. So, Brothers, remember! The land belongs to no one other than ourselves.[1]

Indeed, Charles VII *had* renounced his imperial-dynastic rights in November 1918. A *balik boeono* of sorts *had* followed in both Vienna and Budapest. Béla Kun's Hungarian Communist Party *had* taken power on March 21, 1919, and, in the four months before this regime collapsed in the face of Czech and Romanian invasions, it *did* summarily execute a substantial number of class enemies. But by November 25, the Allies had helped put into power Admiral Miklós Horthy, who proceeded to launch a terror of his own. Misbach was seven months (but only seven!) sadly out of date, whether he was aware of it or not.

Nonetheless, his words were in many ways as new to colonial Central Java as the rally that he was addressing, for he spoke to his audience with the fullest confidence in the existence of the country of "Oostenrijk"—for which his own language had as yet no name, and which he himself had never seen with his own eyes—on the other side of the "world." Furthermore, the revolutionary events he described were depicted as simultaneous with events in Java, and thus, so to speak, coordinated within a single frame of time—the age of the world-turned-upside-down. This coordination allowed him to expect that what had just happened to *radja* and *ambtenaar* in Oostenrijk would imminently happen to their counterparts in the Netherlands Indies. What is still more startling, however, is Misbach's use of the little word *a*. "A" *radja*, "a" *balik boeono*, "a" Republic, "a" former *ambtenaar* —in each case, *a* shows that what follows will be a component of a single category series that spans visible Java and invisible Oostenrijk. That the names of the categories could indifferently be Dutch-European, Indonesian Malay, or Javanese also indicates an understanding of life then very new: that languages are transparent to each other, interpenetrate each other, map each other's domains—at an equal remove from, or proximity to, the material world. For this equality to be possible—and it was not possible during the youth of Misbach's father—Dutch had to descend from its status as the language of colonial power, and Javanese from its position as the language of ancestral truth. Finally, one notes a deep, surely unconscious shift in the semantic load of *boeono*. Its prior meaning was something close to "cosmos," a natural, vertical universe arranged hierarchically from the Deity, or deities, down through kings, aristocrats, and peasants, to fauna and flora and the landscapes in which they were embedded. It was a meaning that explains why petty Javanese princes called themselves by such grandiloquent titles as Paku Buwono (Nail of the Cosmos) and Hamengku Buwono (Upholder of the Cosmos) without finding the terminology at all ridiculous. But Misbach was clearly using *boeono* in the quite new sense of "world," a horizontal universe of visible and invisible human beings from which volcanoes, demons, water buffalo, and divinities had vanished.

One can see vividly the abrupt character of the change involved by considering another Javanese/Netherlands Indies comparison. In *Imagined Communities*, I discuss an exemplary newspaper article of 1913 composed by Soewardi Soerjaningrat, Misbach's aristocratic contemporary and anticolonial comrade-in-arms.[2] It was titled "Als ik eens Nederlander was," which can best be translated as "If I were, for the nonce, *a* Dutchman." The purpose of the article was to point out the incongruity of Dutch colonials celebrating the Netherlands' independence from Napoleonic subjugation while forcing the natives they themselves held in subjugation to contribute to the cost of the festivities.[3] But we can also see that Soewardi's sarcastic rhetoric took nonchalantly for granted this anonymous series: Dutchmen. By contrast, if one looks at the "memoirs" composed in emprisoned exile by his not-too-distant ancestral kinsman, Prince Diponegoro, who led so lengthy a military struggle against Dutch colonialism between 1825 and 1830 that he is today independent Indonesia's premier historical hero, "the Dutch" as such never appear.[4] His successful enemies are recorded, in feudal, "manuscript" style, by personal name and rank. And if these enemies are not part of the series "Dutchmen," neither is he himself "a" prince or "a" Javanese.

There is another word absent from Diponegoro's melancholy reflections, and that is anything that we could honestly translate as "politics." This absence is not in the least idiosyncratic. In almost all of Asia and Africa, neologisms have had to be coined for this concept during the past hundred years, and the birthdate of each coinage is typically close to that of nationalism. For "politics" to become thinkable, as a distinctly demarcated domain of life, two things had to happen: (1) specialized institutions and social practices had to be visible that could not heedlessly be glossed in the old vocabularies of cosmologically and religiously sustained kingship, to wit, general elections, presidents, censors, parties, trade unions, rallies, police, leaders, legislatures, boycotts, and the like—nations too; (2) the world had to be understood as one, so that no matter how many different social and political systems, languages, cultures, religions, and economies it contained, there was a common activity—"politics"—that was self-evidently going on *everywhere*.

Unlike, say, *industrialism*, or *militarism*, which, we know, were terms coined in Europe decades after the phenomena they attempted to denote were in motion, the vocabularies of "politics" almost always preceded their institutional realization in Asia and Africa. They were read about, then modeled from—hence so often the earliest indigenous minidictionaries were "how-to" glossaries to politics.

Newspapers

That such glossaries were typically circulated through early newspapers and periodicals allows one to consider the special character of the modeling process and, as it were, the grammar that underlay it. This modeling worked more basically by serialization than by "copying" in any simple manner. In my 1983 discussion of the newspaper in the genesis of that apprehension of time required for the imagining of nations, I emphasized, one-sidedly I am now sure, the significance of the calendrical simultaneity of apparently random occurrences that each daily edition proffers to its readers.[5] I completely missed two other interconnected principles of coherence. The first is that newspapers everywhere take "this world of mankind" as their domain, no matter how partially they read it.[6] It would be *contra naturam* for a newspaper to confine its reports to events within the political realm in which it is published. Rwandan horrors in Tokyo's newspapers, the eruption of Mount Pinatubo in Stockholm's, the European Football Cup final in those of Rangoon, all seem absolutely natural in exactly the same way. The second is that this "natural universality" has been profoundly reinforced—everywhere— by an unself-conscious standardization of vocabulary that radically overrides any formal division in the newspaper between local and foreign news. This is not a recent development. In Misbach's era, Peru, Austria-Hungary, Japan, the Ottoman Empire—no matter how vast the real differences between the populations, languages, beliefs, and conditions of life within them—were reported on in a profoundly homogenized manner. Tennô there might be inside Japan, but he would appear in newspapers everywhere else as (an) "emperor." Gandhi might be the Mahatma in Bombay, but elsewhere he would be described as "a" nationalist, "an" agitator, "a" (Hindu) leader. St. Petersburg, Caracas, and Addis Ababa—all capitals. Jamaica, Cambodia, Angola—all colonies.

This is not to say that real comparabilities did not exist, as everyday institutional modeling was going on furiously around the planet during the nineteenth and twentieth centuries. Rather, it was the case that the very format of the newspaper precluded anything else from being imagined, by the very randomness of its ceaselessly changing contents. One might even go so far as to say that the periodical appearance of the Lion of Judah and the Son of Heaven—physically invisible to more than two tiny groups of utterly separated courtiers and officials—to the simultaneous imaginations of millions of people around the world, demanded their location in a single categorical series: monarchs. Series of this kind were quotidian universals that seeped through and across all print languages, by no means necessarily in a unidirectional flow. To give only one example: when in the 1950s young Thai Marxists seized the term *sakdina*, which from medieval times had denoted, on bended knee, the traditional monarch-centered status system in Siam, and then critically inverted its meaning, it seemed to them quite normal to use the same term in a universal sense, and thus write of the *sakdina* social system of medieval Europe.[7] *Sakdina* and *feudal* stood in, as it were, for one another (just as, one can see, did *balik boeono* and *revolution*). This does not mean that they "meant" exactly the same thing, but rather that from Bangkok and Birmingham two parallel series were stretching out across, and seamlessly mapping, a singular world. This example is also emblematic of the way in which from the start the new serial thinking could be operated diachronically up and down homogeneous, empty time, as well as synchronically on the newspaper page.

It was from within this logic of the series that a new grammar of representation came into being, which was also a precondition for imagining the nation. The late colonial environment is an especially apt site for appreciating this development because one can there see how the logic was working in the same way, if in separate institutional milieux, among both white rulers and colored ruled. To illustrate this process, let us continue for the moment with the late nineteenth and early twentieth centuries in the Netherlands Indies.

121

Market Performance

Up until this epoch all forms of popular indigenous "theater," including the well-known, traditional shadow play, were grounded in a logic that one might call iconographic. The stories, presented by live actors or by puppets voiced over by puppeteers, were drawn either from local legends or from episodes in the Mahabharata and Ramayana epics, which over the centuries had become so indigenized that only a tiny literate minority was aware of their Indic provenance. Not only were the stories thoroughly familiar to audiences, their presentation was iconographically fixed. Playbills were unimaginable because the "characters" were all meticulously differentiated by standardized body types, coiffures, costumes, speech styles, and gestural repertoires. There was only one Indra or Rama or Arjuna, who was recognizable the very second he came into stage view. Because there was no question of "interpreting" such figures, who were often understood as quite real beings outside the performance, the identities of actors, indeed often their genders, were a matter of indifference. Paradoxically enough, the "iconographic rules" governing what Rama could conceivably say were so strict that scripts were never thought of, and easy improvization was the normal order of the day.

But toward the very end of the nineteenth century, a new form of theater crystallized in newspaper towns that in its own idiosyncratic way drew on the vaudeville and operetta performances of traveling Eurasian and European troupes. When indigenous players began to stage, for salable tickets, vernacular versions of *The Merchant of Venice*, the draw was precisely the easy mystery of the exotic title (Venice? Where was it? But one could find it on any printed map of the "world"—which had no insets for Heaven or Hell).[8] Shylock, like most of the characters in such dramas, could not be presented iconographically. There was as yet no convention as to how he should look, dress, talk, and move his body. No Jews had ever figured in traditional drama—no moneylenders either. Hence there was no way of playing Shylock except, quasi-"sociologically," as a *social type* or combination of types. The actor (by now gender mattered) could no longer improvise, but required the help of script and rehearsal to be able to present a plausible Jewish usurer; and this plausibility depended on persuading audiences of the "social verisimilitude" of Shylock—in other words, his placeability, replaceability too, within such intersecting universal series as cruel moneylenders, doting fathers, and obsessive misers. Yet his representativenesses were not only grounded in experienced colonial life—to be sure, everyone knew moneylenders, misers, and doting fathers personally, yet in the Indies Jews were few and almost invisible—they were also based in the kingdom of representation itself, the world of print. There fictive Shylocks, Hamlets, and Genevièves aligned themselves "grammatically" not only with real, serial capital cities, strikes, elections, and football matches, but also with pictorial advertisements, which are always unintelligible except as beguiling synecdoches for serial cornucupias of desirable commodities.

Seriality Bound

Meanwhile, on high, serialization was advancing from a rather different direction. In 1920, just as Haji Misbach was campaigning for revolution in the sugar belt of Central Java, the colonial regime executed the first "scientific census" in its domain.[9] Doubtless this came a bit late in world time, but not terribly late. The newly independent United States of America had been, with its rough-and-ready *national* population count of 1790, almost the first state to undertake protoscientific and public census activity—preceding France, the Netherlands, and the United Kingdom by a decade.[10] But until 1850, the unit of enumeration was the household, and only the name of the household's head was recorded. Not until 1880 was a central Census Office set up in Washington, and not until 1902 was this office, renamed a bureau, made a permanent, full-time agency of the state. In a broader frame, one observes that it was only in 1853, in the immediate aftermath of the European nationalist upheavals of 1848, that the First International Statistical Congress, held in Brussels, adopted a resolution establishing the basic "scientific" requirements for achieving international comparability of census data and the standardization of census content and techniques.[11]

That such a resolution had to be voted over and over at the Paris Congress in 1855, the London Congress in 1860, and the Florence Congress in 1867 indicates that all was not plain sailing with the statisticians' political campaign to modernize and "transnationalize" the processing of population counts. We should probably not be surprised that it was only in the infancy of the League of Nations that the campaign more or less reached fruition,[12] still less that this coincided with the very abrupt and rapid spread of suffrage for women.

As many observers have noted, not only is the taking of a census an elaborate, expensive, and thoroughly public affair, but, with some nonetheless quite predictable exceptions, census results are highly visible public texts. In principle, then, they should be open to the same kind of "grammatical" scrutiny that we have summarily applied to the newspaper and the popular theater. In this light, I am inclined to focus on three peculiar aspects of the census's conventions.

The first of these conventions is the impermissibility of fractions, or, to put it the other way around, a miragelike integrity of the body. For example, if a simple, hypothetical classificatory system proposes to sort a population into, say, Blacks and Whites, and then runs into the messy reality that a substantial group is of ancestries mixed in varying proportions, one logical option would be to assign halves, quarters, eighths, and sixteenths to the Black and the White columns. But because the convention forbids this possibility, the practical choices are arbitrary assignment to Black or White, or the proliferation of categories and subcategories—as it were, mulattoes, quadroons, and octoroons—in which mixedness, or fractionality, can resume integral status.[13] Naturally, this does not at all mean that each countee does not anonymously reappear in dozens of other classificatory enumerations within the same census, in each instance as an integer, but it does mean that this complex fractionality is inscribed in invisible ink. In one lighting, every countee is an indivisible whole; in another, merely the site of a maze of intersecting series.

The second convention is anonymity. One might say that the names fully recorded in individual census forms are the highly classified sections of these documents that the state keeps jealously to itself. It is a matter for some amusement that in the United States this "top secret" classification lasts for seventy-two years (furthermore, one can be punished for "secretly" lying to the state on one's schedule).[14] The convention of namelessness has two related "reality effects," as Roland Barthes used to say. On the one hand, it shores up the census's truth, in the sense that it becomes nigh impossible for anyone to match the census up with his or her world of personal knowledge and community acquaintance. On the other hand, through the equivalency of integers, it maps a stable (ten-year) social field, sealed by the imposing page-by-page row of identical totals. This nameless, tabularly crisscrossed field, is, say, Denmark—imagined serially, synchronically, and as a self-portrait.

The third convention, totality, contrasts vividly with the effervescent boundlessness of newspapers' serial imaginings. Totality (nicely inflated to "universe" in the argot of social science) is in fact required for most secondary statistical computations. But it has a political ancestry of its own, which it may be useful briefly to recall. Up along one family line is William Petty (1623–87), Hobbes's acolyte and Adam Smith's John the Baptist, who won a certain posthumous immortality in 1691 with the publication of his *Political Arithmetic*, of which the comparable analytic units were then-existing political states.[15] Up along another line was a seventeenth- and eighteenth-century "German" Cameralist tradition of *comparative* study of *staaten*, which eventually permitted Göttingen professor Gottfried Achenwall (1719–72) to coin, by derivation, the very term *statistik*. New-minted, the term speedily crossed the Channel and entered English with John Sinclair's twenty-one-volume *Statistical Account of Scotland*, published—of course serially—between 1791 and 1799.[16] In effect, before it was settled by the internal logic of statistics itself, the politically moated state of the age of enlightened absolutism had given "totality" its primal shape—just in time for the age of nationalism.

Statistical logic and politics, married in the census, sheared off every series at the same temporal edges (in the twentieth-century American census, the westward movements of "females," "Blacks," and "medical practioners" all end isomorphically on the coastline of the Pacific and the Bering Sea). But at the same time, by their mutual interaction, they created something that newspapers were ill equipped to engender: serial, aggregable, counterposed majorities and minorities, which, starting as formal entities, were positioned in due course to assume political reality. (Here is the matrix from which, exactly in the 1830s when statistical associations were being formed in the anglophone states on both sides of the Atlantic, Alexis de Tocqueville commenced feverishly to imagine tyrannies that were ultimately census grounded.)[17]

The linking bridge was, of course, the suffrage. The reason that the infant United States could so get the start of the majestic world was simply its novel republican and federal character. In the absence of monarchy and estates, it seemed that sovereignty could be manifested only in the will of the citizenry expressed through electoral processes. The national counting of 1790 and all later decennial countings up until the age of Haji Misbach were designed primarily to ensure, arithmetically, the fair apportionment of electoral representation in the two houses of the national legislature. It was not that the numbers of voters in any obvious way matched the census count, but suffrageless females and male minors were assumed to be distributed evenly across the states, and thus the household head (whose name, as I have noted, was the only one the census recorded until 1850) could, in a statistical-apportionment sense, "represent" them. Slaves, however, were not distributed evenly. Property they might be, but southern slave owners were not eager to surrender the chance to count them, once every ten years, as persons. Hence the bizarre compromise arrangement—showing that William Petty's political arithmetic had come fully into its own—whereby each unfree "American" recorded through the census was fractionally counted as three-fifths of a person for purposes of congressional reapportionment.

Fanning out from the United States, electoralism exerted an ever-increasing influence on the style of census taking, as notions of popular sovereignty spread, as the state acquired a welfare-and-development mission, and as the suffrage widened. It was not long before voters began to influence the very categories through which the machinery of enumerations whirred.[18] There were, under the new conditions, for the first time good reasons to wish to be counted, if in a certain style, rather than to hope to be overlooked by the tax man, who was the census taker's early shadow. By the beginning of the century the "electoral" mode of population enumeration had assumed such normalcy in the metropoles that it penetrated silently even into the colonial autocracies, where it could only have long-term subversive effects.

The Philippines affords a vivid example of this process. The first serious enumeration was undertaken in 1818.[19] Its category-roster included such strange, unelectoral bedfellows as *difuntos* (the dead), *negros infieles* (infidel blacks), *tributos* (tribute payers), *mestizos españoles* (persons of mixed-Spanish descent), *morenos* (the brown skinned), and *individuos contribu-yentes* (individual taxpayers). Its devisors were clearly thinking, from on high, in primarily ecclesiastical and financial terms. The word *almas* (souls) and the primary opposition between *infieles* and *convertidos* (infidels and converted) showed up for the last, and first, time. Cross-category totals, the necessary basis for majority-minority groupings, were scarce. There was no trace of territorialism, nor of the dozens of ethnolinguistic groups dotted across the islands.[20] The next census, that of 1877, was completely secular, and the shadow of the tax collector had disappeared. The three simple axes on which the count was based marked presence/absence of residents, their character as *españoles* or *extranjeros* (foreigners), and their skin color: *blancos*, *pardos*, and *morenos*.[21] Everything here breathed a backward, but definitely nineteenth-century, autocracy. The 1903 census, however, taken by the Americans within months of the official termination of their brutal war of conquest, was already structured protoelectorally in the peculiar American manner, categorizing (in alphabetic order!) twenty-five "wild" or "civilized" native ethnolinguistic groups, five skin-color tones from white through black, as well as a skein of birthplaces and, where relevant, citizenships.[22] In the publicized pages of *this* census, the words *Tagalog* and *Ilocano* had, for the first time, numbers attached to them, which were perfectly available for Tagalog and Ilocano speakers to read. And the "reality-effect" of the official census, its claim that what was being counted was, socially speaking, profoundly "there," gave these figures a kind of calm monumentality.

More striking still, with a category-structure of this kind, the Americans in the Philippines, who could not imagine *not* counting themselves, given that they so preeminently counted, appeared as a visible, sealed-in, numbered *minority*. Exactly the same thing happened in the 1921 census of the Netherlands Indies, and more generally in the twentieth-century colonial world. From a certain angle, one can see each of these censuses as smoking entrails from which the impending collapse of a particular colonialism lay ready to be deciphered.

Practice

From the contrast between two styles of serialization—one, figured by the newspaper, unbound and unenumerated; the other, figured by the census, bound and numerated—the lineaments of two kinds of politicization and political practice emerge, both of which, however, show how basic seriality always is to the modern imagining of collectivity.

One can get a vivid sense of the dynamic of the first from the following passage, which I have translated from *Dia Jang Menjerah* (She who gave up), a mesmerizing tale published in 1952 by the most celebrated of Indonesian writers, Pramoedya Ananta Toer. It describes how Is, teenage elder sister of the tale's heroine, comes to join the radical organization Pesindo (Socialist Youth of Indonesia) in the revolutionary upsurge that followed immediately after the end of the brutal Japanese occupation of Indonesia (1942–45):

> In such times too the rage for politics roared along like a tidal wave, out of control. Each person felt as though she, he could not be truly alive without being political, without debating political questions. In truth, it was as though they could stay alive even without rice. Even schoolteachers, who had all along lived "neutrally," were infected by the epidemic rage for politics—and, so far as they were able, they influenced their pupils with the politics to which they had attached themselves. Each struggled to claim new members for his party. And schools proved to be fertile battlefields for their struggles. Politics! Politics! No different from rice under the Japanese Occupation. Soon enough courses followed. And those who had only just obtained an understanding of capitalism-socialism-communism competed to give lectures at food stalls, on street corners, and in the buildings that snarled in each of their skulls. And Pesindo too sprang up in the barren, limestone soil of our village. By now, Is knew the society she was entering. She had found a circle of acquaintances far wider than the circle of her brothers,

sisters, and parents. She now occupied a defined position in that society: as a woman, as a typist in a government office, as a free individual. She had become a new human being, with new understanding, new tales to tell, new perspectives, new attitudes, new interests—newnesses that she had managed to pluck and assemble from her acquaintance. And all of this proceeded, untouched, amid the suffering of day-to-day existence.[23]

The circle of Is's brothers, sisters, and parents is without series. But at the revolutionary moment, to which she makes her small contribution, she imagines herself, for the first time in her tender life, serially: as "a" woman, "a" typist, "a" free individual, "a" new human being. This serialization so transforms her consciousness that everything now glows new to her. But these series, in their plasticity and universality, can never appear in a census, and not merely because they cannot be enumerated and totaled.[24] Furthermore, it is clear that she sees these series as of a kind, so that being a woman, a typist, and a new human being fulfill rather than counteract her commitment to the struggle for her country's freedom. We understand, too, that the series mentioned are at any moment available for kaleidoscopic transformation, enlargement and contraction. Nothing is fixed in fated stone. Tomorrow, she may become "a" revolutionary, "a" prisoner, "a" youth, "a" spy, indeed "a" nationalist in that boundless, but grounded, universal series that included, in 1946, Clement Attlee and Jawaharlal Nehru, but only and always on a provisional basis. And if Is understands herself now as a part of the world-in-motion, so to speak summoned by quotidian universals to battle, we too read her under the same signs. We may not share her young womanhood, her typing skills, her native language, her religion, or her culture, but she speaks to us not, ethnographically, as an "informant," but as a member of series that are open to us if we wish to act on them.

It is crucial to note that most of the series into which she sees herself entering require, as their entrance fee, that she act, in both senses of that word. She will have to learn how to "do" a revolutionary member of Pesindo, as others have had to learn how to "do" Hamlet, or strike organizer, or nationalist. But she understands all this as emancipation, and the last thing on her mind is her identity or her roots. (We can from the start sense that she will sweep herself away toward subsequent tragedy.)

The logic of the modern census series appears to move in the opposite direction. One might initially pursue this logic by considering the primal act that censuses appear quietly to elicit: namely, voting. Under optimal conditions, this act requires joining a one-day queue of people, each taking his or her turn to go into an enclosed space as strangely private as a public toilet, and for which the drawn curtains seem to serve as decent clothing. Once inside, these people pull the same levers or write standardized words or signs on identical pieces of paper. At exactly that point they cease, whether they like it or not, to "be" voters, except in an ascriptive sense, until the next movable feast comes around.

The extraordinary minimality and periodicity of the act of voting reminds us of how far the ballot is isomorphic with the census schedule in its refusal of fractions, its studied, aggregable anonymity, and its ensconcement, in due course, in strictly bounded totals. But this also shows us the basis of its real and symbolic political efficacy. This basis is *entitlement* (with all the ironic, antique overtones of its etymology). Before one can "do" voting, one must be entitled to do it, through an act of law of which one is never the singular beneficiary. And one is not simply "entitled" to vote; the very act of voting "entitles" *someone else* to act, on one's behalf. This "someone else," however, operates not by power of attorney, but as the representative of a bounded series. The finite numerology of such series in turn works within overlapping, stratified, majoritarian/minoritarian matrices. It is this that makes possible, for example, the quite normal situation that the minute elections are over, no one but political professionals ascribes any importance to the exact numbers by which a winning candidate defeats her or his opponent, and even voters who voted against the winner feel completely entitled to make claims upon that winner on the morrow of her victory. Encapsulating each level of electoral majority is always a higher whole. Voters have always the totality—the n of entitled voters—in their minds.

Out of this framing have emerged, over the past half century in particular, two signal consequences for the development of collective subjectivities. Both point in the same direction, if for somewhat different reasons.

The first is proportional entitlement, on the ground of n. As the twentieth-century electorally based "service" state multiplied its functions and enlarged its welfare capabilities, the census, ever more elaborate, increasingly became the integrated database from which every type of planning and budgetary allocation departed. Consquently, the census itself became the object of a more visible politicization. Take, for one extreme example, Nigeria, where for years a census was politically out of the question, precisely because of fears as to what it would show about the "true" numbers of the country's self-imagined ethnic groups, and thus imply for the distribution of political power and economic benefits. For another, more agreeable case, note how voter pressure in the turbulent "long" 1960s led to the abolition of the census (the last was held in 1971) in the Netherlands, which to this day remains the one country in the world to have repudiated this powerful instrument of governmentality.[25] The turmoil over the U.S. census of 1980 is still more indicative of the degree to which census definitions of categories have hardened into essentialized political realities through their role in organizing the allocation of economic and other benefits and the expectations of such benefits.[26] Of such categories, none has proven more important than the "ethnic," originally devised a century ago, in a prewelfare age, to monitor disdainfully the flows of immigrants from different parts of Europe. After the shutting off of large new immigrations in the 1920s, however, these categories became, thanks significantly to the revolution in communications, the bases for electoral mobilizations even at the national level. The powerful interlocking effects of census categorization and entitlement politics can be seen from the political emergence of such recent American imaginings as the Hispanic vote and the Asian American constituency, perhaps even in the electoral elision of race into ethnicity in the case of "Blacks."

This kind of late-twentieth-century political identification, in which the census and its young cousin the random-sample survey replace the neighborhood and the hometown, is not only of growing political importance, but enables us to see more clearly that fragile but sharp line between ethnicity and nationalism. Ethnic politics is played out on the basis of people's prior *national* entitlement as voters, and is justified on the basis of proportionality within the framing of the existing census. When, or better if, a *soi-disant* ethnic group remagines itself as a nation (as for, example, has been happening with the Quebecois) and seeks to become an independent nation, then it discards this census in the name of a new one of its own figuring. It is exactly at the moment of independence, however, that the logic of proportionality reemerges, within a new *n*.

The second consequence is reinforcement for identitarian politics. I noted earlier the essentialist implications of the bounded, numbered series that censuses best exemplify. But I suspect that the series operates in the same direction at another level. Consider it this way. Identity is logically a function of duality: it exists at the moment when "b" encounters "= b." This is a dry, algebraic way to gloss Woyle Soyinka's biting dismissal of Léopold Senghor's series *négritude*: The Tiger has no need of Tigritude. In other words, Tigritude appears necessary only at the point where two uncertain beasts mirror themselves in each other's exiled eyes.

The word *exile* is not employed here idly. We are all only too aware of how incessantly people speak not merely of "seeking" "roots," but of "exploring," "finding," and, alas, "coming close to losing" their "identities." But these searches, which rhetorically move inward toward the site that once housed the soul, in fact proceed outward toward real and imagined censuses, where, thanks to capitalism, state machineries, and mathematics, integral bodies become identical, and thus serially aggregable as phantom communities.

In our time, moreover, such communities are no longer confined to the interiors of already existing nation-states. As I have argued at greater length elsewhere, the revolutions in communications and transportation of the post-World War II era have combined with postindustrial world capitalism to produce cross-national migrations on a historically unprecedented scale.[27]

The same forces have worked to create "diasporic" collective subjectivities that are imagined, census-fashion, as bounded series. Few texts give one a more emblematic view of this transformation than the well-meaning *Penguin Atlas of Diasporas*.[28] Opening with more than seventy pages devoted to a Jewish diaspora that begins in the eighth century before Christ, it proceeds through Armenians, Gypsies, Blacks, Chinese, Indians, Irish, Greeks, Lebanese, and Palestinians to end with Vietnamese and Koreans. In each case, the remarkable thing is the authors' insistence on providing numerical totals and subtotals—so to speak, "Total" world-Armenians and "total" Armenians in France, in Georgia, in Australia, or in Argentina. No less instructively, these totals are calmly, if implausibly, rounded off: forty-two thousand "Indians" in Kenya in 1920, forty thousand Jews in Portugal in 1250. Is it necessary to underline that these countings were made by imperial state machineries for their own reasons and by their own peculiar logics, that it is quite uncertain how many of the forty-two thousand "Indians" in fact imagined themselves as such, and that there was every sort of ambiguity and arbitrariness involved in deciding who "was" a Jew in thirteenth-century Portugal? The truth is that an ersatz-historical atlas of this kind, far from depicting historical subjectivities, actually represents a certain contemporary vision of cosmopolitanism based on a quasi-planetary dispersion of bounded identities. Wherever the "Chinese" happen to end up—Jamaica, Hungary, or South Africa—they remain countable Chinese, and it matters very little if they also happen to be citizens of those nation-states. It would occasion no surprise if a book of this kind finds today a warm reception in circles whose members are attracted by the idea of finding themselves "in exile," entitled to belong to ancient bounded communities that nonetheless stretch impressively across the planet in the age of "globalization."

Whether any of this represents a meaningful cosmopolitanism seems to me very doubtful, because it is at bottom simply an extension of a census-style, identitarian conception of ethnicity, and lacks any universal grounding. Nothing offers a greater contrast with the young Javanese girl who imagined herself a "new human being," not a member of a Javanese diaspora, and who enrolled herself, like Haji Misbach, as a firmly local member of the un-bounded series of the world-in-motion.

Notes

1. Quoted in Takashi Shiraishi, *An Age in Motion: Popular Radicalism in Java, 1912–1926* (Ithaca, N.Y.: Cornell University Press, 1990), 193.
2. Benedict Anderson, *Imagined Communities: Reflections on the Origin and Spread of Nationalism*, rev. ed. (London: Verso, 1991), 117.
3. Curiously enough, Soewardi failed to notice the comic and reactionary character of this commemoration. Instead of reminding Dutch men and women of their ancestors' genuinely heroic declaration of independence from Felipe II's empire in 1581, or Madrid's final acceptance of that independence in 1648, after decades of bitter fighting, it celebrated London and Berlin's defeat of Napoléon, the Holy Alliance's imposition of a mediocre monarchy on a people with a long republican tradition, and the forcible inclusion into the new "kingdom" of what is today's Belgium.
4. A substantial part of the text of these verse memoirs appears in Ann Kumar, "Dipanegara (1787?–1855)," *Indonesia* 13 (April 1972): 69–118.
5. Anderson, *Imagined Communities*, 22–36.
6. The English translation of *Bumi Manusia*, the title of the first of the great Indonesian writer Pramoedya Ananta Toer's tetralogy of novels on the origins of Indonesian nationalism.
7. See the sophisticated discussion in Craig J. Reynolds, *Thai Radical Discourse: The Real Face of Thai Feudalism Today* (Ithaca, N.Y.: Cornell University, Southeast Asia Program, 1987).
8. See A. Th. Manusama, *Komedie Stamboel of de Oost-Indische Opera* (Batavia [Jakarta]: n.p., 1922), for a splendid account. Manusama offers a provisional repertoire of forty-three "shows" that, in a nice illustration of my argument above, are thoroughly cosmopolitan-local in thematic character: nine drawn from *The Arabian Nights*, nine from local tales and legends, six from Persia, six from India ("Hindustan"), three from China, and ten from Europe (24–27). In this last group we find not only *The Merchant of Venice* and *Hamlet*, but also *Geneveva* (Geneviève of Brabant). *Somnambule* (La Somnambula), *Robertson de duiker* (probably Robert de Duivel, Robert the Devil), and so on.
9. Peter Boomgaard, *Population Trends, 1795–1942* (Amsterdam: Royal Tropical Institute, 1991), gives a good account of this endeavor and the contrast it forms with previous enumerations for tax and corvée purposes.
10. The reasons for the early start of the United States will be considered below.
11. The 1820s and 1830s have been described as an era of "statistical enthusiasm," in which statistical societies were formed for the first time in the United Kingdom and the United States. See Paul Starr, "The Sociology of Official Statistics," in *The Politics of Numbers*, ed. William Alonso and Paul Starr (New York: Russell Sage Foundation, 1986), 24, 15.
12. Much of the above material I owe to Marc Ventresca of Stanford University.
13. For example, between 1840 and 1910, the major category "Negroes" in the U.S. census contained within it four subcategories: mulatto, quadroon, octoroon, and black. See William Petersen, "Politics and the Measurement of Ethnicity," in *The Politics of*

Numbers, ed. William Alonso and Paul Starr (New York: Russell Sage Foundation, 1986), 208.

14. Information kindly provided, over the telephone, by the New York City office of the Bureau of the Census.

15. As a ruthless young *esprit fort*, he had in 1654 been sent to Ireland by the Lord Protector to make a count of persons and property, that could serve as the basis for systematic colonial exploitation and oppression.

16. See, inter alia, Starr, "The Sociology of Official Statistics," 13–15, and the sources therein cited.

17. See the celebrated chapter 12 in *De la Démocratie en Amérique*, 13th ed. (Paris: Pagnerre, 1850), 226–34, especially 230: "*De nos temps*, la liberté d'association *est devenue* une garantie nécessaire contre la tyrannie de la majorité" (emphasis added). Was a "majority," let alone a tyrannical majority, seriously conceivable under the *ancien régime*?

18. This is probably the right place to remind the reader that, all the same, the census includes two contrasting types of series—the categorical and the scalar. The modal case of the first is gender, for which only two exclusive lifetime possibilities are open; the modal case of the second is income distribution, which proceeds by a long series of graded steps with fuzzy endings so that billionaires and paupers are made invisible. The scalar format offers every possibility for people to "move" up and down these steps in the course of their lives. From this rises the agreeable utopian idea of a census in which gender becomes scalar, with several graded steps, and income binary-categorical—as it were, divided simply between haves and have-nots.

19. It was sponsored, however, not by the colonial government but by the Ayuntamiento of Manila, and relied on the apparatus of the church rather than the state for its implementation.

20. There was no real attempt to count the substantial Muslim and hill-tribe pagan populations residing within what on paper was the Spanish Philippines.

21. In the meantime, first Manila, then other ports, had been thrown open to international trade, so that "foreigners" were now appearing there for the first time. Furthermore, the arrival of the steamship made the presence/absence of residents a real question.

22. The most elaborate discussion available of Philippine population counts, and the politics thereof, is in the appendix to the first volume of Onofre Corpuz, *The Roots of the Filipino Nation* (Quezon City: Aklahi Foundation, 1989), 515–70.

23. This work can be found in Pramoedya Ananta Toer's collection *Tjerita dari Blora* (Tales of Blora) (Jakarta: Balai Pustaka, 1952); the quoted passage is on p. 279.

24. One might think that "a" typist in "a" government office should be occupationally censusable. But the whole passage shows that here "typist" is a planetary series.

25. See J. J. Woltjer, *Recent Verleden* (Amsterdam: Balans, 1992), 414.

26. See the excellent chapters "The 1980 Census in Historical Perspective," by Margo A. Conk, and "Politics and the Measurement of Ethnicity," by William Petersen, in *The Politics of Numbers*, ed. William Alonso and Paul Starr (New York: Russell Sage Foundation, 1986). Petersen's mordant section on "the creation of the 'Hispanics,'" is particularly telling.

27. See Benedict Anderson, "Exodus," *Critical Inquiry*, 20 (Winter 1994): 314–27.

28. Gérard Chaliand and Jean-Pierre Rageau, *The Penguin Atlas of Diasporas* (Harmondsworth: Viking, 1995). The French original, *Atlas des Diasporas*, was published in 1991 by Éditions Odile Jacob.

Flexible Citizenship among Chinese Cosmopolitans

Aihwa Ong

Destabilizing Chineseness

Stories cribbed from the business pages:

> A recent late summer in the Ukraine. An angry mob dragging down a statue of Lenin enacted the political collapse, while vendors selling Bolshevik trinkets reinvented the economy. David Chang, representing The Asia Bank in New York, was in town to snap up apartment houses and real estate before the dust settles. "Governments come and go," he says, "but business stays."[1]

> In California, "the Silicon Valley way of divorce" among new Chinese immigrants results in one failure out of five marriages. A "typical" Chinese couple—he is an engineer, she an accountant—used to live in a half-a-million-dollar house with two well-schooled children. They invested in a second home and vacationed in Lake Tahoe. When the wife asked for a divorce, it was not because her husband had an affair, or at least not with another woman. "My husband works on his computer in the office during the day, comes home at 8 p.m., and continues to sit in front of his computer after dinner. . . . I am a 'computer widow' who is never asked how she was doing, nor what has happened to the family lately."[2]

Postmodern elements jostle for attention: *displacement*—Asians in Western worlds; *fragmentation*—families broken up by emigration and divorce; *difference*—male and female subjectivities; *impermanence*—in everyday arrangements. Were these reports about people other than the Chinese, they would attract no more than a passing glance. But to me, such postmodern snapshots are a jarring reproach to academic descriptions of Chinese identity, family, and cultural practices.

Much scholarship on Chinese subjects has been shaped by Orientalist concerns with presenting the Other as timeless, unchanging culture. Recent attempts to revise the static images of Chineseness nevertheless still confine the analysis of ways of "being Chinese" within clearly defined Chinese contexts of the nation-state or of culture.[3] An essentializing notion of Chineseness continues to dog the scholarship, because the Chinese past, nation, singular history, or some "cultural core" is taken to be the main and unchanging determinant of Chinese identity. Sometimes we forget that we are talking about one-quarter of the world's population. What is conveyed is the sense that people identifiable as "Chinese" exist in their own worlds, and even when they participate in global processes, they continue to remain culturally distinct. I suspect the grand Orientalist legacy continues to lurk in a field, dominated by historians, convinced of the singularity of this great inscrutable Other. Younger scholars and feminists who seek to provide more complex historically and geopolitically contingent accounts of Chinese cultural practices are often merely tolerated, if not marginalized for threatening to disrupt the stable tropes of high Sinology. Perhaps not so ironically, as I have mentioned above, ambitious Asian politicians have made much political capital by borrowing academic representations of Chineseness for their own self-orientializing projects.[4] Grand Orientalist statements are dialectically linked to the petty orientalisms generated by transnational corporate and advertising media that make pronouncements about Oriental labor, skills, values, families, and mystery. The legend for Singapore Airlines used to be "Singapore Girl, what a great way to fly."

But stories about capital, displacements, hybridity explode reigning notions about being Chinese. How do discrepant images reflect changing social, economic, and political relations in which Chinese subjects are important participants? Today, overseas Chinese are key players in the booming economies of the Asia-Pacific.[5] In what ways have their border-crossing activities and mobility within the circuits of global capitalism altered their cultural values and class strategies? In this essay, I explore how the flexible positioning of diasporic Chinese subjects on the edge of political and capitalist empires affects their family relations, their self-representation, and the ways they negotiate the political and cultural rules of different countries on their itineraries. In contrast to Edward Said's unilateral construction of the objects of orientalisms as silent participants in Western hegemonic projects,[6] I trace the agency of Asian subjects as they selectively participate in orientalist discourses encountered on travels through the shifting discursive terrains of the global economy. Yet their countercultural productions should not be interpreted as a self-reproduction of "the ways we are situated by the West," but as complex maneuvers that subvert reigning notions of national self and the Other in transnational relations.

Perhaps more than other travelers and migrants, international managers and professionals have the material and symbolic resources to manipulate global schemes of cultural difference, racial hierarchy, and citizenship to their own advantage. Today, flexibility reigns in business, industry, labor, and financial markets, all technologically enhanced innovations that have effects on the way people are differently imagined and regulated, and on the way people represent and conduct themselves transnationally.[7] But whereas international managers and professionals may be adept at strategies of economic accumulation, positioning, and maneuver, they do not operate in free-flowing circumstances, but in environments controlled and shaped by nation-states and capital markets.

For instance, the form and meaning of citizenship have been transformed by global markets and floods of skilled and unskilled workers crossing borders. Although citizenship is conventionally thought of as membership based on the political rights and participation within a sovereign state, globalization has made economic calculation a major element of diasporic subjects' choice of citizenship, as well as in the ways nation-states redefine immigration laws. I use the term *flexible citizenship* to refer especially to the strategies and effects of mobile managers, technocrats, and professionals who seek to both circumvent *and* benefit from different nation-state regimes by selecting different sites for investments, work, and family relocation. Such repositioning in relation to global markets, however, should not lead one to assume that the nation-state is losing control of its borders.[8] State regimes are constantly adjusting to the influx of different kinds of immigrants, and to ways of engaging global capitalism that will benefit the country while minimizing the costs. For instance, nation-states are reworking immigration law to attract capital-bearing subjects while limiting the entry of unskilled labor. From the perspective of such immigrants as well-heeled Hong Kongers, however, citizenship becomes an issue of handling the diverse rules or "governmentality" of host societies where they may be economically correct in terms of human capital, but culturally incorrect in terms of ethnicity.[9]

In order to understand the tactical practices of this diasporic managerial class, we must locate them within and one step ahead of the various regimes of truth and power to which they, as traveling persons, are subject. Michel Foucault uses *regime* to refer to power/knowledge schemes that seek to normalize power relations.[10] By appealing to particular "truths" developed about science, culture, and social life, these systems of power/knowledge define and regulate subjects, normalizing their attitudes and behavior. The regimes that will be considered here are the regime of Chinese kinship and family, the regime of the nation-state, and the regime of the marketplace, all providing the institutional contexts and webs of power within which Chinese subjects (re)locate and (re)align themselves as they traverse global space.

As Don M. Nonini has argued, each kind of regime requires for its effect "the localization of disciplinary subjects"—that persons be locatable and confinable to specific spaces and relations defined by the various regimes: the kinship network, the "nation," the marketplace.[11] In this sense, "flexible citizenship" also denotes the localizing strategies of subjects who, through a variety of familial and economic practices, seek to evade, deflect, and take advantage of political and economic conditions in different parts of the world. Thus we cannot analytically delink the operations of family regimes from the regulations of the state and of capital. One can say, for example, that Chinese family discipline is in part shaped by the regulation of the state and by the rules of the global marketplace, but the convergence of Chinese family forms with flexible strategies of capital accumulation enables them to bypass or exploit citizenship rules, as the case may be, as they relocate capital and/or family members overseas. So while I talk about flexible citizenship, I am also talking about the different modalities of governmentality—as practiced by the nation-state, the family, capital—that are interconnected and have effects on each other, variously encoding and constraining flexibility in global (re)positioning. By analyzing different modalities of flexibility *and* governmentality under globalization, I identify contemporary forms that shape culture making and its products. I will first discuss the regime of diasporic Chinese kinship and how it structures, deploys, and limits flexible practices.

Middling Modernity: *Guanxi* and Family Regimes in Diaspora

One form of elite Chinese sensibility developed in the context of the late nineteenth century, when interregional commerce flourished under European colonialism in East and Southeast Asia. This entry of Chinese into mercantile capitalism ruptured the traditional links of filiation among Chinese subjects, Chinese families, and the Chinese nation. Alienated from the colonial powers, commercial classes redirected Confucian filiation away from the political system, and paternalism collapsed into an ethos narrowly focused on family well-being and interests, and firmly under male control. Outmigration and the dispersal of family firms outside China exposed emigrants to different possibilities of being Chinese in the world.

A diasporic Chinese modernity—in the "middling" sense of pragmatic everyday practices[12]—developed among emigrant Chinese in the colonial worlds of East and Southeast Asia. In city ports and colonial enclaves, Chinese subjects facing political mistreatment and intense competition for survival evolved an instrumentality in norms concerning labor organization, family practice, links between family and the wider economy, and dealings with political authorities.[13] For instance, in nineteenth-century China, the Confucian ideology of filial piety (xiao) governed the relations of superior and subordinate (father-son, husband-wife, older-younger brothers). Because the family was considered a microcosm of the moral order, xiao relations also figured relations to rules.[14] But European imperial domination in treaty ports like Canton and Shanghai soon undermined Confucian hegemony. One outcome was early modern anti-imperialist, antipatriarchy movements, especially among university students in Beijing. However, the commercial legacy of European rule, which resulted in a family-centered notion of Confucianism, developed among overseas Chinese communities existing under colonial rule in Southeast Asia. Among the new commercial classes, loyalty to the modern state (founded in 1911) was barely formed, and the detested colonial powers were tolerated so long as money could be made. The Chinese comprador class became notorious for the systematic ways its members amassed personal power and wealth at the expense of the new republic. By forming profitable links overseas, merchant and industrial families repositioned themselves as subjects of global trade rather than loyal subjects of the Chinese motherland. The age-old notion of filial piety to the social order collapsed, freeing diasporic kinship systems to adjust to overseas colonial empires.

Modern Chinese transnationalism thus has roots in these historical circumstances of diaspora and European colonial capitalism, and in the postcolonial era, Chinese family enterprises became fully integrated within the larger global economy. Chinese traders recruited labor gangs, organized construction and mining crews, and ran brothels, gambling houses, and opium dens—all activities that transgressed the localizing regimes of colonial powers—while becoming more firmly integrated within the colonial economies.[15] Their regional networks for labor and capital accumulation enabled Chinese traders to be the "wild men" who continually challenged political regimes and eluded their regulation.[16] Many Chinese sojourners did express a residual political loyalty to the Chinese motherland by contributing funds to the leaders of the struggling republic. But in the colonies, paternal bonds and interpersonal relations (guanxi) structured networks for interregional trade and provided the institutional basis for a sense of a larger, diffused "imagined community" of overseas Chinese (huaqiao).[17]

In the postcolonial era, most Southeast Asian states have remained suspicious of the political loyalty of their Chinese citizens, partly because of the economic domination and extensive overseas connections of these citizens. Only Singapore and Taiwan, both possessing a Chinese majority, have promoted Confucian education to inculcate state loyalty as continuous with filial piety in the family. But in most countries, especially in Islam-dominated Malaysia and Indonesia, the discourse of nationalism draws on colonial models of race-based multiethnic nationhood.[18] Thus there are different cultural politics of being Chinese in different countries, but for many overseas Chinese, there is no obvious continuity between family interests and political loyalty (especially given their rather common experience of anti-Chinese discrimination in the host countries). Outside of Taiwan and Singapore, there is a disengagement between Chinese cultural interests and national belonging in host countries identified with dominant ethnicities, such as Vietnamese or Malay. For instance, in Malaysia, lower-class Chinese subjects often seek to evade the localizing mechanisms of the state that stigmatize them as "more Chinese" (i.e., less assimilated than upper-class Chinese) and hence subject to regulation as second-class citizens. This diffused sense of being diasporic Chinese has also been shaped by their flexible, mobile relations across political borders, and by the kinship regime of truth and control.

Launching family businesses on the edges of empires, Chinese subjects depend on a careful cultivation of *guanxi* (interpersonal) relations and instrumentalist family practices. These habits, attitudes, and norms are not a simple continuation or residual of some essentialized bundle of "traditional Chinese" traits. *Guanxi* networks in Southeast Asia are historically contingent, a kind of (post)colonial "habitus"[19]—that is, the dispositions and practices that emphasize pragmatism, interpersonal dependence, bodily discipline, gender and age hierarchies, and other ethnic-specific modes of social production and reproduction in diaspora and under foreign rule. Such overseas Chinese habitus has ensured that the emigrant family survives for generations while evading the discipline of the colonial, and later the postcolonial, state, with its special regimes of othering Chineseness.

Produced and shaped under such conditions, the familial regimes of diasporic Chinese based on *guanxi* are not without their own violence and exploitation of workers, family members, kinsmen, and so on. In the early days of colonial capitalism, *guanxi* networks deployed Chinese emigrants in the "pig trade," supplying coolies to labor camps throughout Asia, thus subjecting many to brutal control, lifelong indebtedness, poverty, and crime while enriching their patrons.[20] *Guanxi*, as a historically evolved regime of kinship and ethnic power, controls and often entraps women and the poor while benefiting fraternal business associations and the accumulation of wealth for Chinese families in diaspora.

In everyday life, however, there is widespread misrecognition of *guanxi*'s violence, while its humanism is widely extolled by ordinary folk, businessmen, and cultural chauvinists alike. Such symbolic violence[21]—or the erasure of collective complicity over relations of domination and exploitation—is also present in academic writings that unduly celebrate *guanxi* as the basis of recent overseas Chinese affluence.[22] Misrecognition of business *guanxi* as basically a structure of limits and inequality for many and enabling of flexibility and mobility for the few to accumulate wealth is part of the ritual euphemization of "Chinese values," especially among transnational Chinese and their spokesmen.[23]

Indeed, *guanxi* regimes and networks have proliferated within the institution of subcontracting industries, the paradigmatic form of flexible industrialization throughout the Asia-Pacific. Many Chinese firms enter light manufacturing by subcontracting for global companies, producing consumer items such as jewelry, garments, and toys in "living-room factories."[24] In recent years, *guanxi* networks have been the channels for subcontracting arrangements between overseas Chinese capital and enterprises in mainland China. A Sino-Thai tycoon who is the largest investor in China invokes *guanxi* to explain the growth of his conglomerate on the mainland compared to what he sees as the inflexibility of Western firms: "American and European companies have adapted themselves to a very sophisticated legal-based society. . . . In China there is no law. There is no system. It is a government by individuals, by people."[25] As such, the *guanxi* institution, as invoked and practiced, is a mix of instrumentalism—fostering flexibility and the mobility of capital and personnel across political borders—and humanism—"helping out" relatives and hometown folk on the mainland. Although patriotic sentiments may be be intermixed with *guanxi* connections, overseas Chinese investors are also moved by opportunities for mobilizing cheap labor in China's vast capitalist frontier.[26] It is probably not possible to disentangle nostalgic sentiments toward the homeland from the irresistible pulls of flexible accumulation, but the logic of *guanxi* points to sending capital to China while shipping the family overseas.

It may sound contradictory, but flexible citizenship is a result of familial strategies of regulation. Michel Foucault suggests that we think of modern power, in its "government" of population and its welfare (biopolitics), as productive of relations, rituals, and truths. I consider the rational, normative practices that regulate healthy, productive, and successful bodies within the family and their deployment in economic activities for economic well-being as family governmentality. The biopolitics of families, however, are always conditioned by wider political economic circumstances.

The rise of Hong Kong as a global manufacturing center was secured after British colonial rule put down and domesticated trade unions and student activitists during the 1960s, a state strategy that was common throughout Asia.[27] In subsequent decades, refugee families in all classes have adapted through hard work, fierce competitiveness, and tight control over the family in order to improve overall family livelihood and wealth. Local social scientists use the term *utilitarian familialism* to describe the everyday norms and practices whereby Hong Kong families place family interests above all other individual and social concerns. One scholar observes that economic interdependency is the basic structuring principle, expressed as "all in the family," a principle that mobilizes the immediate family and other relatives in common interests.[28] An individual's sense of moral worth is based on endurance and diligence in income-making activities, compliance with parental wishes, and the making of sacrifices and deferral of gratification, especially on the part of women and children. In her study of factory women, Janet Salaff found that daughters are instilled with a sense of debt to their parents, which they "repay" by shortening their schooling and earning wages that often goes toward their brothers' higher education.[29] The writers cited above seem to identify such family practices as something inherent in "Chinese culture," ignoring the effects of state discipline and a highly competitive marketplace on refugee families. Such family regimes among the working classes have been responsible for the phenomenal growth of Hong Kong into a manufacturing giant. Among the upwardly mobile, biopolitical considerations inform family discipline in production and consumption. Besides acquiring the habitus of continual striving, children, especially sons, are expected to collect symbolic capital in the form of educational certificates and well-paying jobs that help raise the family class position and prestige. In imperial and republican China, the accumulation of degrees was an established way to rise from peasant to mandarin status, or a way for merchants to rise socially in the eyes of officials.[30] In Hong Kong, the entrepreneur's rise to the highest status is determined solely by his wealth, regardless of how it has been accumulated, although he too may take on the trappings of mandarin learning.[31]

Such familial regimes, which regulate the roles of sons and daughters for the family well-being, can also become discontinuous with or subvert the biopolitical agenda of the state. The British government's laissez-faire policy encourages the population to pursue wealth with "flexibility and vigor"[32] and, until the eve of the return of Hong Kong to China rule, to express political freedom as a market phenomenon. This market-driven sense of citizenship was until recently viewed as the right not to demand full democratic representation, but to promote familial interests apart from the well-being of society.[33] Middling modernity thus places a premium on material goods and an instrumental approach to social life, indexed by the ownership of Mercedes Benzes and market shares. There is a joke that professors spend more time playing the stock market than teaching. Risk taking and flexibility in the entrepreneurial sense induce an attenuated sense of citizenship. A young, single civil servant posted to San Francisco confided to me:

> I don't think I need to associate myself with a particular country. I would rather not confine myself to a nationality defined by China or by the U.K. I am a Hong Kong person, I grew up there, my family and friends are there, it's where I belong. . . . I lack a sense of political belonging due to the British colonial system, but we have thrived on the system—in terms of the quality of life, roughly fair competition, in terms of moving up through the educational system, even though Hong Kong is not a democracy.

This young man plans to get a British passport and try his luck wherever he can practice his talents. Like many savvy Hong Kongers, he is outwardly mobile, aligned more by world market conditions than the moral meaning of citizenship in a particular nation. Such middling, disaffected modernism has been shaped within the politics of colonialism and the nation-states over a refugee and diasporic population, and yet these strategies are adept at subverting the political regimes of localization and control.

English Weather: National Character and the Biopolitics of Citizenship

Since the 1960s, ethnic Chinese from Hong Kong and Southeast Asia have sought residential rights in Western countries in order to escape political discrimination and anticipated upheavals that disrupt businesses and threaten family security. But with the rising affluence of Asian countries and relatively declining economies in the West, they may find that economic opportunities and political refuge may not both be found in the same place, or even in the same region of the world. With the impending return of Hong Kong to mainland rule, many Chinese professionals would like to continue working in Hong Kong and China, but have parked their families in safe havens in Australia, Canada, the United States, and Great Britain. They have soon found that their search for overseas citizenship is constrained by the immigration policies of Western countries equivocating over capital and ethnicity.

The contours of citizenship are represented by the passport, the regulatory instrument of residence, travel, and belonging. Citizenship requirements are the effects of what Foucault calls "biopolitics," whereby state policies regulate the conduct of subjects as a population (by age, ethnicity, occupation, and so on) and as individuals (sexual and reproductive behavior) in the interests of ensuring security and prosperity for the nation as a whole. Under liberal democracy, biopolitical regulation (governmentality) helps construct and ensure the needs of the marketplace, through a policy of acting and not acting on society.[34] For instance, in Hong Kong, British liberal government has always been poised on a boundary between government action and necessary inaction in the commercial realm, in order to maintain the wide-open, capitalist economy. The question of Hong Kong Chinese emigration to Great Britain then must be considered within the dialectics between liberal governmentality and transnational capitalism.

As the residents of a remnant of the empire, Hong Kongers are designated "British-dependent territory citizens" (BDTC), with limitless rights of travel but no rights to reside in Great Britain. After the reimposition of China rule, these same residents will be called "British nationals (overseas)" (BNO), with the conditions of domicile and travel unchanged. Hong Kong Chinese are thus normalized as an overseas population that is in but not of the empire; their partial citizenship rests on differences of territoriality, coloniality, and (unmentioned) British origins.

British immigration policy is at the threshold of structurally determining the relationship between class and race, so that phenotypical variations in skin color can be transformed into social stratification based on the assumed capital and labor potential of different groups of immigrants. Postwar immigration laws institutionalized racial difference through the progressive exclusion of "colored" immigrants from the Commonwealth.[35] In the early 1960s, under public pressure to restrict colored immigrants (said to overwhelm housing and state benefits), the Conservative government withdrew the right of "colored" U.K. passport holders to enter Britain. A few years later, the same government granted the right of entry and settlement to several million "white" people from South Africa. Such action was defended by a government white paper that maintained that expanded Commonwealth immigration creates social tensions; the immigrant presence thus has to be resolved if "the evil of racial strife" is to be avoided.[36] Although the language of immigration law is not explicitly racist, the distinction between whites and coloreds from the Commonwealth, and their assumed differential contribution to racial tensions (*race* is frequently used to mean only coloreds, not whites), clearly reproduces a class hierarchy whereby race is given concrete institutional expression.

In this transnational discursive formation of race, Chinese from Hong Kong are coloreds, yet clearly differentiated from Afro-Caribbean immigrants because of their significant role in overseas capitalism and their perceived docility under British rule in Hong Kong. In the 1960s, restrictions of immigration from the Commonwealth countries limited Hong Kong arrivals mainly to restaurant operators and employees.[37] In addition, thousands of students were sent by their parents for higher education in Britain. By the 1980s, fear of the imminent reversion to China rule and its potential threat to the Hong Kong economy generated steady emigration, mainly to Western countries. Soon the monthly outflow of Hong Kongers had reach one thousand, thus jeopardizing confidence in the Hong Kong financial market, in which British interests were heavily invested. The colonial government saw the problem as one of "brain drain," and fought to stem the outflow by appealing to Orientalist reason. An official commented that "the [Chinese] have an overwhelming pragmatic concern for family and personal development—the same pragmatic self-interest that has made the Hong Kong economy so successful."[38]

In England, immigration policy was modified to grant citizenship to some Hong Kong subjects, mainly as a gesture to stem the outflow and stabilize faith in the Hong Kong economy. Again, biopolicial criteria that would serve market interests determined who was to be awarded citizenship. In 1990, a nationality bill granted full citizenship or "the right of abode" to only fifty thousand elite Hong Kongers and their families (about a quarter million out of a total Hong Kong population of almost six million). The members of this special subcategory of Chinese are carefully chosen from among householders (presumably predominantly male) who have British connections in government, business, or some other organizations. A point system for different occupations, such as accountancy and law, discriminates among the applicants, who must have high education and must presumably speak fluent English. They are mainly in the age bracket of thirty to forty. Thus these individuals are selected for their capacity to be normalized as British citizens and their ability to participate in the generation of transnational capital.

British immigration law thus produces a new discourse on overseas Chinese, who are eligible for citizenship only as *Homo economicus*. Although the British Labour Party criticized the bill's "elitist" emphasis on the immigrants' education and professional backgrounds, it did not address the larger subject of how interest in transnational capital colors the perception of race. Although yet to be fully implemented, the new nationality law constructs a different legal subjectivity of citizenship—as less than *Homo economicus*—for Chinese already in the country.

Homi Bhabha has noted that English weather invokes the "most changeable and immanent signs of national character" and is implicitly contrasted to its "daemonic double": the hot, tropical landscapes of the former colonies. English weather represents an imagined national community under threat of "the return of the diasporic, the postcolonial."[39] Prime Minister Margaret Thatcher, anxious to quiet a restive public over the admission of more coloreds into the "bless'd isle," defended her bill in Parliament by wondering why the Chinese would trade sunny Hong Kong for Great Britain, "a cold and cloudy island." She reminded the British that the nationality bill was intended as an "insurance policy" to keep would-be Chinese citizens in Hong Kong up to and beyond 1997. In other words, full British citizenship for even those Chinese meeting the biopolitical criteria is citizenship indefinitely deferred; the nationality law operates as insurance against their ever becoming full British citizens. It is clear that a cold welcome awaits them.

China Recalls Prodigal Sons

Even before the "tidal wave" of emigration following the Tiananmen crackdown in 1989, China had tried to stem the exodus of capital and professionals from Hong Kong. Through its mouthpiece, the New China News agency office, the People's Republic repeatedly appealed to all Hong Kongers who have gone abroad to reconsider their decision, to "come back, to work for the prosperity of the land of [your] birth." An official blamed the flight of Hong Kong Chinese on the instrumental ethos bred under Western influence. He charged that Chinese residents have been led astray by capitalist countries offering investment opportunities to attract Hong Kong skill and capital.[40] China viewed the British nationality law as an insult to Chinese sovereignty, and a shameless attempt by Britain to cream off Hong Kong's talent. It threatened expulsion of those who possess British citizenship after 1997.[41]

Generally, China takes a paternalistic tone with errant Chinese capitalists who would be "forgiven" for seeking foreign citizenship, and "prodigal sons" who return are favorably contrasted against the "traitors" who would abandon capitalism in China altogether. While China appeals to filial piety and capitalist opportunities to retain Hong Kong subjects, Britain holds out the promise of citizenship and democratic rights, thereby hoping to ensure a place for British interests in the Pacific Rim economies.

Many Hong Kongers have opted to work in China while seeking citizenship outside both countries altogether. Caught between British disciplinary racism and China's opportunistic claims of racial loyalty, between declining economic power in Britain and surging capitalism in Asia, diasporic Chinese seek a flexible position among the myriad possibilities (and problems) found in the global economy. Flexible capital accumulation is dialectically linked to the search for flexible citizenship as a way to escape the regime of state control, either over capital or over citizens. In Hong Kong, a small industry has arisen to disseminate information about the legal requirements and economic incentives for acquiring citizenship abroad. Just as Hong Kong-registered companies seek tax havens in places like Bermuda, well-off families accumulate passports not only from Canada, Australia, Singapore, and the United States, but also from revenue-poor Fiji, the Philippines, Panama, and Tonga (which requires in return for a passport a down payment of U.S. $200,000 and an equal amount in installments).[42] The Hong Kong authorities uncovered a business scam that offered, for a sum of U.S. $5,000, citizenship in a fictitious Pacific island country called Corterra. More well-heeled travelers may seek out actual remote islands, safe havens that will issue passports for little commitment in return. One investor confided in me that his brother is a friend of the king of Tonga, who gave him citizenship in return for a major investment. A political refuge secured, his brother continues to operate the family's multinational hotel business out of their Hong Kong headquarters, managing properties in Britain and China without needing their citizenship papers. Thus for Hong Kong Chinese, for whom the meanings of motherland, country, and family have long been discontinuous and even contradictory, legal citizenship is sought not necessarily in the sites where one conducts one's livelihood, but in places where one's family can pursue the "American dream." Among elites and the not so elite, this means a politically stable and secure environment where world-class education can be found for the children and real estate is available for homesick housewives to speculate in.

Plotting Family Itineraries

Big business families provide the clearest examples of a careful blending of discipline in familial practice and flexibilization in business and citizenship. The likes of Li Ka-Shing and the late Sir Y. K. Pao, who rose from refugee poverty to immense wealth, are considered the most brilliant realization of such innovative entrepreneurial border running in the Chinese diaspora. Many tycoon families emerged in the 1960s, when businessmen amassed fortunes in real estate, just as its manufacturing industries helped make Hong Kong a household word for inexpensive consumer products.[43] In interviews with the sons of some of these wealthy families, I found the familial regime of control to be very firm, even as the family business takes off overseas. Fame and business power relations are inseparable, and the company founding father is a patriarch who regulates the activities of sons who must be trained and groomed to eventually take over the family business. *Xiao* relations are instilled through the force of family wealth. From the top floor of his San Francisco high-rise, Alex Leong,[44] a mild-mannered middle-aged investor, tells me:

I remember, even when I was in junior high [in Hong Kong], my objective was to follow my father's footsteps and be in business . . . to take over the family business rather than to try to work for someone else or to do my own thing. Because I think it is very important for sons to carry on the family business, something that has been built up by your father. To me, that's the number-one obligation. . . . If your family has a business, why would you go work for somebody else, and leave a hired man to look after your family business? To me, that doesn't make any sense.

Alex comes from a prominent family that traces back to a granduncle who was once the governor of Guangdong province. Alex's father went to school in Germany, but after the Communist victory in 1949, he took his family to Australia. His father then explored business opportunities in Brazil, where the family lived for a few years. They finally returned to Hong Kong, where his father went into real estate and set up a firm called Universal Enterprises. *Xiao* dictates that Alex and his brothers take on the roles mapped out by their father. Alex explains that it is a common practice for big business families to distribute their sons across different geographic sites:

The fathers make a very clear subdivision whereby one brother doesn't infringe on the others, fearing that there would be too much fighting among them. For instance, my oldest brother works in Hong Kong. I take care of everything in North America. We always talk, but we know whose responsibility it is here and over there.

In another wealthy family, the eldest son (who obtained a Tonga passport) remains in Hong Kong to run the family hotel chain in the Pacific region, while the second brother, based in San Francisco, takes care of the North American and European hotels. The youngest brother, who came on board later, is managing family business in Southern California. Daughters, no matter how qualified, are never put into management positions in the family business, which is considered their brothers' patrimony.[45] Three Hong Kong-born women are working as investors in the San Francisco Bay Area, but they are running their own firms using seed money from their fathers.

Their businesses are not part of the family enterprises founded by their fathers. Alex refers to one of these women as "one of the men," because she has been highly successful in what is still considered a male vocation.

Although Alex cannot imagine doing anything else, he confesses that he sometimes feels "stifled" by the fact that the reins of control are in his father's hands:

> When you have a father as a boss, to me that's a double boss, right? You can't just say, "I don't agree, I quit, and resign." . . . You can't just walk away from your father. And then a father who has been in business for so long, he'll never recognize you as an equal, so you are always in a subordinate position.

The familial regime is so powerful that even sons who try to slip its nets are sometimes pulled right back into conformity. Alex's youngest brother graduated from college a few years ago, but having observed his older brothers' predicament, has resisted working in the family business. The young man expressed his rebellion by working in a bank, but under the paternalistic eye of one of his father's wealthy friends. Alex expects that "eventually, when my youngest brother joins in, it is our objective to continue to expand here in the U.S. and to wind down in Hong Kong." Scholars of rural China maintain that a man who has inherited family property rather than acquired his own fortune enjoys more power over his sons,[46] but here in the tumult of the global economy, it is the self-made tycoon who appears to exert strong control over his family throughout his lifetime and who directs and regulates the behavior of his sons, who are sent out across the world to carve out new niches for the family business empire. Alex's father has been retired for some years now, but the sons continue to consult him on major selling and buying decisions. A political analogue to this system of boss rule is the continuing power of the former prime minister of Singapore, Lee Kuan Yew, who still appears to exert tremendous *towkay* (boss) power over his state enterprise.[47]

Thus the masculine subjectivity of this elite diaspora community is defined primarily in terms of the individual's role as a father or a son, the role of maintaining the paternalistic filial structure that both nurtures and expands family wealth. Unlike daughters, who will inherit a small share of the family fortune (about 30 percent of what the sons get in Alex's family) and then have nothing to do with the male estate, sons must remain active, integral parts of the family business throughout their lives. To be merely passive, as in drawing an income without involvement in the daily operation of the business, is to play a feminine role, like sisters, who marry out, or wives, who may manage the finances but rarely take on management roles. However, as uncertainties increase in Hong Kong, and more sons can break away and emigrate on their own, a few young women have taken over running their family businesses.[48] But the familial system has been to rely on men, and in families without sons, even "foreign devil" sons-in-law who have proved their loyalty to the family business can take the place of sons. For instance, the business empire of Sir Y. K. Pao, the late shipping and hotel magnate, is now run by his two Caucasian sons-in-law. One can say that *xiao* has been bent and channeled to serve the governmentality not only of the family, but of global capitalism as well.

Families in America, Fathers in Midair

The modernist norms and practices of diaspora Chinese anticipate their relocation, along with capital infusions, into the Western hemisphere. Earlier Chinese immigrants to the United States were largely laborers, with a sprinkling of merchants. Today, Chinese investors and professionals arrive as cosmopolitans already wise in the ways of Western business and economic liberalism.[49] With new modes of travel and communication, familial regimes have become more flexible in both dispersing and localizing members in different parts of the world. Hong Kong papers talk about the business traveler as an "astronaut" who is continually in the air, while his wife and children are located in Australia, Canada, or the United States, earning rights of residence.

The turn toward the United States began in the 1960s, when teenagers from middle- and upper-middle-class families applied to American schools and colleges. Alex's father often told him, "Your future is really going to be outside Hong Kong. So you should be educated outside, as long as you maintain some Chinese customs and speak Chinese." The well-off used their children's overseas education as entrée into a Western democracy, buying homes for the children and setting up bank accounts and exploring the local real estate. Upon graduation, sons are expected to help expand the family business in the country. After graduating from Berkeley and the University of Wisconsin business school, Alex set up a local branch of his father's company in San Francisco. Because he is not yet a citizen, his parents plan to retire in Vancouver, Canada, where residential rights can be had for an investment of C$300,000. They expect to join him eventually in the Bay Area, while the sons take over greater control in running the family empire. This mix of family and business strategies allows them to weave in and out of political borders as they accumulate wealth and security.

Many entrepreneurs, however, continue to shuttle between both coasts of the Pacific (because it is still more profitable to do business in Hong Kong) while their wives and children are localized in North America. The astronaut as a trope of Chinese postmodern displacement also expresses the costs of the flexible accumulation logic and the toil it takes on an overly flexible family system. The astronaut wife in the United States is euphemistically referred to as "inner beauty" (*neizaimei*), a term that suggests two other meanings for "inner person," that is, "wife" (*neiren*) as well as "my wife in the Beautiful Country (i.e., America)" (*neiren zai Meiguo*). Wives thus localized to manage suburban homes and take care of the children—lessons in ballet, classical music, Chinese language—sarcastically refer to themselves as "widows" (and computer widows), expressing their feeling that family life is now thoroughly mediated and fragmented by the technology of travel and business.

In a Canadian suburb, some widows have formed a group called Ten Brothers in order to share domestic problems and chores in the absence of their husbands. "We have to start doing men's work like cutting grass in the summer and shoveling snow in the winter. So we call ourselves 'brothers' instead of 'sisters.'"[50] This sense of role reversal induced by flexible citizenship has also upset other prior arrangements. In the Bay Area, wives bored by being "imprisoned" in America parlay their well-honed sense of real estate property into a business sideline. Down the peninsula, the majority of real estate agents are immigrant Chinese women selling expensive homes to other newly arrived widows. Here also, flexibility reigns as wives keep trading up their own homes in the hot residential market. A Hong Kong industrialist tells me that he has moved five times over the past sixteen years as a result.

In some cases, the flexible logic deprives children of both parents. The teenagers dropped off in Southern California suburbs by their Hong Kong and Taiwan parents are referred to as "parachute kids." One such child left to fend for herself and her brother refers to her father as the "ATM machine," because he issues money but little else from some extraterrestrial space. Familial regimes of dispersal and localization then discipline family members to make do with very little emotional support; disrupting parental responsibility, straining marital relations, and abandoning children are such common practices that they have special terms. They thus challenge claims that the "Confucian affective model" is at the heart of Chinese economic success[51] when the flexible imperative in family life and citizenship requires a form of isolation and disciplining of women and children that is both critiqued and resisted. The logic of flexibilization expresses the governmentality of transnational capitalism within which many elite families are caught up, and their complex maneuvers around state regulations reveal the limits and pathos of such strategies.

American Liberalism, Citizenship, and Pacific Rim Capital

I have argued elsewhere that in the United States, neoliberalism plays a role in shaping our notion of the deserving citizen. The history of racial conflict also tends to produce a perception that different kinds of ethnic and racial groups embody different forms of economic and political risks.[52] Following Foucault, I consider liberalism not merely an ethos but a regime of normalizing whereby *Homo economicus* is the standard against whom all other citizens are measured and ranked.

At the turn of the twentieth century, the Chinese had the dubious distinction of being the first "racial" group to be excluded as undesirable and unsuitable immigrants to the United States. Earlier, Chinese immigrants had been welcomed by capitalists and missionaries as cheap, diligent, and docile laborers, but they were eventually attacked as unfair competitors by white workers in the railroad and mining industries.[53] During the Cold War, the public image of Chinese oscillated between that of the good Chinese, as represented by America's Guomindang allies, and the bad Chinese associated with "Red China."[54] In the 1960s, the emergence of a middle-class Chinese population provided contrast with the growth of a nonwhite "underclass," a term used mainly for inner-city blacks.[55] The media popularized the term *model minority* to refer to Asian Americans, who were perceived as a minority group that collectively raised itself up by its bootstraps, thus fitting the criteria for the good or at least deserving citizen.[56] Images of Oriental docility, diligence, self-sufficiency, and productivity underpin contemporary notions that the Asian minority embodies the human capital desirable in good citizens, in contrast to those who make claims on the welfare program.[57]

Through the next decade, the influx of immigrants from Hong Kong and Taiwan, many of them students bound for college, swelled the middle-class ranks of Asian Americans.[58] The rise of a Chinese immigrant elite—many suburb-living professionals—coincided with the restructuring of the American economy and its increasing reliance on skilled immigrant labor and overseas capital. In the public's mind, the Asian newcomers seemed to embody the desired disciplinary traits of an increasingly passé model of American character. For instance, in the aftermath of the Tiananmen crackdown, a letter to the *San Francisco Chronicle* defended the admission of Chinese (student) refugees:

151

The opportunity to welcome the best and the brightest of China and Hong Kong into our area is fantastic. These are motivated, energetic, courageous people, with strong cultural traditions of taking care of their families, working hard, and succeeding in business. We need more of these values in our midst, not less.[59]

It appears that "traditional" American values are to be found in these newcomers, who are coming with different kinds of capital, but perhaps not so strong "cultural traditions." Earlier images of the Chinese railroad worker, laundryman, houseboy, and garment worker have been replaced by the masculine executive, a *Homo economicus* model inspired in part by the so-called neo-Confucian challenge from across the Pacific.[60]

Increasingly, the reception of skilled and capital-bearing Chinese newcomers represents the triumph of corporate discourses and practices that invoke the "Pacific Rim" and its Oriental productivity and new wealth. For instance, under pressure from corporate and Asian lobbies, U.S. immigration laws were modified in 1990 to attract some of the Pacific Rim capital flowing toward Australia and Canada, where the laws are less stringent. A new "investor category" allows would-be immigrants to obtain a green card in return for a million-dollar investment that results in the creation of at least ten jobs. On Wall Street, seminars directed at Asian Americans offer suggestions on how to "get U.S. citizenship through real estate investment and acquisition." A consultant urges, "Think of your relatives in Asia. If they invest in you, they get a green card and you get a new business."[61] As in other Western countries with finance-based immigration, citizenship has become an instrument of flexible accumulation for the nation-state, as a way to subvert its own regulatory mechanisms in order to compete more effectively in the global economy.

Narrating Cosmopolitan Citizenship

In what ways has the arrival of the diaspora Chinese reworked the cultural meanings of *Asian American* and produced a new discourse of Pacific Rim romanticism, and even symbolic violence? Whereas Said has described Orientalism as a one-sided and self-reifying process, I have tried throughout this essay to represent the discursive objects themselves as cocreators in Orientalism. This has been, after all, part of their flexibility in negotiating the multicultural worlds of European imperialism. For centuries, Asians and other peoples have been shaped by a perception and experience of themselves as the Other of the Western world.[62] The new prominence of Asians in the world markets has enabled Chinese subjects to play a bigger role in identifying what counts as "Chinese" in the West.[63] Diaspora Chinese academics now use Orientalist codes to (re)frame diaspora Chinese as enlightened cosmopolitans who possess both economic capital and humanistic values. Wang Gungwu, formerly chancellor of Hong Kong University, hails overseas Chinese living "among non-Chinese" as "a modern kind of cosmopolitan literati" who have embraced Enlightenment ideals of rationality, individual freedom, and democracy.[64] Perhaps. U.S.-based scholars claim that "Confucian humanism" will create "an Oriental alternative" to the destructive instrumental rationality and individualism of the West[65]—in other words, a kinder and gentler capitalism for the twenty-first century. One wonders whether these scholars have bothered to visit factories run by Chinese "humanists" and observed whether their practices are really that "humanistic" and uninformed by the logic of capital accumulation.

These grand claims circle around and occlude the complex, wide-ranging realities of East Asian capitalism, or at least its Chinese variant. For instance, Hong Kongers hail from a colonial territory where there has been little nurturing of Confucian humanism and democratic values. Until Tiananmen, many had developed a radically apolitical stance toward the state. Just as Hong Kong is viewed as a place to maximize wealth, so the Western democracies to which many are bound are considered "gold mountains" of opportunity. The subcontracting system of production used in Hong Kong and Taiwan, and now in China, is among the most exploitative of women and children in the world.[66] In Hong Kong, "democracy" for many entrepreneurs often means freedom from political constraints on making money, and the state and wider society are of concern only when they can be made relevant to family interests.[67] In the view of the business elite, the modern social order is built upon the domination of those who possess intellectual and economic power, and wealthy people are the models of envy and emulation, rather than enemies of the poor.[68] Like investors all over the world, Chinese businessmen who engage in philanthropy are seeking to escape property taxes and to gain social status as prominent members of society; it is a stretch to construct these as acts of Confucian benevolence. As billionaire Li Ka-shing says, "There is no other criterion of excellence [except money]."[69] But such prideful discourses on diaspora Chinese elites as humanistic citizens persist, and they are intervening in narratives about the role of Asian Americans in the United States.

From across the Pacific, corporate America answers the call to reconsider Chinese immigrants as exceptional citizens of the New World Order imaginary. Of course, the reception is not unambivalent, for global trade is viewed as war.[70] This contradictory attitude was expressed by David Murdock, chairman and CEO of Dole Foods Company, at a conference on Asian Americans in Los Angeles. Murdock personifies corporate America: his company has operations in more than fifty countries and employs thousands of employees in the Asia-Pacific. He warned that in a world of many big economic powers, technological edge has shifted East. There are, however, more than seven million Asian Americans. He continued:

> We need to be more competitive. We need people who understand the languages, cultures, the markets, the politics of this spectacular region. Many Asian Americans have language ability, cultural understanding, direct family ties, and knowledge of economic conditions and government practices throughout Asia. This knowledge and ability can help Americans achieve political and business success in the region. . . . much of their insight and ability can [help] in opening doors for the U.S., building a new structure for peace in the Pacific.[71]

By defining a role for Asian Americans as good citizen and trade ambassadors, Murdock's speech situated them in the wider narrative of the Oriental as trade enemy.

At the same conference, Los Angeles City Councilman Michael Woo, who was then seeking to be the first Asian mayor of Los Angeles, picked up the narrative by reframing the question, "What then is this new person, this Asian American? In the new era of the Pacific?"[72] The question, reminiscent of European queries about Anglos earlier in the century, subverts the view that whites are the undisputed key players on the West Coast. Woo, whose family has close ties with Asian capital, went on to propose "a new hybrid role" whereby new Asian immigrants (rather than long-resident Asian Americans, he seemed to suggest) can act as "translators, go-betweens [between] one culture and another, using skills that have brought us to such prominence and success in the business world and in the professions, and entering into the public arena" to become mediators in community relations.

Asians are "bridge builders," Woo claimed. In his view, the Asian American "middleman minority" is not the besieged ethnic group of academic theorizing.[73] He was using the term in the larger global sense, coming dangerously close to the meaning that evokes compradors, the Chinese elites who acted as middlemen between colonial governments and the masses in Asia. Indeed, such *muchachos*, as Fred Chiu (following Mike Taussig) has pointed out, are "the ideal-typical mediating and (inter)mediating category/force in the reproduction of a world of—out-going as well as in-coming—nationalism and colonialism."[74] And of course the term *bridge* has gained new resonance for overseas Chinese in their new prominence as transnational capitalists. In Chinese, the word for bridge (*qiao*) puns with the term for overseas Chinese (the *qiao* in *huaqiao*), and as I have argued elsewhere, diaspora Chinese have been quick to play on the metaphor of bridging political boundaries in their role as agents of flexible accumulation and flexible citizenship.[75] The bridge-building metaphor appeals to an Asian elite that sets great store in being engineers, doctors, managers, businessmen, and bankers, and who see themselves as self-made men who are now building the infrastructures of modern affluence on both sides of the Pacific. Woo saw a continuity between Asian economic and cultural middleman roles. He noted that trading skills developed in the diaspora, "in the midst of cultures very different from their own," included not just those of use in "the handling of money, but also skills in sizing up people, negotiating a deal, and long-term planning." He suggested that these "survival skills" could be "transferred" to non-Asians. Woo thus echoed the *Homo economicus* construction of Chinese immigrants and elevated their role in the American social order.

Such narrativization is never simply complicit with hegemonic constructions, but seeks to reposition Asian immigrants and Asian Americans as new authority figures, while suggesting declining human capital and leadership qualities among Anglos. By calling Asian Americans the new Westerners, Woo implied that Anglos have been surpassed in diligence, discipline, moral capital, and even knowledge of the changing multicultural world that is critical to America's success. His narrative carves out a space of Asian Americans as mediators in American race and class relations. The bridge-building citizen evokes the tradition of American communities, the ideal of a civil society where neighbors look out for each other.[76] Asian American leaders, Woo seemed to suggest, could build bridges between racial minorities and the government. By identifying Pacific Rim bodies with Pacific Rim capital, the concept of bridge builders gentrifies Asian American identity in both its local and its global aspects, in moral contrast to less privileged minorities and their dependence on the welfare state.[77] When Woo's talked ended, the largely Asian audience rose up and clapped enthusiastically, and voted to replace the *model minority* label with the *bridge-building* minority, a term that apparently enables Asian Americans to share the transnational role of diaspora Chinese building the Pacific century.[78]

Conclusion

The emigration of Chinese corporate elites out of Asia has entailed the cultural work of image management as they seek wider acceptance in Western democracies and in different zones of late capitalism. By revising the academic images of Chinese as money handlers, trading minorities, and middlemen, corporate spokesmen paint a picture that mixes humanistic values with ultrarationalism, values that suggest the ideal-type *Homo economicus* of the next century.[79] Such self-representations are not so much devised to collaborate in the biopolitical agenda of any nation-state, but to convert political constraints in one field into economic opportunities in another, to turn displacement into advantageous placement in different sites, and to elude state disciplining in order to reproduce the family in tandem with the propulsion of capitalism.

Of course, whereas for bankers boundaries are always flexible, for migrant workers, boat people, persecuted intellectuals and artists, and other kinds of less well-heeled refugees, this apparent mix of humanistic concerns and capitalist rationality is a harder act to follow. For instance, Don Nonini has identified the tensions and pathos experienced by middle-class Malaysian Chinese whose familial strategies of emigration are intended to escape second-class citizenship as much as to accumulate wealth overseas.[80] Although small-business-owning Chinese consider themselves locals in their Malaysian hometowns (e.g., as "natives of Bukit Mertajam"), many are vulnerable to anti-Chinese policies and feel that they have no choice but to send their children overseas, where they may feel less discrimination. These businessmen postpone joining their children in places like New Zealand, which do not feel like "home." Their loyalty to home places in Malaysia is ironically disregarded by state policies that discriminate against them as lower-class ethnics in a way that does not affect wealthy Chinese who are viewed as more "cosmopolitan" and open-minded about Malay rule. As Jim Clifford has reminded us, there are "discrepant cosmopolitanisms," and the cosmopolitanism of lower-class Chinese from Malaysia is fraught with tensions between sentiments of home and pressures to emigrate.[81] This is not to say that the Hong Kong Chinese elites do not have patriotic feelings for the Chinese motherland, but rather that the investor emigrants are well positioned to engage in a self-interested search for citizenship and profits abroad, a strategy that will enhance their economic mobility and yet sidestep the disciplining of particular nation-states.[82]

Among this elite group, though not limited to them, such a mix of ultra-instrumentalism and familial moralism reveals a postnationalist ethos. They readily submit to the governmentality of capital, while plotting all the while to escape state discipline. In the most extreme expressions, their loyalty appears to be limited to the family business; it does not extend to any particular country. A Chinese banker in San Francisco explains that he can live in Asia, Canada, or Europe: "I can live anywhere in the world, but it must be near an airport." Such bravado constructs a bearable lightness of being that capital buoyancy can bring. Yet the politics of imagining a transnational identity dependent on global market mobility should not disabuse us of the fact that there are structural limits, and personal costs, to such flexible citizenship.

This essay should not be interpreted as an argument for a simple opposition between cosmopolitanism and patriotism (taken to an extreme, either is an undesirable or dangerous phenomenon). I have noted elsewhere that a Confucian cultural triumphalism has arisen alongside modern Chinese transnationalism in Southeast Asia.[83] Some scholars have been tempted to compare the role of modern Chinese economic elites to that of medieval Jewish bankers, whose activities protected free trade along with liberalism and other Enlightenment values in the Dark Ages. We should resist such comparison. Although contemporary Chinese merchants, bankers, and managers have burst through closed borders and freed up spaces for economic activities, they have also revived premodern forms of child, gender, and class oppression, as well as strengthened authoritarian regimes in Asia.[84] A different kind of cosmopolitical right is at play. The point is not that all Chinese are thus painted with the same broad brush of elite narratives, but that the image of the border-running Chinese executive with no state loyalty has become an important figure in the era of Pacific Rim capital. What is it about flexible accumulation—the endless capacity to dodge state regulations, spin human relations across space, find ever new niches to exploit—that allows a mix of humanistic relations and ultra-instrumentality to flourish? Indeed, there may not be anything uniquely "Chinese" about flexible personal discipline, disposition, and orientation; they are rather the expressions of a habitus that is finely tuned to the turbulence of late capitalism.[85]

Notes

This essay is a revised and expanded version of an earlier article, "On the Edge of Empires: Flexible Citizenship among Chinese in Diaspora," *positions* 1, no. 3 (1993–94): 746–78. I thank Kathleen McAfee, Don Nonini, and Pheng Cheah for their helpful comments.

1. Summary of a story in the *New York Times*, 31 August 1991, A1.

2. Summary of "The Silicon Valley Way of Divorce," *Overseas Scholars' Monthly* (Taipei), January 1991, 71.

3. See "The Living Tree: The Changing Meaning of Being Chinese Today" (special issue), *Daedalus* 120, no. 2 (1991); "China in Transformation" (special issue), *Daedalus* 122, no. 2 (1993).

4. See Aihwa Ong, "'A Momentary Glow of Fraternity: Images of Nation and Capitalism in Asia," *Identities* (Winter 1996): 331–66.

5. A recent volume edited by Ruth McVey, *Southeast Asian Capitalists* (Ithaca, N.Y.: Cornell University, Southeast Asian Program, 1992), explores the emergence of a transnational Chinese bourgeoisie in Southeast Asia, focusing on their making of advantageous political and economic ties, but it does not consider the changing cultural forms and ideological representations that accompany these transitions.

6. Edward Said, *Orientalism* (New York: Pantheon, 1978).

7. David Harvey identifies our era as one of "flexible accumulation," but he underestimates the ways culture shapes material forces and the effects of political economy on culture. David Harvey, *The Conditions of Postmodernity* (Oxford: Basil Blackwell, 1989).

8. This has been suggested by many scholars. See Masao Miyoshi, "A Borderless World? From Colonialism to Transnationalism and the Decline of the Nation-State," *Critical Inquiry* 19, no. 4 (1993): 726–51; Benedict Anderson, "Exodus," *Cultural Inquiry* 20 (Winter 1994): 324–25.

9. Foucault uses *governmentality* to mean the deployment of modern forms of (nonrepressive) disciplining power—especially in the bureaucratic realm—and other kinds of institutions that produce rules based on knowledge/power about populations. See Michel Foucault, "Governmentality," in *The Foucault Effect: Studies in Governmentality*, ed. G. Burchell, C. Gordon, and P. Miller (Chicago: University of Chicago Press, 1991), 87–104.

10. Michel Foucault, *Discipline and Punish: The Birth of the Prison*, trans. A. Sheridan (New York: Random House, 1977); Michel Foucault, *The History of Sexuality*, vol. 1, trans. M. Hurley (New York: Pantheon, 1978).

11. Don M. Nonini, "Shifting Identities, Positioned Imaginaries: Transnational Traversals and Reversals by Malaysian Chinese," in *Ungrounded Empires: The Cultural Politics of Modern Chinese Transnationalism*, ed. Aihwa Ong and Don M. Donini (New York: Routledge, 1997), 203–7.

12. See Paul Rabinow, *French Modern: Norms and Forms of the Social Environment* (Cambridge: MIT Press, 1989), 9–10.

13. For studies on Chinese merchant families in early modern China, when European powers dominated the coastal cities, see Mark Elvin and G. William Skinner, eds., *The Chinese City between Two Worlds* (Stanford, Calif.: Stanford University Press, 1972).

14. Mayfair Mei-hui Yang, "The Modernity of Power in the Chinese Socialist Order," *Cultural Anthropologist* 3, no. 4 (1988): 416; Tani Barlow, "Theorizing Woman: *Funu, Guajia, Jiating,*" *Genders* 10 (1991): 132–60.

15. See Victor Purcell, *The Chinese in Southeast Asia* (Kuala Lumpur: Oxford University Press, 1965); Carl Trocki, *Opium and Empires: Chinese Society in Colonial Singapore, 1800–1910* (Ithaca, N.Y.: Cornell University Press, 1990).

16. See Don M. Nonini and Aihwa Ong, "Introduction: Transnationalism as an Alternative Modernity," in *Ungrounded Empires: The Cultural Politics of Modern Chinese Transnationalism*, ed. Aihwa Ong and Don M. Donini (New York: Routledge, 1997), 3–36.

17. This term was used by the Chinese government to refer to its overseas nationals, but in Southeast Asia it became a generic term used to refer in a diffuse way to diasporic

Chinese in general, regardless of their nationality. In this essay, I use the terms *huaqioa, overseas Chinese,* and *diasporic Chinese* interchangeably.

18. See Benedict Anderson, *Imagined Communities: Reflections on the Origins and Spread of Nationalism,* 2d ed. (London: Verso, 1991). Anderson underplays the centrality of race in colonial-inspired notions of nationalism in Southeast Asia, seeking instead to focus on the "good" kind of anti-imperialist, civic nationalism.

19. Bourdieu, *Outline of a Theory of Practice* (Cambridge: Cambridge University Press, 1977), 90–95.

20. Allen Chun, "Pariah Capitalism and the Overseas Chinese of Southeast Asia: Problems in the Definition of the Problem," *Ethnic and Racial Studies* 12, no. 2 (1989): 233–56.

21. Bourdieu, *Outline of a Theory of Practice,* 190–97.

22. See Peter Berger and Hsia Hsin Huang, eds., *In Search of an East Asian Development Model* (New Brunswick, N.J.: Transaction, 1988); Hung-chao Tai, ed., *Confucianism and Economic Development: An Oriental Alternative?* (Washington, D.C.: Washington Institute Press, 1989).

23. There is a growing popular and academic literature on the centrality and mysticism of *guanxi* in Chinese capitalism, and not just by Asian writers. See, for instance, Joel Kotkin, *Tribes: How Race, Religion, and Identity Determine Success in the New Global Economy* (New York: Random House, 1992); James Fallows, *Looking at the Sun: The Rise of the New East Asian Economic and Political System* (New York: Pantheon, 1994).

24. Ping-Chun Hsiung, *Living Rooms as Factories: Class, Gender, and the Satellite Factory System in Taiwan* (Philadelphia: Temple University Press, 1995).

25. Quoted in Edward A. Gargan, "An Asian Giant Spreads Roots," *New York Times,* 14 November 1995, C3.

26. Aihwa Ong, "Anthropology, China, and Modernities: The Geopolitics of Cultural Knowledge," in *The Future of Anthropological Knowledge,* ed. Henrietta Moore (London: Routledge, 1996), 60–92.

27. See Frederic C. Deyo, ed., *The Political Economy of New Asian Industrialism* (Ithaca, N.Y.: Cornell University Press, 1987).

28. Emily Siu-kai Lau, *Society and Politics in Hong Kong* (New York: St. Martin's, 1983), 72–74.

29. Janet W. Salaff, *Working Daughters of Hong Kong: Filial Piety or Power in the Family?* (Cambridge: Cambridge University Press, 1981).

30. See Ho Ping-ti, *The Ladder of Success in Imperial China* (New York: Columbia University Press, 1962).

31. Lau, *Society and Politics in Hong Kong,* 95–96.

32. Edward K. Y. Chen, "The Economic Setting," in *The Business Environment in Hong Kong,* 2d ed., ed. D. G. Lethbridge (Hong Kong: Oxford University Press, 1984), 3–4.

33. Ibid.

34. Colin Gordon, "Governmental Rationality: An Introduction," in *The Foucault Effect: Studies in Governmentality,* ed. G. Burchell, C. Gordon, and P. Miller (Chicago: University of Chicago Press, 1991), 1–15.

35. Robert Miles, *Race* (London: Routledge, 1989), 84–85.

36. Ibid., 85–86.

37. James L. Watson, *Chinese Lineage and the Emigrant Family* (Berkeley: University of California Press, 1975), 50–78.

38. Quoted in Chan Chi-keung, "Exodus Threat to HK Credibility," *South China Morning Post,* 28 January 1988, 1. The most he could hope for was for them to return to Hong Kong with their shiny new Canadian and Australian passports.

39. Homi Bhabha, "DissemiNation: Time, Narrative, and the Margins of the Modern Nation," in *Nation and Narration* (New York: Routledge, 1990), 327.

40. "Time Running Out to Stop the Brain Drain," *South China Morning Post*, 29 December 1987.

41. Sam Seibert et al., "Hong Kong Blues," *Newsweek*, 16 April 1990, 45.

42. For more details on finance-based immigration programs, see *South China Morning Post*, 20 November 1988.

43. Wong Siu-lun, *Emigrant Entrepreneurs: Shanghai Industrialists in Hong Kong* (Hong Kong: Oxford University Press, 1988).

44. To protect the privacy of all my subjects, I have given them pseudonyms.

45. For discussion of comparable practices in Chinese business families based in Singapore, see Chan Kwok Bun and Claire Chiang, *Stepping Out: The Making of Chinese Entrepreneurs* (Singapore: Simon & Schuster, 1993).

46. See, for example, Sung Lung-sheng, "Property and Family Division," in *The Anthropology of Taiwanese Society*, ed. Emily Martin and Hill Gates (Stanford, Calif.: Stanford University Press, 1981).

47. *Towkey* is a transcription of the Hokkien word for the head of a family business, a term commonly used in Southeast Asia to refer to Chinese entrepreneurs or any successful self-employed Chinese man. In Mandarin, the word is *toujia*.

48. See *New York Times*, 14 January 1996, sec. 3.

49. For a discussion of Chinese cosmopolitans in Vancouver, see Katherine Mitchell, "Transnational Subjects: Constituting the Cultural Citizen in the Era of Pacific Rim Capital," in *Ungrounded Empires: The Cultural Politics of Modern Chinese Transnationalism*, ed. Aihwa Ong and Don M. Donini (New York: Routledge, 1997).

50. The name of Ten Brothers is borrowed from a band of Robin Hood-type robbers in the Chinese classic *The Water Margin*. *South China Morning Post*, 5 February 1994.

51. See Tai, *Confucianism and Economic Development*, 18–19.

52. Aihwa Ong, "Cultural Citizenship as Subject-Making: Immigrants Negotiate Racial and Cultural Boundaries in the United States," *Current Anthropology* 37, no. 5 (1996): 737–62.

53. Roger Daniels, *Asian American: Chinese and Japanese in the United States since 1850* (Seattle: University of Washington Press, 1988), 129–54.

54. Ibid., 301.

55. Gunnar Myrdal, *An American Dilemma: The Negro Problem and Modern Democracy* (New York: Vintage, 1968), 184–85.

56. Minority scholars often miss the ways neoliberal ideas about human worth affected processes of racial formation in the United States. See, for example, Michael Omi and Howard Winant, *Racial Formation in the United States* (New York: Routledge & Kegan Paul, 1986).

57. Actually, the ideological divide thus drawn was not so clear-cut, as Chinatown movements also came to be shaped by the Great Society programs and many Chinese American students were radicalized by the African American struggle for civil rights in the 1960s. This new ethnic consciousness arising out of struggle found expression in storefront programs to provide for the health care, housing, and other needs of new immigrants. Many of the advocates saw Chinese immigrants, most of whom were poor, as victims of racist capitalism, a view that was shaped by the Marxist framework of ethnic studies programs that were being introduced on campuses.

58. The influx of poor immigrants continued, helped by the 1962 law that allowed the reunification of families, a new infusion that revitalized Chinatowns. See Victor G. Nee and Brett de Bary Nee, *Longtime Californ': A Documentary Study of an American Chinatown* (Stanford, Calif.: Stanford University Press, 1972).

59. Letter to the editor, *San Francisco Chronicle*, 16 June 1989, op-ed.
60. Asian American writers like Frank Chin and Maxine Hong Kingston have challenged the model minority image by exploring Chinese American identity as formed from the tension between politics and aesthetics; see J. P. Chan., F. Chin, L. F. Inada, and S. Wong, eds., *The Big AIIEEEEE! An Anthology of Chinese American and Japanese American Literature* (New York: Meridian, 1991). However, such literary works, together with more recent Asian American performative arts, have had less impact on the national consciousness than the media-borne and corporate renditions of Asians at home and abroad.
61. Through this opening, the U.S. government hoped to attracted four billion dollars a year and to create as many as forty thousand jobs annually. Lourdes Lee Valeriano, "Green-Card Law Means Business to Immigrants," *Wall Street Journal*, 21 February 1992, B1. The actual gains so far have fallen short of both goals. Hong Kong investors I spoke to said that the investment figure is too steep, given that they can obtain a Canadian passport for less than $300,000. Furthermore, since the law was passed, great investment opportunities in China have sucked most of the overseas Chinese capital back to Asia. See Ong, "Anthropology, China, and Modernities."
62. Stuart Hall, "Cultural Identity and Diaspora," in *Identity, Community, Difference*, ed. J. Rutherford (London: Verso, 1990), 225–26.
63. The Japanese of course were the first economically significant Asians in the world economy, but other than a few business tracts about superior Asian quality control, they have not participated as vigorously in Western discourses about Orientals as one might expect. But some have become more vocal following the examples of newly assertive Southeast Asian leaders. See Mahathir Mohamad and Shintaro Ishihara, *The Voice of Asia: Two Asian Leaders Discuss the Coming Century* (Tokyo: Kodansha International, 1996).
64. See Wang Gungwu, "Among Non-Chinese," *Daedalus* 12, no. 2 (1991): 148–52. It is interesting that the term *non-Chinese* has emerged as a category in such self-Orientalizing discourses as displayed in the *Daedalus* special issue "The Living Tree." This term seems to herald the elevation of Chineseness to the global status enjoyed by Westerns vis-à-vis less developed parts of the world, commonly referred to as the conceptual and geographic South. By taking the East out of the underdeveloped category, this discursive move reinforces the model of global binarism.
65. Tai, *Confucianism and Economic Development*; Tu Wei-ming, "The Rise of Industrial East Asia: The Role of Confucian Values," *Copenhagen Papers in East and Southeast Asian Studies* (April 1898): 81–97; Tu Wei-ming, "Cultural China: The Periphery as the Center," *Daedalus* 120, no. 2 (1991): 1–32.
66. See Salaff, *Working Daughters of Hong Kong*; Susan Greenhalgh, "De-Orientalizing the Chinese Family Firm," *American Ethnologist* 21, no. 4 (1994): 746–76; Lee Ching Kwan, "Factory Regimes of Chinese Capitalism: Different Cultural Logics in Labor Control," in *Ungrounded Empires: The Cultural Politics of Modern Chinese Transnationalism*, ed. Aihwa Ong and Don M. Donini (New York: Routledge, 1997), 115–42; Hsiung, *Living Rooms as Factories*.
67. Lau, *Society and Politics in Hong Kong*, 118.
68. Ibid., 119.
69. Quoted in Lynn Pan, *Sons of the Yellow Emperor: A History of the Chinese Diaspora* (Boston: Little, Brown, 1990), 366–67.
70. This view is promoted by the bestseller *Rising Sun*, by Michael Crichton (New York: Ballantine, 1992), and suggested by James Fallows's *Looking at the Sun*.
71. Murdock's speech is one of two taped by the Asia Society, "The Asian American Expe-

rience: Looking Ahead. Speeches by Keynote Speakers David Murdock and Michael Woo," Los Angeles, October 1991.

72. Asia Society, "The Asian American Experience."

73. See Edna Bonacich, "A Theory of Middleman Minorities," *American Sociological Review* 38 (1973): 583–94.

74. Fred Chiu, "Non-mediating Forces versus Mediating Forces: New 'Subjecthood' in Local/Regional Resistances against Nation/Global Systemic Drives," paper presented at the workshop "Nation-States, Transnational Publics, and Civil Society in the Asia-Pacific," University of California, Berkeley, 28–30 June 1996.

75. Ong, "Anthropology, China, and Modernities."

76. As a politician with a tiny Asian support base, Woo depended primarily on votes from multiethnic constituencies, especially Anglos and African Americans. There is something about his bridge-building metaphor that suggests the Confucian norm of relations between older and younger brothers, which he seems to suggest as a model for city politics. This representation apparently found some acceptance among Los Angeles citizens, because, despite the failure of interethnic coalitions during the 1992 class and racial rioting, Michael Woo remained for a time the most popular candidate in the mayoral race.

77. See Stuart Hall and David Held, "Citizens and Citizenship," in *New Times: The Changing Face of Politics in the 1990s*, ed. Stuart Hall and M. Jacques (New York: Verso, 1989), 173–88.

78. Citizenship rights are public entitlements, but does a citizen have the material and cultural resources to choose among different courses of action in public life? For Woo, Asian American citizenship seems irrevocably tied to Pacific Rim capital.

79. The academic terms were coined by Maurice Freedman, "The Handling of Money: A Note on the Background to the Economic Sophistication of the Overseas Chinese," *Man* 19 (1959): 54–64; W. F. Wertheim, "The Trading Minorities in Southeast Asia," in *East-West Parallels* (The Hague: W. Van Howeve, 1964), 38–82.

80. Nonini, "Shifting Identities."

81. Jim Clifford, "Traveling Cultures," in *Cultural Studies*, ed. Lawrence Grossberg, Cary Nelson, and Paula A. Treichler (New York: Routledge, 1992), 108.

82. In "Thinking through Transnationalism: Notes on the Cultural Politics of Class Relations in the Contemporary United States," *Public Culture* 7, no. 2 (1996): 353–402, Roger Rouse maintains that American class formation and cultural politics must be analyzed in relation to global capitalism, and yet he neglects to consider the role of foreign capitalists in reworking American race and class relations. Also, while he claims flexible subjectivities are fostered among the working classes by "the bourgeoisie" (391), he does not discuss the flexible strategies of the latter in dealing with both global capitalism and the regulatory power of the nation-state.

83. Ong, "A Momentary Glow of Fraternity."

84. See Aihwa Ong and Don M. Donini, eds., *Underground Empires: The Cultural Politics of Modern Chinese Transnationalism* (New York: Routledge, 1997).

85. See, for example, Michael Lind, "To Have and Have Not: Notes on the Progress of American Class War," *Harper's*, June 1995, 35–47.

Importing Miao Brethren to Hmong America:
A Not-So-Stateless Transnationalism

Louisa Schein

The Trope of Arrival

Driving past the Dairy Queens, White Castle hamburger stands, and Pizza Huts to the outer reaches of suburban St. Paul, Minnesota, U.S.A., one comes upon the Aldrich Sports Arena.[1] Flanked by trim lawns and circled by sprawling parking lots, the stark arena rises as an icon of American leisure. On this Saturday in late August 1995, however, the lots are filling with the vans and roomy sedans that are the vehicles of choice for Hmong Americans with large families. The event is the International Symposium on Hmong People, sponsored in part by Norwest Bank of Minnesota. Dark-suited Asian men and considerably fewer women, comparably well dressed, are streaming to the entrance doors, some with children in tow. Inside the doors there is bustling confusion as preregistered conferees make their way to tables staffed by young Hmong volunteers to pick up glossy folders containing the symposium agenda along with name badges. Nonregistered guests pay ten dollars for one-day admission. Altogether, several thousand people will pass through these doors in the course of the symposium. Before anyone is permitted entry into the arena proper, their bags are searched and their bodies are scanned with handheld metal detectors.

Once admitted, a visitor finds that a perch at the top of the stands affords a comprehensive view. At the entrance door directly below, two lines of eight young people each, dressed ornately in full ethnic festival costume and headdress, stand on either side to greet guests with smiles as they enter the cavernous space. The floor of the arena is half covered with rows of tables and chairs for symposium registrants. At the opposite end, a stage has been erected. A U-shaped configuration at the front of the floor seating is reserved to give dignitaries the best vantage point for viewing the action. Flanking the stage on one side are four banners: U.S.A., China, Vietnam, Canada. On the other side, five more: Argentina, Australia, France, Thailand, Laos. These, in no apparent order, are the countries of both the Hmong homeland and the Hmong diaspora. In their arrangement and in their parity, these banners announce what the symposium promises—to array Hmong from all corners of the globe side by side for, as the master of ceremonies pronounces, "our journey of cultural, economic, and educational development."

There is more. A great din rises from the echoing enclosure. The grand-stand area, designated for a less formal audience, is partially filled with a greater proportion of women, children, and teens in denim and sweats. There are only a handful of white people in the crowd—of these, one is a journalist and one (myself) an anthropologist.[2] Both have worked with the Hmong for many years. A few of the other whites in attendance are in the employ of the symposium, working as technicians, operating sound and light equipment. Others are just "friends of the Hmong." On one side of the arena floor is a length of several tables filled with books on Hmong history, culture, folklore, U.S. resettlement, and so on, for sale by a local Hmong arts, books, and crafts store. Next to that is a set of tables at which conferees can sign up for "site visits"—organized bus tours to the state capitol, the water utility treatment plant, a university neuroscience research lab, General Mills Company, the Science Museum, the Hmong Farming Cooperative, the College of Agriculture, and more. Next to that, two Hmong businesses, Illumination Technologies and L Technology, Inc., have set up promotional displays. On the other side of the arena is a table devoted to "tradition"—on it are arrayed handcrafted objects, from baskets to musical instruments, that are not for sale. Clusters of conferees mass around the book and other object smorgasbords, gazing curiously upon Hmong heritage frozen for posterity in print and artifact.

Transnationality Interrogated

What is at work here? What *is* the International Symposium on Hmong People? In this essay I will set about answering this question—both ethnographically and interpretively. In the process, I will problematize the specific forging of transnationality between Hmong in the United States and their coethnics, the Miao, in China. A close reading of the cultural and economic practices that make up this apparently cosmopolitan project, and attentiveness to the constraints upon it, reveals that it is multiply complicated by the situatedness of Hmong/Miao agents within their respective nations/states. Through a detailed account of the symposium and the maneuverings around it, I work toward theorizing the ways, both current and historical, that state structures and/or nationalisms condition the activities that constitute *trans*nationalisms, both propelling and molding the latter without necessarily dampening them.

Reciprocally, I contribute to discussions of the ongoing production of the "state" by exposing its dialectical relation with the production of the transnational. In other words, the state is not envisioned as a static entity that simply acts upon the flows and currents of transnationalism; rather, it is seen as crystallized in part through its engagement with that which breaches its border control, its putative sovereignty. The occurrence of breaches, however, is not to be taken as straightforward evidence that "the state" has been diminished or rendered obsolete by the proliferation of transnational practices; rather, arenas of engagement are regarded as vital sites for the understanding of how nations/states and cosmpolitanisms articulate in the contemporary historical moment.

What follows are accounts of several dimensions of the symposium that represent such arenas of engagement. I begin with a brief sketch of the Hmong diaspora out of China and of the cultural and economic practices that constitute the contemporary forging of transnationality after decades, if not centuries, of separation. Then, after exploring some theoretical dilemmas posed by the relation between state and society in transnational processes, I proceed to an examination of the modes through which moves toward ethnic autonomy coexisted alongside state enmeshment in the making of the symposium. This is followed by three instances that point to the need for nuancing state-transnational relationships: (1) the effect of Chinese border policing on the composition of the symposium, (2) the ways in which Hmong/Miao positioning within and outside the state produced prestige disjunctures in the event itself, and (3) the mutually constitutive relation between refugee Hmong and "America."

The Vagaries of Hmong/Miao Diaspora

The Minnesota Hmong symposium was the second event in what was envisioned by its creators as a regular meeting that would recur at different sites of Hmong/Miao population around the globe. One of its explicit purposes—encapsulated in the simple slogan "Unity"—was the reunification of far-flung coethnics who had been separated, in some cases for several centuries. This required, among other things, a reconciliation of ethnonyms. In China, *Miao* is a designation for one of the official minority nationalities (*shaoshu minzu*) recognized by state organs since early in the Maoist period. They numbered 7.4 million in China's 1990 census,[3] are scattered over seven of China's southwest provinces, and are primarily highland agriculturalists. Miao common identity has been debatable in ethnological circles both within and beyond China, but the term *Miao* has nonetheless been increasingly calcified as a legitimate category of ethnic agency over the decades since 1949. As a consequence, Miao elites within China now for the most part embrace the Miao name, confounding their coethnics abroad, who reject it as derogatory and imposed by the Chinese. Nonetheless, it is with "the Miao" that Hmong outside China must interact, despite their continuing discomfort with the ethnonym (as discussed below). In the remainder of this chapter, I use *Miao* to refer to members of this ethnic group within China and *Hmong* for those in the diaspora worldwide.

In the eighteenth and nineteenth centuries, conflicts over land and political subjection eventuated in the migration of several waves of Miao out of China into Vietnam, Laos, Thailand, and Burma. These migrations were from those Miao communities close to the Chinese border, and from subgroups who referred to themselves as Hmong. Some of those who had settled in Laos later became embroiled in the Vietnam War, enticed by the chimera of future political self-determination to serve as guerrillas in the CIA's secret war there.[4] It was these Hmong who then became refugees to the West upon U.S. withdrawal in 1975; thence began an exodus from Laos—with most desired destinations in the United States, France, Australia, and Canada—that continued throughout the 1980s, slowing, but not entirely ending, in the 1990s.

Outside China, Hmong migrants have politicized the issue of the ethnonym, renouncing the term *Miao* (and its Southeast Asian cognate *Meo*) as derogatory and imposed by the oppressive majority. In the process, the identification of the China-based group with which U.S. refugees are currently forging solidarity has become increasingly complicated. Only a subset of the official 7.4 million Miao in China speak the same dialect as and wear ethnic costumes similar to the Hmong migrants to Southeast Asia and beyond. Other cultural markers, such as folklore, music, dance, and food, are also widely divergent. Hence Hmong connections with the Miao can often be negotiated only through interpreters (via English and Chinese) and through great cultural leaps of faith. Links—to use Amitav Ghosh's formulation for the Indian diaspora—must be "lived within the imagination."[5] Mutual recognition between the Miao in China and the Hmong overseas has been an ongoing productive enterprise, one that, as Stuart Hall has phrased it, "is never complete, always in process, and always constituted within, not outside representation."[6] Specifically, it has been elaborated out of the heightened exposure that has characterized the past decade. This increased contact has been a direct consequence of the relaxing of travel restrictions that has come with post-Mao Chinese liberalization, and of the gradual acquisition of green cards and sufficient economic resources that has come with long-term Hmong resettlement in the United States.

The solidarity that has been painstakingly crafted out of the confusion of linguistic and cultural disidentification, then, has been premised more on political and economic bonds than on cultural uniformity.[7] Homeland logics of nostalgia, intact tradition, heritage preservation, and the like have been supplemented with identitarian politics based on shared minority status and the deployment of collective memories of persecution. And the accompanying imperatives of fraternal cooperation and mutual assistance have in turn been extended to large-scale economic schemes. Plans are afoot for joint-venture investments in small manufacturing plants in the labor-rich Miao Chinese countryside, and for import-export arrangements for specialty goods produced in Miao areas.

Heartland Meets Homeland: Culture and Profit

Culture itself has become an object of intense commodification as economic schemes intersect those of cultural production. Cottage industries have sprung up in China to mass-produce Miao costumes in the customary style to be exported for sale in U.S. Hmong communities by entrepreneurial culture brokers. A panoply of performing troupes have been formed by Miao in China with high hopes of garnering invitations to perform at some of the myriad Hmong festivals held all over the United States at regular intervals throughout the year. Indeed, for Hmong American sponsors of these cultural events—who are concerned with marketing—a major box-office draw is precisely the promise of displays of "traditional culture" direct from the longed-for homeland. Yet another lucrative venture is the production of slickly packaged videotapes—usually in a travelogue style, based on individual Hmong excursions—that document the lives of Miao brethren in China, both urban and rural.[8] They feature copyright warnings, are narrated entirely in Hmong language, and sell for the steep price of about thirty dollars each within the Hmong American community.

These practices of cultural commodification exemplify the transnational cultural flows about which Appadurai and Breckenridge have written.[9] Their trajectories reveal a central contradiction engendered at the interface of culture and economics. In one sense, their messages are of horizontal fraternity, of the dissolution of boundaries that separate Hmong and Miao around the globe. But in another sense, they have been constructed on a bedrock of inexorable disparity. It is the residence of Hmong Americans in gray urban sites, dislocated from the Asian land and purported cultural integrity of their memories, that makes the imported Miao and their romanticized images from China so consumable—almost as "traditional" palliatives for the experience of discomfiting "modernity." At the same time, it is the relative prosperity of such metropolitan Hmong, compared to the stark lives of their co-ethnics in Asia, that makes possible their ventures in packaging culture in ways that intensify accumulation in U.S. Hmong sites. Diasporas, as Clifford puts it, are "never clear of commodification."[10] These transnational flows, for all their multivectorality and putative kin bonding, are inescapably conditioned by global asymmetries that yield advantage and the potential for internal exploitation.

It was the conjunctures between culture and commerce, the discrepant but reciprocal desires of Hmong and Miao across the Pacific, that propelled the inception of the first International Symposium. There had been academic meetings held by Miao in China to which U.S. Hmong had been invited, but it was not until Hua Laohu, a highly placed Miao literary scholar and composer from Hunan province, visited the United States that the Hmong International Conference Committee was formed to plan the first jointly organized event. The meeting, which was held in the fall of 1994, was convened in Jishou, the capital of the Xiangxi Tujia and Miao autonomous prefecture in Hunan province, and attended by approximately fifty U.S. Hmong.[11] The promise of "business opportunities" for Hmong Americans was the factor that swelled the numbers.[12]

Thus a relationship was consolidated, highly resonant with that of core and periphery, in which Miao in China offered cultural riches, raw materials, and cheap labor to U.S. Hmong, who in turn brought capital along with their desires to garner greater returns from it. This unequal positioning, however, was also crosscut by the production of an ethos of transnational ethnic solidarity that sought to render these disparities insignificant. Hua Laohu's initial visit to the United States, for instance, was sponsored and funded by the Hmong Youth Association of Minnesota, which footed the bill for his $1,800 airfare. Constructed as a bearer of "traditional" values, he had originally been imported as corrective to an anomie that had been plaguing Hmong communities, inciting youth gangs and criminal activities. Some young Hmong, as detailed below, have taken the path of the Boy Scouts. Others have become increasing cause for concern among Hmong parents and community leaders as they drift from family life into all-Hmong or multiethnic gangs that are organized around the same logics of rivalry and violent conflict for which other American youth gangs are known. The Youth Association's "intent was to promote Hmong culture/heritage and to instill self-esteem in today's Hmong youth community in order to further prevent crime and drug involvement."[13]

Intact culture, then, was to be disseminated around the globe through these particular linkages and was to effect a vigorous and restorative cosmopolitanism based on the active fusing of divergent materials from a variety of sites and the eventual and hoped-for effacement of divisive differences. These strategies were pursued on the surface level by, for instance, the U.S. Hmong adoption of imported Chinese Miao costumes as a new kind of "festival chic." At a much more intimate level, they involved the arranging of marriages of Miao young women to U.S. Hmong men in search of "traditional" wives. Refraction through the gender lens underscores once again the contradictory conjuncture of unity and asymmetry: in keeping with the age-old practice of trafficking in women,[14] trans-Pacific kin ties were forged through these marriages, but it was nonetheless the Chinese Miao homeland that offered up brides for the nostalgia-driven desires of Hmong American men—and not the other way around.

The State versus the Transnational: Paradigm Wars

When I first encountered these multiplex strategies of transnationalism between China and the United States, I theorized them cumulatively as "oppositional cosmopolitanism." Following Robbins's reworking of Clifford, I considered them as possible instances of a nonelite cosmopolitanism, one that was premised on distance from, rather than implication in, that conventional cosmopolitanism marked by privilege and affluence.[15] I interpreted Hmong/Miao practices as incited by common identification on the basis of minority status and as tactics for overcoming or countering the marginalization imposed upon the Hmong/Miao people by their respective states. The Minnesota Hmong symposium of 1995, however, complicates this reading because of its dense enmeshment with the Chinese and American states, both in terms of historical shaping and in terms of its actualization. The account of the event that follows reveals the imbrication of "the state" both as obstacle and as enabler in making the conference happen. On the other hand, it considers what role the conference might have played in making "the state."

My inquiry is informed by two streams of contemporary criticism. First, I consider the consternation that has met formulations such as *postnationalism* and *postsovereignty*, on the part of adversaries who assert the intractable and ongoing, if not renewed, relevance of the nation-state to global processes.[16] Rather than take up the very fraught debate as to whether or not the world is "post-" anything, I want to draw attention to a pernicious zero-sum logic that portrays transnationalism and the "nation-state" as mutually exclusive and as locked in competition for paradigmatic primacy. Why, instead, can these debates not work toward imagining nation-state and transnational as interlocked, enmeshed, mutually constituting? In the process, nation and state would need to be vigilantly delinked, making room for the notion of deterritorialized nationalisms, loosed from their moorings in the bounded unit of the territorial state, and coalescing at both local and translocal levels.[17]

The project of delinking state and nation throws any unexamined and unitary character of the state into question and points to the second critical stream I want to engage. This resides in recent efforts to destabilize "the state" conceptually, to unmask it (to invoke Taussig's invocation of Radcliffe-Brown), or to deconstruct it. If scholarship on the state could be shown to contain the same "peculiar sacred and erotic attraction, even thralldom, combined with disgust, which the State holds for its subjects," what alternatives could be envisioned for an intellectual praxis that resists this mystification?[18] One approach, following Gupta, is to pursue microinvestigations of particular local constructions of and encounters with "the state," thereby exposing its discursive and contextual specificity. Gupta's ethnographic approach would "problematize the relationship between the translocality of the state and the necessarily localized offices, institutions, and practices in which it is instantiated."[19] Anna Tsing's thick descriptions of the appropriation and deployment of icons of state power among otherwise remote mountain-dwelling people (the Meratus Dayaks in Indonesia) also demonstrates this approach.[20]

A corollary tactic, if the reification (Gupta) or fetishization (Taussig) of "the state" is to be unraveled, would be to question the original bifurcation of state/civil society into two antagonistic categories. This questioning has been carried out both from the perspective of critiques of the Eurocentrism of the conceptual binary and from the perspective of particular sites in which the saturation of "society" by the state (Ben Lee on China) or the so-called conviviality between state and masses (Achille Mbembe on postcolonial Africa) renders the clean divide between state and society virtually inoperable.[21] Ethnographic and other types of site-specific studies will continue to push the question of whether or to what extent the binary holds or whether it is better conceived as a situated artifact that has gained transnational currency precisely through its production at a center of imperialist cultural export.

When I theorized Hmong/Miao transnational practices as "oppositional cosmopolitanism," my analysis was tacitly complicit with the state/civil society binary. Oppositional to what? Opposition was conceived in relation to the respective states in which Hmong and Miao were situated; these states were by definition repressive, limiting, and marginalizing. Although this latter aspect is without doubt a part of Hmong/Miao perceptions and experiences of their relevant states, it falls short of the whole picture. What remain, among many trajectories to be explored, are (1) the production of states in the course of transnational practice and (2) the analytic blurring of boundaries between state and nonstate that is evidenced through studies of lived instances involving putative or imagined state presence.

The Making of the International Symposium

The International Conference Committee is envisioned by organizers as an ongoing entity that will convene regular meetings at sites of Hmong/Miao settlement around the globe.[22] At present the committee appears to be centered in China and the United States, although there are gestures toward inclusion of representatives from France, Thailand, Laos, Canada, Australia, and so on, as emblematized by the nine banners circling the stage in St. Paul. Hua Laohu, the then fifty-eight-year-old Miao writer-composer and chair of the committee, put together the first meeting in 1994 with an amalgam of resources, including those from U.S. Hmong organizations and those from Chinese official bureaus. These resources proved to be critical; a Miao studies organization had convened a meeting in Guizhou province the previous year and invited numerous Hmong representatives from the United States, but had lacked funds for publicity and to support conferees in China. The result was that not one Hmong from overseas attended.

But Hua Laohu's ability to marshal resources did not come only from individual fund-raising efforts. An accomplished member of the literati in China, Hua Laohu was also a member of the government of the Xiangxi Tujia and Miao Autonomous Region Prefecture in Hunan. Reminiscent of the scholar-official status category of the imperial era, intellectuals who had been cultivated under the Maoist state were also regularly in the business of governance. Nor was organizing for Hmong/Miao transnational solidarity considered incompatible with Hua Laohu's post as a vice prefectural official. Indeed, it was an artifact of several decades of Maoist nationality policy that minorities in dense aggregations should have both representation in higher government and regional autonomy, including control over regional funds. And Hua Laohu was not alone in his strategic positioning: listed as members of the "leading body" (including "consultants" and "chairmen") of the conference committee were eleven other Miao representatives, all of whom listed titles such as "provincial official," "ministry official," and "vice-governor."[23] Far from simply being agents of a centralized state apparatus, then, these officials could also be seen as self-designated ethnics working openly and with government funds on behalf of their own group, both within and beyond China.

The language in which the meeting was formulated was nonetheless not stridently separatist or adversarial. On the contrary, promotional materials emphasized that the meeting had been "ratified by the Cultural Ministry of the People's Republic of China" and held closely to the post-Mao formula of marketization. Consistent with the moment of economic opening that China has been pursuing, the somewhat long-winded title of the conference explicitly conjoined culture with trade: "The International Miao (Hmong) Culture Symposium and Economic and Trade Cooperative Conference." Other titles that appeared in the evolution and planning of the meeting had included "International Symposium on the Miao People and International Economy and Trade Talks of West Hunan, China," and "International Symposium on Miao (Hmong) and Conference for Promoting World Miao (Hmong) Culture, Economy, Trade, Communication and Cooperation."

Forming transnational economic alliances, then, was both seen as advantageous intraethnically *and* framed in terms of respective state priorities. The Hmong American chair of the symposium committee, Vang Xang, articulated the relationship as follows in his comments on "doing business overseas," embedded in his lecture at the 1994 meeting:

> Doing business overseas is not as easy as we Hmong originally thought. When we want to do business country to country, we have to think who we are and what country we are in. . . . If we want success in business we have to go through both the United States and China's Department of Commerce and Trade. It may take time for us to learn, but when we have built our business route there will be no one who has unfairly lost money and our government will gain more confidence in letting us do things on our own.[24]

Likewise, the text of Hua Laohu's speech handout to the St. Paul symposium fused accommodation or even obeisance to respective governments with a kind of ethnic uplift philosophy. I quote at length to demonstrate how densely these themes were interwoven:

> Ladies and gentlemen: it has been common knowledge that the Hmong is a great, ancient, world spread nation with brilliant culture and a long history. It is a brave, industrious and transnational people with outstanding wisdom. . . . should we Hmong people stay behind and remain poor? No, we should, under the leadership of the government, rouse up ourselves again to catch

up with the mainstream nations of the countries in which we live. We should give full play to our spirit of hardworking and walk to the wealthy road together with our brother nations. . . . I think no matter what country we live in, we should obey the law of the country and submit to the administration of the government. We Hmong should not only strengthen our internal unity, but also get along well with other nations, help each other and make joint efforts to maintain the social stability of the country we live in. . . . I will never change my mind, that is: the approximately 10 million Hmong people around the world should walk hand in hand, strengthen unity and contribute to the promotion of cooperation and development of culture, education, science, technology, economy, and trade between the Hmong worldwide.[25]

A Not So Borderless World?[26]

Hua Laohu's comments can be read as very pointed in a more particular sense—one that forces the question of relationship to state. The text of the above speech had to be delivered by his representative, because Hua Laohu himself had been prevented from attending the second symposium, the one convened in the United States. Nor were the perhaps 100–150 Miao in China who had arranged to attend ultimately able to make the trip. At the last minute, less than three weeks before the conference was to begin, and after nearly a year of planning and securing of permissions, the Chinese government—in the form of the Foreign Affairs Ministry (Waijiao Bu) and the Public Security Ministry (Gongan Bu), issued a blanket denial of exit visas for all Miao planning to participate. The St. Paul International Symposium went on in the absence of all but a handful of Miao from China. Efforts at transnational solidarity notwithstanding, at this critical moment, state borders were all that mattered.

There are several ways to read this summary exercise of state power. The stated official reason, as relayed to me by conference organizers, was that the Chinese government "couldn't increase the internal contradictions and conflicts among Hmong Americans [bu nenggou zengjia Meiguo Miaozu neibu maodun he fenqi]." To what did this refer? At first, it was interpreted in terms of the fact that a different group of Miao from China had already been granted permission to visit St. Paul around the same time. The inference was that allowing two contemporaneous events with delegations from China to take place in the same city would foment competition and ill will. But later it was revealed that some U.S. Hmong antagonistic to the conference and its organizers had written a letter, ostensibly to Hua Laohu, intimating that the U.S. conference chair was a spy, involved in U.S. intelligence work, and that the Chinese delegates' safety could not be guaranteed were they to attend. Copies of the letter were circulated by the authors to China's Foreign Affairs Ministry, Nationalities Affairs Ministry, and Cultural Ministry, as well as to the U.S. Embassy and relevant provincial governments—the same offices that had earlier received and approved proposals for the event. The impression was created that conflict and factionalism were so explosive among the U.S. Hmong that these would only be exacerbated were China to facilitate this event.

This vision of China as the arbiter of internal U.S. Hmong politics has an aura of incongruence around it, perhaps because of an assumption as to the impermeability of levels—state, ethnic, and so on. How, in other words, could it make sense that the Chinese state could have a remote hand in shaping, or suppressing, the machinations of Hmong factional politics "internal" to the United States? But there were other possible explanations for why China might have taken such extreme action. The moment—early August 1995—was one of heightened antagonism in U.S.-China relations, strained by the Chinese detention of journalist Harry Wu, the visit of Taiwan president Lee Teng-hui to Cornell University, and the uncertainty of Hillary Rodham Clinton's attendance at the upcoming United Nations Women's Conference. With issues of Tibet and Chinese minority policy lurking just beneath the surface of U.S. human rights discourse on China, it is not implausible that Beijing officials considered the exodus—even purportedly temporary—of more than a hundred members of a minority group to an overseas ethnic event that was about global solidarity to be inopportune, given the prevailing tensions. From that perspective, any U.S. government sponsorship of the meeting would likely have been a liability for Hmong organizers. The potential, at least from the official vantage point, for the symposium to become a venue for the voicing of critique of minority policies within China might have been enough to warrant Beijing's caution.

Organizers' formal responses to the visa decision were, notably, calculated to stress the nongovernmentality of the event. In this context—in which the respective states were coming into conflict—their strategy, unlike the earlier stress on enmeshment and obedience to the state, was to affirm the *private* character of the symposium. In the words of one Chinese Miao would-be delegate, the conference should be seen as a "nongovernmental" (*minjian*) and "scholarly" (*xueshu*) activity in which the delegates' travel to the United States was not "spending government money [meiyou hua guojia de qian]." In the words of one of the U.S. Hmong organizers, the conference was "public," "nonpolitical," "nonpartisan," and "educational," and the Chinese government should understand that U.S. government involvement was only in the form of expressing support, and not in supplying funds or organizing activities. Whereas the agenda for the Minnesota conference had proudly boasted attendance and "welcoming addresses" on the part of the state governor, the St. Paul mayor, a U.S. congressman, and two U.S. senators, this political turn of events called for the downplaying of association with "government" in favor of a popular—and implicitly less potent—ethnic celebration.

What emerges from the contradictions between the discourses of enmeshment with state and those of disavowal? First, they illustrate the complexity and multiplicity of interests that intersect at the site of the symposium and its planning. Transnational ethnic solidarity was not necessarily synonymous with ethnic autonomy. In some instances, participants were quick to point out the close identity with the state inherent in the event. In other instances divisiveness between states divided the ethnic organization itself, and a strategy of disassociation was called for in an attempt to salvage the symposium. But what might also be pondered further in interrogating the Chinese government action is the following: Must there not have been some degree of perceived oppositionality for Beijing to take the attendance of Chinese Miao so seriously? And if oppositionality was perceived, was it not *in effect* there?

Hierarchies of Prestige: Hmong and Miao Leadership

Despite the absence of the Miao delegation, the symposium proceeded with pomp and grandeur. A handful of delegates from China had trickled through, either because they had come to the United States earlier or because their exit visas had been granted earlier and were not subsequently revoked. The ritual activities that accompanied the conference proceedings were replete with dramatizations of international friendship—especially that between China and the United States. In some ways these rituals affirmed horizontal unity, but in others they were about the internal rankings and prestige systems that organized Hmong and Miao social-political lives. These systems differed by national site, conditioned by the respective histories of Hmong/Miao from China, Laos, and elsewhere. Some striking disjunctures emerged as they came into contact in the course of the symposium.

Hmong/Miao social organization—usually described as "clan" or "lineage" based and comprising patrilineal surname groups and their leaders—has been variously crosscut by intersecting political systems.[27] Indeed, it

175

hardly makes sense to characterize any unitary form of social organization in the language of the "ethnographic present," given that a range of political engagements have shaped Hmong/Miao internal politics for centuries. There is, however, a strong recurrent vision of leadership that supersedes the clan or lineage unit—that of a "king"—that has taken multiple forms in different contexts and different historical moments. Anthropologists have analyzed recurrent myths of the king in terms of Miao/Hmong statelessness throughout history and have linked instances of messianism and Christian conversion to the desire to have a form of political leadership equivalent in stature to or rivaling that of the states in which they have lived as minorities.[28] Nicholas Tapp ties this imagining of a state and/or a supreme autocrat to the maintenance of Hmong/Miao ethnic autonomy:

> A long process of historical marginalization, when rationalised in terms of a myth which projects the possibilities of participation in a state formation into an idealised past and future, can serve to disguise real structural contradictions between democratic, autocratic, and stately forms of social organisation, and sustain a remarkably homogeneous and resilient ethnic community.[29]

The famed Miao rebellions that peppered the history of China's southwest in the eighteenth and nineteenth centuries and in Laos in the first half of the twentieth were typically incited under the charismatic leadership of a "Miao *Wang*" or Miao King (Hmong *Vaj* in Hmong dialect).[30] In the 1950s and 1960s, there were several messianic movements among the Hmong in Southeast Asia. One was focused on the invention of a new script to replace the one that, according to legend, had been tragically lost in ancient migrations. Another prophesied that "Christ would come to the Hmong in a jeep."[31] It is this vision that some scholars have interpreted as accruing to the great prestige of Lieutenant Colonel Vang Pao, the CIA-armed and -funded commander of the Hmong "secret army" that waged guerrilla warfare against the Communist Pathet Lao during the Vietnam War.[32] To this day, this U.S.-created military commander, now based in California, is referred to by Hmong as "the General" and is associated with the cause under which he had always rallied support—that of establishment of an autonomous homeland for his people. Vang Pao's military prestige, then, although rivaled and contested within the U.S. Hmong refugee context, has carried over for twenty years outside Laos and has sustained him as a "Hmong leader" despite the non-Hmong history of his original ascension to power.

This syncretic aspect of Hmong leadership is highly characteristic of the forms that have developed in the United States and elsewhere as internal strivings for autonomy and self-determination have fused with the larger structures with which the Hmong and Miao have of necessity engaged. Indicative of this hybrid quality and ongoing complexification of Hmong leadership is the plural definition given by a sociologist researching U.S. "Hmong leaders" as

> Hmong who make decisions affecting the Hmong community and shape opinions of community members: traditional leaders, such as clan heads; directors and staff in mutual assistance associations; and important public sector employees like school counselors and community organizers.[33]

If state-bestowed positions, from CIA to U.S. municipality, were sources of prestige and paths to legitimate leadership for Hmong refugees who landed in the United States, what was the analogue in China? Historically, Miao leaders did not emerge only in oppositional relation to state power in times of rebellion; they were also appointed by the state under the *tusi* system used to govern China's ethnic others through the designation of indigenous headmen to collect taxes and exact corvée labor. Indeed, Miao historians argue that many of the Miao rebellions of the Ming and Qing Dynasties (1368-1644-1911) were a reaction against the replacement of the indigenous *tusi* with Chinese officials from outside.[34] Likewise, under Mao, party membership and party leadership became legitimate paths to prestige, coexisting alongside the roles of clan elders and ritual experts in the countryside who also retained authority, despite its being suppressed during certain political movements, particularly the Cultural Revolution.

By the 1980s, Miao and members of other minorities occupied some very high posts in the Party and government, particularly in autonomous regions and other areas where minorities were populous. Miao were especially numerous in the higher government echelons of Guizhou province, the site of their densest aggregation. Popular Miao regard for these high-status posts merged with the "Miao *Wang*" legends of old, spawning renewed hopefulness about Miao leadership—a leadership not linked to insurrection or ultimate autonomy, but to ethnic well-being and some degree of self-determination within the Chinese state. Such aspirations were pinned on those with the highest-level appointments—those closest to the central government; thus, in 1988, when a Miao scholar and I spotted the then Miao governor of Guizhou province, Wang Chaowen, on the street in the provincial capital, the former remarked: "There goes our Miao king."[35]

The Agenda for the International Symposium, printed before the Chinese government's denial of exit visas, closely reflected but also mutated these state-bestowed hierarchies, whether Chinese or American. The individuals included in the formal ceremonies were those who figured highest within the respective national and military systems in which they operated or had operated earlier in their careers. Indicative of how heavily shaped the Minnesota meeting was by its being situated in the United States, a parallel Chinese prestige system of high-ranking scholars, some even from Beijing universities, was given no positioning on the formal program of the first two days. Also indicative of the importance of the U.S. location was the sequencing of the presenters. The listing on the Agenda can be read closely for its imagining of the world order of Hmong/Miao officialdom as envisioned by Hmong Americans. The first session, held on a Saturday afternoon, after opening with a dance performance by the United Laotian Artists Troupe, an arraying of international delegates on stage, and a presentation by a Hmong Boy Scout troop of the flags of the countries represented, featured the following list (notations in parentheses are mine):

- Mr. Vang Lee, President Hmong Youth Association of Minnesota (present)
- Mr. Xang Vang, International Symposium on Hmong People Chairman (present)
- Praya Noraparmork, Major General Vang Pao, former Royal Lao Second Region Military Commander (present)
- Mr. Norm Coleman, Mayor of the City of St. Paul (speech by a representative)
- Mr. Arne Carlson, Governor of the State of Minnesota (speech by a representative)
- Mr. Bruce Vento, U.S. Congressman from the State of Minnesota (present)
- Mr. Paul Wellstone, U.S. Senator from the State of Minnesota (speech by a representative)
- Mr. Rod Grams, U.S. Senator from the State of Minnesota (absent)
- Mr. Jim Campbell, Norwest Banks representative (speech by a representative)

Sunday, after a Saturday evening of "cultural performances" that included traditional-style dances in Hmong/Miao costume, contemporary American dances to rock music, Hmong singing, Chinese juggling and gymnastics, and Chinese lion dancing, as well as dancing for all conferees to

Hmong rock bands, the formal program continued with the following lineup
of "Speeches by Conference Country Representatives":

- Hualaohu, Symposium Founder and Chair (speech by representative)
- Moua Ge Mouanoutoua, Hmong-American representative (present)
- General Chen Jing Wu, Hmong-Chinese representative (absent)
- Mr. Ly Pao, Hmong Australian representative (present)
- Mr. Chalern Chai Sae Yang, Hmong-Thai representative (present)
- Mr. Vuong Quynh Son, Hmong-Vietnamese representative (absent)
- Mr. Chaolen Her and Mr. Xay Ker Yang, Hmong-Lao representatives
  (speech by a representative)
- Mr. Nao Pao Vang and Mr. Ly Chao, Hmong-French representatives
  (speech by a representative)
- Mr. Pao Lee Moua, Hmong-Canadian representative

Following the country representatives, the Agenda promised three major
speeches—by Vang Pao, by the wife of the former Miao governor Wang
Chaowen, and by Praya Tou Geu Lyfuoung, former chief justice of the royal
Lao government.

Although the Agenda offered a structure in which the U.S. representatives were arranged in parallel to the "country representatives" on two con-
secutive days, what in fact happened with the restructuring of the program
because of absences was that Hmong Americans from Laos, and especially
Vang Pao, punctuated the conference with speeches at the beginning and
end, with the various "country representatives" effectively subsumed within
this framework. The effect was of the "country representatives," arrayed for
the perusal of the Hmong American audience, offering up their respective
country reports in a hierarchy structured by the supremacy of the Hmong
American leadership. This was epitomized by the ceremonial presentation
made by one of the few delegates from China—a young Miao scholar hailing
from Guangxi province. The gift—or tribute?—was two books published in
China: *The Culture of the Miao of China* and *A History of Miao Origin and
Development*.[36] They were not offered to the international Hmong/Miao
community, nor to the chair of the symposium, but rather to Vang Pao and
Praya Tou Geu Lyfuoung, luminaries from the days of Lao political struggle.
What in another context might have been constructed as the center of
Miao/Hmong culture and population—namely, the Chinese homeland—had
become a form of quaint symbolic capital to be offered up to the First World
Hmong, whose consumption of it would in turn affirm their positional supe-
riority. At the level of structure, then, the symposium produced a startlingly

close replication of an American vision of a global order, in which non-Western others supplied exotic culture and raw material for core desires. From the perspective of the Chinese social order in which Miao functioned daily, this relationship might have seemed at the very least disjunctive with their experience, if not altogether absurd. Their current rankings in Chinese academic and political institutions did little to dislodge them from their role as cultural conservators whose prestations to Vang Pao amounted to a reiteration of the U.S. power to plunder in the name of celebration. Tellingly, Vang Pao, in concluding his talk, the closing speech of the symposium, switched from Hmong language to English to proclaim: "Thank you. God Bless America." He received a standing ovation.

The Hmong Making of America

If the global centrality of the United States was reiterated through the structure of the symposium, several other components of the event illustrate ways in which the symposium itself could be seen as contributing to the making of the American nation. They demonstrate further that in addition to the state merely acting upon and shaping transnational phenomena, transnational processes may in turn reinforce or produce national or state projects. These processes contravene straightforward and unidirectional paradigms of immigrant assimilation, suggesting instead that what constitutes the nation is altered not simply by the "diversity" that immigrants import, but also by the way their presence and their transnational ties come to recast the imagining of the nation itself.

The first two instances involved white American politicians. On Sunday night, amid the festivities, the arena enlivened with loud dance music and a long revue of performances, young people mingling in shimmering evening gowns and outlandish suits, a white middle-aged man ascended the stage to make a short campaign speech. He was running for senator from the state of Minnesota and seized this opportunity to work toward creating a voting bloc among Hmong immigrants, who are increasingly constructed as a political constituency in the areas of their dense concentration—Minnesota, California, Wisconsin. His enjoinder for all Hmong to "become citizens and get involved in politics" worked to situate the Hmong as players in the American scene.

A second politician, U.S. Congressman Bruce Vento, was pursuing a project more extensive than simply garnering votes. He addressed the symposium on the opening day, and began by chronicling the sacrifices that Hmong had made in fighting with the CIA in Laos:

In order to secure a positive future for Hmong people, we must first heal the wounds of the past.

- During the Vietnam War, tens of thousands of Hmong men, women, and children served in American Special Guerrilla Units organized by the CIA.
- Hmong pilots flew thousands of dangerous rescue and ground support missions and bore the brunt of the fighting without being enlisted as servicemen and -women.
- 10,000 to 20,000 gave their lives and over 100,000 were forced to flee to refugee camps to avoid further persecution and death.

The bill he was proposing was proffered as compensation, almost as apology for Hmong exclusion from "normal" status in the U.S. military by offering a special niche for them among the American citizenry. The "Hmong Veterans' Naturalization Act" would

acknowledge and honor the contribution of the Hmong people at that crucial time in the past and help to make it possible for them to continue making contributions as American citizens.
- The bill would make the attainment of U.S. citizenship easier for those who served in American special units by waiving the English language test and residency requirements for naturalization.
- The bill recognizes the loyalty of the Hmong and helps repay their sacrifice by easing the adjustment of Hmong into American society.

These forms of political incorporation framed in the idiom of citizenship contain multiple valences. Ostensibly a mainstreaming into the unitary category that signifies belonging to America (i.e., citizen), their particular formulations encode other messages as well. Following Ong's notion in which what she calls "cultural citizenship" is awarded differentially to immigrants by slotting them into particular positionings with particular expectations vis-à-vis the nation, it is evident that Hmong were being incorporated both in and because of their specificity.[37] On the one hand, Vento's bill individuated the Lao Hmong refugees in the rhetoric of dedication and sacrifice, singling them out as entitled to membership not so much by virtue of their current participation in United States economics and civic affairs, but rather on the basis of their clientelist "service" to the United States in the past. On the other hand, the lore around the vote-seeking candidate for office was that one of his campaign strategies was to highlight his marriage to a Vietnamese woman. This suggests a tacit amalgamation of Hmong with Vietnamese and, by extension, a classification of Hmong as Asian American replete with the accompanying responsibility to uphold the standards of America's "model minority."[38] The socialization of Hmong as unique but proper participants was also echoed in the speech by the representative from Norwest—the symposium's sponsoring bank:

> It is our job to fill [Hmong] needs. We have done this by recognizing that those needs are different from many others living in the community. For example, many Hmong living in the area work in factories on assembly lines. It is very hard to cash a check without a savings account. With our free checking, it saves money for customers who would have to pay to get their checks cashed. . . . We know that it is difficult for many Hmong in the community to use a bank. Many are used to borrowing money from family. It is our job to communicate how a bank can help all people and to build trust between our bank and the community. Kou [a Hmong "personal banker"] has helped do this by talking with Hmong customers in their own language to explain how their money is safe and insured in the bank. . . . This brings me to my third point. Why banks are important for our communities. Banks play a vital role in the economy. We make commitments to serve the people by reinvesting into the community. We accept deposits from our customers, pay interest on those deposits and then reinvest those deposits in our communities in the form of loans to finance businesses. We also help individuals achieve their financial dreams.

In each case, as the quote makes abundantly evident, Hmong were being compartmentalized as discrete entities in the constitution of Americanness, not simply framed as targets for blanket homogenization. This was diaspora discourse in "constitutive tension with nation-state/assimilationist ideologies."[39]

National Renewal from Boys to Men

The final component that illustrates the Hmong making of America concerns the famed Hmong Boy Scout troop that ornamented the proceedings at several intervals. In highly militaristic processional, as mentioned above, the Boy Scouts helped open the meeting by marching onstage bearing the flags of the relevant countries from which Hmong/Miao hailed. When Vang Pao concluded his closing speech, they once again appeared, this time for a "salute"—again, not to the assembly of international delegates and luminaries, but exclusively to Vang Pao. About twenty Scouts, neatly uniformed in khaki shirts adorned with insignias and red epaulettes and tucked into army green slacks, some of the older ones sporting the characteristic yellow-and-blue kerchief around their necks, arrayed themselves onstage. Then one of them ceremoniously presented "the General" with a gift—his own Boy Scout kerchief placed respectfully around Vang Pao's neck. This was followed by a demonstration of tent building. Then the Scouts' white American troop leader, a Minnesotan high school teacher who had become deeply involved with the Hmong, gave a speech to elucidate how the troop had become so successful and well-known, both in Minnesota and all over the country.[40]

The speech ranged over a number of issues, including Hmong immigration history and the spirit of the Boy Scouts. Its overarching theme was the convergence between Hmong experience and values and those of the Boy Scouts. Scouting "teaches boys to be good boys, to take care of each other, to work hard and respect their elders," the troop leader asserted. Citing the story of a five-year-old Hmong boy who "carried a rifle in Laos and lived in a hole for a year," he extolled the Hmong boys' military background in terms of how it conditioned them for Scouting. "Soldiers know how to think what is best for the group, not just themselves."

Contradicting the notion that membership in the Boy Scouts would function simply to train Hmong boys to be good boys American style, the troop leader emphasized instead what he (and implicitly other Americans) could learn from Hmong boys, their exotic and culturally scripted skills:

> Hmong boys run the Scouting. I don't teach the Hmong boys how to cook—
> I don't know how to cook rice. I don't know how to cook chicken and fish on
> a stick. I don't know how to catch fish, but these Hmong boys can catch fish
> when no one else can.

He went on to stress the "family values" that Hmong children are said to exemplify, referencing, somewhat obliquely, the fears of juvenile degeneracy that haunt so many contemporary U.S. parents:

> I work with a Hmong troop and an American troop. Parents of the American
> troop want to know what the Hmong secret is. They want to know how you
> raise such good children, how you get them to work hard, be serious about
> school, listen to adults, be so polite. . . . Hmong Scouting builds on what par-
> ents teach.

Borrowing Hmong "tradition" as instructive for all American children, he lauded their values and then went further, situating scouts in a position of apprenticeship with regard to the strengths of this ancient and resilient culture:

> The last thing I've learned about Hmong Scouting is that you must teach Hmong traditions. Many of the boys in the troop have grown up with Power Rangers, Michael Jackson, Michael Jordan, Mortal Kombat. They want to learn about Hmong traditions. We invite their fathers down to teach about music and stories. We've changed from teaching refugee kids about America to teaching Hmong American kids about Hmong tradition.

Who is importing what here becomes an intriguing question. It is tempting to read these comments by a white American man in terms of what they intimate about how American malehood is responding to shifts in the global economy, to the rise of the Pacific Rim, and to the earlier "defeat" of the United States in Vietnam. MacDonald has chronicled the ideological currents at play around the founding of the Boy Scouts in Britain over the period 1890-1918.[41] He found a conjunction of several factors pushing a crisis. First, the shakiness of the British Empire led to a questioning of the very civilization on which it was built. Second, urban migration, slum crowding, and poverty gave rise to a perception of the working class as weak, vice-ridden, and slovenly from the perspective of a middle class desperately trying to hold on to its own youth. Third, the image of the frontier, whether African or American, peopled with cowboys, "Red Indians," and "Zulu warriors," was upheld as a redemptive site of martial virility, where freedom and adventure conjoined with obedience and discipline to forge an alternate, more hopeful masculinity.

In the wake of the many ways that "Asia" has destabilized American dominance in the past few decades, one wonders if the appropriation of Hmong into Boy Scout formulations of value does not parallel in striking ways the kind of process MacDonald describes. With youth gangs and video games threatening the "moral fiber" of urban American youth, the Boy Scouts appear as a compelling remedy, and the Hmong boys, already well trained in filial duty through their Asian "heritage," emerge as especially inspiring, effectively out-Scouting white Scouts in their respect for elders and offering a new spin on the notion of Asians as "model." Furthermore, their military savoir faire, instead of symbolizing what America "lost" in Vietnam, can be transmuted into just what is called for in a refurbished Scout/white manliness, armed and ready. That Hmong fought *as guerrillas* coincides neatly with the spirit of freedom and adventure that constituted the lure of Scouting, embodied in earlier days in the "Red Indians" and "Zulu warriors."

At the same time, their "traditions," their cache of cultural otherness, intimates, among so many other things, just that intact male supremacy that so many white men have tried to recuperate by importing Asian women as brides.[42] For so many intersecting reasons, then, Hmong boys in Scouting might be read as a more metaphorical counterpart to the Asian female imports, but one that nonetheless deftly restores a threatened martial virility to white Americans.

Conclusion: Revisiting the Heart of Whiteness

What, then, does this final instance, in which Asian refugees join the American Boy Scouts to teach Americans better American values on the one hand and to learn about their own traditions on the other, tell us about Hmong/ Miao transnationalism? About the contours of nonelite cosmopolitanism? And about ways that the transnational jostles up against the nation and the state?[43]

Commentary on the transnational has regularly figured "diasporics" (Appadurai), "transmigrants" (Basch et al.), or "exile communities" (Tölölyan) as conceptually opposed to nations or states, as necessarily contravening or undermining them or, at minimum, breaking the "nation-state" apart at the hyphen (Appadurai).[44] My project here has been to pursue, through microethnography of an ostensibly transnational event, the development of a vision less structured by oppositionality. This entails, first, looking closely at what constitutes "the diasporics" and "the migrants" and potentially complicating these categories. Likewise, it entails rigorously avoiding a privileging of state-based nationalisms as paradigmatic identity formations. This in turn means unpacking what Liisa Malkki has underscored as the moral character of *internationalist* discourse—a vision that imagines the globe as entirely occupied by parallel and equivalent nation-states and, in the process, deauthorizes or even questions the humanity of those "ambiguous . . . social and political locations that are cast beyond [national] bounds."[45]

A couple of things take place conceptually when peoples cross state borders and maintain ties beyond them. First, they take on a degree of internal homogeneity that may be an artifact of their analytic separation from the national centers from which they have become distinguished by their mobile status. They become recognizable as "peoples" who putatively possess as much internal congruence as those territorial nationalisms from which they have purportedly broken away.[46] Second, their internal relationships come to be standardized in terms of certain regular features, such as homeland nostalgia and remittances. Third, they take on the status of minority in contradistinction to a majority or mainstream that is purportedly more territorially centered and more formative of dominant discourse. This minority/dominant relationship often assumes a predictive quality characterized by certain conventions; it is, for instance, those in the dominant category who are seen as having the potential to become cosmopolitans from the security and affluence of their "home" base.

Hmong/Miao history and practices fall outside these standard formulations in many ways and, as a result, force a number of questions. To begin with, the divisions and political struggles around the ethnonyms *Miao* and *Hmong* highlight the obstacles to internal unity and the extent to which solidarity is a fragile edifice constructed upon the ground of tenuous identifications. Much cultural production and identity formation is entailed in the forging of transnationality. In the case of Hmong migrants from Laos, the putative homeland splits, and they are torn between yearning for the land of their own recent memory (i.e., Laos) and the land of originary myths (i.e., China). More important in terms of the project of this chapter, political histories position members of this fledgling transnational network in dissonant hierarchies, structures that both derive from and reiterate the importance of the relevant states to the elaboration of suprastate organization. Only at certain times, as in the case of China's denial of exit visas, does the state appear as an external limiting or facilitating agent in relation to the initiatives of "stateless" minorities. At other times, as in the case of Hua Laohu's organizational clout and resources for bringing off the Hunan meeting, the state was virtually indistinguishable from the transnational agents involved.

Moreover, what *is* the state in relation to these practices? Robbins asserts that "these days we can take for granted neither the durable power of the state (vis-à-vis international capital, on the one side, and the rise of new racisms and nationalisms, on the other) nor its political malevolence, however comfortable for those who warm themselves in friction with it."[47] The project of resisting comfortable friction in favor of questioning the "state's" power and malevolence can be extended to querying how to situate and demarcate it at all. My hope is that the detail offered here will push in the direction of dismantling the state as agentive and as categorically distinct from those putatively nonelite practitioners of migrant transnationalism. In qualifying the scales at which agency might be located both in and around a less static, more processual nation/state, Hmong/Miao practices emerge provocatively, then, as at once sub- and supranational.[48] But if the level of the state is not assumed to be commensurate with that of the nation, then do the *sub-* and *supra-* prefixes denote an operable taxonomy of scales at all? This in turn should bring territorialized nationalisms under scrutiny. I think that Hmong enmeshment with the Boy Scouts tells us more than that "America" has moved from being an assimilationist melting pot to being a salad bowl of multiculturalism in which Hmong become the latest contributors to an ever more diverse sense of what constitutes America. I think this syncretism, this hybrid constitution of Boy Scout values, intimates the shortcomings of the categories upon which nationalisms are hung, nationalisms that are still thought to be premised on some kind of unexamined cultural continuity, even if it is that of invented tradition.[49] The Boy Scouts may instead be an example of an institution that—in the very process of rehearsing values that are designated as Hmong and American—is enacting an unnamed cosmopolitanism in the space of a very specific institutional site. This would be a cosmopolitanism marked not by the privilege of border-crossing mobility and affluence, but rather by the identity slippage that renders untenable the fixity of nations and their political/cultural constituents.

Notes

I am deeply grateful to the Hmong acquaintances who facilitated my full participation in the International Symposium, especially Vang Xang and Yuepheng Xiong. For incisive comments on earlier drafts of this essay, I thank Debra Curtis, Akhil Gupta, Michael Moffatt, Bruce Robbins, and Caridad Souza. All opinions and errors remain, of course, my responsibility.

1. See Mary Louise Pratt, "Fieldwork in Common Places," in James Clifford and George E. Marcus, eds., *Writing Culture: The Poetics and Politics of Ethnography* (Berkeley: University of California Press, 1986), 27–50, for a sustained discussion of the "arrival story" in classical ethnographies. There is some play in what follows, because what the reader—through the eyes of the ethnographer—is arriving at is not the strange and far-away destination of the classics, but instead the American heartland, a site that should feel highly familiar—or does it?

2. Jane Hamilton–Merritt, a photojournalist, covered the Hmong in Laos during the Vietnam War and, more recently, authored a book on their involvement during and after that period. See Jane Hamilton–Merritt, *Tragic Mountains: The Hmong, the Americans, and the Secret Wars for Laos, 1942–1992* (Bloomington: Indiana University Press, 1993). My anthropological research on cultural politics in China and in the Hmong diaspora began in 1979 among Hmong refugees in Providence, Rhode Island, and has been conducted in the United States, France, Thailand, and primarily China. For support of this research I am grateful to the Committee on Scholarly Communication with the People's Republic of China, the Fulbright-Hays Doctoral Dissertation Research Abroad Program, the Samuel T. Arnold Fellowship Program of Brown University, the University of California at Berkeley, and the Rutgers University Research Council, as well as numerous institutions and individuals in China who sponsored or otherwise facilitated my research. For research on the symposium, I thank the Rutgers Anthropology Department and the Douglass College Fellows Opportunity Program.

3. See "Major Data of the 1990 Census (3): Population of China's Ethnic Nationalities," *Beijing Review* 33, no. 52 (December 24–30, 1990): 34.
4. For a sampling of historical accounts of this period from divergent political stand-points, see Nina S. Adams and Alfred W. McCoy, eds., *Laos: War and Revolution* (New York: Harper Colophon, 1970); Wilfred Burchett, *The Second Indochina War: Cambodia and Laos* (New York: International, 1970); Geoffrey C. Gunn, *Rebellion in Laos: Peasant and Politics in a Colonial Backwater* (Boulder, Colo.: Westview, 1990); Hamilton–Merritt, *Tragic Mountains*.
5. Amitav Ghosh, "The Diaspora in Indian Culture," *Public Culture* 2, no. 1 (1989): 76.
6. Stuart Hall, "Cultural Identity and Cinematic Representation," *Framework* 36 (1989): 68.
7. This is the position I took in a lecture I gave at a Miao symposium in China, at which I was asked to speak on the future of the Miao/Hmong globally. Louisa Schein, "On the Conditions for Transnational Identification of the Miao and Hmong," paper presented at the Guizhou Miao Studies Association Conference, Tongren, Guizhou, China, October 18, 1993.
8. See Hamid Naficy, "The Poetics and Practice of Iranian Nostalgia in Exile," *Diaspora* 1, no. 3 (1991): 285–302, for an exploration of a comparable production of nostalgic homeland representations by Iranian exiles in Los Angeles.
9. Arjun Appadurai, "Global Ethnoscapes: Notes and Queries for a Transnational Anthropology," in Richard G. Fox, ed., *Recapturing Anthropology: Working in the Present* (Santa Fe, N.M.: School of American Research Press, 1991), 191–210; Arjun Appadurai, "Disjuncture and Difference in the Global Cultural Economy," *Public Culture* 2, no. 2 (1990): 1–24; Arjun Appadurai and Carol A. Breckenridge, "Why Public Culture?" *Public Culture* 1, no. 1 (1988): 5–9.
10. James Clifford, "Diasporas," *Cultural Anthropology* 9, no. 3 (1994): 313.
11. An autonomous prefecture is an administrative unit encompassing several counties and granted political and cultural "autonomy" in the form of policies such as minority quotas for representation in government and the use of minority language in education.
12. To my knowledge, four international meetings have been convened thus far. The first, put on by the Guizhou Miao Studies Association, was held in 1991 in the city of Kaili, Guizhou province, and attended by only a handful of U.S. Hmong. The second, organized by the same association, took place in 1993 in Tongren, Guizhou, and none of the U.S. Hmong invited elected to attend. The third, in 1994, was the first effort of Hua Laohu and the International Committee and took place in Jishou, Hunan province, attended by perhaps fifty Hmong from the United States and other non–Asian countries. The fourth was the St. Paul meeting in August 1995. I attended the second and the fourth meetings, and collected data on the other two through personal communications, correspondence, videotapes, and printed materials.
13. Fong Lee, "Coloured Tiger Visits US Hmong Community," *Hmong Diaspora: Asia–Hmong Development Organization Newsletter* 1, no. 1 (1995): 11.
14. See Gayle Rubin, "The Traffic in Women," in Rayna R. Reiter, ed., *Toward an Anthropology of Women* (New York: Monthly Review, 1975), 157–210.
15. Bruce Robbins, *Secular Vocations: Intellectuals, Professionalism, Culture* (London: Verso, 1993); James Clifford, "Traveling Cultures," in Lawrence Grossberg, Cary Nelson, and Paula A. Treichler, eds., *Cultural Studies* (New York: Routledge, 1992), 96–116. See my "Forged Transnationality and Oppositional Cosmopolitanism," *Comparative Urban and Community Research* (forthcoming).
16. Arjun Appadurai, "Patriotism and Its Futures," *Public Culture* 5, no. 3 (1993): 411–29; Michael Shapiro, "Moral Geographies and the Ethics of Post–Sovereignty," *Public Culture* 14 (1994): 479–502.

17. "Deterritorialized nationalisms" here implies a dissociation from existing states, a phenomenon sharply distinct from the "deterritorialized nation-states" detailed by Basch, Glick-Schiller, and Szanton Blanc, in which existing nation-states claim loyal constituencies among "transmigrants" living abroad. See Linda Basch, Nina Glick-Schiller, and Cristina Szanton Blanc, *Nations Unbound: Transnational Projects, Postcolonial Predicaments and Deterritorialized Nation-States* (Basel, Switzerland: Gordon & Breach, 1994).

18. Michael Taussig, "Maleficium: State Fetishism," in *The Nervous System* (New York: Routledge, 1992), 111.

19. Akhil Gupta, "Blurred Boundaries: The Discourse of Corruption, the Culture of Politics, and the Imagined State," *American Ethnologist* 22, no. 2 (1995): 375–76.

20. Anna Lowenhaupt Tsing, *In the Realm of the Diamond Queen: Marginality in an Out-of-the-Way Place* (Princeton, N.J.: Princeton University Press, 1993).

21. See Partha Chatterjee, "A Response to Taylor's 'Modes of Civil Society,'" *Public Culture* 3, no. 1 (1990): 119–32; and Gupta, "Blurred Boundaries"; Ben Lee, "Critical Internationalism," *Public Culture* 7 (1995): 559–92. On conviviality, see Achille Mbembe, "The Banality of Power and the Aesthetics of Vulgarity in the Postcolony," *Public Culture* 4, no. 2 (1992): 1–30. The slippage here between "civil society" and "society" is pointed; it highlights the way in which the binarizing tendency effectively hardens the edges of the state and in turn homogenizes that which is thought to be nonstate, whether political, apolitical, civil, social, or other. For discussions that focus on China in order to move toward complicating the categories, see, for instance, Craig Calhoun, "Civil Society and Public Sphere," *Public Culture* 5, no. 2 (1993): 267–80; Craig Calhoun, "Tiananmen, Television and the Public Sphere: Internationalization of Culture and the Beijing Spring of 1989," *Public Culture* 2, no. 1 (1989): 54–71; Tony Saich, "The Search for Civil Society and Democracy in China," *Current History* 93, no. 584 (1994): 260–64.

22. Statements such as this one that concern the perceptions or actions of those involved in the conference are based on personal communications unless otherwise referenced. I refrain from identifying the informant where (1) I am referring to a collective vision or action or (2) it would be politically imprudent for the informant to be named.

23. Here and below, in order to retain their character and where available, I use the translations from Hmong/Miao/Chinese to English that were provided by members of the symposium, rather than translating myself.

24. Vang Xang, speech to International Symposium on Miao (Hmong), in "International Miao (Hmong) Culture Symposium and Economic and Trade Cooperative Conference Topic and Precis of Treatises," unpublished conference materials (1994), 11.

25. Hua Laohu, speech to '95 American International Symposium on Hmong People, conference handout (1995).

26. Masao Miyoshi's "borderless world" image of the decline of the importance of nation-states in the face of transnational corporations remains compelling, highlighting the almost surprising character of the instance of state border policing to be discussed here. Masao Miyoshi, "A Borderless World? From Colonialism to Transnationalism and the Decline of the Nation–State," *Critical Inquiry* 19 (1993): 726–51.

27. See Yang Dao, "The Hmong: Enduring Traditions," in Judy Lewis, ed., *Minority Cultures of Laos* (Rancho Cordova, Calif.: Southeast Asia Community Resource Center, 1992), 249–326; Nicholas Tapp, "The Relevance of Telephone Directories to a Lineage-Based Society: A Consideration of Some Messianic Myths among the Hmong," *Journal of the Siam Society* 70, nos. 1–2 (1982): 114–27.

28. See Nicholas Tapp, "The Impact of Missionary Christianity upon Marginalized Ethnic Minorities: The Case of the Hmong," *Journal of Southeast Asian Studies* 20, no. 1

(1989): 70–95; Cheung Siu-woo, "Millenarianism, Christian Movements, and Ethnic Change among the Miao in Southwest China," in Stevan Harrell, ed., *Cultural Encounters on China's Ethnic Frontiers* (Seattle: University of Washington Press, 1995), 217–47.

29. Tapp, "The Relevance of Telephone Directories," 125.

30. See Concise History of the Miao Editorial Board, *Miaozu Jianshi* (Concise history of the Miao) (Guiyang: Guizhou Nationalities Press, 1985); Cheung, "Millenarianism"; Robert D. Jenks, *Insurgency and Social Disorder in Guizhou: The "Miao" Rebellion, 1854–1873* (Honolulu: University of Hawaii Press, 1994); Gunn, *Rebellion in Laos*, 149–60.

31. William Smalley, *Mother of Writing: The Origin and Development of a Hmong Messianic Script* (Chicago: University of Chicago Press, 1990); W. E. Garrett, "The Hmong of Laos: No Place to Run," *National Geographic* 145, no. 1 (1974), 83, cited in Tapp, "The Relevance of Telephone Directories," 116.

32. Gunn, *Rebellion in Laos*, 170.

33. Jeremy Hein, "From Migrant to Minority: Hmong Refugees and the Social Construction of Identity in the United States," *Sociological Inquiry* 64, no. 3 (1994): 287.

34. Concise History of the Miao Editorial Board, *Miaozu Jianshi*.

35. Significantly, this same man, now retired from his post as provincial governor, but still on the provincial People's Political Consultative Conference, has recently replaced a Miao academic as the new chair of the Guizhou Miao Studies Association. The hope is that he will have more political clout and command more resources in domestic and international organizing for the association (personal communication, February 1996).

36. Guo Zhu, *Zhongguo Miaozu Wenhua* (The culture of the Miao of China) (Nanning: Guangxi Nationalities Press, 1994); Guo Zhu, *Miaozu Yuan Liu Shi* (A history of Miao origin and development) (Nanning: Guangxi People's Press, 1994).

37. Aihwa Ong, "Cultural Citizenship as Subject-Making: Immigrants Negotiate Racial and Cultural Boundaries in the United States," *Current Anthropology* 37, no. 5 (1996): 737–62.

38. See Wendy Walker-Moffatt, *The Other Side of the Asian American Success Story* (San Francisco: Jossey-Bass, 1995), for a problematization of this in terms of the educational expectations applied to Hmong immigrants.

39. Clifford, "Diasporas," 308.

40. See David L. Moore, *Dark Sky, Dark Land: Stories of the Hmong Boy Scouts of Troop 100* (Eden Prairie, Minn.: Tessera, 1989), for a collection of anecdotal accounts and oral history of the Minnesota Hmong Boy Scouts.

41. Robert H. MacDonald, *Sons of the Empire: The Frontier and the Boy Scout Movement, 1890–1918* (Toronto: University of Toronto Press, 1993).

42. Ara Wilson, "American Catalogues of Asian Brides," in Johnetta Cole, ed., *Anthropology for the Nineties* (New York: Free Press, 1988), 114–24.

43. In this final section I implicitly reflect upon Appadurai's characterization of the United States as a one-time "heart of whiteness" that is also marked by "its uneasy engagement with diasporic peoples, mobile technologies, and queer nationalities." Appadurai, "Patriotism and Its Futures," 412.

44. In addition to the works of the other authors mentioned, see Khachig Tölölyan, "The Nation-State and Its Others," *Diaspora* 1, no. 1 (1991): 3–7.

45. Malkki offers, as the remedy to this totalizing image of the world order, a greater attentiveness to hybridity and liminality as "the very quick of contemporary political and social life" (57). I question, however, whether these notions can do the work required of them here, or if they don't in the end reiterate the purity and boundedness of the nation form as essential to their analytic evasion of it. Liisa Malkki, "Citizens of Humanity: Internationalism and the Imagined Community of Nations," *Diaspora* 3, no. 1 (1994): 41–68.

46. This internal congruence is particularly unstable when it concerns amalgam categories such as that of Asian American, to which the Hmong are at present uneasily linked. See Lisa Lowe, "Heterogeneity, Hybridity, Multiplicity: Marking Asian American Differences," *Diaspora* 1, no. 1 (1991): "Asian American discussions of ethnicity are far from uniform or consistent; rather, these discussions contain a wide spectrum of articulations that includes, at one end, the desire for an identity represented by a fixed profile of ethnic traits, and at another, challenges to the very notions of identity and singularity which celebrate ethnicity as a fluctuating composition of differences, intersections and incommensurabilities. The latter efforts attempt to define ethnicity in a manner that accounts not only for cultural inheritance, but for active cultural construction, as well" (27).

47. Robbins, *Secular Vocations*, 210. The "we" here may prove problematic to demarcate. Is there a universalism implied in this statement that elides precisely that *differential* consequentiality of states that conditions Hmong and Miao practice in different moments? My thanks to Akhil Gupta for emphasizing the perspectival in considering the state and the transnational.

48. For discussions of the importance of scale in the consideration of the relations among the local, the national, and the cosmopolitan, see Neil Smith, "Contours of a Spatialized Politics: Homeless Vehicles and the Production of Space," *Social Text* 33 (1992): 54–81; Bruce Robbins, "Cutting Cosmopolitanism Down to Size," unpublished manuscript (n.d.).

49. See Eric Hobsbawm and Terence Ranger, eds., *The Invention of Tradition* (London: Cambridge University Press, 1983).

Ruth, the Model Émigré:
Mourning and the Symbolic Politics of Immigration

Bonnie Honig

And we Americans are the peculiar, chosen people—the Israelites of our time.
▸ *Herman Melville*

Immigrants are one of the chief dangers against which Americans are trying to defend their home country these days. And yet immigrants or foreigners have at other times provided some of the energy that has helped shape the character of the United States. How should we think about this ambivalence?

Some suggest that today's immigrants are less welcome and perceived to be more dangerous to the unity of the republic because they tend not to be white.[1] There is some truth in that. But it should also be noted that ethnics now thought of as white were not so identified when their grandparents first came to the United States as immigrants. Irish immigrants, southern Italians, and others were thought of as black.[2]

It is also said that the human capital of contemporary immigrants is lower than that of their predecessors. Recent arrivals tend to be less educated and less wealthy than those who entered the United States prior to the loosened 1965 Immigration Reform and Control Act.[3] Others stress the self-selection of immigrants: those who make the journey tend to be the boldest, most resourceful members of their communities.[4] Ample data support all sides of the human capital debate, and so far there is no resolution in sight. That may say something about the inadequacy of the data or about the politics of their collectors and interpreters. Or it may say something about the power of the symbolic politics at work here: Would concerns about immigration simply disappear if it could be shown conclusively—as some claim it has been—that (for example) immigrants put more into the economy than they take out? Or that they tend to assimilate into the dominant culture by the third generation of residence in the United States, rather than form separatist enclaves in perpetuity?

Rational arguments about the costs and benefits of foreigners fail to settle (though they may inform) the politics of immigration because the issue has as much to do with identity as with interests.[5] Periodic politicizations of immigration are often occasioned by tensions in the economic or political order, but they are also always symptoms of a perpetual public anxiety about national identity and unity. The felt need (never wholly satisfied) for national identity frames the way regimes treat foreigners and gives rise to vastly different stories about them. Contemporary American newspapers are filled both with anxious reports of foreigners fragmenting domestic institutions and with approving reviews of immigrant memoirs celebrating "hybridity," a nonassimilative, hyphenated, bilingual and bicultural identity. This ambivalence about foreigners stems from the regime's determination to recuperate foreignness for a national project and not just from the nature of the immigrants or ethnics in question.

The political and cultural demand for a shared identity can be the ground of democracy (as Rousseau thought) or it can generate demands for social unity that are, particularly in multicultural settings, in tension with liberal democratic principles. In this essay, I explore the role of foreigners in fostering and hindering the development of shared identity and institutions. I argue that democratic principles are best realized at this moment in a commitment to a *politically engaged, democratic cosmopolitanism* in which the will to national unity or identity is attenuated and democratic actors have room to seek out political, cultural, and other forms of not just identity-based affiliation at the subnational, national, and international registers. Increasingly, democratic practice exceeds the states it seems to presuppose; democracy's *demos* is dispersed.

I approach these issues by way of the biblical Book of Ruth, a text deployed by Cynthia Ozick and Julia Kristeva in some recent reflections about identity, immigration, nationalism, and cosmopolitanism. I develop my account of cosmopolitanism by way of a critique of Kristeva's version of that ideal and by way of a new reading of Ruth that emerges out of an engagement with Ozick's and Kristeva's readings of that text. Like Ozick and Kristeva, I see the Book of Ruth as a generative, potentially very powerful source of new ethics and dispositions. My aim, then, is not to read Ruth in a contextualist fashion but to intervene and participate in *contemporary redeployments* of the Book of Ruth as part of a symbolic politics of immigration.

Ruth

The Book of Ruth begins with a flashback. A few years earlier, a man named Elimelech, his wife, Naomi, and their two sons left Bethlehem to escape famine. They moved to Moab, having heard that Moab was flourishing while Bethlehem suffered. The move to Moab is controversial. Elimelech has abandoned his community in a time of need and, worse yet, he has gone to live in Moab, the home of the historical enemies of the Israelites. This terribly forbidden move, and the famine that occasions it, suggests that the Israelites have fallen away from their fundamental moral principles.

The Moabites are lacking virtue as well, but theirs is no temporary corruption. They refused water to the Israelites as the Israelites wandered in the desert from Egypt to the Promised Land. And when the Israelites camped at Beth Peor, some Moabite women tried to seduce the Israelite men into illicit relations and idol worship. For this, Deuteronomy's prohibition against intermarrying with Moabites is uncompromising: "None of the Moabites' descendants, even in the tenth generation, shall ever be admitted into the congregation of the Lord" (23:4).

Elimelech dies soon after settling in Moab. His sons marry two Moabite women, but these men also die within ten years, leaving behind three childless widows, Naomi and her Moabite daughters-in-law, Ruth and Orpah. Naomi hears that the famine in Bethlehem is over and she decides to return home. Her daughters-in-law accompany her initially, but she soon tells them to "turn back, each of you to her mother's house" in Moab (1:8). They refuse, Naomi insists, and finally Orpah, weeping, agrees to return to Moab. Ruth remains, however, and when Naomi tells her again to leave ("See, your sister-in-law has returned to her people and her gods; return after your sister-in-law"; 1:15), Ruth responds poignantly:

> Whither thou goest, I will go
> Whither thou lodgest, I will lodge
> Thy people shall be my people
> Thy god shall be my god
> Whither thou diest, I will die, and there I will be buried. (1:16-17)

Naomi says nothing in response, but she stops protesting and Ruth accompanies her on her journey.

In Bethlehem, Naomi is welcomed back by the women of the community. She announces her losses to them and declares her name changed from Naomi (which means "pleasant") to Mara (which means "bitter") (1:20). Naomi and Ruth establish a joint household. Ruth supports them by harvesting the remnants left in the field of a man named Boaz, who, as it turns out, is a relative of Naomi. Having heard of Ruth's remarkable loyalty to Naomi, Boaz welcomes Ruth to his field and sends her home with extra grain.

But Naomi and Ruth conspire together to achieve a more certain protection than that. Ruth seeks out (and perhaps seduces) Boaz one night on the threshing-room floor and calls on him to extend his protection to her through marriage, while also redeeming a piece of land that was left to

Naomi by Elimelech. Boaz notes that there is another male relative who has prior right or obligation to redeem the land, but he promises to do what he can for Ruth. He goes the next morning to find the next of kin and convenes a meeting of the town elders to resolve the question of Elimelech's land. The next of kin's interest in redeeming the land dwindles when he hears that Boaz intends to marry Ruth. Knowing that if they have a son, the child could claim the redeemed land as his own inheritance without recompense, the next of kin offers his option/obligation to Boaz.[6]

Boaz and Ruth marry and have a son who is given to Naomi to nurse. The women's community celebrates, proclaims the child *Naomi's* son and protector in old age, pays Ruth the highest compliment, declaring her to be of more value to Naomi than seven sons, and names the child Obed. Ruth never speaks again, and she is, of course, absent from the Book of Ruth's closing patrilineal genealogy, which ends with David, later to be the king of Israel. Ruth's precarious position in the Israelite order is stabilized by a marriage and birth that provide the founding energy for a new monarchic regime. In turn, Ruth's migration seems to be the vehicle of this welcome regime change. The Book of Ruth opens "in the days when the judges ruled," a time of famine, barrenness, and corruption, and closes amid plentiful harvest and a newly born son, with a genealogy anticipating the coming monarchy.

But this regime founding leaves us nonetheless uncertain about Ruth's status as an immigrant. How should we read Ruth's closing silence? Has she been successfully assimilated or has she been left stranded? More generally, what connections between immigration and founding are presupposed and consolidated by this great short story? What is a Moabite woman—a forbidden foreigner—doing at the start of the line of David?

Immigration and Founding

According to two of the Book of Ruth's recent readers—Cynthia Ozick and Julia Kristeva—Ruth is a model immigrant. Ozick reads Ruth as a tale of reinvigoration by way of conversion or assimilation. (This is in line with the dominant, traditional reading of the story.) Ruth's conversion to Judaic monotheism from Moabite idolatry testifies to the worthiness of the Jewish God. Ruth's devotion to Naomi exemplifies Ruth's virtue, which is an example for everyone and a ground for the rule of David. Ruth, the model immigrant and convert, supplements the Israelite order and saves it from its wayward rule by judges by founding a new sovereign monarchy.

For Kristeva, by contrast, Ruth unsettles the order she joins. Israelite sovereignty is secured by Ruth, but it is also riven by her, by the moment of otherness she personifies as a Moabite. Whereas Ozick's Ruth completes the Israelite order, Kristeva's Ruth makes it impossible for the order ever to attain completeness. And this, Kristeva argues, is Ruth's great service to the Israelites: she disabuses them of their fantasies of identity and makes them more open to difference and otherness. But Kristeva's Ruth does not only disrupt the order she joins; she also adopts its customs and rituals and tries to get along. From Kristeva's perspective, that makes Ruth a valuable model for those contemporary Muslim immigrants who tend to resist absorption into their receiving regimes.[7]

Ozick's and Kristeva's redeployments of Ruth both combine two of the dominant and enduring responses we have to immigrants. Either immigrants are valued for what "they" bring to "us"—diversity, energy, talents, industry, innovative cuisines, and new recipes, plus a renewed appreciation of our own regime, the virtues of which are so great that they draw immigrants to join us—or they are feared for what they will do to us—consume our welfare benefits, dilute our common heritage, fragment our politics, undermine our democratic or cosmopolitan culture. Both responses judge the immigrant in terms of what she will do for—or to—us as a nation.

The first (welcoming) response models immigration as an occasion for citizens (who are perhaps jaded) to reexperience the fabulous wonder of founding, the moment in which the truth or power of their regime was revealed or enacted for all the world to see. Notably, Moab is (as President Clinton put it in a speech in the Middle East in the fall of 1994) "the land where Moses died and Ruth was born." Ruth is the vehicle through which the Law comes alive again generations after the death of the lawgiver, Moses. Ruth's immigration and conversion reperform the social contract of Sinai and allow the Israelites to reexperience their own initial conversion, faith, or wonder before the Law. Ruth's choice of the Israelites re-marks the Israelites as the Chosen People, a people worthy of being chosen. Here, the immigrant's choice of "us" makes us feel good about who we are. (In the American context, the pleasure and reinvigoration of having been chosen is illustrated and produced, for example, by the *New York Times*'s periodic publication of photographs of new citizens taking the oath. That pleasure is further protected by the failure to keep any continuous official statistics on remigration or emigration.)[8]

The second (wary) response to immigrants also suggests a reexperience of the founding. Highlighted here, however, is the impulse to secure a regime's identity by including some people, values, and ways of life and excluding others.[9] Here, the immigrant's choice of us *endangers* our sense of who we are. We might see the Book of Ruth as an effort to reinvigorate Israelite identity without also endangering it by combining the story of Ruth's immigration with the story of Orpah's decision not to emigrate. The contrast between Ruth and Orpah highlights the extraordinariness of Ruth's border crossing, as Cynthia Ozick points out.[10] But the contrast also has another effect: it suggests that Ruth's migration to Bethlehem does not mean that Israel is now a borderless community open to all foreigners, including even idolatrous Moabites. Israel is open only to the Moabite who is exceptionally virtuous—to Ruth, but not to Orpah.

Together, then, Ruth and Orpah personify the coupling of wonder *and* fear, opportunity *and* threat, the sense of supplementation *and* fragmentation that immigrants often excite in the orders that absorb or exclude them. (Is Orpah not threatening? Traditional interpreters give expression to their fears when they claim that Goliath is her descendant.) Personified by the two distinct characters of Ruth and Orpah, these impulses may seem to be attached to different objects, the good immigrant versus the bad, for example. But what if we read Orpah as part of Ruth, a personification of the part of Ruth that cannot help but remain a Moabite even in Bethlehem? The story might then illustrate the deep and abiding ambivalence that (even democratic) regimes tend to have about the foreigners living in their midst.

Ruth's foreignness is what makes her fabulous conversion possible. Her conversion is really worth something because she is a Moabite. It is her foreignness that enables her to re-mark the choiceworthiness of the Israelites and to refurbish their identity as a Chosen People. But Ruth's foreignness also makes her threatening to the order she might otherwise simply reinvigorate. There is no way around it: a *Moabite* has come to live in Bethlehem!

In short, Ruth figures the deep undecidability of the immigrant whose foreignness both supplements and threatens the receiving regime *at the same time.* Kristeva looks to the Book of Ruth for an alternative, seeking a way to welcome the foreignness we find so threatening, but her cosmopolitanism ultimately succumbs to a kind of national chosenness of its own. I, too, turn to the Book of Ruth seeking alternatives.

Ozick's Ruth: Convert or Migrant?

Ozick's reading of Ruth is indebted to the traditional rabbinical interpretations, but departs from them significantly. "I mean for the rest of my sojourn in the text to go on more or less without [the rabbis]," she says (219–20). Where earlier readers interpreted Orpah in terms of her unfavorable comparison with Ruth, Ozick pauses to look at Orpah in her own right. "Let us check the tale, fashion a hiatus, and allow normality to flow in: let young stricken Orpah not be overlooked" (221). Orpah is noteworthy not just for her failure, by contrast with Ruth, to emigrate to Bethlehem for the sake of Naomi and monotheism. Orpah stands out for her own admirable action: she married an Israelite in Moab (not a popular thing to have done, certainly) and came to love Naomi. Orpah may not have been up to the tests of monotheism and emigration, but she was an "open-hearted" woman (224), beyond the confines of "narrow-minded," conventional prejudice (222).

Ozick's Orpah is special, but ultimately, in the crucible of the decision to emigrate or not, the true principle of her character is revealed. She represents "normality," not "singularity" (220). Her wants are mundane; her imagination does not soar. In returning to her mother's house, she returns also to her idols. Orpah "is never, never to be blamed for" her choice, Ozick says, but she suggests nonetheless that history has, indeed, judged Orpah ("Her mark is erased from history; there is no *Book of Orpah*"; 221). Ozick resists the judgment of history by pausing to reflect on Orpah, but she also consolidates history's judgment by depicting Moab's (and Orpah's) disappearance from the world stage as deserved rather than contingent and by figuring Orpah's decision as ordinary and immature by contrast with Ruth's decision, which is "visionary" (224): "Ruth leaves Moab because she intends to leave childish ideas behind" (227).

The contrast between Ruth and Orpah, though softened by Ozick's appreciative hiatus, instantiates Ozick's distinction between the normal and the singular. But it also does something else. Ozick's contrast between Ruth and Orpah effectively works to undo the undecidability of the immigrant who both supports and threatens to undermine the order that both depends upon and is threatened by her. Ozick positions Ruth, the immigrant, to reinvigorate the Israelite order without at the same time threatening to corrupt it. The threat of corruption, along with the specter of unconvertible foreignness, is projected onto Orpah, whose failure to emigrate symbolizes a failure to convert (and vice versa). If by staying home Orpah stayed with her gods, then by leaving home, Ruth left her gods behind. The contrast leaves no doubt about Ruth's conversion. There is no danger in her presence in Bethlehem. She is surely one of "us."

The unthreatening character of Ruth's reinvigorative immigration is further consolidated by another moment in Ozick's essay. In a lovely insight into Naomi, Ozick sees her instruction to Ruth to follow Orpah and return to "her people and to her gods" as evidence that Naomi "is a kind of pluralist" *avant la lettre* (223). Naomi is not a zealot, Ozick says. Orpah has her gods, Naomi has hers, and Naomi knows and accepts that. But Naomi's acceptance of Moabite idolatry is tied to the fact that Moabite idol worship occurs in Moab. Her pluralism is territorial. When Naomi says that Orpah has returned to her people and to her gods, Naomi implies (and Ruth surely picks up on this) that it is not possible to go to *her* people in Bethlehem with Moabite gods. In Naomi's pluralism, people and their gods are tied together and positioned in their proper territorial places. Ozick is right that this is a valuable pluralism by contrast with the forms of imperialism and zealotry that will tolerate difference nowhere on earth. Its limits are more evident, however, by contrast with forms of pluralism that demand a more difficult toleration, that of differences that live among us, in our neighborhoods, right next door, in our own homes.

Ozick's positioning of Ruth and Orpah as personifications of singularity and normality, combined with her territorialization of cultural difference, establishes a safe and secure distance between Ruth and Orpah. This distance works (intentionally or not) to enable Ruth to serve as a vehicle of the reinvigoration Ozick seeks without also jeopardizing the identity of the Israelites. Ozick's Ruth is able to supplement the Israelite order without at the same time diluting or corrupting it because the undecidable figure of the (Moabite) immigrant, both necessary for renewal and dangerous to the community, has been split into two: Orpah—the practical, material Moabite who stayed at home with her idols, in her "mother's house"[11]—figures the Other whose absence keeps the community's boundaries and identity secure, while Ruth—loyal, devoted to Naomi, possessed of the mature, abstract imagination needed to be faithful to the one invisible God—refurbishes the order's boundaries through her conversion to it. This splitting protects the Israelite order from Moabite corruption while allowing it to profit nonetheless from the supplement of Ruth's migration. In short, Ozick does not see the undecidability of the immigrant, and the lingering foreignness of Ruth, so taken is she with the inspiring supplement of Ruth's reinvigorating virtue.

Ozick's disambiguation of Ruth and Orpah follows from two contestable interpretive claims: first, that the sole object of Ruth's choice was monotheism, and second, that Ruth's exceptional virtue won for her an easy assimilation into the Israelite order, which was, in turn, only improved (and not also threatened) by her supplement. Ozick's reading, she herself says, is "spotty and selective, a point here, a point there" (219), less an interpretation than a retelling. Her goal is not exhaustive analysis. Rather, she seeks to reinvigorate this ancient text, to deploy it for particular, inspirational purposes. Nonetheless, I want to trace the multiple possibilities borne by this text but hidden by Ozick's particular treatment because such a tracing illustrates the complexity of the symbolic politics of immigration.

Emphasizing Ruth's famous speech to Naomi, Ozick says that Ruth acted not only out of an impressive love for Naomi but also out of a deep monotheistic faith. Why would Ruth say, "Thy god shall be my god," if she was not moved by faith? Why would she even move to Bethlehem? "Everything socially rational is on the side of Ruth's remaining in her own country" (225). But the social rationalities of the situation are unclear. It cannot have been easy to return to Moab as the childless widow of an Israelite. Contra Ozick, Orpah's course was courageous too.[12]

Was Ruth moved by faith alone? Ruth may infer from Naomi's instruction—"See, your sister-in-law has gone back to *her people* and to *her gods*"— that Naomi is concerned about Ruth's unacceptability and unassimilability in Bethlehem. Do not worry, Ruth responds. I may not know all the customs but I will go where you go, live where you live, *your people shall be my people*, and *your god shall be my god*. Is Ruth converting disingenuously, then? Not necessarily. As far as the text is concerned, it is not clear that she is converting at all. She may simply be reassuring Naomi—as so many immigrants have reassured their hosts and sponsors before and since—that she will cause no trouble for her. Faith may also have played a role in Ruth's decision, but the text gives us no reason to think it was dispositive. Most likely, Ruth's motives were multiple and complex; this is clear if we see Orpah as personifying one dimension of Ruth's impossible conflict.[13]

Intent upon recuperating Ruth's potentially disturbing migration for a national project, Ozick reads the Book of Ruth as a fable of reinvigorative assimilation and overlooks the evidence that Ruth's presence within the Israelite order was never unproblematically supportive but always also threatening to it at the same time. Where Ozick sees virtue, conversion, and assimilation, the text of Ruth also suggests complication, recalcitrant particularism, and prejudice. Ruth not only reinvigorates the order she joins, she also taints and troubles it. The Book of Ruth refers to her as "Ruth, the Moabitess" several times (1:22, 2:2, 2:6, 2:21, 4:5, 4:9), suggesting that she, in some sense, stays a Moabite, forbidden, surely noticed, and perhaps despised by her adopted culture even while also celebrated by it for the virtue she brings to it.

And (contra Ozick) Ruth is not only a virtuous character, she is also transgressive. According to some commentators, she boldly seduces Boaz on the threshing-room floor.[14] The seduction, though dreamed up by Naomi, is compatible with Ruth's identity as a Moabite, from whom the Israelites expected seduction. For Ozick, this scene (in which Ruth lies down next to Boaz in the middle of the night and uncovers his "feet") depicts "a fatherly tenderness, not an erotic one—though such a scene might, in some other tale, burst with the erotic" (229–30). But the text does not side with Ozick.[15] It leaves open the question of what happened that night.[16]

Finally, why does Ruth not mother Obed? Why does Naomi come in to take her place? One commentator argues that this is because childbirth was never Ruth's desire, but rather Naomi's all along.[17] Alternatively, or additionally, an alertness to Ruth's status as an (undecidable and therefore potentially dangerous) immigrant suggests that Naomi may step in to inculcate Obed properly in the ways of the Israelites because his Moabite mother would not be able—or could not be trusted—to do so. As an immigrant, Ruth has the power to reinforce the order's sense of wonder and faith by effectively reperforming the social contract of Sinai. As an immigrant, she also has the power to unsettle, dilute, and perhaps even fragment the community's sense of identity. The community's appreciation of Ruth's reinforcement finds expression in the women's community's celebration of her. The community's fear of fragmentation may find expression in its transfer of Obed from Ruth to Naomi: Ruth may not mother Obed because she is a Moabite.[18]

These complications are absent from Ozick's reading because she sees the undecidable figure of the immigrant as two distinct figures: the one who supplements the order (Ruth) and the one who might dilute or corrupt it (Orpah). Ozick sees things this way because she counts on Ruth to perform a function not unlike that of the legislator in Rousseau's *Social Contract*, whose combination of foreignness (he comes from elsewhere) and exemplary virtue enables him to restore a wayward order to its forgotten first principles. Rousseau solves the problem of the stranger's dangerous undecidability by having him leave as soon as his restorative work is done. (There is no provision for the office of the legislator in the regime's constitution; Book II, Chapter 7.) Ozick tries to solve the same problem many multicultural Western democracies have tried to solve since: by having the helpful (part of the) foreigner/stranger (Ruth) assimilate and by ensuring that the dangerous (part of the) foreigner (Orpah) leave or stay behind.

Orpah's departure to Moab is not Ozick's doing. It is reported by the text. But the text does not tell us how to position ourselves in relation to Orpah's disappearance. We might mourn, regret, resist, or accept it. Nor does the text tell us how to conceive of the relationship between Ruth and Orpah. We might emphasize their commonalities and seek out their connections or stress the distances between them. Perhaps in order to attain closure and profit most from Ruth's supplement, Ozick does the latter, domesticating Ruth's absorption and occluding the Orpah-like differences that (according to the text, anyway) still touch Ruth's character.

Kristeva's Ruth: The Ideal Immigrant

Julia Kristeva tries to (re-)capture the undecidability of the immigrant in her own reading of the Book of Ruth as a potentially alternative model of a founding myth.[19] She points out that Ruth, "the outsider, the foreigner, the excluded," founds a monarchic line that is riven by difference from the beginning.[20] The rift is generative: "If David is also Ruth, if the sovereign is also a Moabite, peace of mind will never be his lot, but a constant quest for welcoming and going beyond the other in himself" (76).

There is, however, no trace of this idealized ("welcoming") relation to the other in David's lament (cited by Kristeva) that "the people often speak to him wrathfully, saying 'Is he not of unworthy lineage? Is he not a descendant of Ruth, the Moabite?'" nor in David's wish (also cited by Kristeva) to be rid of his Moabite ancestry so that the people might properly revere him (74). David was more zealous than Kristeva suggests in dealing with Others. He certainly outdid Saul in his willingness to destroy his enemies. Later rabbinic interpreters imagine David complaining about being identified with Ruth because he thinks (certainly the later interpreters think) the foundation of his regime will be more stable and more secure without her. At the same time, however, David needs Ruth, not to "worry" his sovereignty (as Kristeva puts it; 75), but to supplement his own well-known deficiencies with the story of her exceptional virtue and also to support his efforts to expand Israel's sphere of influence to Moab.

Kristeva argues that Ruth's gift to the regime *is* her foreignness and its worrying of Israelite sovereignty. But this misses the fact that for the Israelites, as for Ozick, Ruth's virtue is in spite of her foreignness or apart from it. Her gift to the regime is her exemplary character and faith, manifested in her willingness to leave Moab for Naomi and to convert to monotheism. Ruth's foreignness, per se, is no gift.

Kristeva is right, however, to see some promise in the Judaic embrace of Ruth and in the various biblical requirements charging Israel with hospitality to strangers or foreigners (65–69). But she reads Ruth without Orpah (who is barely mentioned), and so Kristeva's Ruth easily becomes (as in Ozick's reading) a figure of virtue for her willingness to convert to Israelite monotheism while leaving all really disruptive differences behind in Moab. Without Orpah and all she represents (e.g., the recalcitrance of difference, the home yearning of immigrants, the forbiddenness of Moabites), Kristeva loses hold of the immigrant's undecidability.

Orpah's absence from Kristeva's retelling of the story is significant. Kristeva seems to count on the ethics-generating power of stories about strangers to move us out of our insistence on national or ethnic self-identity, but in the end her own acceptance of strangeness turns out to depend upon the stranger's willingness to affirm the existence and the worth of the order she supplements and disturbs. Ruth is the model immigrant, for Kristeva no less than for Ozick, because of Ruth's willingness to swear fidelity to Naomi, her people, and her god. Indeed, Kristeva's cosmopolitanism depends upon similar pledges of allegiance from French citizens and immigrants alike.[21]

Kristeva's Orpahs: Cosmopolitanism without Foreignness

In *Nations without Nationalism*, Kristeva returns to Ruth, the border-crossing convert, to figure a cosmopolitanism that Kristeva directs at French nationalists and at recent immigrants to France such as the Magrebi denizens and citizens who "wear the Muslim scarf to school" (36). These immigrants resemble Ruth in their willingness to emigrate from their original homes, but they also resemble Orpah insofar as they remain attached to the particular cultures of their home countries (*Strangers*, 194). Is there nothing French to which immigrants might feel allegiance (*Nations*, 60)?

The enduring attachment of many Algerian immigrants to their culture and homeland and their option since 1963 of citizenship in an independent Algeria have led many of them either to reject French citizenship or to relate to it in purely instrumental terms. In response, those on the French Right have in the past ten years been calling for tighter controls on immigration and demanding that citizenship be awarded only to those who relate to France affectively. Those on the French Left resist efforts to control immigration and reject attempts to inscribe citizenship as an affective practice.[22]

Charging that the first response is too "nationalist" and the second too "world-oriented," (the Left is too ready to "sell off French national values"; *Nations*, 37), Kristeva carves out a middle ground between them and offers up a cosmopolitanism that is distinctively French in which the nation is still an important but not all-encompassing site of identity, centered not on *Volk* but on compact (40). Kristeva resignifies the nation from a final site of affiliation to, in psychoanalytic terms, a *transitional object*. (The object is a device, such as a favorite blanket or stuffed animal, that empowers the child to separate from the mother[land] and eventually, in theory, anyway, move on to an independent—blanketless/postnationalist—existence.) Brilliantly cutting across the French Right/Left divide, Kristeva's cosmopolitanism is rooted and affective, but attached finally to a transnational, not a national, object.

Kristeva's cosmopolitanism secures and is secured by affective relations to a series of "sets"—specifically, self, family, homeland, Europe, and Mankind—in which each set operates as a transitional object for the next (41). By locating the sets in a progressive, sequential trajectory of transition, Kristeva avoids the issue of possible conflicts among them. She also avoids the question of a specifically French affiliation by using the abstract term "homeland" for *that* set. But her call for an identification with *Europe* positions French and Magrebi subjects asymmetrically in relation to her cosmopolitanism.[23] And because her cosmopolitanism (as Kristeva says repeatedly) "make[s] its way through France" (*Nations*, 38), specifically by way of Montesquieu, it works to shore up a uniquely French identity, even while claiming to overcome or transcend it. "There is no way for an identity to go beyond itself without first asserting itself in satisfactory fashion," she says (59). (But this generous recognition of the need to affirm identity before overcoming it is not extended to France's immigrant communities.)

There is surely no way out of this paradox, in which cosmopolitanism must be striven for through the particular, albeit heterogeneous, (national) cultures that shape us. But Kristeva does not explore the paradox, and she tends to leave the heterogeneity of France behind in her embrace of one particular strand of French Enlightenment thought. She is right to say we must "pursue a critique of the national tradition without selling off its assets." But her account of French cosmopolitanism ultimately protects (what she sees as) the nation's assets from critique and from critical engagement with others: "Let us ask, for instance, where else one might find a theory and a policy more concerned with respect for the *other*, more watchful of citizens' rights (women and foreigners included, *in spite of blunders and crimes*), more concerned with individual strangeness, in the midst of national mobility?" (46–47; emphasis added).

The limits of Kristeva's cosmopolitanism emerge again when, echoing Ozick's preference for Ruth over Orpah, Kristeva suggests that the "'abstract' advantages of a French universalism may prove to be superior to the 'concrete' benefits of a muslim scarf," implying that the scarf, unlike the nation, is essentially a fetish and is therefore unable, as such, to serve as a healthy transitional object (*Nations*, 47).[24] She seems to have those who wear the scarf in mind when she says there "are mothers (as well as 'motherlands' and 'fatherlands') who prevent the creation of a transitional object; there are children who are unable to use it" (41–42). Kristeva sees these veiled women much as Ozick sees Orpah: tethered to their idols, their mothers and motherlands, capable of some bold mobility but ultimately incapable of proper and mature transition, they mark (what Kristeva calls) the "melancholy" of nationalism (43).

Kristeva quite rightly sees a generative possibility in a differently conceived French *nation* (47). Why not accord the same possibility to the Muslim scarf? In *Women and Gender in Islam*, Leila Ahmed highlights the transitional properties of veiling in a particular context, arguing that for Muslim women in contemporary Egypt the veil, worn increasingly by professional and university women, operates as a kind of transitional object, enabling upwardly mobile women to move from the familiar settings of their rural homes "to emerge socially into a sexually integrated world" that is "still an alien, uncomfortable social reality for both women and men."[25] Ironically, if Ahmed is right and veiling *can* function as a healthy transitional object, then Kristeva's figuring of the veil as a concreteness that may have to give way to the welcome abstraction of cosmopolitanism puts her in the very position of those mothers she criticizes, those "mothers (as well as 'motherlands' and 'fatherlands') who prevent the creation of a transitional object."[26]

The pleasing irony of this insight should not, however, blind us to the fact that the problem with Kristeva is not simply her failure to explore the transitional properties of veiling while managing nonetheless to see the transitional possibilities of the nation. Were that the case, she could simply change her position on veiling and the problem would be solved.[27] Instead, the problem with Kristeva is her failure to engage Others in her deliberations about the project, goals, and instruments of a cosmopolitanism she values too much to risk by including it in the conversation as a question rather than as the answer. Kristeva ends up in this awkward position because she neglects what Judith Butler calls the "difficult labor of translation," an ongoing project of political work that always also involves a critical self-interrogation and courts the risk of transformation.[28] Without a commitment to such a labor, Kristeva's cosmopolitanism already knows what it is—and what it is not—and so it *risks* becoming another form of domination, particularly when it confronts an Other that resists assimilation to it, an Other that is unwilling to reperform for "us" the wonder of our conversion to world (or French) citizenship.

When Kristeva does invite an exchange with "foreigners, [which] we all are (within ourselves and in relation to others)," she imagines it will "amplify and enrich the French idea of the nation" (*Nations*, 47). But this imagined exchange, in which Others join to complete the French idea, calls attention to the need for a different cosmopolitanism in which cosmopolitans risk their cosmopolitan (and nationalist) principles by engaging Others in their particularities while *at the same time* defending and discovering located universalisms such as human rights and the equal dignity of persons. There is not enough evidence of such a risk in the questions put to immigrants by

Kristeva: "What does each immigrant community contribute to the lay concept of *national spirit as esprit general* reached by the French Enlightenment? Do these communities recognize that *esprit general* or not?" (60).

A democratic cosmopolitanism may, together with Ozick and Kristeva, find ethical renewal in the engagement with foreigners, but the energy of that renewal will not come from the foreigner's affirmation of our existing categories and forgiveness of our past "blunders and crimes" (*Nations*, 46). Instead, the renewal of cosmopolitanism, the site and source of its energies, will come from engagements with foreigners who seem to threaten but with whom joint action is nonetheless possible—not easy perhaps, but possible.

Mourning, Membership, Agency, and Loss: Ruth's Lessons for Politics

The Book of Ruth may inspire a democratic cosmopolitanism. I return to Ruth by way of a psychoanalytic account of transitional objects so as to explore the experience of loss and mourning in projects of transition and translation. I focus on transitional objects in particular because the issue here is transition to a future democratic cosmopolitanism and because that device plays a central role both in Kristeva's account of immigration and in Ozick's reading of Ruth, in which Naomi is in effect the transitional object that enables Ruth to make the (progressive) move from Moab to Israel (227–28). I treat psychoanalysis not as a universal method but as a particular cultural paradigm that explores experiences of compensation and loss in a way that resonates with certain communities and cultures, not just individuals. That the cultural-symbolic connections among nationalism, immigration, psychoanalysis, and transitional objects are well established was evidenced by the *New York Times Book Review*'s use in its summer 1995 issue of an illustration depicting a U.S. flag-stuffed baby bottle to accompany a review of Michael Lind's *The Next American Nation*.

Modeling issues of separation and autonomy in terms of the child's developing independence from the mother, the object relations school of psychoanalysis emphasizes the role of transitional objects in the process of individuation. I borrow from one version of this account, but I distance myself from its reliance on the model of an original maternal relation so as to affirm the permanence of issues of separation. Separation and transition are issues not just for children or immigrants, but for all of us throughout our lifetimes. I also seek to avoid the progressive trajectory of developmental accounts. That trajectory infantilizes the immigrants whose transitions are part of what is at issue here, and it works to affirm Western receiving regimes' perceptions of sending regimes as a "past that the West has already lived out" and that can be left behind without loss.[29] (Kristeva's and Ozick's progressive accounts tend to feed these prejudices too.)

In a Winnicott-indebted analysis emphasizing the loss that attends and occasions individuation and separation, Eric Santner argues that transitional objects enable separation in a healthy way only if certain necessary conditions are met. First, the separation must not be traumatic; it must be temporary. Second, there must be a healthy environment conducive to transitional object play. And third, that play must have an intersubjective dimension; that is to say, it must be witnessed periodically by the figure whose (temporary) absences are being borne. If these conditions are met, the space of object play can serve as a site of healthy mourning for the loss entailed by transition. At play with the transitional object, the subject acts out her bereavement and is thereby empowered for separation and individuation (as in the "fort-da" game—a kind of peekaboo—described by Freud). There is empowerment here, not just mourning: the play provides the subject not simply with a substitute (for the loss being mourned) but with a lesson in what Peter Sacks calls "the very means and *practice* of substitution." At best, the subject learns *agency* in the face of loss (perhaps even as a result of it, if the conditions are right for such learning).[30]

If these conditions are not met, neither mourning nor empowerment will ensue. Instead, the subject will first make a fetish of the object, engaging it in a furious and hyperbolic play that signals her denial of her loss. Second, the object will ultimately lose all meaning for the subject and she will abandon the object entirely, leaving it stranded. The evacuation of the object's meaning can result in "signification trauma," which leaves the subject stranded, silent and speechless, outside the world of language, play, and mourning. Emphasizing all three dimensions of transitional object play—mourning, empowerment, and intersubjectivity—Santner summarizes Winnicott's view with the aphorism "Mourning without solidarity [i.e., transitional object play in the absence of intersubjectivity or an intersubjective witnessing] is the beginning of madness."[31]

How does this account apply to the Book of Ruth? By pointing out that successful transitions are determined not by the nature of the transitional object itself but by the context in which it operates, Santner calls attention to the role of institutions, culture, community, and politics in projects of transition and translation, something to which Kristeva does not adequately attend in her critique of immigrant particularism. And Santner's focus on mourning, empowerment, and intersubjectivity calls attention to the fact that none of these three components of successful transition is available in Ruth's case. Ruth's separation from Orpah (who, in my account, personifies

Moab) is traumatic. There is no healthy space for transitional object play, no intersubjective witnessing, and no possibility of proper mourning because Ruth is not given cultural, juridical, or psychological permission to mourn Orpah-Moab. Nor are we. Ruth made the right choice. Ozick and Kristeva agree on that. What could there be to mourn?

Ozick and Kristeva both seem to assume that their affirmation of the rightness of Ruth's choice (and their marginalization of Orpah) secures Ruth's transition from Moab. But, if Santner and Winnicott are correct, the opposite is true: the insistence on the rightness of Ruth's choice leaves her (and us) unable to mourn Orpah-Moab and, in the absence of the proper work of mourning, Ruth's transition is jeopardized, even subverted, not secured. Naomi's power as a transitional object for Ruth *depends upon* the proper mourning of Orpah and upon a kind of continued (perhaps hyphenated?) relation with her. At least, it depends upon the recognition that Orpah (Moab) is part of Ruth. Cast in Ozick's and Kristeva's terms, we might say that Ruth's insight into a universality remains touched by a particularity with which it may be in tension but by which Ruth and her insight are nonetheless also nourished.

Indeed, contra Ozick and Kristeva, the Book of Ruth can be read as a tale of incomplete mourning, a fable of failed transition. Through the lens provided by Santner, Ruth's famous loyalty to Naomi exceeds the idealist and pragmatic interpretations considered above. No longer can it signal simply the selfless devotion of a virtuous woman, nor can it be only a mark of Ruth's immigrant practicality.[32] It is now undeniably also possible that this clinging is a symptom of Ruth's denial of her loss of Orpah-Moab, a sign of Santner's first stage, the stage in which the subject's denial of her loss leads to a frenzied attachment in which the transitional object is fetishized.

And Ruth's closing silence can no longer be taken to signal merely successful and complete absorption. Another possibility presses itself upon us: that silence may be a mark of Santner's second stage, the stage in which the subject suffers from a "signification trauma." In Ruth's case, the trauma is produced by the separation from Orpah-Moab and the corresponding loss of any meaningful relationship to Naomi, Ruth's adopted (transitional) mother. That second loss is finally symbolized by Naomi's adoption of Obed in place of Ruth, but it is foreshadowed much earlier by, among other things, Naomi's failure to introduce or even mention Ruth to the women who welcome Naomi back to Bethlehem.

These two moments in Ruth's story mark two familiar moments of immigration dynamics as they are modeled in contemporary multicultural democracies: (1) a furious and hyperbolic assimilationism (or assimilative cosmopolitanism) in which all connections to the motherland are dis-avowed, and (2) a refusal of transition and a retreat into a separatist or na-tionalist enclave that leaves the immigrant stranded in relation to the receiv-ing country *and* in relation to the lost homeland. The two moments are figured developmentally by Santner and Winnicott, but they actually make simultaneous claims upon immigrants and receiving regimes.

This binary of absorption versus enclavism is generated by efforts to re-cuperate foreignness for national(ist) projects. Is there a way out of this predicament? Two directions are suggested by this analysis. First, we must respond constructively to the invocations of the privileges of hosts over guests that are so popular today (e.g., Kristeva, *Nations*, 60). In the United States at the moment these invocations find expression in the resurgence of the English-only movement; the scapegoating of immigrants for the failure of the domestic and international capitalist economy to reproduce the American Dream; the blaming of immigrants and ethnics for the fragmenta-tion of high culture, perversely enough at a time when the homogenizing powers of American popular culture are at their height; and the identifica-tion of enclavism with immigrants and ethnics at a time when the propensity to withdraw from public services and public culture is most characteristic not of foreigners but of the wealthy.

In response to all this, we must vouchsafe spaces that were not there for Ruth, spaces that meet the need for a certain kind of, as it were, transitional object play. The term *play* here should not mislead. These are spaces of seri-ous political work and negotiation in which the proper work of mourning can be initiated while other needs of living together are pursued. Mourning is not the exclusive provenance of incoming immigrants in this account. Suc-cessful democratic transitions and expansions depend upon the willingness of *both* receiving populations and immigrants to risk mutual transformation, to engage and attenuate their home yearning for the sake of each other and their political life together. Such actions in concert may occur by way of sec-ondary associations that do not require citizenship for membership, though citizens participate in them too: neighborhood groups, local school board politics, immigrant advocacy organizations such as the Workplace Project on Long Island,[33] even those renowned, supposedly withdrawalist, immigrant mutual assistance organizations can be sites of transformative, absorptive democratic participation, solidarity, and de facto (if not de jure) citizenship.[34]

These secondary associations must be complemented by the education of residents to be citizens of the world whose diversity is replicated inside the nation's territorial borders, to acquire second and even third languages, to understand their own cultures and political arrangements as part of a

larger network of democratic possibilities, to see those arrangements as plat-
forms from which to form subnational and international coalitions, and to
see their democratic institutions as still in the making and amenable, therefore, to the amendments that might be the results of immigrant (and even
"foreign") *participation* in democratic practices and movements at subnational, national, transnational levels. The United States has a long history
of alien suffrage ("finally undone by the xenophobic nationalism attending
World War I")[35] in which democratic participation is linked not to the juridical status of citizenship but to the fact of residence. At present, several cities
allow noncitizen residents to vote in local, school board (Chicago and New
York), and municipal (several Maryland localities, such as Takoma Park)
elections.[36] Alien suffrage is an important symbolic and political resource for
those involved in immigration politics and cosmopolitan projects seeking to
attenuate the identification of democratic agency solely with the privileged,
juridical status of citizenship.

A second direction suggested by this analysis is transnational rather than
subnational, but it is also associational and affective. Ruth's severed sororal
relation to Orpah calls to mind the sister city movement, a movement that
in some ways exemplifies and may yet help build a future democratic cosmopolitanism. Sister city relationships, affective sites of located, institutional transnationalism, are usually founded by local civic energies and initiatives. Their transnationalism makes them an important and potentially
energizing complement to the subnational solidarities noted above.[37] And the
fact that sister cities establish relationships that are not limited "to carrying
out a single project" makes them an important complement to more temporary, issue-oriented forms of local and international solidarity that are coalitional.[38] Most important, sister cities interrupt projects of (re-)nationalization
by generating practices of affective citizenship that exceed state boundaries
(and sometimes even violate state foreign policy).[39] Together, subnational
and transnational associations enact a cosmopolitan practice. They provide
sites of leverage in national(-ist) politics, while also serving as settings in
which mourning, empowerment, solidarity, and agency can develop and find
expression.

Retold, the Book of Ruth is not only a fable of founding and immigration; it is also—appropriately—a parable of mourning and membership. It
gives an account of the institutional and cultural conditions for the proper
work of mourning and teaches the importance to a meaningful and empowered agency of intersubjective spaces, actions in concert, multiple solidarities, civic powers, and (always contested) connections to the past. Because
such spaces, actions, powers, and connections are available to Naomi in

Bethlehem, she is restored to plenitude and agency. Ruth's fate is different because Bethlehem positions her and Naomi asymmetrically in relation to their losses. The women's community provides Naomi with support and sympathy. They witness her ritually mournful name change to Mara (though they never call her by that name), and she is empowered for agency (symbolized by maternity).

"The homeopathic constitution and (reconstitution) of the self takes place not in a vacuum," Santner says, "but always in a particular social context."[40] Ruth is provided with no such resources and no such context because her losses are not seen as such and her transnational connections to Orpah-Moab (a potentially alternative site of support and power) are severed. Like Antigone's mourning of Polynices, Ruth's mourning of Orpah is forbidden for the sake of a regime's stability and identity. Thus Ruth's mourning—like Antigone's—is endless, melancholic. Her losses get in the way of the closure this community seeks to attain through her *and* in spite of her. Indeed, the fact that Naomi's restoration to the community is finally marked by her occupation of Ruth's position as mother to Obed suggests that the reinvigoration of this community and the stabilization of David's monarchy depend not only upon the supplement of Ruth's inspiring example but also, and at the same time, upon her marginalization.

The lessons of the Book of Ruth exceed those of (Ozick's) assimilation and Kristeva's cosmopolitanism. This great short story calls upon us to move further toward a democratic cosmopolitanism that seeks to secure for both immigrants and receiving populations the cultural and institutional, ethical, and political conditions for the proper work of mourning—and living—together.

Notes

This essay is dedicated to my grandmother, Sara Wolloch, on the occasion of her 100th birthday. For their comments on earlier drafts of this essay, I am very grateful to Seyla Benhabib, Jane Bennet, William Connolly, Richard Flathman, Jill Frank, Patchen Markell, Martha Minow, Hanna Pitkin, Michael Rogin, Michael Sandel, Tracy Strong, Michael Whinston, and, especially, Linda Zerilli. I also owe thanks to the many others in attendance when I presented this material at Rutgers, Princeton, Northwestern, Harvard, the Center for Advanced Study in the Behavioral Sciences, and the American Bar Foundation. For financial support, I am indebted to the National Science Foundation Grant SES-9022102.

1. Sanford Ungar, *Fresh Blood: The New American Immigrants* (New York: Simon & Schuster, 1995), 20–21.

2. Noel Ignatiev, *How the Irish Became White* (New York: Routledge, 1995), 2.

3. George Borjas, *Friends or Strangers: The Impact of Immigrants on the U.S. Economy* (New York: Basic Books, 1990).

4. Alejandro Portes and Ruben G. Rumbaut, *Immigrant America: A Portrait* (Berkeley: University of California Press, 1990).

5. As Alan Wolfe puts it: "A framework organized around a balance sheet approach in which the assets and liabilities are added up is too rooted in utilitarianism to address why immigration has such symbolic importance for most Americans." Alan Wolfe, "The Return of the Melting Pot," *New Republic*, December 31, 1990, 32.

6. There is some debate about the details of this scene. Is the next of kin being asked to redeem the land through purchase or to redeem Ruth through marriage? See Danna Fewell and David Gunn, *Compromising Redemption: Relating Characters in the Book of Ruth* (Louisville, Ky.: Westminster/John Knox Press, 1990), for a summary of the debate and the single best reading of the scene.

7. Some doubt that the Book of Ruth can be a resource for an account of immigration politics because the text tells the story of a single migrant, whereas the contemporary issue involves hordes of people. My own view is that the text's success at dramatizing enduring issues of immigration politics is due partly to its use of the device of personification. Moreover, the story of Ruth has established connections to immigration politics that precede my analysis. Marjorie Garber (personal communication) recalls playing Ruth in the late 1940s in a series of fund-raisers sponsored by Hadassah to help Jewish refugees make their way to Palestine after the war. Interestingly, given Kristeva's use of the head scarf to mark the recalcitrance of Muslim immigrants, Garber, as Ruth, wore a head scarf to mark her character's European (refugee) identity.

8. It has been estimated that 195,000 U.S. residents emigrate annually; see Priscilla Labovitz, "Immigration: Just the Facts," *New York Times*, March 25, 1996, op-ed. I discuss in detail the symbolic functions of the iconic new citizen photograph in "Immigrant America? How Foreignness 'Solves' Democracy's Problems," in *No Place Like Home: Democracy and the Politics of Foreignness* (Princeton, N.J.: Princeton University Press, forthcoming).

9. Toni Morrison calls particularly sharp attention to the exclusionary dimension of the (re-)founding effect of American immigration in relation to American Blacks. Toni Morrison, "On the Backs of Blacks," in Nicolaus Mills, ed., *Arguing Immigration* (New York: Simon & Schuster, 1994).

10. Cynthia Ozick, "Ruth," in Judith A. Kates and Gail Twersky Reimer, eds., *Reading Ruth: Contemporary Women Reclaim a Sacred Story* (New York: Ballantine, 1994), 221. Page numbers for further cites of this volume appear in text.

11. In psychoanalytic terms, Orpah's (over)attachment to her mother(land)—represented by the phrase her "mother's house" (an unusual locution for the Bible)—prevents her, as it did Antigone (who clung to Polynices, the displaced site of her longing for her mother, Jocasta), from entering the (paternal or monotheistic) Law, the realm of the Symbolic. Luce Irigaray notes the displacement in *Antigone* but, moved by a sensibility more tragic than Ozick's, Irigaray finds a subterranean location for Antigone, who eternally unsettles the dominant order. Ozick pauses to reflect momentarily on Orpah, but she does not look to Orpah as a source of eternal dissonance or (in Irigaray's appropriation of Hegel's term) irony. Luce Irigaray, *Speculum of the Other Woman* (Ithaca, N.Y.: Cornell University Press, 1985).

12. The difficulties of such a return are occluded by Ozick, who comments on the unusualness of Orpah's exogamy but then assumes that Orpah's life in Moab will be unproblematic: "Soon she will marry a Moabite husband and have a Moabite child" (224). Fewell and Gunn have a better grasp of the situation: "What are Ruth's opportunities in Moab? Who would want to marry a barren widow, much less one that had been living with a foreigner? And would she be known as the 'Israelite-lover,' the one too good

for her own people? . . . In the end, we might ask, what takes more courage, the staying or the leaving?" *Compromising Redemption,* 97–98. See also Rosa Felsenburg Kaplan, "The Noah Syndrome," in Susanna Heschel, ed., *On Being a Jewish Feminist* (New York: Schocken, 1983), 167.

13. Jack M. Sasson notes this device of personification elsewhere in the Book of Ruth: "A didactic device frequently resorted to by Biblical writers is to limit the spectrum of choice to two alternatives, only one of which will prove to be correct. An obvious method of putting such a concept in effect is the creation of two brothers, only one of whom will ultimately fare well. Mahlon marries Ruth—he will live on" (through the posterity of Obed). Other biblical examples noted by Sasson are Cain and Abel, Jacob and Esau, Ishmael and Isaac, all male. Why does Sasson not include Ruth and Orpah in his list? Perhaps because of his Proppian assumption that Orpah is a merely marginal character, not central to the tale and not worthy, therefore, of further interpretive attention. Jack M. Sasson, *Ruth: A New Translation with a Philological Commentary and Formalist-Folklorist Interpretation* (Sheffield, England: JSOT, 1989), 16–17.

14. See Judith A. Kates, "Women at the Center: *Ruth* and Shavuoth," in Judith A. Kates and Gail Twersky Reimer, eds., *Reading Ruth: Contemporary Women Reclaim a Sacred Story* (New York: Ballantine, 1994), 194–95.

15. Ozick's claim echoes Hegel's that the brother-sister relation, of which he takes Polynices and Antigone to be exemplars, is unerotic. As Jacques Derrida points out, the claim is astonishing given the incestuous origins of this pair: "Antigone's parents are not some parents among others." Jacques Derrida, *Glas* (Lincoln: University of Nebraska Press, 1986), 165.

16. The Hebrew term used here for "feet" is a pun for genitals. Jack Sasson gives a wonderful reading of the scene in which Boaz is said to mistake Ruth for a "Lillith" (a demonic woman/spirit thought to be responsible for nocturnal emissions and male impotence). "Upon awakening, Boaz discerns the figure of a woman. Fearing that it might be that of a Lillith, he shudders in fear. The storyteller's joke is that Ruth turns out to be equally as aggressive in her demands to be accepted as a mate. In this case, we shall be shortly reassured (if we do not know it already) that matters will turn out well for all concerned." *Ruth: A New Translation,* 78.

The "joke" of the scene depends upon Boaz's misidentification of Ruth as a "Lillith." What Sasson does not note is that the error is overdetermined not simply by Ruth's sex/gender, but also by her Moabite identity. Moabite women were particularly feared by the Israelites as temptresses and seductresses. This scene is much more (or less) than a joke, then. It allows Boaz to experience his worst fears about Ruth—that, her conversion/immigration notwithstanding, she is truly a Moabite after all, a bearer of desire that will not respect the proper boundaries of male, Israelite subjectivity. Boaz experiences those fears precisely in the moment of his misidentification of Ruth (whom he already desires) because in that moment his fears are safely displaced onto a Lillith.

17. Gail Twersky Reimer, "Her Mother's House," in Judith A. Kates and Gail Twersky Reimer, eds., *Reading Ruth: Contemporary Women Reclaim a Sacred Story* (New York: Ballantine, 1994), 105.

18. I am reminded here of the not quite analogous story of the "Pelasgian inhabitants of Lemnos, who carried off Athenian women from Brauron and had children by them. When their mothers brought them up in the Athenian way, the fathers became afraid and killed both the mothers and their children. Because of both these deeds, the word 'Lemnion' was associated with anything bad." Gail Holst-Warhaft, *Dangerous Voices: Women's Laments in Greek Literature* (New York: Routledge, 1992), 211 n. 54, citing Herodotus, *Histories* VI, 6, 138.

19. Noting Ruth's love for Naomi, Kristeva calls attention to the woman-to-woman passion at the base of the Davidic line, a passion that flies in the face of structuralist assumptions about the order-constituting function of the male homosocial exchange of women. One might well add to this the observation that the order-constituting exchange in this text is that of a male—Obed—who is passed from one woman, Ruth, to another, Naomi.
20. Julia Kristeva, *Strangers to Ourselves*, trans. Leon S. Roudiez (New York: Columbia University Press, 1991), 75. Page numbers for further cites of this volume appear in text.
21. Julia Kristeva, *Nations without Nationalism*, trans. Leon S. Roudiez (New York: Columbia University Press, 1993), 63. Page numbers for further cites of this volume appear in text.
22. See Rogers Brubaker, *Citizenship and Nationhood in France and Germany* (Cambridge: Harvard University Press, 1992), 138–64; James Hollifield, *Immigrants, Markets and States: The Political Economy of Postwar Europe* (Cambridge: Harvard University Press, 1992), chaps. 6–7.
23. Norma Moruzzi, "A Problem with Headscarves: Contemporary Complexities of Political and Social Identity," *Political Theory* 22, no. 4 (1994): 665.
24. Kristeva does note the tenuousness of the distinction between fetish and transitional object, however, when she concedes that the transitional object is "any child's indispensable fetish" (*Nations*, 41).
25. Leila Ahmed, *Women and Gender in Islam: Historical Roots of a Modern Debate* (New Haven, Conn.: Yale University Press, 1993), 223–24.
26. Ahmed discusses veiling in Egypt, not France, but her argument was recently echoed by France's Federation of Councils of Parents of Pupils in Public Schools (FCPE), which opposed the expulsions of more than seventy girls who wore head scarves to their schools in Lille and the Paris region: "These expulsions carry with them 'the immense inconvenience of confining these young girls to within their family circle and of limiting any possibility of emancipation.'" *Migration News Sheet*, November 1994, 2. Kristeva never questions why she (like so many others) expresses her concerns about Muslim particularism through Muslim *women*. This is not a new question. It was posed by Fanon in "The Unveiling of Algeria." Winifred Woodhull hazards an answer to it, albeit not with Kristeva in mind. Echoing Fanon, she says, "In the eyes of many French people, girls of Maghrebian descent are generally diligent students and compliant people—in short, the most assimilable element of the immigrant population; if they begin to defend their right to 'difference,' the whole project of integration seems to be jeopardized." Winifred Woodhull, *Transfigurations of the Maghreb: Feminism, Decolonization, and Literatures* (Minneapolis: University of Minnesota Press, 1993), 48.
27. My thanks to Pratap Mehta on this point.
28. Judith Butler, "Kantians in Every Culture?" *Boston Review*, October–November 1994, 18.
29. Shiv Visvanthan, "From the Annals of the Laboratory State," *Alternatives: A Journal of World Policy* 12 (1987): 41.
30. Eric L. Santner, *Stranded Objects: Mourning, Memory and Film in Postwar Germany* (Ithaca, N.Y.: Cornell University Press, 1990), 19–26; Peter Sacks, *The English Elegy: Studies in Genre from Spenser to Yeats* (Baltimore: Johns Hopkins University Press, 1985), 8.
31. Santner, *Stranded Objects*, 26–27.
32. This is a possibility I myself raised earlier, along with Fewell and Gunn in *Compromising Redemption*.
33. Jennifer Gordon, "We Make the Road by Walking: Immigrant Workers, the Workplace

Project, and the Struggle for Social Change," *Harvard Civil Rights-Civil Liberties Law Review* 30 (1995): 407–50.

34. Camilo Perez-Bustillo, "What Happens When English Only Comes to Town? A Case Study of Lowell, Massachusetts," in James Crawford, ed., *Language Loyalties: A Sourcebook on the Official English Controversy* (Chicago: University of Chicago Press. 1992), 201.

35. James B. Raskin, "Legal Aliens, Local Citizens: The Historical, Constitutional and Theoretical Meanings of Alien Suffrage," *University of Pennsylvania Law Review* 141 (1993): 1397.

36. Ibid., 1429–30. It should be noted, however, that residency can be a restrictive rather than a permissive requirement. Other cities, such as Long Island, use stringent proof of residency requirements to keep immigrants out of public schools. See Doreen Carvajal, "Immigrants Fight Residency Rules Blocking Children in L.I. Schools," *New York Times*, August 7, 1995, A1, B4.

37. The potentially empowering if also controversial connections that may be forged by sub- and transnational groups in coalition are illustrated by the following case, which also militates against the impression that sister cities are benign and unimportant associations. In late 1988, the Lion's Club International of Taipei donated ten thousand Chinese-language books to the Monterey Park, California, public library, intending the gift to "reinforce the closeness they felt with their sister-city, which many [had] begun to call 'Little Taipei.'" Mayor Barry Hatch saw in this gift an assault on American values and fought to refuse it, but he ultimately lost out to a coalition made up of local civic groups and Chinese American community leaders. James Crawford, *Hold Your Tongue: Bilingualism and the Politics of "English Only"* (Reading, Mass.: Addison-Wesley, 1992), 1–3.

38. Wilbur Zelinsky, "The Twinning of the World: Sister Cities in Geographical and Historical Perspective," *Annals of the Association of American Geographers*, 81, no. 1 (1991): 1.

39. Liz Chilsen and Sheldon Rampton, *Friends in Deed: The Story of U.S. Nicaraguan Sister Cities* (Madison: Wisconsin Coordinating Council on Nicaragua, 1988).

40. Santner, *Stranded Objects*, 24.

The Borders of Europe

Etienne Balibar

Translated by J. Swenson

The "borders of Europe": Does the "of" indicate an objective or a subjective genitive? As we shall see, both are necessarily involved, and what is at stake is precisely the "Europeanness" of Europe's borders.

A reflection on the borders of Europe might well be the least abstract way at our disposal to leave behind a continually ruminated philosopheme, which has been given renewed youth by the proliferation of discussions about the future, the meaning, the culture, and the cultural exceptionalism of Europe: namely, the antithesis of the particular and the universal. But it might also be, more speculatively, a way to understand how a certain conception of the universal and the particular as opposites has imposed itself among those who want or believe themselves to be "Europeans," a conception that has assigned philosophy the task— its highest task, even—of sublating the abstraction of this opposition in a superior "synthesis." The figure of the unity of opposites (which is itself in many ways subtended by the schema or metaphor of the border) has never abolished this conception. On the contrary, it has confirmed that what can be demarcated, defined, and determined maintains a constitutive relation with what can be thought. Putting into question the notion of the border—indissociably "concept" and "image," or rather prior to the very distinction (must we call it "European"?) between concept and image—thus always in some sense implies a confrontation with the impossible limit of an autodetermination, a *Selbstbestimmung* of thought. It implies an effort to conceptualize the line on which we think, the condition of possibility or the "hidden art" of distributions and delimitations.

One might wonder why this task should be any easier today than in the past. Indeed, it may not be any easier. But it is all the more inescapable insofar as we are living in a conjuncture of the vacillation of borders—both of their layout and their function—that is at the same time a vacillation of the very notion of border, which has become particularly equivocal. This vacillation affects our very consciousness of a European "identity," because Europe is the point of the world whence border lines set forth to be drawn throughout the world, because it is the native land of the very representation of the border as this sensible and supersensible "thing" that should be or not be, be here or there, a bit beyond (*jenseits*) or short of (*diesseits*) its ideal "position," but always somewhere.[1]

This observation of an uncertainty in the representation of borders is not contradicted by the insistence (which can be violent or peaceful) on the unsurpassable or sacred character of borders, and may even explain it.[2] The conjuncture in which we are currently living in Europe—from the Atlantic to the Urals, unless it be to the Amur River, from the Nordkapp to the Bosporus, unless it be to the Persian Gulf, wherever the representation of the border as particularization and partition of the universal reigns—is producing a brutal short-circuit of the "empirical" and "transcendental" dimensions of the notion of the border. This conjuncture immediately makes questions of administration and diplomacy, politics and policing, into philosophical questions. It confers a practical import on speculative decisions about the meaning of defining an "interior" and an "exterior," a "here" and a "there," and generally about everything that Kant would have called the amphibologies of reflection.

In such a conjuncture, it is necessary to try to think what it is difficult even to imagine. But it can also be fruitful to work on the imagination itself, to explore its possibilities of variation. In an admirable recent book, the psychoanalyst André Green notes, "One can be a citizen or an expatriate, but it is difficult to imagine *being* a border."[3] But isn't this precisely what, all around us, many individuals, groups, and territories must indeed try to imagine? It is precisely what they are living, what most intimately affects their "being" insofar as it is neither this nor that. This is perhaps what all of Europe, and not just its "margins," "marches," or "outskirts" must today imagine, for it has become a daily experience. Most of the areas, nations, and regions that constitute Europe had become accustomed to thinking that they had borders, more or less "secure and recognized," but they did not think they were borders.

I will sketch out this variation around three aspects of the problem (in a sense the "real," the "symbolic," and the "imaginary" of the border): (1) the current vacillation of borders, (2) the interiority and ideality of borders, and (3) the conflict or the overlapping of "cultures" around what, taking up an old archetype, I will call the European *triple point*.

The Vacillation of Borders

That borders are vacillating is a matter of experience: first and foremost, that they are no longer at the border, an institutional site that can be materialized on the ground and inscribed on the map, where one sovereignty ends and another begins; where individuals (ex)change obligations as well as currency; where in peacetime customs examinations, verifications of identity, and payment of duties and tolls are carried out; where in wartime armed populations converge, coming to defend the fatherland by attacking the enemy's expansionism. I will not discuss here the question of whether this institutional form of the border is ancient or recent, universal or particular. I shall recall, rather, that it is the result of a long gestation, of a series of choices no one of which was necessary, but that led to one another, and that coincide with the universalization of a very particular form of state, originating in Europe: the national state. And I shall be content to note that this institution, today, is irreversibly coming undone.

With respect to the question that concerns us, this situation did not begin when the Maastricht Treaty came into effect, nor with the announced application of the Schengen accords. The malady—if such there is— "comes from further afield."[4] It comes from the transformation of the means of international communication, which has relativized the functions of the port of entry and by contrast revalorized internal controls, creating within each territory zones of transit and transition, populations "awaiting" entry or exit (sometimes for several years, sometimes in a periodically repeated fashion), individually or collectively engaged in a process of negotiation of their presence and their mode of presence (that is, their political, economic, cultural, religious, and other rights) with one or more states.[5] It comes from the fact that the speed of purchase and sale orders and monetary conversion, executed in "real time" (even integrating "rational anticipations" of the behavior of public and private agents into the computer's imaginary), has gone far beyond the possibilities of control on the part of administrations (to say nothing of control on the part of citizens). It comes from the fact that the appropriation of "natural" (or natural-cultural) factors "common to the human race" by individuals or groups themselves controlled and appropriated by states has encountered its limits. The cloud generated by Chernobyl cannot be stopped at the border, nor can the AIDS virus, despite the reinforced control that some dream of imposing on its "bearers," which means virtually on all of us. Nor can one stop CNN's images, even by regulating the sale of satellite dishes. At most one can try to superimpose other images on them by jamming signals on a worldwide scale. It comes from the fact that the methods of modern warfare no longer cross borders in the strict sense (let us recall such archaeological formulas and images as the "violation of Belgian neutrality" and tanks knocking over boundary posts), but virtually (and actually, as the Gulf War proved) overhang them, that is, negate them. It comes from the fact that the class struggle, as we used to say (or as we would say today, the managing of phenomena of inequality and exclusion and of the flows of active and inactive populations), has definitively escaped the jurisdiction of national states, without thereby coming under the control of apparatuses that could be called "global." It comes from the fact that there has occurred a tendential inversion of power relations in the hierarchy of idioms in which the formation of individuals and the cultural recognition of groups, and consequently the very evolution of languages, are carried out. (This hierarchy has always combined the three levels of the national, the dialectal—or "vernacular," whether socially or regionally defined—and the transnational—easily baptized the "universal.")[6] It comes from the fact that the possibility of concentrating in a single place ("capital," "metropolis") the exercise of political power, economic decision making, and the production of aesthetic models has definitively disappeared. And, to conclude, it comes from the fact that the response by some European nations, or rather by their ruling classes, to these different processes of "globalization" has been to initiate a transfer of institutions to the supranational level, a process whose very signification (the juridico-political status and the value that it confers on the idea of "community") continues and probably will continue to divide them on the question of union for an unforeseeable time to come.

Thus borders are vacillating. This means that they are no longer localizable in an unequivocal fashion. It also means that they no longer allow a superimposition of the set of functions of sovereignty, administration, cultural control, taxation, and so on, and consequently a conferral on the territory, or better, on the duo of territory and population, of a simultaneously englobing and univocal signification of "presupposition" for all other social relations.[7] Further, it means that they do not work in the same way for "things" and "people"—not to speak of what is neither thing nor person: viruses, information, ideas—and thus repeatedly pose, sometimes in a violent way, the question of whether people transport, send, and receive things, or whether things transport, send, and receive people: what can in general be called the empirico-transcendental question of *luggage*. Finally, it means that they do not work in the same way, "equally," for all "people, and notably not for those who come from different parts of the world, who (this is more or less the same thing) do not have the same social status, the same relation to the appropriation and exchange of idioms."[8] This properly social differentiation is already in the course of powerfully disaggregating the modern equation—whose identitarian logic is fundamentally based on the concept of the border[9]—of citizenship and nationality, and consequently of irreversibly transforming the very notion of people, *peuple*, *Volk*, *narod*, *umran*, and *açabiyya*, and so on, for this equation presupposes that we can maintain, at

219

least as a legal fiction (but all right is fictive, or fictional), the equality of citizenships as an equality of nationalities.[10]

Borders are vacillating. This does not mean that they are disappearing. Less then ever is the contemporary world a "world without borders." On the contrary, borders are being both multiplied and reduced in their localization and their function, they are being thinned out and doubled, becoming border zones, regions, or countries where one can reside and live. The quantitative relation between "border" and "territory" is being inverted. This means that borders are becoming the object of protest and contestation as well as of an unremitting reinforcement, notably of their function of security. But this also means—irreversibly—that borders have stopped marking the limits where politics ends because the community ends (whether the community is conceived of in terms of "contract" or "origin" has only a relative importance here, to tell the truth, because the practical result is the same), beyond which, in Clausewitz's words, politics can be continued only "by other means." This in fact means that borders are no longer the shores of politics, but have indeed become—perhaps by way of the police, given that every border patrol is today an organ of "internal security"—objects or, let us say more precisely, things within the space of the political itself.

The Interiority and Ideality of Borders

This situation gives us the means to return to the border's past and to correct a representation that seems natural, but that is nonetheless manifestly false, or in any case too simple: the representation that makes the border the simple limit between two territorial entities, similar but independent of one another. Contemporary globalization is certainly bringing about what can be called an underdetermination of the border, a weakening of its identity. But the border is no less troubled by the recent memory, the insistent afterimage of the inverse figure: that of the overdetermination of borders. By this I mean to designate the fact that, at least in Europe (but this model is one that "we" have proposed to and imposed upon the entire world, through conquest and colonization, then decolonization and the establishment of the "league of nations"), state borders, understood equally as the borders of a culture and an at-least-fictive identity, have always been immediately endowed with a global signification. They have always served not only to separate particularities, but always also at the same time, in order to fulfill this "local" function, to "partition the world," to configure it, to give it a representable figure in the modality of the partition, the distribution and attribution of regions of space, or, to put it better, of the historical distribution of the regions of space, which would work like the instantaneous projection of the progresses and processes of its history. Every map in this sense is always a world map, for it represents a "part of the world," it locally projects the *universitas* that is *omnitudo compartium absoluta*.[11]

We would need time here to illustrate this thesis by a series of examples, to linger on the succession of figures of the symbolic overdetermination of borders, which is present here as the immediately global import of the slightest bend of a border. We would have to enumerate all of its theologico-political names, from the first division of the world made by Pope Alexander VI between the Spanish and the Portuguese at the Treaty of Tordesillas (1494),[12] immediately contested by others (the English, the French), up to its modern equivalents: the division of Africa at the Conference of Berlin (1895), or the division of Yalta. We would need to show—this time taking up the analyses of Braudel and Wallerstein—how the division of the world between Europeans or quasi-Europeans has always been the condition of the (at least relative) stabilization of the borders that, in Europe itself, separated states from one another and constituted the condition of their "equilibrium." And we would have to notice the same figure everywhere: that of a binary division of world space (of the "sphere" or the whole) that is disturbed not so much by the fluctuations of the balance of power between "camps" as by the intervention of a *third*, which can be manifested as aggression, resistance, or even a simple "passive" presence that renders the partition invalid. We would then have to write the history of the successive "Third Worlds"—even before the invention of the expression—and see how, each time, they blurred the local question of the partition of the world because, ideologically as much as strategically, they blurred the representation of the globe. But above all, we would have to show that such an overdetermination is never—however decisive this aspect may be—a simple question of external power, of relations of force and the distribution of populations between states, but always also, as Derrida has correctly emphasized, a question of idealities: a "spiritual" question, therefore, or better yet, a symbolic question.

National borders would not be capable of securing (or trying to secure) identities, would not be capable of marking the threshold at which life and death are played out (in what in Europe is called "patriotism");[13] in brief, to take up the decisive formulation elaborated by Fichte in the *Addresses to the German Nation* (1807), they would not be capable of being "internal borders" (internalized borders, borders for interiority) were they not idealized. And they would not be idealized, conceived of as the support of the universal, if they were not imagined as the point at which "worldviews"

(*Weltanschauungen, conceptions du monde*), and thus also views of man, were at stake: the point at which one must choose, and choose oneself.

But the term *worldview* is much too vague. Or more precisely, it is frighteningly equivocal. For it can cover, as need be, the notion of cultural difference (whether it be a question of rights, manners, or traditions): a fundamentally imaginary notion since the principle of its definition is the perception of "similarities" and "dissimilarities," the principle of proximity and distance. Or it can cover the notion of symbolic difference, for which, in order to make myself understood, I will reserve the name of a difference in civilization: a difference that does not bear upon resemblance but upon the reconcilable and the irreconcilable, the compatible and the incompatible.

Everyone can feel, to take only one example from contemporary situations, that when the French (although certainly not all of them) indignantly decry the sentencing of two children found guilty of murder to "indefinite detention" ("detention at Her Majesty's pleasure"—it being by no means certain that this sentence is unanimously approved by the English), at the exact moment that their own minster of justice presents himself as the spokesman for a public opinion demanding a "genuine life sentence" for murderers and rapists of children,[14] it is not a cultural difference that is at play, but a symbolic trait, or a trait of civilization, that bears upon the way in which "subjects" relate themselves to childhood and adulthood, innocence and perversion, the relation between "act" and "intention," "responsibility" and "irresponsibility" in the definition of crime. Everyone can thus understand that such differences have little or nothing to do with "cultural distance," or rather that they are probably all the more marked where the cultural proximity is greatest, and thus that it is much more difficult to imagine a harmonizing of the French and English (or Anglo-American and Franco-German) judicial systems than to resolve the question of the acceptance or rejection of the so-called Islamic veils worn by certain young women in the schools of the French Republic. I will even risk the hypothesis that in this respect each fraction of Europe, however restricted it may be, still contains, actually or potentially, as the result of history and the subjective choices it has occasioned, the same diversity and divisions as the world considered in its totality.

Traditionally, the disciplines of history and sociology have assigned the differential traits of civilization, in this sense, to the domain of the religious. This is no doubt a consequence of the properly European identification of the general notion of the symbolic with religious idealities, in other words of the fact that the master signifiers in whose name the interpellation of individuals as subjects occurs, in Europe or more precisely in the Mediterranean basin, are religious words or words with a religious background. "Patriotism" and "law" are good examples. It is thus also a consequence of the fact that the establishment (and later crisis) of secular state hegemonies, whose form of universality is above all juridico-political, does not simply succeed in a linear way upon the establishment and crisis of religious hegemonies or universalisms. The crisis of the nation-state has begun in today's Europe, without any foreseeable end, whereas the crisis of religious consciousness is by no means completed or resolved. However, the same precautions are necessary with respect to the notion of "religion" as that of "border": no one knows what religion in general is, or rather no one can define the difference between a religious symbol and a profane symbol other than by a tautological reference to what has gradually been identified as "religion" in the history of Europe. And everywhere that history has been rethought on the European model.

The Conflict or Overlapping of Cultures around the European Triple Point

Let us nevertheless admit an identification of the religious and the symbolic, at least as a provisional working hypothesis. The symbolic overdetermination of borders will then appear in a new light. We can reformulate a number of our observations—that borders are always double, that they can separate particular territories only by structuring the universality of the world, and that this doubling is the very condition of their internalization by individuals and thus of their function as constitutive of identities—by saying that every instituted, demanded, or fantasied border must be both a political border and a religious border in this sense. And, inversely, we can say that the only way to realize the border as an absolute separation is to represent it as a religious border—even when this religion is a lay, secularized religion, a religion of language, school, and constitutional principle.[15]

I believe that an idea of this sort is at work, for example, in the recent book by Rémi Brague, *Europe, la voie romaine*—one of the few that might survive the current overproduction of historico-philosophical works on the theme of "European identity."[16] Brague seeks the definition of European identity in an interplay of splits, successive religious demarcations, which he sees as having fractured the proto-European, circum-Mediterranean space between antiquity and our own time: Orient and Occident, North and South, with each of these axes being capable of reduplicating itself one or more times. The "definition" of Europeanness that he arrives at is of the greatest interest. In many respects it rejoins, across other teleologies, the Hegelian concept of historicity, that is, the conflictual movement that projects each "principle" of civilization outside of itself, toward a sublation that will call for its own sublation, and so on. This definition characterizes Roman-Latin-European identity neither by an origin, nor a foundation, nor a fidelity to authentic roots that would be proper to it, but by tradition itself: the betrayal and transmission of a heritage (which supposes its betrayal), which he calls "belatedness" (secondarité). Europeans, according to Brague, are properly speaking neither "Jews" nor "Greeks" (the great dilemma that inflamed the nineteenth century from Renan to Matthew Arnold), but still and always "Romans," because they inherit from the Greeks and the Jews (or the Semites) a Logos that is not their own, and that as a consequence they can only appropriate on the condition of endlessly transforming it and transmitting it again—which, we know, can mean imposing it—beyond every preestablished border. At the limit, we can say: on the condition of losing it.

Nevertheless, Brague manifestly believes in "Latinity" or "Romanity" understood in this sense, and he believes in it for reasons that are as much properly religious as "cultural." For him, the center of the orbis is indeed in the urbs, and more precisely in the Loggia of Saint Peter's Square, whence shines forth the splendor of truth (splendor veritatis). This is why, after having defined identity in terms of a structural schema, which as such is formal or differential (a fact expressed by the perfectly universalizable notion of "belatedness," a phenomenon whose best contemporary examples are no doubt given by North America and even more by Japan, the double inheritor of the foreign civilizations of China and the Occident), he nonetheless ends up considering the structure of transmission and betrayal as specifically attached to a site, to a space, in brief as having its historico-natural site on one side rather than the other of the split between Orient and Occident (namely, in the West), on one side of the split between North and South (or Christianity and Islam), namely, on the northern, "Christian shore" of the Mediterranean. For him as for so many others the thought of structure ends up repeating a thought of substance.

It does not seem to me that we can escape the constraints of this sort of repetition without difficulty. But personally I prefer to work directly with another schema of the configuration of the world, which moreover seems to me to be subjacent to Brague's own argument. I call this schema the *triple point*,[17] or triple point of heresy (in the etymological sense of *heresy*, which is also the foundation of its theological, or theologico-political, sense: to choose one side rather than the other in the symbolic order, and thus to represent error for truth and truth for error). We do not have the time here to give its full genealogy.[18] We should still recall that this figure is constitutive of the very representation of Europe as a "part of the world" comparable to Africa (or Libya) and Asia. It is thus at the origin of a cartography that engendered the very notion of the border, in its different uses. It begins with the inscription of the letter *tau* within a circle ("schema T/O") that the Greeks, and notably Herodotus, opposed to the figure of earth and ocean as concentric circles, and in which the Christians later believed that they saw Christ's cross, as if inscribed in a predestined way upon the very face of the earth.[19] It is still to be found in the great romantic myth of the "European Triarchy," as displayed in the title of Moses Hess's book (1841), which in Marxism will become the interpretive schema of the "three sources" (economics, politics, philosophy: England, France, Germany). One can find in it one of the privileged figures of the mirroring by which the figure of the world can be found in the constitution of Europe, in such a way that the universality of the world exhibits in return, at every moment, its essential Europeanness. One finds it again, to be sure, in the three empires of Orwell's *1984*, which today many imagine as the United States, Western Europe, and Japan (or China).

I am only proposing a slight variation on this traditional figure. (Even more than traditional, it is archetypal, and in that sense imprescriptible, but not necessarily inalterable, for its contours and its point of application can shift.) But I believe that this variation is sufficient to put back in motion the representation of borders. I propose that Europe is not and never has been made up of separate regions ("empires," "camps," "nations"), but rather of overlapping sheets or layers (*de nappes qui se recouvrent*), and that its specificity is this overlapping itself: to be precise, an East, a West, and a South. This was already the case in Herodotus's time, and it is not necessary to subscribe to all of Martin Bernal's hypotheses[20] in order to suppose that the triple point constituted by the meeting of the Mediterranean, the Nile, and the Tanaïs (the Don) is much more a zone of interpenetration of "Germanic," "Semitic," and "Egyptian" (or "Libyan") cultures than a line of segregation. This is even more so the case today, when—European nations having conquered the world and then having had to officially withdraw, but without burning their bridges—it is *from the whole world* that the discourse, capitals, labor powers, and sometimes the weapons of Europe come back to us, as an aftershock.

I see advantages to working and playing with representations of this sort, rather than allowing them to act on us unperceived, outside of our consciousness and our grasp. The primary advantage is to alert us to the significations that are at work in every tracing of a border, beyond the immediate, apparently factual determinations of language, religion, ideology, and power relations. One cannot but feel that it is an idea, an image, and a fantasy of Europe that, under our very eyes, are producing their deadly effects in the "partition" and "ethnic cleansing" of Yugoslavia generally and of Bosnia in particular, and that Europe is in the course of committing suicide by allowing the suicide in its name of these fragments of a single "people," whose whole history is constituted by the repercussions of its own divisions.

But it is necessary to say more: "Croats," "Serbs," and "Muslims" are definitely neither nations nor religions. For their misfortune they are much more—voluntary or involuntary incarnations of "irreconcilable" civilizations—and also much less—simple clan solidarities, reappearing as the ultimate recourse against the ravaging of the political identities of "modernity." In reality I see only one name that is fully appropriate to them: they are races. By this we should understand reciprocal racisms, as "Semites" and "Aryans" were "races" in Europe. Yugoslavia is a "triple point" of European racial relations. As a consequence, what is being played out there, before us and by us, is the question of whether a state, a nation, a democracy, a society is constructed by the dissociation or by the combination, the overlapping, of the components of every "European" culture, on the scale of the continent as on the scale of each of its parts, its local projections.

But what can be read, as a far-off trace and as a current dilemma, in greater Europe or in each little Europe, can now also be found in many other parts of the world. This is why I will suggest that today around the world there are many other Europes that we do not know how to recognize. We are always narcissistically in search of images of ourselves when it is structures that we should look for. Ever since the dichotomy of the two camps, which collapsed from its very success, was officially abolished, triple points have been reappearing everywhere: Easts, Souths, Wests. To put it plainly, these are the cultural or identitarian overlappings in which the possibility of constructing political singularities are played out today. Each of these figures has its own history and its own dynamic, but all of them are constituted by working on European schemata of partition and the border and adapting them to their own contingencies.

This is why they all teach us that Europe is everywhere outside of itself, and that in this sense there is no more Europe—or that there will be less and less of it. But, in this dissemination without recourse, there is never more to be lost than to be gained—not in terms of the essence or substance of Europe, but in terms of the capacity of thinking and the project of governing oneself that it also represented.

Notes

This essay was first presented at the conference "L'idée de l'Europe et la philosophie," sponsored by the Association des professeurs de philosophie de l'académie de Poitiers, in Poitiers, France, December 2–4, 1993.

1. Here again, there would be occasion to undertake a reflection of thought upon itself, and to pose the question of the intimate relation between the representation of the border, often the site where life and death are played out, and the idea of a unique "passage" between "life" and "death," the "other of life" and the "other life," which has determined all "European" theology and ethics—with the proviso that it was the Egyptians who first thought it under the form that we have inherited. See Yvette Conry, "Frontières de vie, frontières de mort," *Raison présente* 85 (1988): 49–70.

2. "The rehabilitation of the border is today the condition of any politics, as it is the condition of any true exchange." Philippe Séguin, "La république et l'exception française," *Philosophie politique* 4 (1993): 45–62. [Séguin was at the time, as he is today, the president of the French National Assembly. Trans.]

3. André Green, *La folie privée: Psychanalyse des cas-limites* (Paris: Gallimard, 1990), 107.

4. [See Racine's *Phèdre*, act 1, scene 3: "Mon mal vient de plus loin." Trans.]

5. See on this point the volume edited by Marie-Claire Caloz-Tschopp (with a preface by François Julien Laferrière), *Frontières du droit, frontières des droits: L'introuvable statut de la "zone internationale"* (Paris: L'Harmattan/ANAFE, 1993).

6. For the complete history of the decisive event in the representation of universalism and particularism in the element of language—that is, the proclamation by the Academy of Berlin in 1784 of the "universality of the French language"—see Ferdinand Brunot, *Histoire de la langue française* (Paris: Librairie Armand Colin, 1935), t. VII.

7. This is what Gilles Deleuze and Félix Guattari described not long ago in *A Thousand Plateaus: Capitalism and Schizophrenia*, trans. Brian Massumi (Minneapolis: University of Minnesota Press, 1987), in a half realist, half fantastical way, as the entry into the era of "deterritorialized flows," a new era of "nomadism," which can be a nomadism *on the spot*.

8. If I may be permitted a personal memory here, I first became conscious of this question the day when, after we had shared beer and chocolate, an old Indian fisherman from the shores of Lake Pátzcuaró (state of Michoacán, Mexico) explained to me in perfect Spanish (by which I mean Spanish that I understand without difficulty) that he had finally figured out why his attempts to emigrate to the United States had always failed: because, he told me, "there is a letter missing" in Tarasca (his maternal language); "hace falta una letra, entiendes amigo." This letter, lost since time immemorial, can never be recovered. And this letter is the one you have to have to cross the northern border. But the situation is not reciprocal, for never in his life will the gringo tourist recover the letter that is missing in English, or French, or German, and nonetheless he will cross the border as often as he wants for as long as he wants, to the point that it will lose its materiality.

9. See Gérard Noiriel, *La tyrannie du national: Le droit d'asile en Europe (1793–1993)* (Paris: Calmann-Lévy, 1991).

10. On citizenship as a status in current international space, see my essay, "L'Europe des citoyens," in *Les étrangers dans la cité: Expériences européennes*, ed. Olivier Le Cour Grandmaison and Catherine Wihtol de Wenden (Paris: La Découverte, 1993), 192–208. [The equation of the terms is sufficiently strong that in contemporary American usage *citizenship* most often covers both concepts. Under the word *citizen*, the *American Heritage Dictionary* (Boston: Houghton Mifflin, 1992) lists "citizen," "national," and "subject" as synonyms, commenting, "the central meaning shared by

these nouns is 'a person owing allegiance to a nation or state and entitled to its protection.'" In Balibar's usage, *nationality* is the *status* of belonging, generally in an exclusive fashion, to a particular nation, by birth or naturalization; *citizenship* has a more active sense, designating rights and in particular a "right to politics." Trans.]

11. Immanuel Kant, *De mundi sensibilis atque intelligibilis forma et principiis* (Inaugural Dissertation, 1770), sec. I:2, iii; translated as "On the Form and Principles of the Sensible and the Intelligible World," in *Theoretical Philosophy, 1755–1770*, trans. and ed. David Walford (Cambridge: Cambridge University Press, 1992), 382: "entirety, which is the absolute totality of its component parts."

12. See Régis Debray, *Christope Colomb, le visiteur de l'aube, suivi des Traités de Tordesillas* (Paris: La Différence, 1991).

13. See Ernst Kantorowicz, *"Pro Patria Mori* in Medieval Political Thought," in *Selected Studies* (Locust Valley, N.Y.: J. J. Augustin, 1965), 308-24.

14. [Pierre Méhaignerie, Garde des sceaux (minister of justice) in 1993, had proposed a sentence of "perpétuité réelle," that is, life without parole, in cases of the murder of children aggravated by rape, torture, or other "barbaric acts." Trans.]

15. The question is often posed as to exactly what constitutes the internal link, which is historically manifest but theoretically enigmatic, between French scholarization and colonization, both of which are symbolized by the name of Jules Ferry. I believe that this link passes through the religious institution of the border. In the nineteenth century, the border of the French nation, indissolubly ideal and real, is a double border: a European contour (the "hexagon," the "natural borders" of the Rhine, the Alps, and the Pyrenees) and a global contour (the limits of the French Empire, an eminently "republican" empire, a new Roman Empire). These two contours are infinitely close by right but infinitely distant in practice (not only because thousands of miles separate them, but because one encloses French citizens and the other essentially French subjects, referred to as "natives." The interstice between them, colored pink on old French globes, is the zone of missions, where the recruitment of soldiers for the defense of the mother country has as its counterpart the diffusion of a sacred heritage of civilization: the Rights of Man, the French language, universal secularism. This allows us to better understand the forms that the battle against "fundamentalism" (*l'intégrisme*) can take in certain of the Republic's schools, for example, episodes that might seem disproportionate, such as the unanimous mobilization of a junior high school's teachers against the admission to the Republican school of a few young girls more or less voluntarily wearing "Islamic veils," or the obdurate resistance to granting excuses from gym class, which in other cases are to be had for the asking. This is because the internal border is at stake: the "Empire" no longer exists, but its idea is still present, as is the ghost of its "subjects," with their "superstitions" or "fanaticisms." Every veil that crosses the door of a school above which is inscribed "Liberty, Equality, Fraternity" (to which we have long since learned to add the words "free, secular, and mandatory") is the proof, not only that we had to renounce the empire, which is fundamentally secondary, but above all that we had to withdraw from it without having accomplished the mission that we believed we were fulfilling there: liberating peoples from their ignorance and their intolerance, teaching the French version of secular religion to all.

16. Rémi Brague, *Europe, la voie romaine* (Paris: Critérion, 1992).

17. [In thermodynamics, the triple point designates the relation between temperature and pressure at which solid, liquid, and vapor states coexist in equilibrium. Trans.]

18. For some complementary developments, see my contribution "Quelles frontières de l'Europe?" in the volume *Penser l'Europe à ses frontières*, Géophilosophie de l'Europe/Carrefour des Littératures européennes de Strasbourg (La Tour d'Aigues: Editions de l'Aube, 1993), 90–100.

19. "See Christian Jacob, "Le contour et la limite: Pour une approche philosophique des cartes géographiques," in *Frontières et limites*, ed. Christian Descamps (Paris: Editions du Centre Pompidou, 1991).
20. Martin Bernal, *Black Athena: The Afroasiatic Roots of Classical Civilization* (New Brunswick, N.J.: Rutgers University Press, 1987).

Part III ▸ Toward a Cosmopolitan Cultural Studies

The Varieties of Cosmopolitan Experience

Scott L. Malcomson

"Cosmopolitan" has never been an academic post. Cosmopolitanism has its origins in the Greek words for "order, world," and "citizen." There was no school of cosmopolitanism; it was more an attitude. As so often in the ancient world, the real fun seems to have been over early, before empire acquired a certain bureaucratic firmness, a time when the line between philosopher and lunatic was appealingly thin. Consider Diogenes the Cynic, nicknamed the Dog (*kyon*, the origin of the word *cynic*), living in an earthenware tub; or his follower Crates, the public copulator. It was Diogenes whom Alexander the Great visited on his way to conquering everything in sight. Alexander asked the tub-bound philosopher if he could do anything for him, and Diogenes famously replied, "Yes, stand aside; you're keeping the sun off me." As Peter Green has noted, the two men shared "a stubborn and alienated intransigence. But whereas Diogenes had withdrawn from the world, Alexander was bent on subjugating it; they represented the active and passive forms of an identical phenomenon."[1]

Alexander and Diogenes were both, in their ways, extreme cosmopolitans. The tension between active and passive continued through the Greek and Roman periods. Cosmopolitans, most of them influenced by Stoicism, took their universal citizenship as a license either to withdraw from the world or to master it. Of those who withdrew, not much more can be said. Those who did not tended to use their citizenship toward one of two purposes: to study the world or to control it. Stoic cosmopolitans were first among the ranks of ancient geographers and ethnographers; they were likewise prominent among the defenders of empire, particularly during the Roman period. When the Roman cosmopolitans were patriotic, their patriotism contained multitudes.

In English, *cosmopolite* came into frequent use only in the seventeenth century, and seems to have been an unobjectionable term. That changed in the early nineteenth century, when the idea of being a citizen of the world became defined as the opposite of patriotism. In 1857, Carlyle contrasted cosmopolitanism with "the old home feeling"; thirty years later, Tennyson, in *Hands All Round*, tried to square the circle with "That man's the best Cosmopolite, who loves his native country best." In the context of European nationalism in the nineteenth century and the twentieth, cosmopolitans gradually acquired an odor of scholastic, probably harmless, aestheticism, at best—or, at fascist worst, of rootless elders of Zion plotting the subjugation of nations. In the postwar pax Americana, the term *cosmopolitan* became merely quaint, almost a refined synonym for *indecisive*.

This is now changing. Since the end of the Cold War, nationalism has acquired some fresh legitimacy in intellectual circles and, partly as a reaction, cosmopolitanism has likewise been reinvigorated. The new cosmopolitans usually have a left, or at least liberal, bent, and a desire to change the world, however modestly. I remember about a decade ago Gayatri Spivak speculating that the deconstruction of fixed identities had gone too far, leaving oppressed groups without the groupness they needed to fight back; maybe, she thought, it was time for a "strategic bargain with essence." The new cosmopolitanism is rather the opposite—a strategic bargain with universalism. The left academy, camped as it has been in the forests of multiculturalism, the cultural studies suburbs, or the postcolonial city, seems to be mobilizing itself for another look at the monism that was meant to be buried by *Of Grammatology*. The idea is to show a purposeful concern for all humanity without ignoring "difference." It may amount to a highly provisional universalism, more method than conclusion, something like Isaiah Berlin's liberalism but with more bite. Whether the new cosmopolitans will be more (or less) effective than their predecessors remains to be seen, for, as ever, the key political question with cosmopolitans is: What do they *do*?

One option for American cosmopolitans is to dwell on the specialness of our nation as, to use the poststructuralist slang, always already cosmopolitan. In this way, one can perhaps be a cosmopolitan and a patriot at the same time. Such is the position of David Hollinger in *Postethnic America*. A dissatisfaction with vulgar multiculturalism is the animating force behind his book. He sees multiculturalism as dangerously provincial and politically minimalist. Like Michael Lind and others, he trawls back through the work of Horace Kallen and Randolph Bourne, two forgotten early twentieth-century figures currently being revived, and argues for a "national culture" that, given the peculiarity of the United States as a multiethnic country with strong democratic traditions, will not be just a cover for the rule of a single ethnicity (e.g., white people). In order to reach this stage, he advocates "postethnic" thinking.

Why postethnic and not cosmopolitan? Because cosmopolitanism is too "generic."

> As "citizens of the world," many of the great cosmopolitans of history have been proudly rootless. But postethnicity is the critical renewal of cosmopolitanism in the context of today's greater sensitivity to roots. "Rooted cos-

mopolitanism" is indeed a label recently adopted by several theorists of diversity whom I take to be moving in the direction I call postethnic.[2]

The reference is to Mitchell Cohen in *Dissent* and Bruce Ackerman in *Ethics*, though the term itself seems weak enough to be applied liberally; none of the new cosmopolitans seems to want an entirely unrooted cosmopolitanism.[3]

At any rate, if we need a new national cultural ideal, I suppose this is as good as it can get. What would this United States be like? When Michael Lind tried to imagine it in *The Next American Nation*, he achieved an opiated, Coleridgean vision, with Frederick Douglass swooping alarmingly among the clouds. Hollinger is on more familiar terms with the man from Porlock; he speaks prosaically of "voluntary affiliations" and the multiple, shifting constituents of an individual American's identity.[4] And he speaks of love, citing Edwin Markham's "The Man with the Hoe" (1899): "He drew a circle that shut me out— / Heretic, rebel, a thing to flout. / But love and I had the wit to win: / We drew a circle that took him in!" "We are all," Hollinger concludes, "left with the responsibility for deciding where to try to draw what circles with whom, and around what."[5]

More internationally minded cosmopolitans such as Bruce Robbins and Martha Nussbaum share this preference for voluntary associations. In a noted *Boston Review* essay, Nussbaum took cosmopolitanism on the attack against Richard Rorty's *New York Times* op-ed defense of patriotism.[6] Instead of Edwin Markham, she used the Stoic philosopher Hierocles, to nearly identical effect:

> [The Stoics] suggest that we think of ourselves not as devoid of local affiliations, but as surrounded by a series of concentric circles. The first one is drawn around the self; the next takes in one's family. . . . Outside all these circles is the largest one, that of humanity as a whole. Our task as citizens of the world will be to "draw the circles somehow toward the center" (Hierocles) . . . making all human beings more like our fellow city dwellers, and so on.[7]

Robbins's take is more supple and lacks the technocratic arrogance of "making all human beings more like our fellow city dwellers"—Which city? What about farmers?—not to mention the even more worrying "and so on." Robbins speaks of an "affiliation with universalism" in his effort to

> shake loose terms like cosmopolitanism and internationalism from the rationalist universality with which each has been entangled since Kant, and thus

to perform the delicate work of defining, nurturing, revising, and propagating a cosmopolitan or internationalist politics that will be more self-limiting and more efficacious than any we have yet seen.[8]

Robbins seems to be advocating a cosmopolitanism of *humility* rather than what I take to be Nussbaum's cosmopolitanism of pedagogical *patience*.

Both Robbins and Nussbaum, as internationalists, have been influenced by the dramatic rise in numbers and power of nongovernmental organizations (NGOs), voluntary associations that have begun to provide a third way in international affairs that avoids both Western-dominated globalism (commonly represented by the World Bank) and the opportunistic "difference"-mongering of despotic states (currently represented, for debating purposes, by Nigeria and Singapore). For Robbins, the 1993 Vienna summit was the turning point, when both non-Western cultural relativists and Western universalists were ambushed by an alliance of African, Latin American, and Asian NGOs. Among the direct and indirect results of the Vienna insurrection were a U.N. declaration on violence against women, which included language touching on such delicate issues as marital rape and incest; the inclusion of human-rights monitors in U.N. peacekeeping operations; and the creation of a special rapporteur on violence against women. The NGOs in Vienna argued in particular for women's rights as human rights. They preserved their anti-Western bona fides while bravely confronting their own governments; they did this by taking universalism into their own hands, thereby gaining some power that neither the Western governments nor their own wanted them to have. Such a neither-one-nor-the-other cosmopolitanism could have a long life ahead of it. As the *New York Times* reported about a Sisterhood Is Global conference in May 1996:

> Women in the Islamic world say they draw on universal concepts of human rights—and often on Western educations—while insisting that they are Muslims first and that this will always affect their thinking and methods. Many, including women who might consider themselves secularists, defend others who chose to veil themselves and adopt a conservative theology.[9]

This was not, certainly, what Immanuel Kant had in mind when he wrote his essays "Perpetual Peace" and "Idea for a Universal History with a Cosmopolitan Purpose." Kant believed that it is nature's plan for nations to come to their senses (in the distant future) and join in a federation that will create a global civil society subject to universal law. He admitted that things at present looked bad, and knew that contemporaries might find him

Pollyannaish, but he believed that any other conclusion about the direction of history would require permanent irrationality. It was his hope that "a universal cosmopolitan existence" would eventually be understood by all as "the highest purpose of nature" for man.[10] So cosmopolitans have been quoting him ever since.

Unfortunately, Kant also thought that Europe would be at the helm of nature's world historical adventure. His progressive "system" begins in Greece and on to Rome, skips past the notoriously disappointing fourteen hundred years that followed Constantine, and ends up in Enlightenment Europe, from which he is able to discern "a regular process of improvement in the political constitutions of our continent (which will probably legislate eventually for all other continents)."[11]

The new cosmopolitans are keenly aware of the imperial pedigree of universalism and, thus, of cosmopolitanism. Some do, it is true, tend to be overly selective in their choice of quotes. That last parenthesis is rarely found on new-cosmopolitan pages; it also marks the basic fear among left academics, and not only academics, of what a new cosmopolitanism could degenerate into—namely, a Eurocentric, "rationalist," secular-democratic jihad. The recipe might begin with the GATT negotiations, add some World Bank nostrums about international civil society and environmentally sensitive industrialism, mix in a few Vaclav Havel speeches about the Idea of the West, then define all Third World exports as "dumping." It isn't hard to imagine.

I remember spending an evening several years ago at the American Research Institute in Turkey (ARIT). This was in Istanbul, in the summer. ARIT is a sort of dormitory-with-library for visiting scholars. We all sat around watching the nightly television news bulletins delivered in, I think, English, French, and German, following the Turkish broadcast. This was a quick and competitive way to find out who understood German. (Most of us knew only a little Turkish; English and French didn't count.) On this particular night, it was announced that some group in Europe—could it have been an OSCE committee?—had decided that it was indeed an excellent idea to determine international trade policies according to human-rights standards as set down by whatever European committee this was. I searched for a notebook to jot down the news—of particular interest to Turks, who might anticipate a new tactic for keeping them out of the European Union—but by the time I found a pen the English was gone, the French too, and we were on to the German, at which I was, sadly, hopeless.

So I went to the window and looked out on the twilit city and enjoyed a cigarette (not, at that time, a universal human-rights violation). ARIT had a spectacular view of Istanbul, which was, of course, the headquarters of two cosmopolitan empires in that difficult period between Constantine and Kant, but which was now, in the 1990s, obviously far from the center of power. The cosmopolitan ideals of Byzantines and Ottomans—and, for that matter, Greeks and Romans—were sometimes used coercively. Some Roman Stoics advocated conquest on the principle that Romans were simply more virtuous than anyone else.[12] There's little reason to think that a new, Western, Kantian cosmopolitanism would entirely escape this tendency.[13] It may be that a cosmopolitan is simply someone empowered to decide who is provincial; Robert Pinsky cautions, in his response to Nussbaum's essay, against "the arrogance that would correct *your* provinciality with the cosmopolitanism of *my* terms."[14] Legislating cosmopolitans, to transcend this arrogance, might need to have a degree of self-understanding that would exceed any so far seen in history.

Personally, my favorite neglected Kant quote comes from his popular lectures on anthropology. No, I'm not referring to his insight that Jews have "a not unfounded reputation for being cheaters," or even his belief (expressed in another essay) that blacks are inherently "stupid." I'm thinking of his remarks on the German character: "[The Germans] have no national pride, and are too cosmopolitan to be deeply attached to their homeland."[15] Is this merely further evidence that philosophers know themselves least? Perhaps. But it also suggests to me that philosophy is of limited use in thinking about cosmopolitanism. The cosmopolitan's challenges are not in theory but in practice, and in practice Kant and the cosmopolitan Stoics of classical Greece and Rome are not of great use.

The cosmopolitanism debate has tended to neglect actually existing cosmopolitanisms, an understandable failing in academic discussions. Philosophers and theorists specialize in abstraction. They are fact gatherers only on weekends. But this high-level approach misses much of interest. What are some actually existing cosmopolitanisms? Several of the oldest came about as a result of religio-military expansion, a process of both brutality and subtlety. People of mainly local sympathies encounter Islam, Buddhism, or Catholicism (or Arrianism) and begin reaching out to a wider world of which, through faith, they become something like citizens. This kind of spiritual cosmopolitanism is less common today than previously, though I recall watching, in 1995, a group of young Christians at JFK Airport preparing, with whoops, high fives, and prayers, to fly to Africa—and, in Africa, meeting Muslim propagators on their way to JFK.

A second type of existing cosmopolitanism might be described as antiimperial or extranational—the cosmopolitanism of ideologues and more normal people, left and right, who look outside their situations for social or po-litical models. This is extremely common in politics, whether when a Sene-galese reads Sartre or a Canadian reads Gandhi. (Or, it has to be admitted, when a Calcuttan reads Burke.) Rare indeed is an entirely indigenous politi-cal leader, much less an entirely indigenous politics.

"The market," that First Cause of contemporary thinking, brings about cosmopolitanisms of varied types. (It should be remembered that both Seneca the Younger and Kant referred to increased global trade as leading toward a cosmopolitan world.) There is, of course, merchant cosmopoli-tanism, in which, as Marx put it, the bourgeois is (systematically) chased around the world. Its milieu is the overseas affiliate and the hotel, its coat of arms three laptops rampant beneath the motto "Buy in Bulk." Like religious cosmopolitanism, the mercantile variety is very old. It is somewhat limited in its universalism by virtue of class restraints on membership.

The frequent-flier merchant is not the only traveler, however. There are also smaller merchants, carrying their stuffed suitcases on and off airplanes or buses. Around the northern Mediterranean shores, for example, one sees countless traders stumbling blearily off buses with their loads, or selling out of their cars. They may not be certain where they are at any given moment, but they always know the exchange rates. They resemble in many ways the old seaman culture that preceded the internal combustion engine—the sailors who would evolve cosmopolitan languages, such as the lingua franca of the Levant, never heard before and not to be heard again. Below the petty merchant is the average immigrant, who has only his or her labor to sell. Current anti-immigrant thinking does not see this population as cosmopoli-tan, but as stubborn—unwilling to assimilate. This is simply foolish, as any-one who is an immigrant, or spends time with immigrants, knows. Certainly, immigrants preserve many old ways—that's why American cooking remains superior to English—but immigrant life, especially at the lower social levels, where class membership has fewer entry requirements, is a model of cos-mopolitanism. One need not search long in an American city to find a stock-room worker or janitor who can communicate successfully in more lan-guages than can most Ivy League graduates. I only hope that, when some white population finds itself at a grave disadvantage and must send emi-grants to a prosperous nonwhite country, the economically exiled whites will behave with as much grace and sensitivity as have their brothers and sisters currently come to Europe and America.

Entertainment has also created an actually existing cosmopolitanism. There are the icons—Bruce Lee, Michael Jackson, Madonna (though these, as the Sylvester Stallone case proves, can change rapidly)—but there are also those figures who are less than global, or whose presence in cultures not their own cannot be explained simply by U.S dominance of entertainment production. Bob Marley is one example, as is Jim Reeves, a white Christian crooner whose popularity in Africa and parts of its diaspora finds no decisive explanation in global capitalism.[16] Moreover, Euro-American product can be turned to the most unlikely uses outside its normal circuits, not only in cargo cults but in, for example, a Saipan nightclub, where I heard a nationalist singer go through one of his biggest hits, "Whiter Shade of Pale." (I asked him why it was so popular; he couldn't explain it.) On Saipan, incidentally, the patriot's breakfast has as its centerpiece a slab of Spam. One could accuse the Saipanese nationalists of having a "colonized mind," but that is generally a pejorative, and I don't think it becomes cosmopolitans to humiliate powerless people for their tastes.

All of these actually existing cosmopolitanisms involve individuals with limited choices deciding to enter into something larger than their immediate cultures. The decision to enter into a larger religion than one's own is perhaps the freest of these choices, though physical and material compulsions are often part of the mix. The decision to enter a political realm larger than the local may sometimes be taken at leisure, but is more often made under force of circumstances. More narrowly market-driven choices usually derive from a desire not to be poor, or simply not to die. Entertainment choices are based on a range of options frequently beyond the control of the individual consumer. Such compulsions may explain in part why the mass of real cosmopolitanisms rarely enters into scholarly discussions of cosmopolitanism: to argue that the choice of cosmopolitanism is in some sense self-betraying and made under duress takes away much of its ethical attractiveness. If cosmopolitanism is both indeterminate and inescapable, it becomes difficult to theorize. Yet such is, I think, normally the case.

Sociologically speaking, the new cosmopolitanism of the American academic left may itself be a forced cosmopolitanism. Multiculturalism and postmodernism have become fashion-challenged; based on purely anecdotal evidence, I have the impression that resentful white men on tenure committees, longing for a return to their own parochial universalism, have begun to seize their historical moment; campuses have become significantly less white over the past decade; and, most important, since the end of the Cold War global capitalism is no longer something left academics can merely swear at. On one hand, the global market has become a much more real presence in the lives of developed-world leftists; on the other hand, opposition to market globalization has become, to a great extent, a right-wing activity, and that makes any simple anticapitalism a dangerous pursuit. When the enemy's forces seem more universal than ever, some leftists will naturally want to turn from the particular to the universal—especially when the enemy has, simultaneously, begun to promote its own, nationalist particularisms. Even communitarian theorists are talking about retaining a dose of universalism.

It has become a commonplace that the "global market" is homogenizing the world's cultures. (I'm taking a wait-and-see attitude, because some Stoics said the same thing, and that was a long time ago.) It is also a commonplace that capital must become more heterogeneous, or multicultural, in order to find new markets and so continue expansion. This is the kind of contradiction on which an international economy thrives. How does a cosmopolitan fit into it? Americans supposedly have the option of patriotic cosmopolitanism, which seems fine to me as long as we don't fool ourselves into believing that it has any importance beyond our shores. (Michael Lind's version seems to come with a cutoff date—an isolationist cosmopolitanism, which just shows how a good idea locally can go wrong when applied globally.) A second option—seeking out and praising those cultures, whether multinational or purely local, that "resist" the market—is often attractive but can seem curiously self-subverting. After all, if you honor only cultures that resist some notion of global capitalism, then you are still reproducing the idea that an economic system provides the basic measure of cultural value. When Arjun Appadurai writes of "imagined worlds" that, ideally, "are able to contest and sometimes even subvert the imagined worlds of the official mind and of the entrepreneurial mentality that surround them," he may be damning with faint praise.[17] Cultures defined in terms of the global market are just that, and the sad results of such a mind-set are easy to find: since 1989, a growing number of thinkers have followed Francis Fukuyama in arguing that "culture" is the determinant of economic success, a belief that can quickly lead to an extreme conservatism and the writing-off, so to speak, of loser cultures.

Cosmopolitanism has a long history of arrogance, as Pinsky has noted. It seems to me that the best thing the new cosmopolitanism has going for it is the glimmerings of a fine humility. As far as cosmopolitanism is concerned, I would venture that the rest of the world has almost nothing to learn from the West. Those aspects of Western culture that make sense as universals are already well-known and, to the extent they can operate as universals, are inherently non-Western. As for the extension of cosmopolitan ethical practice, I tend to think that will come from the non-Western world, which is today the more natural forcing ground of cosmopolitanism. Among other things, those outside the West have a far greater self-interest in true—that is, non-imperial (and non-"rational")—cosmopolitanism.

One hot afternoon in Dakar, I happened to be at the U.S. Embassy during a meeting on human rights. The visiting civilian experts spoke about democracy and free speech and so on, an entirely predictable address to which the assembled Senegalese listened politely. Then their turn came. One military man started talking about the precious uniqueness of Senegalese culture on his way to a defense of polygamy, but he undermined his argument by giggling from time to time and did not seem to believe it himself. Everyone else, male and female, just laughed at him. The rest of the Senegalese participants' remarks centered on one simple question: Is it a human right not to die of starvation? The visiting American experts had seen this coming, but they nevertheless had little to say except *no*. And the Senegalese kept on asking, until everyone, realizing what was happening, began to laugh. The joke, of course, was that we were supposed to be discussing universal human rights, but it had become apparent that one big right was missing from the list. From the Senegalese perspective, this was due to an unfortunate shortcoming distinctive to the ethnic group of white people, a shortcoming for which this blindered Western tribe had to be pitied. The Senegalese did not attack the American experts. They reached out to them, with generosity and humor, in a manner that can only be described as cosmopolitan.

Notes

1. Peter Green, *Alexander of Macedon, 356–323 B.C.: A Historical Biography* (Berkeley: University of California Press, 1991), 123.
2. David A. Hollinger, *Postethnic America: Beyond Multiculturalism* (New York: Basic Books, 1995), 5. I do wonder how new this sensitivity to roots is. Post-Alex Haley genealogy research is indeed newish, but there are many kinds of roots, and many types of sensitivity. A little more than thirty years ago, several states were still under Jim Crow laws that were quite sensitive to roots. Some private clubs still are. Sensitivity about genealogy per se—a concern with lines of descent—is probably characteristic of most societies in most times. This is worth keeping in mind, as polemicists against multiculturalism sometimes behave as if a sensitivity to roots really is a juvenile mood inspired by a TV miniseries, and therefore has no place in serious pursuits such as scholarship and journalism.

   I should also emphasize that being a "citizen of the world" is not always a matter of proud choice. Oliver Goldsmith's narrator, Lien Chi Altangi, in *The Citizen of the World* (1762), is saddled with his universal status to the point where some English dinner partners refuse to admit he's Chinese: an author "attempted to prove that I had nothing of the true Chinese cut in my visage; showed that my cheek-bones should have been higher, and my forehead broader. In short, he almost reasoned me out of my country, and effectually persuaded the rest of the company to be of his opinion." Being reasoned out of one's country must have seemed no small possibility in those Enlightenment times. Goldsmith wrote his parody following on the success of Montesquieu's *Persian Letters*.

3. Mitchell Cohen, "Rooted Cosmopolitanism," *Dissent* (Fall 1992); Bruce Ackerman, "Rooted Cosmopolitanism," *Ethics* 104 (1994): 516–35; both cited in Hollinger, *Postethnic America*, 5. Does anyone want a truly rootless cosmopolitanism? Even Fougeret de Monbron, author of *Le Cosmopolite ou le citoyen du monde* (1750), hate-filled as he was, and an ardent uprooter, found after his wanderings: "I hated my homeland, and all the uncivilities of the various peoples among whom I have lived have reconciled me with it. If I had reaped no other profit from my travels save that one, I should regret neither their cost nor the strain they caused." He is cited in Julia Kristeva's *Strangers to Ourselves*, trans. Leon S. Roudiez (New York: Columbia University Press, 1991), 142. Kristeva herself leans more toward Montesquieu's famous passage, from *The Spirit of the Laws*, that begins with the relation between self and family and ends, "If I knew something useful to my homeland and detrimental to Europe, or else useful to Europe and detrimental to Mankind, I would consider it a crime."

4. Michael Lind, *The Next American Nation: The New Nationalism and the Fourth American Revolution* (New York: Free Press, 1995). The voluntarism of which Hollinger writes seems both ethically appealing and historically dubious. For a very different approach to both the ethics and the historiography, see Joseph R. Levenson's *Revolution and Cosmopolitanism: The Western Stage and the Chinese Stages* (Berkeley: University of California Press, 1971), especially Frederic Wakeman's foreword concerning the relationship between Levenson's choosing, so to speak, of Jewishness and his approach to Chinese cosmopolitanism.

5. Hollinger, *Postethnic America*, 170–72.

6. Martha C. Nussbaum, "Patriotism and Cosmopolitanism," *Boston Review* 19, no. 5 (1994). Some of the *Boston Review* material, plus six new essays, has been published in Nussbaum's *For Love of Country: Debating the Limits of Patriotism* (Boston: Beacon, 1996). Rorty's essay appeared in the February 13, 1994, issue of the *New York Times*.

7. Nussbaum, "Patriotism and Cosmopolitanism," 4. This is a more aggressive tack than Nussbaum takes in her *The Therapy of Desire: Theory and Practice in Hellenistic Ethics* (Princeton, N.J.: Princeton University Press, 1994), where she worries about the wispiness and class exclusivity of the Greek pedagogic model: "What does one do with the real people of the world, while waiting for politics to become rational? It may be true that philosophy can speak to the design of institutions; but it can rarely do anything to make its conceptions reality. Alexander the Great was not a good Aristotelian pupil, and that was a better shot at shaping the world than most philosophers will ever get" (100–101). It certainly was; and the example of Alexander would preoccupy later generations, because his mad dash east toward Ocean symbolized a whole set of burning issues. Should one—as a Greek, or Roman—build an empire, or stay home? How can one know when the pursuit of glory crosses into madness? Since Nussbaum emphasizes the Stoics as cosmopolitans, we might look at the Senecas, father and son, and their thoughts on empire. Seneca the Elder made the question "Should Alexander sail Ocean?" the first of his rhetorical exercises, the *Suasoriae*. A deep anxiety about the possible impiety of such a sailing comes vividly across, and is, indeed, frequently aired in classical literature (e.g., Lucan in *The Civil War*, Pliny in *The Natural History*). Seneca quotes Pedo (on Germanicus rather than Alexander): "Are we looking for races / Beyond, in another clime, a new world untouched by breezes? / The Gods

call us back, forbid us to know the end of creation / With mortal eyes. Why do our oars violate seas that are not ours, / Waters that are holy? Why do we disturb the quiet home of the Gods?" (1.15). Seneca the Younger, cited by Nussbaum as a representative Stoic cosmopolitan, kept his father's worries, and in *Natural Questions* states, "The greatest contribution to human peace would be for the seas to be closed off." He is quoted in James S. Romm's excellent *The Edges of the Earth in Ancient Thought: Geography, Exploration, and Fiction* (Princeton, N.J.: Princeton University Press, 1992), which sensitively explores the tragic element in classical imperial thought. It is worth recalling that the later Stoics tended to believe that the Roman Empire was an earthly manifestation of divine reason working itself out in the lives of men.

Stoic or not, classical writers had, of course, many and varied opinions on the desirability of empire and the related question of cosmopolitanism. One prominent belief was that expansion undertaken to increase the stock of knowledge could be defended as good. (As noted earlier, Stoics were prominent in the ranks of classical geographers, natural scientists/ethnographers, and world historians.) The coupling of an extension of political-economic power with natural-scientific ambition would also characterize much European thinking in the Renaissance and Enlightenment and, eventually, in North America. Colonial intellectuals and intellectual politicians very much saw ethnography as both a true branch of the natural sciences and a political activity. William Bartram (1739–1823), like Montesquieu, both pursued this science and, memorably, parodied it: "I am not for levelling things down to the simplicity of Indians, yet I may be allowed to conjecture that we may possibly better our condition in civil society, by paying some more respect to and impartially examining the system of legislation, religion, morality, and economy of these despised, persecuted *wild people*, or as they are learnedly called, *bipeds*—I suppose meaning a creature different from quadrupeds." William Bartram, *Travels and Other Writings* (New York: Library of America, 1996), 550. Bartram, unusually for any era, deeply admired both Montesquieu and the Creeks, speculating at one point that "the same spirit that dictated to Montesquieu the idea of a rational government, seems to superintend and guide the Indians" (536).

To my mind, an attractive cosmopolitanism would have to have a sense of tragedy, a sense of humor, and a sense of limits—that is, a strong sense of history.

Actually, Alexander was not that poor a pupil of Aristotle, who wrote in *Politics:* "Those who live in a cold climate and in Europe are full of spirit, but wanting in intelligence and skill; and therefore they retain comparative freedom, but have no political organization, and are incapable of ruling over others. Whereas the natives of Asia are intelligent and inventive, but they are wanting in spirit, and therefore they are always in a state of subjection and slavery. But the Hellenic race, which is situated between them, is likewise intermediate in character, being high-spirited and also intelligent. Hence it continues free, and is the best-governed of any nation, and, if it could be formed into one state, would be able to rule the world" (VII.1327b).

8. Bruce Robbins, "The Weird Heights: On Cosmopolitanism, Feeling, and Power," *differences* 7, no. 1 (1995): 167.

9. *New York Times*, May 12, 1996, A3.

10. Immanuel Kant, "Idea for a Universal History with a Cosmopolitan Purpose," in *Kant's Political Writings*, trans. H. B. Nisbet (Cambridge: Cambridge University Press, 1970), 51.

11. Ibid., 52.

12. Karl Galinsky, for example, in his *Augustan Culture: An Interpretive Introduction* (Princeton, N.J.: Princeton University Press, 1996), writes of "a steady tradition, developed especially by Stoic philosophers friendly to Rome, such as Posidonius, of

equating the justifiable conquest of other peoples not with the right of the stronger, but the duty of the better, 'better' entailing, among other things, higher moral and ethical standards" (133).

13. In 1791 we find William Bartram wondering whether the Indians "were deserving of the severe censure which prevailed against them among the white people, that they were incapable of civilization. In the consideration of this important subject it will be necessary to inquire, whether they were inclined to adopt the European modes of civil society? Whether such a reformation could be obtained, without using coercive or violent means? And lastly, whether such a revolution would be productive of real benefit to them, and consequently beneficial to the public?" *Travels*, 24.

14. Robert Pinsky, response to Nussbaum, "Patriotism and Cosmopolitanism," *Boston Review* 19, no. 5 (1994): 12.

15. The references to Jews and to the German cosmopolitan character are in Immanuel Kant, *Anthropology from a Pragmatic Point of View*, trans. Mary J. Gregor (The Hague: Martinus Nijhoff, 1974), 77, 180. Kant refers to blacks as stupid in his *Observations on the Feeling of the Beautiful and the Sublime*, trans. John T. Goldthwait (Berkeley: University of California Press, 1960), 113. "The Negroes of Africa," he notes earlier, "by nature have no feeling that rises above the trifling" (110). Interestingly, the *Observations* end with these and other passages concerning blacks and American "savages" as a *quos contra* buildup for Kant's urging of cosmopolitan education. Having finished with Native Americans, he briefly surveys Europe's long decline from classical civilization into triviality and barbarism, and its recent recovery in his own day, then unwinds a final sentence: "Nothing now is more to be desired than that the false glitter, which so easily deceives, should not remove us unawares from noble simplicity; but especially that the as yet undiscovered secret of education be rescued from the old illusions, in order early to elevate the moral feeling in the breast of every young world citizen to a lively sensitivity, so that all delicacy of feeling may not amount to merely the fleeting and idle enjoyment of judging, with more or less taste, what goes on around us" (116).

16. See Mark Schone, "Gentleman Juju," *Journal of Country Music* 18, 1 (1987): 5–8.

17. Arjun Appadurai, "Disjuncture and Difference in the Global Cultural Economy," *Public Culture* 2, no. 2 (1990): 7.

Comparative Cosmopolitanisms

Bruce Robbins

In the much-publicized backlash against the left's influence in the academy, there has been a strange coincidence. On the one hand, literature departments are accused by the right of abandoning "Culture," capital C, in favor of *multiculturalism*, defined by a writer for the *New York Times Magazine* as "the drive to include non-Western materials in every possible course."[1] On the other hand, in variants of the sad, familiar story of academicization-as-decline, literature departments are also accused of falling from the commonness of culture into the privacy of *professionalism*—self-enclosed, jargon-ridden, hypertheoretical, ignoring the common reader and lacking any general human concern. Academics as a professional "conspiracy against the laity," minority constituencies who blindly insist on seeing their numbers and cultural differences recognized in the curriculum, without concern for the value of their cultural exhibits as judged by any more general standard—in each case the target is the same: the particular as opposed to the universal, the "special interest" pressing for its own advantage at the expense of the common good.

There is some reason to be skeptical about any version of the common good that can ally against it two such unlike terms as *non-Western cultures* and *American professionals*. But this is just the alliance that I want to examine. My premise will be that the right is right. Not in its opposition of the universal and the particular, about which more below, nor in its tendentious versions of professionalism or multiculturalism. It is right in the (perhaps unconscious) implication that the new worldliness of the Anglo-American humanities, our recent reaching out to world literature and to colonial, postcolonial, and minority discourse, is somehow related to the local self-interest, the social or institutional being of critics as a group.[2] To this premise must be added, however, the question of whether to relate them is, as both right and left often assume, necessarily to make an accusation. I will answer that it is not. Cultural criticism in the United States has often claimed to be oppositional by virtue of its *un*worldliness—its joint appeal to a restricted, elevated canon and to Arnoldian or Weberian disinterestedness. Both appeals have been largely discredited in recent years (perhaps because it became increasingly difficult to believe, with the increasing academicization of intellectual life, that institutions servicing so many thousands of people a year could be entirely staffed by, and engaged in producing, mavericks and outsiders). But the brouhaha in the press over multiculturalism and the continuing vulnerability of tenured and untenured radicals to attack, not least from themselves, suggest that no alternative description of where intellectuals think they stand (especially when they are not being Eurocentrists) or what intellectual activities they engage in (especially when they are speaking about other cultures) has successfully taken the place of the former ideal. This essay is an attempt to explore an alternative description. Now, perhaps, it is time to consider the new brand of intellectual oppositionality that might be emerging from what I call our new worldliness—worldliness in the two senses of (1) planetary expansiveness of subject matter on the one hand, and (2) unembarrassed acceptance of professional self-interest on the other.

Belonging, Being Situated, Being Specific

The right is clearly wrong—indeed, it is contradicting itself—when it suggests that multiculturalism and professionalism are related as parallel versions of particularism. Applied to these two objects, the charge of particularism indicates not a parallel but an intersection. For if professional critics *were* hermetically sealed in an ivory tower, then why *would* they respond to "pressure" from "minorities"? If academics were as self-enclosed as we are told (and as some of us appear on occasion to believe), then why would they *support* multiculturalism? Between these two cases of supposed particularism, there would in fact seem to be some sort of communication, some common language, common interest, common ground. But what ground could that be?

When we speak today of world literature or global culture, we are not naming an optional extension of the canon. We are speaking of a new framing of the whole that revalues both unfamiliar and long-accepted genres, that produces new concepts and criteria of judgment, and that affects even those critics who never "do" world literature or colonial discourse at all—that affects all critics, that is, by shifting criticism's whole sense of intellectual enterprise. In an unprecedented and somewhat mysterious way, what it means to be an intellectual or a critic seems to have become worldly or transnational or—to use a willfully provocative word—cosmopolitan. But this cosmopolitanism does not yet seem to have moved forward to the stage of conscious self-definition, nor has it been seized upon, therefore, as a possible means of self-legitimation or self-defense. If the neoconservatives have been quick to attack the emergent or perhaps already dominant sensibility that supports multicultural inclusiveness, they have been allowed to keep the term *cosmopolitanism* for themselves. Contrasting it to particularism or "cultural egocentricity," Dinesh D'Souza, for example, cites it with full approval.[3] But the left meanwhile, groping for a line of defense stronger than "diversity for diversity's sake," has almost completely shunned the term.[4] And this is in large part, I think, *because* it connects international or global subject matter with the embarrassingly local placement of intellectuals in relatively privileged institutions.

Beyond the adjectival sense of "belonging to all parts of the world; not restricted to any one country or its inhabitants," the word *cosmopolitan* immediately evokes the image of a privileged person: someone who can claim to be a "citizen of the world" by virtue of independent means, expensive tastes, and a globe-trotting lifestyle. The association of cosmopolitan globality with privilege—classy consumption, glossy cleavage, CNN, modems, faxes, Club Med, and the Trilateral Commission—is so deeply unattractive to us, I think, because deep down we tend to agree with the right that, especially when employed as academics, intellectuals *are* a "special interest" group representing nothing but themselves.

This is not to say that the privileges associated with cosmopolitanism can be, as the saying goes, left unexamined. The first entry under "cosmopolitan" in the *Oxford English Dictionary*, from John Stuart Mill's *Political Economy*, suggests why left-wing critics have recoiled from it: "Capital," Mill wrote in 1848, "is becoming more and more cosmopolitan." Cosmopolitanism would seem to mimic capital in seizing for itself the privilege (to paraphrase Wall Street) of "knowing no boundaries"—which is also the gendered privilege of knowing no bodies, of being, in Donna Haraway's words, "a conquering gaze from nowhere," a gaze that claims "the power to see and not be seen, to represent while escaping representation."[5] We may also remember that the gendered and classed privilege of mobile observation in a world of tight borders and limited visibility corresponds to a traditional self-image of criticism itself—criticism as disinterestedness, neutrality, objectivity—that the left rightfully shies away from. The very act of comparison, as in comparative literature, can seem to signal a liberation from insularity and national prejudice into the one true judgment. And when the international range of comparison suddenly and dramatically expands to include the world outside Europe, there is the danger that, under cover of the most democratic intentions, what will be reinvented is the old "free-floating intellectual," or an even older version of privileged impartiality. The most visibly ineligible example is perhaps V. S. Naipaul, who has recently been singing the praises of what he calls "our universal civilization."[6] Naipaul presents himself (in Rob Nixon's words) as "the ultimate literary *apatride*, the most comprehensively uprooted of twentieth-century writers and most bereft of national traditions." And he does so in order to lay claim to

Arnoldian objectivity, to a "secure, reputable tradition of extratraditional-ism"—that is, to "detachment" in the geographic, empirical, and political senses of the word.[7]

As an image of criticism, detachment is deservedly obsolete. It is an article of our contemporary faith that, like Naipaul, intellectuals and academics are not detached but *situated*—for many of us, say, situated as metropolitans, or situated as professionals. To say this, however, is already to feel some impious stirrings of doubt. What precisely do we mean by the situatedness we devoutly claim to believe in? What excess baggage does it carry? How tightly does it restrict access to the other places we may come from, the other places we communicate with? How far can this metaphor of locality be reconciled with the expansive awareness or worldliness to which we also aspire?

In an effort to begin thinking through this piece of piety, let us consider, for example, Tim Brennan's application of the term *cosmopolitan* to Salman Rushdie. Brennan speaks of the "almost boastful cosmopolitanism" of "third world metropolitan celebrities," including Rushdie, who are celebrated at the expense of "the domestic or indigenous artist in the process of an actual anticolonial struggle."[8] In another article, he places Rushdie in a group of "cosmopolitan commentators on the Third World, who offer an *inside view* of formerly submerged peoples for target reading publics in Europe and North America in novels that comply with metropolitan tastes." The message of such cosmopolitans—a critique of Third World nationalism and Third World elites—"is very familiar to us," Brennan concludes, "because it has been easier to embrace in our metropolitan circles than the explicit challenges of, say, the Salvadoran protest-author Manlio Argueta." Thus the metropolis understands the Third World in terms of a "disengagement" and a "rootlessness" that are "not at all characteristic of the 'counter-hegemonic aesthetics' of much Third World writing."[9]

This argument might be classified as strongly reader or reception determined. According to Brennan, the decisive reality of the text, a social reality pinpointed with the authority of a lexicon borrowed from market research, is the "target reading publics" of Europe and North America: the "tastes" of the metropolitan consumer. In much the same way, Rob Nixon argues that Naipaul is not an exile but *really* a metropolitan. "The introduction of the category 'metropolitan' helps dispel the myth of Naipaul's homelessness."[10]

To catch an author in the act of belonging to the metropolis, even one who claims to belong nowhere, is a two-finger exercise, given that we believe in advance that everyone belongs somewhere, that there is no alternative to belonging. But the exercise becomes more complicated as soon as we ask what it *means* to belong, or how many different ways of belonging there may be. Absolute homelessness is indeed a myth, and so is cosmopolitanism in its strictly negative sense of "free[dom] from national limitations or attachments"—as the doctrine, in George Boas's words, "that nationality is insignificant from every point of view."[11] But this negative sense of "cosmopolitan" coexists from the outset in tension with more positive ones: with the scientific sense of "worldwide distribution," and with the more general sense of "belonging" to parts of the world other than one's nation. In any given case, it seems reasonable to try to sustain this tension, valuing the negative relation to nationality without giving up an insistence on belonging—an insistence that includes the possibility of presence in other places, dispersed but real forms of membership, a density of overlapping allegiances rather than the abstract emptiness of nonallegiance.

After all, we know that in other contexts "grounding," "placement," and "location" are tricky metaphors. Whether mediated by the Marxist global division of labor or the psychoanalytic model of selfhood, the notion that we are where we are not is an equal and opposite constituent of the new common sense. If our supposed distances are really localities, as we piously repeat, it is also true that there are distances *within* what we thought were *merely* localities. No localization can be assumed to determine absolutely. If it could, then the charge of "metropolitanism" that falls on "celebrities" like Naipaul and Rushdie would also have to fall on the metropolitan critic who *makes* that charge, whatever his or her own political intentions and degree of celebrity.[12] Situatedness would indeed be our faith, in the most dogmatic sense, if we allowed it to suggest the surrogate divinity of a single, absolutely determining cause and if we did so, moreover, largely as a masochistic means of punishing and paralyzing ourselves.

Not enough imagination has gone into the different modalities of situatedness-in-displacement. And one of the places where we must learn to see a more complex function or office of placement is the university. It says something about the humanities as institutionalized in the university, for example, that they can both overappreciate the rootlessness of the world's Naipauls and, *for reasons that are no less institutional,* feed off what Brennan calls "protest-authors" as well. It says—and this is the beginning of an answer to the right's charge that professional scholars esoterically ignore the general welfare—that critics have to legitimate themselves to the public, that they do so as transmitters of cultural artifacts whose value to the public is a site of interpretive contest, and that those who criticize Naipaul as a metropolitan are simply engaging in that contest, which is to say behaving in no less professional a manner, obeying no less professional a logic, than those who delight to see their prejudices confirmed by Naipaul's trashing of the postcolonial nations. The political differences that count are not differences about professionalism as such.[13]

Professional self-legitimation can of course proceed by universalizing those values ("Western culture") of which the critic is custodian and transmitter. But professional self-legitimation can also base itself on the premise that all universals are merely particulars in disguise. The anticosmopolitan jargon of the authentically particular and the authentically local provides no escape from or political alternative to the realm of the professional. It simply conceals the exemplification, representation, and generalization in which any intellectual work, professional or not, is inescapably involved, its own included.

Consider, to take another example, how the piety of the particular functions within the most basic and apparently neutral of scholarly concepts: the concept of specificity. In her seminal essay "Under Western Eyes: Feminist Scholarship and Colonial Discourses," Chandra Mohanty objects that First World feminist scholarship has often used the category "woman" in a universalizing way "with little regard for historical specificities." Her objection to "ethnocentric universalism" in the name of specific situations was extremely useful then, and it remains indispensable now.[14] Nevertheless, it entitles one to inquire into the specific situation in which it itself is formulated and received. What about the (presumably "Western") logic that values and rewards this insistence on ("Eastern"?) specificity? Why should the professional discourse of metropolitan critics greet the call for specificity with such suspiciously unanimous enthusiasm?

One answer to these questions appears in Mohanty's counterexample of scholarship that is *not* "ethnocentric universalism," the example of a "careful, politically focussed local analysis" of lacemakers in Narsapur, India. This analysis leads to the conclusion, Mohanty says, that

> there is no easy generalization in the direction of "women" in India, or "women in the third world"; nor is there a reduction of . . . the exploitation of the lacemakers to cultural explanations about the passivity or obedience that might characterize these women and their situation. . . . These Narsapur women are not mere victims of the production process."[15]

I am in full sympathy with what I take to be Mohanty's intent here, but the possible consequences of her phrasing go far beyond that intent. If we agree that there is "no easy generalization," don't we want to retain the right to *difficult* generalization? Critics other than Mohanty might easily conclude, otherwise, that generalization *as such* is politically undesirable, whereas generalizing is precisely what Mohanty is doing. What she uncovers among the Narsapur women is not so much a set of particulars as an instance of a rather general rule: the rule that exploitation will always be met with resistance. As Mohanty herself notes, the finding of active agency among the Narsapur women registers nothing but that specific generalization that symmetrically opposes Orientalist generalizations about women's "passivity" and "obedience." "Specificity," in other words, functions here as an innocuous mask that hides not only a claim to epistemological authority, but also, more significantly, the unnecessarily camouflaged transmission of *counter-universals, alternative* generalizations.[16]

I am trying to suggest three things. First, that the act of finding "agency" in text after text corresponds to a logic that is as much a part of our professional or metropolitan situatedness as the act of neglecting or denying it would be. Second, that a critic's transmission of this (or any other) cultural value should not disguise itself as a defense of the particular, the local, and the specific, because it involves generalizations that are no less dramatically synthetic—the people united will never be defeated, the unconquerable human spirit, or whatever—than the Orientalist stereotypes they are marshaled against. And third, that if we do not need "easy generalizations," we do need difficult ones—for example, the more difficult though less pious procedure of *not* assuming agency to be everywhere present, but trying to explain why it is where it is and why it isn't where it isn't.

It is arguable that, as a critical procedure or paradigm, the formulaic recovery of inspirational agency may foster political quiescence, whereas a more politicized criticism might in fact result from a focus on vaster, less anthropomorphic, less hortatory structures. After all, why *do* we all value agency so highly? As an abstraction that lends itself equally well to the Marxism of Lukács and the humanism of Matthew Arnold, agency legitimates the specific politics of neither one. What it does legitimate is the public representativeness of criticism as such, its responsiveness to the active voice or will of the people. When the academic humanist pulls this particular rabbit from his or her text, the point is both that the people make their own history and, however implicitly, that the academic who is representing them as so doing, by transmitting this tidbit of the cultural heritage, is him- or herself acting in the interests of the people thereby, including the people who make much of that academic's own immediate history—the public legislators and private funders who pass judgment on academic legitimacy.

However desirable agency may be, there is at any rate no inherent connection between it and the particular, the specific, the local.[17] Here an edifyingly unliterary parallel presents itself: the so-called localities debate that has raged over the past few years among radical geographers. The move in geography to study the smaller, subregional units known as localities came at a time when the worldwide restructuring of the capitalist economy seemed at once to be increasing the scale of global interconnectedness and, in direct proportion, decreasing the power of the human agents concerned to grasp or resist its operations. In scaling down the size of the units studied, geographers were hoping to draw on the empirical authority of the particular, or rather were hoping *through* that authority to sustain a waning illusion of agency. Hidden away in the miniaturizing precision of "locality," with its associations of presence and uniqueness, empirical concreteness, complete experience, and accessible subjectivity, has been the nostalgia for a collective subject-in-action that is no longer so easy to localize. As one essay in the debate concludes, *"We do not have some privileged access to understanding patterns of human agency simply by studying localities."*[18] Thinking small is not enough; agency is not to be had so predictably. The unit of coherence where transformative energies have the best chance of seizing hold is not predictable in advance; it might well be larger, not smaller. As Neil Smith writes: "It is not clear in the current restructuring that, in economic terms at least, coherent regions continue to exist as subdivisions of the national rather than international economy."[19]

This suggests the case for a certain cosmopolitanism—not one obsessed with embodying a preconceived totality, but one that does not judge in advance the macropolitical scale of its units, that sees "worlding" as a process, to quote Gayatri Spivak, and a process in which more than one "world" may be realized, where "worlds" may be contested.[20] *Cosmos* (world) in *cosmopolitan* originally meant simply "order" or "adornment"—as in cosmetics—and was only later extended metaphorically to refer to "the world." Cosmetics preceded totality. Worlding, then, might be seen as "making up" the face of the planet—something that can be done in diverse ways. At the same time, the case for this more modest cosmopolitanism is also a case for a certain professionalism—a professionalism that, without presumption of ultimate totalizing certainty, believes in its own intellectual powers of generalization, abstraction, synthesis, and representation at a distance, and in the process of putting them to use—that believes, one might say, in its own *work*.

Discrepant Cosmopolitanisms: James Clifford

Here, then, is a task: to drop the conversation-stopping, always-reversible charge of "privilege" and instead to discriminate degrees of complacency, degrees of service to the general welfare, within an overarching acknowledgment that the professional producers and transmitters of knowledge are *of course* not motivated solely (if at all) by pure, disinterested altruism. This effort can begin where the cosmopolitan's privileges are most grossly accepted. In an essay titled "Cosmopolitans and Locals in World Culture," Ulf Hannerz defines the figure of the cosmopolitan by a series of exclusions. "Anybody who moves about in the world," he writes, is not a cosmopolitan.[21] Nor is it sufficient to have "a willingness to engage with the Other" (239). Cosmopolitans are not tourists, for whom they are likely to be mistaken, because "tourists are not participants" (242). They are not exiles, because the exile's involvement with another culture has been *"forced"* (242). "Most ordinary labour migrants are not cosmopolitans either. For them going away may be, ideally, home plus higher income; often the involvement with another culture is not a fringe benefit but a necessary cost, to be kept as low as possible" (243). "The perspective of the cosmopolitan must entail relationships to a plurality of cultures understood as distinct entities" (239).

At this point, if not before, one becomes aware of how self-serving this process of definition is. Imagining cultures as "distinct entities" makes them into objects of artistic appreciation for the passing connoisseur; it is a way of imagining that all privileges of mobility and comparison inhere in the cosmopolitan observer. As the definition narrows further, it accumulates still more privileges. Cosmopolitans, like expatriates and ex-expatriates, "are people who have *chosen* to live abroad" (emphasis added). They know "that they can go home when it suits them." Today, this knowledge is less often guaranteed by independent means than by the individuals' occupations. "Transnational cultures today tend to be more or less clearcut occupational cultures" (243). What occupations? The climactic example of transnational occupational culture is—to no one's surprise—the intellectuals.

This more or less shameless use of the new global culture to reinvent or relegitimate Mannheim's "free-floating" intellectuals seems to corroborate, once again, the fear that cosmopolitanism is only a screen for privilege and self-aggrandizement. But this is not the precise moral I draw from it. Hannerz's criteria for true cosmopolitanism share a good deal with traditional aesthetics. In his view, cosmopolitanism becomes an autonomous, unforced appreciation of coherence and novelty among distinct cultural entities. The editor of the volume in which Hannerz's essay appears, Mike Featherstone, stresses the same point when he describes "transnational intellectuals" as those who "seek out and adopt a reflexive, metacultural or *aesthetic* stance to divergent cultural experiences."[22] In my own view, it is this aestheticism, with its presumption of inequality and its spectatorial absence of commitment to change that inequality, that disqualifies Hannerz's essay from representing the new transnationality of intellectual work. What we have to object to is the particular position that the essay tries to legitimate, and not the effort of self-legitimation itself.

By producing a new, international pedigree for the old idea of the intellectual as autonomous critic, Hannerz's essay joins the genre of the allegory of vocation. What I call allegories of vocation are critical works that, while doing whatever other interpretive tasks they set themselves, also perform a second, most often implicit, function: they invent and arrange their concepts and characters so as to narrativize and argue for the general value and significance of the intellectual vocation they exemplify. Examples include Raymond Williams's *Culture and Society*, which tells the story of how leftist critics like Williams himself arose from romanticism to write works like *Culture and Society*, and Gilbert and Gubar's *The Madwoman in the Attic*, which turns *Jane Eyre* into a paradigm for the rise of the twentieth-century feminist critic.[23] But I have not *criticized* any of these works by identifying the genre to which they belong. If we accept the premise that we *want* to do significant work—that we want the privilege, if you like, of doing work that is more significant than earning a living—then we must desire and value texts that help explain, to ourselves and to others, why a particular sort of work is meaningful and valuable. We can criticize the aestheticism of this cosmopolitan, in other words, but not the fact that the essay makes a case for intellectuals. What should be set against it is another case for intellectuals that mobilizes cosmopolitanism differently.

As a more desirable alternative within the same genre, then, I will take up the rich and influential work of historian of anthropology James Clifford, which has been inspiring to students seeking a sense of intellectual vocation in the confusingly transnational space of contemporary knowledge. It has been as inspiring as it has, I think, in part because it has struggled in an exemplary way not only with our ambivalence about cosmopolitanism, but also, less visibly, with our ambivalence about professionalism.

Clifford's position on cosmopolitanism seems to be expressed unequivocally in his influential review of Edward Said's *Orientalism* (1980).[24] There the term *cosmopolitan* is unmistakably derogatory. "Said's basic values," Clifford says, "are cosmopolitan." This statement concludes Clifford's case that "humanist common denominators . . . are meaningless, since they bypass the local cultural codes that make personal experience articulate." "The privilege of standing above cultural particularism, of aspiring to the universalist power that speaks for humanity . . . is a privilege invented by a totalizing Western liberalism" (263). What must always be avoided, Clifford declares, even if the concept of culture itself is eventually abandoned, is "the positing of cosmopolitan essences" (274-75).

In this context, "totalizing Western liberalism" seems to name what is wrong both with cosmopolitanism and with professionalism. Clifford's essay "On Ethnographic Self-Fashioning: Conrad and Malinowski," first published in 1985, has thus been taken as an undermining of the scientific model of ethnographic authority that Malinowski did so much to make the professional standard, an undermining carried out in large part by invidious juxtaposition with the messily literary, unsystematic, unprofessional figure of Conrad. "By professionalizing fieldwork," Clifford writes, "anthropology transformed a widespread predicament into a scientific method" (95). Conrad, who acknowledges the same (cosmopolitan) predicament without escaping into scientific method, thus seems to embody the literary as an alternative to the professional.

If this were all, it would be manifestly insufficient, for, as Paul Rabinow points out, it would leave Clifford no way of acknowledging the fact that, however "literary" his style, in relation to the anthropologists who are his subjects, he too is playing a professional role. "There is only one 'professional,' so to speak, in the crowd," Rabinow comments. "For, whereas all the others mentioned are practicing anthropologists, James Clifford has created and occupied the role of ex officio scribe to our scribblings. . . . Clifford takes us as his natives." A "new specialty is currently in the process of self-definition," Rabinow says. But Clifford's "own writing and situation," which define this specialty, "are left unexamined."[25]

This sort of tit for tat, in which injurious epithets like "specialist," "professional," and "metropolitan" are asked to stand in for substantive political judgment, must always be the result as long as it is assumed that to go ahead and *examine* one's professional "writing and situation," to open one's eyes finally and painfully to the "situatedness" of a metropolitan or a cosmopolitan, is ipso facto to judge oneself intolerably contaminated and self-contradictory. One of the extraordinary strengths of Clifford's work is that this is an assumption he has come to question. If one looks more closely at the Conrad/Malinowski essay, one sees that in fact neither "professional" nor "cosmopolitan" functions there as a term of opprobrium. A struggle with "cosmopolitanism" (95), we are told, is something Conrad and Malinowski have in common. And the essay is about a "difficult accession to innovative *professional* expression" (96; emphasis added) that they also have in common.

And Clifford himself has this in common with them as well. The last line of this extremely moving essay is an ambiguous quotation from Conrad's Marlow: "You see me, whom you know." The point of the ambiguity seems clear: the essay is itself an allegory of vocation describing a "difficult acces-sion to innovative professional expression" shared not only by Conrad and Malinowski, but by Clifford too, along with many of his readers. One might think of the essay, then, as just that act of professional self-examination that Rabinow found lacking in his "Representations Are Social Facts." Much of its power comes from the extra work it does to redescribe and legitimate the work of the *historian* of anthropology along with that of the anthropologist, the professional, second-order work of criticism as well as the "primary," "unprofessional" work of the novelist.

In Clifford's allegorical reading of Conrad, *Heart of Darkness* becomes an alternative model of writing that is no less professional than Malinowski's professional ethnography. The decisive difference between them is that Conrad includes the experience of fashioning and self-fashioning, the activ-ity of selecting and discarding, that is usually suppressed from ethnographic writing. His fiction includes the exclusions—the Lie to the Intended, the tearing off of Kurtz's "Exterminate the brutes!" from the official report—that are inevitable in all professional discourse. Professional discourse, the moral would seem to go, cannot be purified; it can be saved only by its ironic self-consciousness of its impurity.

We may or may not feel that this solution "works"—that it rises above, say, irony as a mode or style of living with exclusion too comfortably. But in fact this is only one of two resolutions to the dilemma of professional exclu-siveness that the essay explores. Why *is* exclusion inevitable? On the one hand, Clifford suggests that, like fiction, even the most scientific discourse selects and fashions and invents. Here only self-consciousness will help. On the other hand, however, he also suggests that the Lie to the Intended and the tearing off of "Exterminate the brutes!" are exclusions produced not by representation in general, but more precisely by the writer's or profes-sional's deliberate act of loyalty to the arbitrary limits of his chosen culture. Marlow, Clifford says, "learns to lie—that is, to communicate within the col-lective partial fictions of cultural life" (99). Clifford tries to restrict the damage this will do as a paradigm of professional ethnography. The "ethno-graphic standpoint" is better represented, he adds, not by Marlow but by the second narrator, silently listening to him, who "salvages, compares, and (ironically) believes these staged truths." But this distinguishing of narrators does not seriously affect the result: professional writing seen as "local, par-tial knowledge," or more strongly (but relegated to a footnote), as "a positive choice for the 'lie of culture'" (99). "Like Marlow's account aboard the *Nel-lie*, the truths of cultural descriptions are meaningful to specific interpretive communities in limiting historical circumstances" (112). The arbitrary, ex-

clusive cultural wholeness that Malinowski imposes upon the Trobriands results from an arbitrary, even absurd act of self-defining allegiance to the professional community of English anthropologists. The ethnographer lies about
his cultural objects, presenting them as more "local" than they are, in order
to make himself a member of the "local" culture of his fellow professionals.

This is a dead end of professional self-definition from which ironic self-
consciousness offers no hope of rescue. But Clifford does trace a way out of
it. The logic of self-rescue goes from "culture" to the "postcultural" and finally back to the "cosmopolitan." If it is no longer feasible to think of the
cultures studied by ethnography as distinct entities, as Clifford repeatedly
suggests, then why assume that the professional culture *of ethnographers* is a
distinct entity? If we must learn to see other cultures not as distinct, different wholes, but as mobile, fluid, hybrid, and inclusive, then why insist on a
necessary and absolute exclusiveness in studying the culture that studies
those cultures? In writing himself out of "culture" as an absurd but necessary
(and necessarily exclusive) order, Clifford also writes himself out of "the
profession" as a similarly necessary (and exclusive) absurdity. Instead of a dichotomy of professional describers of culture on the one hand and their non-
professional objects of description on the other, Clifford now assumes a
"postcultural" space where the subjects and objects of description are at
least potentially reversible, where the mobility required for observation and
comparison is not monopolized by one side, where the word *local* has lost
much of its contrastive force. His name for this space—a space that is not
exclusively professional—is "cosmopolitanism."

In the work that has followed *The Predicament of Culture*, Clifford has
radically revised his opinion of cosmopolitanism.[26] Rather than speaking in
the name of the local, as in the review of *Orientalism*, he has been pointing
out the manifold abuses of "thinking local," the distortions involved in taking
"the field" and "the village" as localizations of culture. He has been calling
on anthropologists to bring back into their ethnographies the "cosmopolitan
intermediaries" who intervene in and help constitute them, and "to focus on
hybrid, cosmopolitan experiences as much as on rooted, native ones." Clifford can approve of cosmopolitanism because he has been seeing it, and
teaching others to see it, as neither the consequence nor the prerogative of
"totalizing Western liberalism." He has been seeing it as something he himself shares with his subjects. It is not only gentlemen travelers, but the people of color who were the servants of those travelers, who have "specific cosmopolitan viewpoints." Even the organized coercion of migrant labor
produces "cosmopolitan workers." "The notion that certain classes of people
are cosmopolitan (travellers) while the rest are local (natives)" is only "the

ideology of one (very powerful) travelling culture" (107–8). Questions of power aside, "they" and "we" can no longer be divided as "local" and "cosmopolitan."

Thus the latter term becomes available again for general use. Instead of renouncing cosmopolitanism as a false universal, one can embrace it as an impulse to knowledge that is shared with others, a striving to transcend partiality that is itself partial, but no more so than the similar cognitive strivings of many diverse peoples. The world's particulars can now be recoded, in part at least, as the world's *discrepant cosmopolitanisms*.

How can comparative attention to discrepant cosmopolitanisms help us respond to the current backlash? In an article in the *New Yorker*, which does its bit for this backlash, Cynthia Ozick comes to the following conclusion on multiculturalism: "I would not wish to drop Homer or Jane Austen or Kafka to make room for an Aleutian Islander of lesser gifts, unrepresented though her group may be on the college reading list."[27] I take Clifford's reversal on cosmopolitanism as a hint that one of the various moves we might make against this use of the Aleutian Islander as an empty figure for pure particularity, and against the label of cultural particularism in general, is to fill the figure in, not just *as* a particular (worthy of the same respect as every other particular), but also, perhaps, as the carrier and embodiment of a certain cosmopolitanism. One might, for example, bring forward an essay by Claude Lévi-Strauss called "Cosmopolitanism and Schizophrenia," which discusses the syncretic mythology of native Americans along the Pacific Northwest coast.[28] Or, apropos of the putative Westernness of the Great Ideas, one might emphasize the word *Egypt* on the first page—unfortunately, *only* on the first page—of an article titled "The Greek Origins of the Idea of Cosmopolitanism," in which the author notes: "The earliest recorded formulation of this idea is supplied by modern archaeological discovery at Tell el-Amarna, in Egypt. Inscriptions have been found there, written by Akhnaton (pharoah of Egypt from 1375 to 1358 BC)."[29] Or one might counter ethnocentrisms both right and left with cosmopolitanism like that of the last page of *I, Rigoberta Menchú*: "My commitment to our struggle knows no boundaries nor limits. That's why I've travelled to many places."[30]

The scholarly project of accumulating instances of cosmopolitanism from around the globe—in Arjun Appadurai's words, "to fish for cosmopolitanism in the raw"—would help clinch the point that the concept is neither a Western invention nor a Western privilege.[31] When the right suggests that after all, there is ethnocentrism everywhere, that is, in the Third World too, the inevitable prelude to the suggestion that, after all, only in the West has there been any move away from it, we can then say not just that unequal power has made Eurocentrism qualitatively different in its effects from other ethnocentrisms. We can also say that we *value* the move away from ethnocentrism—in all the many places, Western and non-Western, where it has occurred. To take an empirical route out of the overly simple binary of universal and particular, rather than performing a merely logical or deconstructive exercise on it, would put the matter across to a broader audience, and it would also have the advantage of distinguishing cosmopolitanism from an abstract, ahistorical universalism,[32] for it would bring out many diverse and overlapping syncretisms and secularisms for which the term is an umbrella.[33] (The opposition between religion and secularism itself might be one casualty of such a project.)

The limits of the term are among its conjunctural virtues. No one actually is or ever can be a cosmopolitan in the sense of belonging nowhere. Who can say, in Jonathan Arac's helpful twisting of a familar phrase, "I am an alien; everything human is alien to me"? Nor can anyone be a cosmopolitan in the sense of belonging everywhere. If such a thing were conceivable, it would not be desirable, for, as Donna Haraway has pointed out, it could exist only in the form of complete cultural relativism.[34] The interest of the term *cosmopolitanism* is located, then, not in its full theoretical extension, where it becomes a paranoid fantasy of ubiquity and omniscience, but rather (paradoxically) in its local applications, where the unrealizable ideal produces normative pressure against such alternatives as, say, the fashionable *hybridization*. Its provocative association with privilege is perhaps better understood, in this context, as the normative edge that cosmopolitanism tries to add to the inclusiveness and diversity of multiculturalism—as an attempt to name a necessary but difficult normativeness.

The term is not as philosophically ambitious as the word *universalism*, though it does some of the same work. (It makes room for moments of generalizing, one might say, without offering license for uninhibited universalizing.) Nor is it as politically ambitious as the word *internationalism*. But it does start us asking what form such an internationalism might best take. The academy-bashing journalists have been suggesting that multiculturalism is nothing but an attempt to revive the naive Third Worldism of the 1960s, with its automatic division between Imperialist Bad Guys and Newly Independent Good Guys. It seems to me that the term *cosmopolitanism* better describes the sensibility of our moment. Now, as opposed perhaps to two or three decades ago, anti-imperialism has been and must be newly careful, skeptical, measured in its support of any nation. Recently and paradigmatically, it has had to learn to oppose Bush's war in the Persian Gulf without defending Saddam Hussein. More generally, it has been to school with movements in the name of gender, class, and sexual orientation that, in Jean Franco's words, "have sprung up on the margins of the nation state" and "no longer couch cultural or political projects in national terms."[35] Our moment, one might say, is that of the globalizing of such movements—a moment to which there would correspond, ideally, some new, denationalized internationalism.

If cosmopolitanism cannot deliver an explicitly and directly political program, it is at least a step toward this sort of internationalist political education. By suggesting that there is no right place to stand, it can take some of the moralism out of our politics. Better still, by doing so it can liberate us to pursue a long-term process of translocal connecting that is both political and educational at once. And in the midst of the short-term politico-educational crisis in which we now find ourselves, it can designate a teaching of culture capable of mobilizing the energy and enthusiasm of a broad front of people who are not all or even predominantly leftists, whatever the right may think. As a practice of comparison, a range of tolerances and secularisms, an international competence or mode of citizenship that is the monopoly of no one class or civilization, it answers the charges of "particularism" and "loss of standards." As a positive ideal of interconnected knowledge and pedagogy, it elevates rather than lowers existing educational standards. It presents multiculturalism as both a common program and a critical program.[36]

The cosmopolitanism of the contemporary American academy invites more cynical analyses: as the expression of an elite of apparently disinterested class aliens who refuse national limits, along with all other social membership, only to the extent that capital does, for example, or as the expression of an older class hierarchy that resists America's imperial nationalism in part because it sets its cultural standards above and against those of ordinary citizens. I prefer a third option: cosmopolitanism as the provocatively impure but irreducible combination of a certain privilege at home, as part of a real belonging in institutional places, with a no less real but much less common (and therefore highly desirable) extension of democratic, anti-imperial principles abroad. As Neil Smith has suggested, rethinking the imperfections of democracy requires rethinking space: the pertinent subnational and supranational units of agency and communication, differentials of scale that rule out many of our most frequent moralizing, universalizing gestures and demand a politics that is also differential. The most generous and useful way to begin rethinking cosmopolitanism, it seems to me, is neither as ideal unplaceableness nor as sordid elitism, but as a way of relativizing and problematizing the scale and the units of democracy.[37] As the invocation of citizenship in a unit that is phantasmatic or impossible, the term keeps us from forgetting that what is democratic progress at home is not necessarily democratic progress abroad—and that what may seem privileged on one scale may elsewhere be recognized as an extension of the constituency of knowledge, a genuine and even unprecedented pushing back of democracy's borders.

Notes

I am grateful to Jean Franco, Dominick LaCapra, Satya Mohanty, Sara Suleri, Jennifer Wicke, Carolyn Williams, Bob Utley, and Larry Rothfield for kind invitations to talk through earlier versions of this essay. A slightly different version appeared in *Social Text* 31–32 (Summer 1992); an expanded version appeared in *Secular Vocations* (London: Verso, 1993).

1. Anne Matthews, "Deciphering Victorian Underwear and Other Seminars," *New York Times Magazine*, February 10, 1991, 57. The sensational overstatement ("every possible course") is evidence that Matthews is shooting to kill—as she does again in her summary of current dogma in the Modern Language Association, when she pretends that culture and multiculturalism are natural antagonists locked in a one-on-one struggle to the death: "The 'classic books' approach to literary study is bankrupt. Multiculturalism is essential."

2. As the word *our* suggests, I am primarily interested here in addressing people who, like myself, earn an uneasy living from cultural work in professions and institutions that sometimes seem aimed against the political and ethical principles that give that work such meaning as it has. Those who work elsewhere, or who escape such contradictions between work and politics by sustaining their radicalism without the help or hope of tenure, will I hope pardon what may look like the self-indulgent narcissism of this exercise. Others will, I hope, excuse what they may see as my evasion of personal detail.

3. Dinesh D'Souza, "Illiberal Education," *Atlantic Monthly*, March 1991, 51–79. D'Souza (54) quotes (with approval) Michael O'Brien, "A Paradox of Our Intellectual Life since the 1960s: We Are Cosmopolitans, Our Scholarship Is Not," *Chronicle of Higher Education*, November 30, 1988, B1, B2.

4. Outside the United States, there are many exceptions to this rule. Robin Blackburn, for example, speaks of the new European union as "a rare and ambitious experiment, of great moment for that radical and democratic cosmopolitanism which might be able to contain and defeat those global forces of division and destruction that stalk the new world order." Robin Blackburn, "The Ruins of Westminster," *New Left Review* 191 (January–February 1992): 29.

5. Donna J. Haraway, "Situated Knowledges: The Science Question in Feminism and the Privilege of Partial Perspective," in *Simians, Cyborgs, and Women: The Reinvention of Nature* (London: Free Association, 1990), 188. Haraway's remarks leave the question of what precisely happens—how far the undesirable consequences of panopticism are undone—when bodies are *returned* to visibility—a question for the so-called experimental ethnography. Would a "panopticism" in which the viewer would be visible remain unacceptable? Would a cosmopolitanism that would be forced to know boundaries and bodies still be one?

6. V. S. Naipaul, "Our Universal Civilization," *New York Review of Books*, January 31, 1991, 22–25.

7. Rob Nixon, "London Calling: V. S. Naipaul and the License of Exile," *South Atlantic Quarterly*, 87, no. 1 (1988): 1, 11, 3. Note the beautiful phrase "comprehensively uprooted," which recognizes diversity of uprootings and encourages discrimination of

more or fewer, greater or lesser uprooting, rather than an overly simple dichotomy of rooted or not.

8. Tim Brennan, "India, Nationalism, and Other Failures," *South Atlantic Quarterly* 87, no. 1 (1988): 134, 135. Brennan usefully argues for a discrimination of nationalisms: "The cosmopolitan writers very often cannot accept the virtues of nationalism in this postcolonial setting, are unable to see it as a defensive bulwark, and therefore fail to distinguish between monstrosities like Pakistan or Kenya . . . and Cuba and Vietnam" (144).

9. Tim Brennan, "The National Longing for Form," in Homi K. Bhabha, ed., *Nation and Narration* (London: Routledge, 1990), 63, 64.

10. Nixon, "London Calling," 27.

11. George Boas, "Types of Internationalism in Early Nineteenth-Century France," *International Journal of Ethics* 38, no. 1 (1927): 152.

12. It seems possible that the vocabulary of "celebrity" functions in cases like this to tarnish a given writer obliquely, that is, to do so without invoking the vocabulary of *class*, which is more seriously contaminating, on the one hand, but also too visibly contaminating for one's allies as well as one's enemies, hence often unusable.

13. This point has been forcefully articulated by Stanley Fish in "Anti-Professionalism," in his *Doing What Comes Naturally: Change, Rhetoric, and the Practice of Theory in Literary and Legal Studies* (Durham, N.C.: Duke University Press, 1989), 215–46.

14. Chandra Mohanty, "Under Western Eyes: Feminist Scholarship and Colonial Discourses," *boundary 2* 12–13 (Spring–Fall 1984): 340, 336. This essay has been reprinted in Chandra Mohanty, Ann Russo, and Lourdes Torres, eds., *Third World Women and the Politics of Feminism* (Bloomington: Indiana University Press, 1991). Regarding "ethnocentric universalism," one thinks of the extraordinary universalizing of Jean-François Lyotard's use of the Cashinahua as figures for all of non-Western humanity in *The Postmodern Condition: A Report on Knowledge*, trans. Geoff Bennington and Brian Massumi (Minneapolis: University of Minnesota Press, 1984).

15. Mohanty, "Under Western Eyes," 340.

16. Agency occupies much the same place in another equally classic polemic on behalf of Third World specificity, Kumkum Sangari's "The Politics of the Possible," *Cultural Critique* 6 (Fall 1987): 157–86.

17. For anyone involved in literary theory, this point will be familiar as the burden of "intertextuality"—the arbitrariness of any text's limits and the way the negotiating of those limits is also the negotiating of the text's meaning and value.

18. Simon Duncan and Mike Savage, "Space, Scale, and Locality," *Antipode* 21, no. 3 (1989): 187.

19. Neil Smith, "Dangers of the Empirical Turn: Some Comments on the CURS Initiative," *Antipode* 19 (1987): 63.

20. Gayatri Chakravorty Spivak, "Three Women's Texts and a Critique of Imperialism," *Critical Inquiry* 12 (Autumn 1985): 243–62.

21. Ulf Hannerz, "Cosmopolitans and Locals in World Culture," in Mike Featherstone, ed., "Global Culture" (special issue), *Theory, Culture & Society* 7 (1990): 238. Page numbers for further cites of this work appear in text.

22. Mike Featherstone, "Global Culture: An Introduction," in Mike Featherstone, ed., "Global Culture" (special issue), *Theory, Culture & Society* 7 (1990): 9; emphasis added.

23. Raymond Williams, *Culture and Society*, 2d ed. (New York: Columbia University Press, 1983); Sandra M. Gilbert and Susan Gubar, *The Madwoman in the Attic: A Study of Women and the Literary Imagination in the Nineteenth Century* (New Haven, Conn.: Yale University Press, 1979).

24. James Clifford, "On Orientalism," in *The Predicament of Culture: Twentieth-Century Ethnography, Literature, and Art* (Cambridge: Harvard University Press, 1988), 255–76. Page numbers for further cites of this work appear in text.

25. Paul Rabinow, "Representations Are Social Facts," in James Clifford and George E. Marcus eds., *Writing Culture: The Poetics and Politics of Ethnography* (Berkeley: University of California Press, 1986), 242, 244. Rabinow offers "critical cosmopolitanism" as a desirable position: "Let us define cosmopolitanism as an ethos of macro-interdependencies, with an acute consciousness (often forced upon people) of the inescapabilities and particularities of places, characters, historical trajectories, and fates." "We are all cosmopolitans" (258).

26. James Clifford, "Traveling Cultures," in Lawrence Grossberg, Cary Nelson, and Paula A. Treichler, eds., *Cultural Studies* (New York: Routledge, 1992). Page numbers for further cites of this work appear in text.

27. Cynthia Ozick, "A Critic at Large: T. S. Eliot at 101," *New Yorker*, November 20, 1989, 125. I discuss this passage at greater length in "Othering the Academy: Professionalism and Multiculturalism," *Social Research* (June 1991): 355–72.

28. Claude Lévi-Strauss, "Cosmopolitanism and Schizophrenia," in *The View from Afar* (New York: Basic Books, 1985), 177–85.

29. Hugh Harris, "The Greek Origins of the Idea of Cosmopolitanism," *International Journal of Ethics* 38, no. 1 (1927): 1.

30. Rigoberta Menchu, *I, Rigoberta Menchu: An Indian Woman in Guatemala*, ed. Elisabeth Burgos-Debray, trans. Ann Wright (London: Verso, 1984), 247.

31. Arjun Appadurai, "Global Ethnoscapes: Notes and Queries for a Transnational Anthropology," in Richard G. Fox, ed., *Recapturing Anthropology: Working in the Present* (Santa Fe, N.M.: School of American Research Press, 1991), 201.

32. There is a great deal of pressure right now to reconsider the resistance to universals that for some time has seemed to be an article of faith on the cultural left. In a recent speech, Cornel West declared: "The power of the civil rights movement under Martin Luther King was its universalism. Now, instead of the civil rights movement being viewed as a moral crusade for freedom, it's become an expression of a particular interest group. Once you lose that moral high ground, all you have is a power struggle, and that has never been a persuasive means for the weaker to deal with the stronger." Quoted in *New York Times*, April 3, 1991, 1. The paradox of a case for universalism based on historical conjuncture and rhetorical advantage suggests how unsettled our relation to universalism remains. Without taking a position on universalism, I want to agree however that *some* sort of "high ground," some description of radically expanded and diverse cultural knowledge that is also of positive value and at least possible commonality, has to be part of our self-definition and strategy. The term *cosmopolitanism* makes this point.

33. The word *secular* would probably be a matter of dispute.

34. Haraway, "Situated Knowledges," 191.

35. Jean Franco, "The Nation as Imagined Community," in H. Aram Veeser, ed., *The New Historicism* (New York: Routledge, 1989), 205.

36. Sylvia Wynter's critique of California's new, insufficiently multicultural history texts uses the power of this slogan. Wynter calls for a new framework that "seeks to go beyond the model of a nation-state coterminus only with Euro-immigrant America, to one coterminus as a 'world' civilization, with all its peoples; and therefore, for the first time in recorded history, coterminus (as a land that's not been yet but must be) with humankind." Sylvia Wynter, quoted in Robert Reinhold, "Class Struggle," *New York Times Magazine*, September 29, 1991, 47. But see George Yudice, "We Are Not the World," *Social Text* 31–32 (1992): 202–16, for reservations about the hidden U.S. nationalism of any such formulation.

37. This issue in political theory requires more work. Within what borders, in what scale of unit, is democracy more or less possible?

Cosmopolitanism, Universalism, and the Divided Legacies of Modernity

Amanda Anderson

One of the more remarkable developments in contemporary cultural criticism has been the surge of interest in the idea and history of universalism, a concept that has frequently been viewed as unrecuperable by practitioners of poststructuralism, postmodernism, and cultural studies more broadly. Partly in reaction to the excesses of identity politics, and partly in response to the political and ethical impasses of a strictly negative critique of Enlightenment, a number of theorists have begun to reexamine universalism, asking how we might best combine the critique of partial or false universals with the pursuit of those emancipatory ideals associated with traditional universalism. I have in mind here not the neo-Kantian versions of universalism promoted by Jürgen Habermas and his followers, which in any event already have a lengthier history, but rather the more guarded, poststructuralist-inflected analyses forwarded by critics such as Etienne Balibar, Judith Butler, Ernesto Laclau, Naomi Schor, and Joan Scott.[1]

In some respects, the reconsiderations of universalism reenact the strategies and approaches that characterized reconsiderations of essentialism in the late 1980s and early 1990s. That is to say, like the advocates of "strategic essentialism," the current theorists frequently adduce universalism's practical necessity, political efficacy, or sheer unavoidability. Similarly, many of these theorists deploy the double gesture characteristic of the essentialism debates, arguing on the one hand that universalism is necessary or practically desirable, and on the other that exclusion and violence will nonetheless attend any projection of unity or commonality.[2]

Still, one cannot simply assimilate the recent discussions of universalism and particularism to the earlier debates over essentialism and constructionism. First, essentialism and constructionism are sharply opposed to each other, whereas universalism and particularism are more easily articulated in a nuanced, mutually constitutive relationship. It is for this reason, I think, that the exchanges over universalism hold more promise than the highly polarized essentialism debates. Second, there is a long and significant history of universalism within Marxism, a body of thought to which many progressive poststructuralists feel some allegiance, however tempered or conditional. Consequently, there is less need to formulate one's relation to universalism in overwhelmingly strategic or suspicious terms. Indeed, it is no accident that some of the most developed contemporary poststructuralist thought on universalism is emanating from critics deeply versed in Marxism, such as Ernesto Laclau and Etienne Balibar. Third, and I think most important, the reconsiderations of universalism are being made in the face of grave concerns over resurgent nationalisms and the often atomizing politics of identity. Whereas the reconsiderations of essentialism sought to address the felt needs and insistent self-understandings of marginalized groups, the reconsiderations of universalism are frequently responses to the limitations and dangers involved in a too-protectionist approach to assertions of identity or primary affiliation. In this sense, the recuperation of universalism is diametrically opposed to the recuperation of essentialism, insofar as the new universalism focuses on those ideals and practices that propel individuals and groups beyond the confines of restricted or circumscribed identities.

There is of course a term that throughout its long philosophical, aesthetic, and political history has been used to denote cultivated detachment from restrictive forms of identity, and that term is *cosmopolitanism*. Interestingly, despite a prevalent prejudice in favor of neologisms, this rearguard term with close ties to universalism is itself making provocative appearances across a range of writings in anthropology, cultural studies, literary criticism, intellectual history, and contemporary theory broadly construed. Many of these appearances are simply gestural or nonce-descriptive, and involve no sustained analysis or endorsement of the term. Such appearances are often passing moments within a larger attempt to describe or promote self-consciously global perspectives and methodologies. But there have been more sustained recuperative analyses of the term, which together considerably complicate and enrich the reconsiderations of universalism.

In this essay, I want to try to characterize the new appeals to cosmopolitanism, and to situate them in relation to both the new poststructuralist versions of universalism and the neo-Kantian universalisms of Habermas and the proponents of communicative ethics. My premise is that the idea of cosmopolitanism is worthy of a focused genealogy in its own right, and that current endorsements of the term have valuable contributions to make to contemporary academic and cultural debates about the politics of identity. A rigorous genealogy of cosmopolitanism would, I believe, contribute to more calibrated analyses of the history of universalism, rendering reductive oppositions between modernity and countermodernity obsolete by bringing into sharp relief modernity's own divided histories, and by disallowing any easy identification of modernity with abstract universalism. For the present purposes, however, I intend to concentrate on the current manifestations of cosmopolitanism, with only passing discussion of the history of Enlightenment and classical cosmopolitanism, to name just two Western forms of cosmopolitanism.

Unlike the reconsiderations of universalism, which have been undertaken by some of the most theoretically ambitious and philosophically inclined of contemporary thinkers, the new cosmopolitanism has tended to emerge within the more exoteric, historically minded disciplines and modes: anthropology, cultural criticism, history of the intelligentsia. To take three prominent examples, sustained recuperative analyses of the term occur in James Clifford's "Traveling Cultures" (anthropology), Bruce Robbins's *Secular Vocations* (cultural criticism; history of the intelligentsia), and David A. Hollinger's *Postethnic America* (American cultural and intellectual history).[3] Within this disciplinary matrix there is a tendency toward more popular venues and more casual genres. Moreover, many proponents of cosmopolitanism who may otherwise produce highly esoteric writings honor the topic by seeking a wider audience through both choice of publisher and style of address. Thus Julia Kristeva deliberately recast the self-avowedly cosmopolitan ideas in *Strangers to Ourselves* in the more journalistic and accessible essays of *Nations without Nationalism*, and Martha Nussbaum and the editors of the *Boston Review* saw "Patriotism and Cosmopolitanism" as the occasion for a wide-ranging forum.[4]

Before going on to consider individual arguments in favor of a rehabilitated or reconfigured cosmopolitanism, I want to sketch briefly some of the main features of the concept. It is important to realize that cosmopolitanism is a flexible term, whose forms of detachment and multiple affiliation can be variously articulated and variously motivated. In general, cosmopolitanism endorses reflective distance from one's cultural affiliations, a broad understanding of other cultures and customs, and a belief in universal humanity. The relative weight assigned to these three constitutive elements can vary, as can the cultural identities against which "reflective distance" is defined. In antiquity, with the initial elaborations of cosmopolitanism by the Cynics and Stoics, cosmopolitan detachment was defined against the restricted perspective and interests of the polis. In the Enlightenment, it was defined against the constricting allegiances of religion, class, and the state. In the twentieth century, I think we can fairly say that it is defined against those parochialisms emanating from extreme allegiances to nation, race, and ethnos. In very recent defenses of cosmopolitanism, the ethnos rhetorically reaches to include any identity politics conceived along the model of the ethnic enclave.[5]

Yet the forms of distance from cultural identification that are advocated within specific cosmopolitanisms can range from the rigorously negative or exclusionary, as in the Stoic position of eschewing petty allegiances in favor of a universal standard, to the expansively inclusionary, as in those cosmopolitanisms that promote understanding of many different cultures and experiences.[6] In exclusionary cosmopolitanism, little to no weight is given to exploration of disparate cultures: all value lies in an abstract or "cosmic" universalism. In inclusionary cosmopolitanism, by contrast, universalism finds expression through sympathetic imagination and intercultural exchange. This tension, between bracketing affiliations on the one hand and appreciating and sometimes integrating them on the other, appears throughout the history of cosmopolitan thought, including its contemporary articulations, which tend to argue for a redefined dialectic between the two.

Cosmopolitanism also typically manifests a complex tension between elitism and egalitarianism. It frequently advances itself as a specifically intellectual ideal, or depends on a mobility that is the luxury of social, economic, or cultural privilege. In the eighteenth century, the cultivation of international communication and travel among scholars was often embraced as the symbolic or even actual enactment of cosmopolitan ideals. Here, privileged mobility among elites synecdochally masquerades as global community, or the coming together of humanity, bespeaking a profound investment in the exceptional individualism of the intellectual class, their enabling but anomalous detachment from ordinary, provincial loyalties. At the same time, the cosmopolitan identification with the larger sphere of the world, or with humanity, or with standards assumed to transcend any locale, is ostensibly inspired by the deep-seated belief in the humanity of all, wherever positioned.[7]

Still, despite its awkward elitism, which can manifest different degrees of self-consciousness, one virtue that cosmopolitanism has over a more abstract universalism is that it situates the question of universalism in relation to the position and role of the intellectual and the intellectual enterprise. It is also commonly articulated in relation to new geopolitical configurations and within the context of destabilizing experiences of intercultural contact and exchange. In the context of Stoical cosmopolitanism, the sense of an expanded world traces to Alexander the Great's program of cultural fusion and his far-reaching world conquests. Likewise in the eighteenth century the opening up of trade routes and the advancement of imperial ventures caused powerful self-interrogation among thinkers in Europe. The results of such interrogations often appear naively unaware of their own imbrication in relations of power, or their relation to the logic of capitalist expansion, as instanced in the common Enlightenment view that international commerce would foster world peace. But if we truly wish to historicize universalism, and locate it within an international framework of cultural contact, exchange, and conflict, then we must trace, and analyze, the specificity of cosmopolitanism in relation to the history of universalism.

Cosmopolitanism also tends to be exercised by the specifically ethical challenges of perceived cultural relativisms; it aims to articulate not simply intellectual programs but ethical ideals for the cultivation of character and for negotiating the experience of otherness. It is no accident, in this regard, that one primary site for the elaboration of a new cosmopolitanism is within contemporary anthropology, whose intellectual project perforce involves complex ethical questions. Although cosmopolitanism has strongly individualist elements (in its advocacy of detachment from shared identities and its emphasis on affiliation as voluntary), it nonetheless often aims to foster reciprocal and transformative encounters between strangers variously construed. In this respect, it partakes of the same intersubjective turn with regard to liberal autonomy as communicative ethics does with regard to Kantian moral theory. Its ethical values frequently result in a mood of optimism that contrasts rather sharply with the hermeneutics of suspicion dominating much work on the cultural left. Although this optimism can appear at times to shade into cultivated naïveté, it is often an acutely self-conscious departure from prevailing practices of negative critique, and moreover is often offset by a sophisticated attentiveness to geopolitical and multicultural complexities.

In *Secular Vocations*, Bruce Robbins provides one of the more thoughtful and developed defenses of cosmopolitanism that has appeared in recent years, one that attempts self-consciously to reconfigure the tension between elitism and egalitarianism. Invoking Edward W. Said's concept of "secular criticism," as well as Clifford's idea of "discrepant cosmopolitanisms," Robbins sketches an intellectual and professional ideal that is very far indeed from the universal humanism of the Enlightenment philosophes.[8] Robbins finds the disparate connotations of the word *cosmopolitanism* exactly suited to his goal of articulating a self-conscious professionalism among academics that acknowledges its own privileges and interests, but without imagining that such an acknowledgment irrevocably taints its practices, or fundamentally disarms its attempts to forward progressive principles and strive against prejudice and partiality. He wants cosmopolitanism to cover a less anxious though by no means complacent acknowledgment of the intellectual's inability to transcend relations of power. Cosmopolitanism enables an embrace of worldliness in two senses: "1) planetary expansiveness of subject-matter, on the one hand, and 2) unembarrassed acceptance of professional self-interest, on the other" (181).

Robbins, that is, acknowledges and accepts the privilege associated with the term. He does so in the knowledge that a significant Marxist tradition, still very much alive, uses the term against intellectuals pejoratively, precisely to describe forms of illusory or politically disastrous detachment from important affiliations. For example, drawing on Antonio Gramsci, Tim Brennan has recently used the term *cosmopolitan* to describe Third World metropolitan intellectuals such as Salman Rushdie, Isabel Allende, and Bharati Mukherjee. In "Cosmopolitanism and Celebrities," he argues that these writers have been selected by Western reviewers as interpreters and public spokespersons for the Third World.[9] "Cosmopolitans" are writers who make Western audiences less uncomfortable, and whose work importantly shares the following characteristics:

> a harsh questioning of radical decolonisation theory; a dismissive or parodic attitude towards the project of national culture; a manipulation of imperial imagery and local legend as a means of politicising "current events"; and a declaration of cultural "hybridity"—a hybridity claimed to offer certain advantages in negotiating the collisions of language, race and art in a world of disparate peoples comprising a single, if not exactly unified, world. (7)

While not dismissive of the important pedagogical and mediating roles of celebrity cosmopolitans, Brennan believes that their attitudes toward the collective popular struggles of national peoples, and their Western reception, must be analyzed in political and cultural terms. To begin this analysis of cosmopolitanism, he invokes Gramsci's critical conception of the cosmopolitan intellectual, whose historically determined emergence thwarts the crucial task of developing "national culture" (10).[10]

According to Gramsci, the Italian intellectual's disconnected relation to national culture traces back to the culturally homogenizing effects of the Roman Empire:

> [It is] necessary to go back to the times of the Roman Empire when Italy, through the territory of Rome, became the melting pot of the cultured classes from throughout the Empire. Its ruling classes became ever more imperial and ever less Latin: they became cosmopolitan. (quoted in Brennan 12)

Cosmopolitanism here translates into a culturally conditioned, disastrous detachment, which is specifically linked to imperialism, the false universal ecumenicism of the Catholic Church, and the development of a rootless, intellectualized, managerial class. Over and against this Gramsci sets the activist intellectual, one who helps to forward the development of national culture through the vigorous and direct expression not of some nostalgically unified national mythos, but of the complex intercultural engagements that define the national history. Here, against Rome, Gramsci invokes ancient Greece and Renaissance England, both cultures whose distinctiveness was achieved through rich intercultural exchange. A contrast is developed, then, between a lifeless imperial disengagement—what Gramsci pejoratively calls "cosmopolitanism"—and a more local and agonistic intellectual practice. Along a Gramscian model, the development of national culture is conceived not in romantic terms, as the recognition of inward essence, a *Volksgeist*, but rather as the dynamic product of social transfer across borders of ethnicity, language, class, taste, and scientific outlook.

Brennan's fascinating though selective genealogy of cosmopolitanism enables a careful situating of the intellectual in relation to geopolitical history and, in particular, the *disparate* histories of various empires. The fact that he uses the term critically does not diminish the analytic richness of his arguments. It is striking to note, however, that the Gramscian alternative to a negative "cosmopolitanism" actually comes close to positive versions of the idea. Although cosmopolitanism manifests, or can be constructed as manifesting, varying degrees of detachment and engagement, the salient point here is that as an analytic category it tends to invite a layered geopolitical understanding. This does not mean that all conceptions of cosmopolitanism—whether positive or negative, naive or sophisticated—achieve a high level of analytic insight, but simply that they tend to be self-consciously articulated in the context of intercultural contact and exchange. Precisely for this reason, a fresh look at the history of cosmopolitanism, including its current manifestations, promises to enrich certain revisionary projects aimed at the analysis of terms such as *modernity* and *universalism*.

Take for example Paul Gilroy's recent study, *The Black Atlantic*.[11] This book resituates the cultural history of slavery, as well as the history of the West, by insisting on an antinational transcultural rubric, the black Atlantic. Gilroy's study is an exemplary instance of the new attempts to do cultural analysis within a genuinely transnational frame, and accordingly, Gilroy is critical of cultural studies' investment in the topos and integrity of *national* histories. He also announces as one of the book's main goals the attempt to rethink seriously the project of modernity. He thus analyzes the racist logics and rhetorics at work in the theorists of modernity beginning with the Enlightenment, while at the same time affirming the promise of the universalist project. In an eloquent introductory passage describing why he focuses so persistently on the dislocating image of the ship—with its illumination of transmigration, intercultural contact, and the middle passage—Gilroy remarks:

> Getting on board promises a means to reconceptualise the orthodox rela-
> tionship between modernity and what passes for its prehistory. It provides a
> different sense of where modernity might itself be thought to begin in the
> constitutive relationships with outsiders that both found and temper a self-
> conscious sense of western civilisation. (17)

This idea central to the rethinking of modernity—that its claims to a culturally superior form of self-consciousness are inseparable from its consti-tutive relations to otherness—can be further refined, and rendered immedi-ately more vivid, through an examination of the history of cosmopolitanism. Gilroy's profound reframing of cultural history reinforces the limitations of a too-restrictive conception of modernity. I want to suggest as well that the cosmopolitan tradition usefully complicates the idea of an insular Western modernity and, moreover, may provide resources for the critique of moder-nity within modernity itself. To reiterate, cosmopolitanism is characteristi-cally elaborated within an experience of cultural multiplicity and at least limited self-reflexivity, and against a specific form of parochialism. Cos-mopolitanism has repeatedly emerged at times when the world has suddenly seemed to expand in unassimilable ways; it is at these moments that univer-salism needs the rhetoric of worldliness that cosmopolitanism provides. Contemporary revitalizations of universalism, and the frequency with which the imperative of *translation* is invoked in current theoretical debates, can be seen as an instance of the same moment of radical destabilization.[12] This is not to say that articulations of cosmopolitanism will magically be less likely to impose their own particulars as a false universal. The Enlighten-ment conception of horizon-expanding travel and communication among scholars was often narrowly limited to Europe, even as many of their re-searches extended to other regions of the world. Likewise the philosophes' constructions of universal human nature often bore all too markedly the im-print of European culture and history. These points are by now ones that we expect to be made. What is more interesting is to follow out the complex forms of cultural positioning, and the more radical potentialities, that are implicit and explicit in the articulation of different cosmopolitan ideals.

Many of the new cosmopolitanisms aim to realize such radical potential-ities through the studied integration of their intellectual and ethical ideals. And whereas the balancing of intellectual and ethico-political principles may be said to characterize a vast range of contemporary work in the human sciences, I want to argue that cosmopolitanism has carved out a distinctive place for itself in regard to this animating tension. Let me begin to address this issue by elaborating more fully the contributions of Robbins and Clifford, paying attention now to the ways in which their egalitarianism reconfigures the traditional elitism of cosmopolitanism. One might view Robbins's text as symptomatic of the new cosmopolitanism insofar as what looked like an intellectual or pedagogical project, "planetary expansiveness of subject-matter," slowly develops into a suggestive ethical meditation. Robbins's ethical orientation begins to announce itself when he makes clear that he is not advocating cosmopolitanism as a negative detachment from any and all affiliations, stressing instead "a density of overlapping allegiances" (184). He then goes on to present favorably Clifford's notion of "discrepant cosmopolitanisms."

Clifford himself argues for an expanded conception of cosmopolitanism, one that extends beyond its usual associations with the West, the metropolis, and the intellectual. His central claim is that "the normative practices of twentieth-century anthropology" have "privileged relations of dwelling over relations of travel" (99). He rejects stabilizing conceptions of "native" culture by drawing out the many ways in which "natives" are travelers within complex webs of intercultural communication and exchange. Clifford employs descriptive terms such as "hybridity" and "diaspora cultures," and commends the work of Paul Gilroy, Marcus Rediker, Kobena Mercer, and Stuart Hall. Although he does not shy away from the more current theoretical terms, it is clear that a redefined cosmopolitanism is his term of choice. After citing Mercer's and Hall's provocative work on how diasporic cultures unsettle conventional conceptions of ethnicity and identity, Clifford writes:

> Such cultures of displacement and transplantation are inseparable from specific, often violent, histories of economic, political, and cultural interaction, histories that generate what might be called *discrepant cosmopolitanisms*. In this emphasis we avoid, at least, the excessive localism of particularist cultural relativism, as well as the overly global vision of a capitalist or technocratic monoculture. (108)

The virtue of Clifford's work, for Robbins, lies in its skillful dismantling of the opposition between cosmopolitan and local, its insistence on multiple cosmopolitanisms partly rooted in local cultures, partly positioned in global networks. No longer conceivable as the prerogative of the West, cosmopolitanisms manifest themselves in any instance of sustained intercultural contact and exchange. Robbins draws this conclusion from Clifford:

273

Instead of renouncing cosmopolitanism as a false universal, one can embrace it as an impulse to knowledge that is shared with others, a striving to transcend partiality that is itself partial, but no more so than the similar cognitive strivings of many diverse peoples. (194)

As an integral part of an intellectual program, then, Robbins attempts to formulate an ethos, a receptive attitude toward otherness that will stimulate what he at one point calls "mobile, reciprocal interconnectedness" (197). The term functions as an umbrella for all attempts to get beyond ethnocentrism, and for the multiple secularisms and syncretisms of a complex world. Robbins also advocates the retrieval and circulation of non-Western formulations of cosmopolitanism, citing among a few other tantalizing examples Lévi-Strauss's essay called "Cosmopolitanism and Schizophrenia," which presents "the syncretic mythology of Native Americans along the Pacific Northwest Coast" (194). Ultimately, Robbins's cosmopolitanism aims to foster communication and to promote a "long-term process of trans-local connecting that is both political and educational at once" (196).

Robbins's cosmopolitanism attempts to mediate between the particular and the universal in both intellectual and ethical terms. First, there is an insistence on a plurality of situated cosmopolitanisms: the variously willed and forced detachments from local or restrictive identities do not issue in a gray universalism but rather a vivid spectrum of diverse dialectics of detachment, displacement, and affiliation. Second, cosmopolitanism is seen to involve a vigilant attentiveness to otherness, an ethical stance that cannot be separated from the will to knowledge: "transcending partiality" is fundamentally both an ethical and an intellectual ideal. Thus, despite the appeal to multiplicity, this cosmopolitanism deliberately contrasts itself with moral relativism: "transcending partiality" is the regulative ideal against which both intellectual projects and intersubjective practices can be judged.

Robbins himself does not make the principles underlying his claims quite as explicit as I have rendered them, however. Indeed, he claims that cosmopolitanism "better describes the sensibility of our moment" in part because "the word is not as philosophically ambitious as the term 'universalism'" (196). He thereby would appear to dissociate himself from a program of explicit normative justification. Yet at the same time, Robbins asserts provocatively at one point that cosmopolitanism "produces normative pressure against such alternatives, as, say, the fashionable hybridization" (196). It is important to recognize that this is not a simple case of inconsistency or underdevelopment of ideas. There exists a genuine tension between the universalist ethical assumptions of the new cosmopolitanisms and their simultaneous desire to cultivate ethical practices that do not impose false universals. It is precisely this tension that has led to the distinctly casual normativity of the cosmopolitan.

In contrast to neo-Kantian universalism, then, proponents of cosmopolitanism simply do not appear anxious about justification: they want to assert a strong normative claim against other positions seen to be normatively weak or undeveloped, but do so through a process of incremental, casual description rather than philosophical justification (or, to anticipate, deconstructive double gestures).[13] This casual normativity may be seen as both stemming from and potentially dictating issues of genre and address. Cosmopolitanism generally invites a description from the perspective of the participant as he or she negotiates a dense array of affiliations and commitments. Although there are developed and ongoing philosophical debates on cosmopolitanism and nationalism, the articulations of cosmopolitanism often occur not within a philosophic or high theoretical mode, but rather within genres more classically literary or eclectic: the essay, the autobiography, travel writing, and works of literature generally.

Ultimately, a too rigorous or bald universalism seems at odds, for the cosmopolitan, with the requisite moral task of developing a delicate intersubjective competence within a culturally diverse horizon. I deliberately use this somewhat jarring phrase, "delicate intersubjective competence," which joins the language of universalist ethics with an emphasis entirely foreign to that tradition—the emphasis on tact, sensibility, and judgment (*phronesis*), which seem fundamental to the cosmopolitan's reconfigured relation to universality. Obviously, one can read this element of cosmopolitanism as itself insufficiently conscious of its investment in an elitist habitus, yet the refinement advocated here is precisely an attentiveness to the "uninhibited generalizing" that is itself an elitist prerogative (Robbins 196). Normative explicitness is felt, somehow, to violate the cosmopolitan spirit, even though the cosmopolitan project is animated by the conviction that delicate intersubjective competence derives from our shared commonalities. As Paul Rabinow writes, when describing "critical, cosmopolitan intellectuals" as one among four loosely federated groups with which he as an anthropologist identifies:

> The ethical is the guiding value. This is an oppositional position, one suspicious of sovereign powers, universal truths, overly relativized preciousness, local authenticity, moralisms high and low. Understanding is its second value, but an understanding suspicious of its own imperial tendencies. It attempts to be highly attentive to (and respectful of) difference, but is also wary of the tendency to essentialize difference. What we share as a condi-

275

tion of existence, heightened today by our ability, and at times our eagerness, to obliterate one another, is a specificity of historical experience and
place, however complex and contestable they might be, and a worldwide
macro-interdependency encompassing any local particularity. . . . Although
we are all cosmopolitans, *Homo sapiens* has done rather poorly in interpreting this condition. We seem to have trouble with the balancing act, pre-
ferring to reify local identities or construct universal ones. We live in-
between.[14]

The cosmopolitan manifests an acute awareness of living in between, dis-
playing a temperamental (one might even say principled) discomfort with a
too-explicit affirmation of the universalism that nonetheless prompts suspicion of "overly relativized preciousness" or "local authenticity." Most of the
current articulations of cosmopolitanism exhibit some version of this balancing act.[15]

As the preceding discussion makes clear, the ethical stance characterizing new articulations of cosmopolitanism has been especially influenced by
the disciplinary crises of (post)modern anthropology. Partly because of this
influence, cosmopolitan ethics can appear at times to be narrow and con-
trived, modeled as they are on a relatively bracketed encounter between
strangers or travelers. Even given the demand for historical and geopolitical
analysis in the "discrepant cosmopolitanisms" of Robbins and Clifford, the
cosmopolitan encounter can appear restrictively dyadic, transient, thin, and
protected, unlikely to have any effect on larger political structures and
forces, to which it can seem culpably inattentive in its valorization and cultivation of "mobile, reciprocal interconnectedness."

But one must guard against giving disproportionate emphasis to the anthropological ethics influencing current articulations of cosmopolitanism. As
I also stated at the outset, the new interest in cosmopolitanism stems largely
from a concern with the question of nationalism and, by extension, with attendant issues of domestic governance and international politics. Hollinger's
Postethnic America engages precisely this matrix of cosmopolitan concerns,
while simultaneously giving voice to those intersubjective ideals I have just
been articulating. The debate in the *Boston Review* over Martha Nussbaum's
"Patriotism and Cosmopolitanism" also brings larger political issues to the
fore. Indeed, the conflicts generated by Nussbaum's piece, which dramatically opposes cosmopolitan ideals to the dangers of provincial patriotism,
symptomatically register tensions over nationalism internal to the new cosmopolitanisms. Lastly, Julia Kristeva has written with insight and eloquence
on the relation between cosmopolitanism and nationalism. Because her ap-

proach in many ways reconciles the oppositions driving the divergences between cosmopolitanism and the new universalisms, I will reserve discussion of her work until the end of the essay.

Although Hollinger describes and endorses a form of cosmopolitanism that he sees operative in the current debates over multiculturalism, the phrase *postethnic perspective* ultimately stands in as his ethico-political ideal, partly, I believe, because it more readily adopts the lexical features of our time: the obligatory *post-* and the recognition of the centrality of the category of ethnicity to many people's self-understandings. But Hollinger underscores the continuities between his postethnic perspective and the cosmopolitanism articulated by American intellectuals earlier in the twentieth century. Indeed, Randolph Bourne's 1916 essay, "Trans-National America," a remarkably resonant endorsement of hyphenated identities, serves as a kind of touchstone for Hollinger's entire study.[16]

Hollinger advocates cosmopolitanism because it places a check on the proliferation of ethnic enclaves and the divisive idea of race-based descent. At the same time, he affirms the value of civic nationalism for a historically multicultural United States. One virtue of Hollinger's argument is that he does not engage in the facile and quixotic rejection of nationalism *tout court*, but rather follows out Liah Greenfeld's distinction between ethnic and civic nationalism in an attempt to preserve the values of the latter: its emphasis on voluntary association, democratic will formation, and tolerance of cultural difference.[17] He specifically argues that the importance of civic nation-states in protecting rights and providing basic welfare programs such as health care and social security is undervalued by proponents of postnationality such as Arjun Appadurai.[18]

As evidenced particularly in the *Boston Review* forum, many thinkers have affirmed a mutually reinforcing relationship between cosmopolitanism and patriotism. This argument can take different forms. One can simply enfold patriotism into an inclusive cosmopolitanism, arguing that individuals' affiliations can be multilayered and nonantagonistic. A corollary of this argument is often that humans need to make identifications on a scale smaller than the "world" or "humanity"; by this account, an exclusionary cosmopolitanism is "thin," "bloodless," "airless," "superficial." One can also assert an affinity between civic nationalism and cosmopolitanism: both share liberal-humanist values and privilege democratic practices, voluntary associations, and a self-reflective relation to cultural heritage and cultural difference.[19] This is the route Hollinger predominantly takes, though within the context of an elaborate endorsement of inclusive cosmopolitanism.

Of course, as Jacques Derrida has argued in the case of France and Europe, it is quite possible for the alliance between nationalism and cosmopolitanism to support a cultural imperialism that is difficult to distinguish from a refurbished ethnic nationalism. Ventriloquizing this position, Derrida writes: "I am (we are) all the more national for being European, all the more European for being trans-European and international; no one is more cosmopolitan and authentically universal than the one, than this 'we,' who is speaking to you."[20] Yet a potentially problematic rhetoric of exemplarity can attend not only cosmopolitanism but also endorsements of postnational or transnational identity. Indeed, Appadurai himself looks hopefully to the United States as a place where postnationality might particularly thrive. The problem is not, however, with aspiration to exemplarity per se, but rather with the forms of unexamined elitism or complacent universalism that such aspiration may, but certainly need not, generate. The more promising and vigilant versions of cosmopolitanism avoid this danger (as do, for that matter, provocative articulations of postnationality like Appadurai's). If the coimbrication of nationalism and cosmopolitanism issues in claims to be the universal subject, then the excesses of a narrow universalism have overwhelmed the promising openness of cosmopolitanism. But this is not necessarily what is happening when one makes appeal to particular national histories; there are reasons the democratic traditions of the United States and France might have something to teach us about cosmopolitan ideals.

Hollinger aims to highlight cosmopolitanism as a significant intellectual and political tradition in the United States, whose current manifestations are sometimes lost within an insufficiently analyzed multiculturalist debate. Hollinger argues that there are two distinct strains within contemporary discourse on ethnicity: the cosmopolitan and the pluralist. He believes that although both strains have been united in their struggle for greater tolerance and diversity, they have different inflections:

> Pluralism differs from cosmopolitanism in the degree to which it endows with privilege particular groups, especially the communities that are well established at whatever time the ideal of pluralism is invoked. While cosmopolitanism is willing to put the future of every culture at risk through the sympathetic but critical scrutiny of other cultures, pluralism is more concerned to protect and perpetuate particular, existing cultures. . . . If cosmopolitanism can be casual about community building and community maintenance and tends to seek voluntary affiliations of wide compass, pluralism promotes affiliations on the narrower grounds of shared history and is more quick to see reasons for drawing boundaries between communities.

> Cosmopolitanism is more oriented to the individual, whom it is likely to understand as a member of a number of different communities simultaneously. Pluralism is more oriented to the group, and is likely to identify each individual with reference to a single, primary community. (85–86)

In keeping with his inclusive cosmopolitanism, Hollinger takes pains to say that his notion of postethnicity is not meant to constitute an absolute break with ethnic identifications; rather, it develops cosmopolitan ideals of voluntary affiliation in light of "the past quarter-century's greater appreciation for a variety of kinds of ethnic connectedness" (4). From a postethnic perspective, one does not dissociate oneself from particular attachments in a purely negative way, but rather reflectively relates to overlapping communities, and sees the individual's relation to its multiple attachments as voluntary, shifting, and part of an ongoing process. Hollinger thus does not want to rule out practices of reflective return to ethnic and other communities, but he wishes such practices to be undertaken in light of broader commitments to civic-democratic culture at the national level.

Clearly, though like Robbins he does not really flesh this out, Hollinger sees cosmopolitanism exerting normative pressure when it questions attachments that are unquestioned from the pluralist perspective. Individuals or groups that threaten civic-democratic ideals, such as neo-Nazis and advocates of ethnic cleansing, can presumably be condemned from the cosmopolitan perspective, but not so straightforwardly from the pluralist one. Hollinger thus articulates a cosmopolitanism that serves as the basis for a specific form of national government, civic democracy; moreover, he argues that his nationalist perspective is compatible with increased global awareness and the fostering of international relations modeled on democratic institutions.

In its advocacy of specific political institutions that promote cultural self-reflexivity, voluntary affiliation, and openness to diversity, Hollinger's program shares affinities with the ambitious ethico-political agendas of Habermas and Seyla Benhabib, both of whom he cites approvingly. Habermas differs from the cosmopolitans insofar as he attempts a justification of democratic institutions through appeal to a universal conception of communicative reason and its attendant ideals of equality and reciprocity. His formalistic approach, as I have already suggested, is temperamentally at odds with the new cosmopolitan sensibility, which feels that formal universalism violates the very diversity it aims to accommodate. Hollinger voices this concern about universalism quite directly: "We can distinguish a universalist will to find common ground from a cosmopolitan will to engage human diversity" (84). Interestingly, Seyla Benhabib, who has been critical of the extreme formalism of traditional communicative ethics, particularly its privileging of a generalized and rationalistic conception of otherness over a more attentive and at least in part *felt* relation to the specificity of the other, has articulated a new "interactive universalism" that moves communicative ethics closer to the spirit of the new cosmopolitanisms with their "recognition, acceptance, and eager exploration of diversity" (Hollinger 84).[21] Indeed, the possible convergence of a more culturally sensitive universalism and a more politically ambitious cosmopolitanism reveals the potential complementarity of these two self-conscious inheritors of the divided legacies of modernity.

Thus far I have been discussing cosmopolitanism's relationship to universalism conceived in traditionally humanist, Enlightenment, or neo-Kantian terms. I now want to pursue the relationship between the new cosmopolitanisms and those poststructuralist reconsiderations of universalism that I invoked at the beginning of this essay. I will do so by briefly comparing the new cosmopolitanisms to two recent approaches to universality, Judith Butler's discussion in *Feminist Contentions*, "For a Careful Reading," which in fact largely replicates her response to Nussbaum in the *Boston Review*, and Etienne Balibar's arguments in "Ambiguous Universality," an essay that appeared in a special issue of *differences* devoted to reconsiderations of universalism. By way of conclusion, I will then turn to Kristeva's provocative and potentially bridge-building arguments in *Nations without Nationalism*.

In "For a Careful Reading," Butler's assertions about universality take place in the context of her general belief that modern identity formation is fundamentally exclusionary insofar as it takes place within a normative heterosexual regime. In keeping with arguments that structured influential poststructuralist responses to the essentialism debates, and actually in contrast to her own earlier arguments in *Gender Trouble*, Butler enacts a double gesture.[22] On the one hand, she insists, we must rigorously critique and expose the exclusions that attend any attempt to assert individual and collective identity. On the other hand, we must recognize that we cannot and ultimately should not avoid such acts of identity assertion: "To set norms, to affirm aspirations, to articulate the possibilities of a more fully democratic and participatory political life is, nevertheless, a necessity. And I would claim the same for the contested status of 'universality'" (129).

As in the case of Ernesto Laclau, Butler's recuperated universalism is articulated almost exclusively in relation to rights, the claim for which is assumed as the primary political act. According to Butler, any actual claim for rights will always be situated and hence can never be truly universal: we can never know that we have achieved a full articulation of universality because we might always encounter a divergent or contestatory articulation of what it means to be universal. There are always cultural conventions that delimit, in her phrase, "the scope of rights considered to be universal" (130). Still, despite this fact, and as the earlier quote indicates, this does not mean that we should not deploy the term *universal*; we should in fact continuously attempt to give it a fuller articulation, so as to include groups that have hitherto been excluded from its purview. One key way to forward this goal is to set different conceptions of universality and of rights in dialogue with one another, in order to aggravate our awareness of cultural divergence and to hone our capacity for transformative intercultural encounters. Thus emerges the call for *translation*: we must engage in the task of

> [articulating] universality through a difficult labor of translation, one in which the terms made to stand for one another are transformed in the process, and where the movement of that unanticipated transformation establishes the universal as that which is yet to be achieved, and which, in order to resist domestication, may never be fully or finally achievable. (130–31)

A double awareness of what we might call an ideal universality on the one hand and actual (and thereby inevitably false) universalities on the other conditions the political attitude Butler advocates. The elusiveness of the universal, its function as a receding goal, keeps the political process vital for Butler, and she specifically opposes her position to the normative philosophy of communicative ethics, which for her is too certain of its claims for the universality of communicative reason. Butler views appeals to shared rationality as attempts to secure in advance those political principles that need to take shape through the very enactment of political struggle and conflict; this is why the universal must be construed as a horizon rather than a foundation. For Butler, a universality that is true to the primacy of political struggle must be articulated in terms of the immediate political claims of oppressed or excluded groups.

The democratic forms of cosmopolitanism differ from Butler's reconstructed universality in that they favor those political institutions seen to ensure the autonomy and freedom required for critically reflective practices of affiliation, disaffiliation, and reaffiliation, for the fullest expression of what we might call hybrid individuality in a multicultural context. Although democratic cosmopolitanism certainly can encompass those forms of political struggle and conflict that seek to secure the democratic conditions for the

full flowering of cosmopolitanism, it nonetheless imagines democratic institutions as a desired precondition (if never fully secure) rather than a necessarily receding horizon. This emphasis on securing the conditions for the free
enactment of individuality places cosmopolitanism closer to liberalism than
to the radical traditions of critique on which Butler relies.

Butler's emphasis on rights claims might be seen as falling within the
logic of pluralism described by Hollinger, because it would appear to aim
simply for greater inclusivity of already constituted groups. But Butler
clearly wishes this to be not merely an additive but a radically transformative process. The sense of the human will alter radically and remain unstable
as competing versions come into contact and seek to translate one another.
One might be tempted to claim that the emphasis on translation constitutes
an ethos analogous to the one characterizing the new cosmopolitanisms, but
there are significant differences between this conception of translation and
the cultivated intersubjective sensibilities promoted by Robbins and Clifford. It is important to notice that Butler locates the enabling disruption of
any given universality at the linguistic level: it is the conflicting *terms* of universality that are transformed in the process of translation, and it is that
"unanticipated transformation" that effectively thwarts any static universalism. A linguistic destabilization guarantees the vitality of the political
process. The discussion of universality thus focuses on a semiological level,
where the disruptive vicissitudes of the given norms of universality are more
primary than an elaboration of intersubjective conduct in a diverse world. It
is precisely this abstractive ascent to a level that exceeds the interpretive
and interactive practices of individuals and groups that cosmopolitan ethics
so assiduously refuses.

Balibar's discussion of universality enables us to press these distinctions
further. He provisionally specifies three different types of universality: real
universality, fictive universality, and ideal universality. *Real universality*
refers to the fact that given the global reach of economic, political, cultural,
and communicative structures, we exist within a world that has effectively
become unified. For this reason, the historic ideal of "establishing universality by connecting humankind with itself, creating a cosmopolis" is now obsolete because it is redundant. Balibar stresses, however, that real universality
has exacerbated rather than alleviated social and cultural differences, antag-
onisms, and conflicts. *Fictive universality* is closer to what we think of when
we discuss the ideals of the Enlightenment: it is for Balibar entirely constructed, but felicitous insofar as it leads dominated groups to struggle for
inclusion under the rubric of the Rights of Man. The price to be paid for

such inclusion is, however, normalization. In acceding to the status of a subject guaranteed rights under the banner of universality, the subject also is constrained to be "normal" by various regimes of power. *Ideal universality* can be set against the constraints of fictive universality. It refers to the fundamental insurrection of individuals and collectivities against normalcy and in the name of noncoercion and nondiscrimination (what for Balibar is collected under the term *equaliberty*, an ideal of freedom and equality together).

Both Butler and Balibar rearticulate the universal ideals that inform political struggle and drive political critique, while at the same time acknowledging the historicity, the fictiveness, of any particular universalism. Like the new cosmopolitanisms, the reconsiderations of universalism are marked by heightened sensitivity to the potential violence and coerciveness of imperial thinking. But, importantly, the ideals of intersubjective recognition and engagement so prominent within cosmopolitanism do not emerge forcefully in these discussions of universalism. I attribute this in part to the fact that the non-normalizing universal, or ideal universality, is so fundamentally linked to a conception of negative freedom rather than the complex negotiations of multiple affiliations that characterize cosmopolitanism. Butler and Balibar foreground what one might call the drama of subjection entailed by fictive universality: its normalizing and hence exclusionary effects. What serves as the condition of possibility for a vital political struggle is a subversive force of negative freedom: the instability precipitated by the act of translation in Butler's case, and the insurrectionary force that resists all coercion and normalization in Balibar's. A less radical conception of freedom animates the cosmopolitan desire for reflective relations to cultural heritages and for noncoercive, reciprocal exchanges between variously situated people.[23] The new universalisms, by contrast, tend to oscillate between a profound conviction that all intersubjective encounters are marked by exclusion and violence, saturated with power-laden effects, and an assertion of radical potentialities for transformation or subversion.

Julia Kristeva presents a special case in this regard, because her writings on cosmopolitanism actually integrate elements of both the new universalisms and the new cosmopolitanisms, and in a way that vivifies the tensions that I have been drawing out. To put it simply, she shares the suspiciousness of the new universalisms and the utopianism of the cosmopolitans. Here, first, is Kristeva's defense of cosmopolitan universalism:

> It would seem to me that to uphold a universal, transnational principle of
> Humanity that is distinct from the historical realities of nation and citizen-

ship constitutes, on the one hand, a continuation of the Stoic and Augustin-
ian legacy, of that ancient and Christian cosmopolitanism that finds its place
among the most valuable assets of our civilization and that we henceforth
must go back to and bring up to date. But above all and on the other hand,
such upholding of universality appears to me as a rampart against a nationalist, regionalist, and religious fragmentation whose integrative contractions
are only too visible today. (26–27)

Kristeva eloquently articulates the need for a renewed cosmopolitanism
and aims to vindicate its earlier traditions. In general, *Nations without Nationalism* defends the ideals of the Enlightenment against reductive and overwhelmingly negative critique, arguing that we should resuscitate some of its
most promising ideas and writers. Kristeva focuses especially on Montesquieu's *esprit général*, suggesting that the concept might aid us in articulating new transitional nationalisms that will hasten the development of international or polynational confederations. Like Hollinger, she finds invocations
of postnationalism quixotic, and believes we must support national forms
that protect democratic practices and the voluntary affiliations that promote
cosmopolitanism generally. That is, she too defends civic forms of nationalism over and against the dangerous destructiveness of ethnic nationalisms.

Yet, unlike some proponents of cosmopolitanism, Kristeva remains wary
of the potentially exclusionary effects of universalist programs. Indeed, her
own highly developed psychoanalytic theory of abjection, which claims that
coherent identity is achieved through the process of excluding and denigrat-
ing forms of otherness, has been fundamental to Butler's arguments about
the violence of heteronormativity. Thus Kristeva goes on to sound an important caveat directly after asserting the importance of universalism:

> Yes, let us have universality for the rights of man, provided we integrate in
> that universality not only the smug principle according to which "all men are
> brothers" but also that portion of conflict, hatred, violence, and destructive-
> ness that for two centuries since the *Declaration* has ceaselessly been un-
> loaded upon the realities of wars and fratricidal closeness and that the
> Freudian discovery of the unconscious tells us is a surely modifiable but yet
> constituent part of the human psyche. (27)

Kristeva's sense of the modifiability of a nonetheless universal destructiveness acts as a wedge of hope enabling belief in the ethical efficacy of cosmopolitanism. Derived from psychoanalysis, Kristeva's cosmopolitanism is
defined both by detachment from provincial identities and by the therapeu-

tic exploration of strangeness within and outside of the self. It serves as the foundation for an individual ethical practice and as the primary principle animating the democratic and fundamentally liberal practices of civic and transitional "nations without nationalism." For Kristeva, only through the exploration of otherness, and the crucial acknowledgment of strangeness within the self, can people begin to "give up hunting for the scapegoat outside their group" (51). Psychoanalysis can contribute to a renewed universalist project insofar as it teaches the ethically enabling truth that "only strangeness is universal" (21). By acknowledging this truth, we will cease to consolidate the self over and against a foreign other.

Kristeva thus sublates the opposition, articulated by Hollinger, whereby universalism asserts sameness and cosmopolitanism explores and embraces diversity and otherness. She may at times sound too optimistic about the seemingly magical capacity of therapeutic transformations to transfigure national politics, yet she also tempers the idealism of cosmopolitanism with a stern warning about the power of psychically driven forms of destructiveness, violence, exclusion, and hatred. This element in Kristeva's writings, I think, distinguishes her sharply from many current articulations of cosmopolitanism, and in fact renders more obtrusive their generally low levels of anxiety and suspicion. Cosmopolitanism embraces rather than scrutinizes its fascination with otherness, resisting the idea that it is tainted by aestheticist or erotic elements. It values interest in otherness for its own sake, and does not think that such interest either can or should be reduced to self-interest, or some monolithic conception of pervasive power. In part, such optimism and casualness must be viewed as a studied reaction to the forms of negative critique dominating much cultural criticism. But absence of anxiety can also indicate absence of duress and, by extension, certain forms of privilege or unacknowledged elitism.

Let me stress here that the current manifestations of cosmopolitanism all tend to be highly self-reflexive about the problem of elitism. One impulse behind using the term *cosmopolitanism* seems to be, as I have indicated, an attempt to situate clearly the putatively universal Western observer or metropolitan intellectual, at the same time that one sees the mobility and self-reflexivity associated with the ideal as characterizing any number of positions hitherto cast as local or native.[24] Still, one might reasonably ask whether the avowal of cosmopolitanism is destined to have a retrograde effect in the current debates. Why dredge up this tainted and problematic word? Robbins probably has the most defensible answer when he says, in effect, dredge it up so we know our hands are always dirty anyway. Clifford would undoubtedly say that when the term is extended to multiple cultural

285

positions, it ceases to be the elitist epithet it once was. Hollinger and Kristeva would be more adamant about the honorable tradition of cosmopolitanism, and its applicability to the ethico-political challenges of our time; indeed, neither Hollinger nor Kristeva is particularly troubled by the way in which the word might be said to be irrevocably invested in its own cultural capital.[25]

There are obvious dangers that attend the new elaborations of cosmopolitanism. The narrowly ethical versions can sometimes appear to over-emphasize a heroicized individual cultivating its relation to otherness and to global diversity: here cosmopolitanism risks becoming an art of virtue for the nineties that stands in for broader-based political programs. The skittishness over more rigorously justified philosophical arguments is also, I believe, ultimately misplaced, if understandable. The continuing refinement of communicative ethics avoids many of the problems plaguing strict Habermasian formalism, and a closer scrutiny of that philosophical dialogue could have much to offer the new cosmopolitanisms, which so far seem content with an ad hoc pragmatic stance. But despite these limitations, there are many aspects of the reconfigured cosmopolitanism that are appealing and certainly analytically useful: its promotion of descriptive analyses from a participatory perspective that is nonetheless self-reflexive and critical; its exoteric genres and modes; its suggestive way of articulating relations among disciplinary formation, global position, and lived ethos; its flexibility as a term that can describe various aesthetics, ethics, and intellectual programs; its desire to exert normative pressure and to refuse the fastidious pieties of negative critique; its linking of self-conscious positioning to the tasks of translation, receptivity to otherness, and the ongoing project of universalism. But apart from the question of how fully the new cosmopolitanisms should be endorsed, it remains clear that we do need to recognize and analyze its manifestations, and to distinguish them from universalism on the one hand and localism on the other. As I stated at the beginning of this essay, focusing on the term will also help pluralize the effects and sites of Enlightenment discourse, and complicate our ongoing histories of modernity's effects. Most significantly, I think that attending to a hybrid concept such as this will allow for a more complex conception of detachment, which is often reductively opposed to a valorized conception of situatedness or, alternatively, too easily celebrated as negative freedom.

Notes

An earlier version of this essay was given as a talk at the Incorporations Conference sponsored by the Unit for Criticism and Interpretive Theory at the University of Illinois, Urbana–Champaign, March 9–10, 1996. I especially want to thank the two conference organizers, Melissa Deem and Chris Kamrath, for providing the initial occasion for pursuing this project, and the conference participants for their engaged reactions to the topic. This chapter has also benefited from readings by Dilip Gaonkar, Allen Hance, and Bruce Robbins.

1. See Etienne Balibar, "Ambiguous Universality," *differences* 7, no. 1 (1995): 48–74; Judith Butler, "Kantians in Every Culture?" *Boston Review* 19, no. 5 (1994): 18; Judith Butler, "For a Careful Reading," in Linda Nicholson, ed., *Feminist Contentions: A Philosophical Exchange* (New York: Routledge, 1995), 127–43; Ernesto Laclau, "Universalism, Particularism, and the Question of Identity," in John Rajchman, ed., *The Identity in Question* (New York: Routledge, 1995): 93–108; Ernesto Laclau, "Subject of Politics, Politics of the Subject," *differences* 7, no. 1 (1995): 146–64; Naomi Schor, "French Feminism Is a Universalism," *differences* 7, no. 1 (1995): 15–47; Joan Scott, "Universalism and the History of Feminism," *differences* 7, no. 1 (1995): 1–14. The spring 1995 issue of *differences* in which several of the above-cited works appear is a special issue devoted to the topic of universalism.
2. For an overview and analysis of the essentialism debates, see Amanda Anderson, "Cryptonormativism and Double Gestures: The Politics of Poststructuralism," *Cultural Critique* 21 (1992): 63–95.
3. James Clifford, "Traveling Cultures," in Larry Grossberg, Cary Nelson, and Paula A. Treichler, eds., *Cultural Studies: Now and in the Future* (New York: Routledge, 1992), 96–112; Bruce Robbins, *Secular Vocations: Intellectuals, Professionalism, Culture* (London: Verso, 1993); David A. Hollinger, *Postethnic America: Beyond Multiculturalism* (New York: Basic Books, 1995). Page number references to these three studies will be made parenthetically in the text.
4. "[In] the present context, a reflection involving an audience wider than that of academic circles seems necessary where the concept of the nation is concerned—a concept that has welded the coherence of individuals in Western history since the eighteenth century." Julia Kristeva, *Nations without Nationalism*, trans. Leon S. Roudiez (New York: Columbia University Press, 1993), 6. Further page number references to this work will be made parenthetically in the text. See also Julia Kristeva, *Strangers to Ourselves*, trans. Leon S. Roudiez (New York: Columbia University Press, 1991). Nussbaum's essay "Patriotism and Cosmopolitanism," along with twenty-nine responses, appeared in *Boston Review* 19, no. 5 (1994): 3–34. It was subsequently published in book form, along with eleven of the original replies and five additional ones. See Martha Nussbaum with Respondents, *For Love of Country: Debating the Limits of Patriotism*, ed. Joshua Cohen (Boston: Beacon, 1996).
5. This brief sketch of the historical shifts in cosmopolitan detachment is partly indebted to Max H. Boehm, "Cosmopolitanism," in *Encyclopedia of the Social Sciences*, vol. 4 (New York: Macmillan, 1931), 457–61.
6. For a useful discussion of the difference between exclusive and inclusive cosmopolitanism in the eighteenth century, see Alan D. McKillop, "Local Attachment and Cosmopolitanism: The Eighteenth-Century Pattern," in Frederick W. Hilles and Harold Bloom, eds., *From Sensibility to Romanticism* (New York: Oxford University Press, 1965). I am indebted to McKillop's terminology here.
7. For discussion of the tension between elitism and egalitarianism in Enlightenment cosmopolitanism, see Thomas J. Schlereth, *The Cosmopolitan Ideal in Enlightenment*

Thought: Its Form and Function in the Ideas of Franklin, Hume, and Voltaire, 1694–1790 (Notre Dame, Ind.: University of Notre Dame Press, 1977), 14.

8. See Edward W. Said, *The World, the Text, and the Critic* (Cambridge: Harvard University Press, 1983), 1–30; Clifford, "Traveling Cultures."

9. Tim Brennan, "Cosmopolitans and Celebrities," *Race & Class* 31, no. 1 (1989): 1–19. Page number references to this work will be made parenthetically in the text. A somewhat expanded version of this essay appears in Tim Brennan, *Salman Rushdie and the Third World* (New York: St. Martin's, 1989).

10. This obviously has resonances with Fanon as well, which Brennan discusses. See "Cosmopolitans and Celebrities," 16–18.

11. Paul Gilroy, *The Black Atlantic: Modernity and Double Consciousness* (Cambridge: Harvard University Press, 1993). Page number references to this work will be made parenthetically in the text.

12. For invocations of the need for translation, see Jacques Derrida, *The Other Heading: Reflections on Today's Europe*, trans. Pascale-Anne Brault and Michael B. Naas (Bloomington: Indiana University Press, 1992); Butler, "Kantians in Every Culture?"

13. Cosmopolitanism's casual normativity might also be described as a kind of pragmatism, a position with which it appears to share some affinities. For a discussion of the connections between cosmopolitan ethics and liberal pragmatism, see Tobin Siebers, "The Ethics of Anti-Ethnocentrism," *Michigan Quarterly Review* 32, no. 1 (1993): 41–70. Siebers especially emphasizes the fundamental optimism and hopefulness characterizing both.

14. Paul Rabinow, "Representations Are Social Facts: Modernity and Post-modernity in Anthropology," in James Clifford and George E. Marcus, eds., *Writing Culture: The Poetics and Politics of Ethnography* (Berkeley: University of California Press, 1986), 258.

15. The concern with how to conduct oneself amid a destabilizing diversity of cultures and norms also exercised the eighteenth-century cosmopolites. In key ways this was linked to their aspirations to develop a science of human nature, a humanist project that is not really in the same spirit as some of these new articulations of cosmopolitanism. But there was also the sense that being a "citizen of the world" required a specific form of character and a rigorous cultivation of virtue. The altruistic, expansive form of cosmopolitanism so linked to our notion of eighteenth-century sentimentalism is partly an attempt to express an ideal of sympathetic encounter of broad varieties of experience. The eighteenth-century elaboration of codes of conduct, manners, and mores is far too momentous and complex a cultural development to go into here, and was linked to the breakdown in aristocratic privilege and the rearticulations of the concept of virtue in the midst of a developing bourgeois ideology. There are of course deeply suspicious readings to be done—and that have been done—of all of this. But such rigorous attention to conduct and manners also was tied to attempts to facilitate the challenges of intercultural contact and exchange. See Schlereth, *The Cosmopolitan Ideal*; Peter Gay, *The Enlightenment: An Interpretation*, 2 vols. (New York: Alfred A. Knopf, 1966, 1969).

16. Interestingly, Bourne also is held up as exemplary in Mitchell Cohen, "Rooted Cosmopolitanism: Thoughts on the Left, Nationalism, and Multiculturalism," *Dissent* (Fall 1992): 478–83.

17. See Liah Greenfeld, *Nationalism: Five Roads to Modernity* (Cambridge: Harvard University Press, 1992).

18. Hollinger specifically takes on the arguments in Arjun Appadurai, "Patriotism and Its Futures," *Public Culture* 5 (1993): 411–29.

19. For examples of these arguments in the *Boston Review* forum, see the responses by

Anthony Appiah, Robert Pinsky, Benjamin R. Barber, Leo Marx, Paul Berman, Charles Beitz, Charles Taylor, Anthony Kronman, and Lawrence Blum. For an argument that takes on the charge that cosmopolitanism will somehow fail to promote the emotionally rich forms of affiliation associated with nationalism or communities of smaller scale, see Bruce Robbins, "The Weird Heights: On Cosmopolitanism, Feeling, and Power," *differences* 7, no. 1 (1995): 165–87.

20. Derrida, *The Other Heading*, 48.
21. "Interactive universalism acknowledges the plurality of modes of being human, and differences among humans, without endorsing all these pluralities and differences as morally and politically valid. While agreeing that normative disputes can be settled rationally, and that fairness, reciprocity and some procedure of universalizability are constituents, that is, necessary conditions of the moral standpoint, interactive universalism regards difference as a starting point for reflection and action. In this sense, 'universality' is a regulative ideal that does not deny our embodied and embedded identity, but aims at developing moral attitudes and encouraging political transformations that can yield a point of view acceptable to all. Universality is not the ideal consensus of fictitiously defined selves, but the concrete process in politics and morals of the struggle of concrete, embodied selves, striving for autonomy." Seyla Benhabib, *Situating the Self: Gender, Community and Postmodernism in Contemporary Ethics* (New York: Routledge, 1992), 153.
22. Judith Butler, *Gender Trouble: Feminism and the Subversion of Identity* (New York: Routledge, 1990). In enacting this double gesture, Butler here is closely following Gayatri Chakravorty Spivak's position on essentialism, a position Butler earlier sought to sublate through the more exclusive emphasis on the unremitting subversion of identity, and on the need to derive politics directly and consistently from a constructionist position. For a discussion of Butler's earlier position in relation to Spivak, see Anderson, "Cryptonormativism and Double Gestures."
23. Cosmopolitanism as a deliberate alternative to "hybridity" bears on this discussion insofar as many poststructuralist appeals to hybridity rely on a similar conception of destabilizing subversion.
24. Of course this immediately raises the question of the relation between the terms *cosmopolitan* and *postcolonial*, especially as descriptors for individuals. Although there are sharp debates about the perceived diluting effect of the term *postcolonial* and its lack of clear positioning in relation to Third World struggles, it nonetheless may seem more attentive to situatedness than the word *cosmopolitan*, which celebrates mobility, detachment, and voluntary identification. But it is important to recognize that cosmopolitanism is an ethico-political ideal as well as a description of global positioning, and thus is open to appropriation by those situated more specifically as postcolonial. For debates on the term *postcolonial*, see Ella Shohat, "Notes on the 'Post-Colonial,'" *Social Text* 31–32 (1992): 99–113; Arif Dirlik, "The Postcolonial Aura: Third World Capitalism in the Age of Global Capitalism," *Critical Inquiry* 20 (1994): 328–56.
25. Hollinger's own investment in the cultural capital of the term, as opposed to the crassly economic resonances that Robbins likes so much, becomes apparent when he feels compelled to rant for a moment against Helen Gurley Brown, insisting that a Grand Canyon separates his ideal from the Cosmo girl, which must be blamed for giving the idea much of its current "lightness" (103). Kristeva's own lack of self-reflexivity might be said to indicate itself when she avows, "I am a cosmopolitan" (15), a form of expression that, though certainly conventional within cosmopolitan traditions, is strikingly absent from the current instances, where writers evince a reluctance to claim the term directly in this way. Cosmopolitanism is an advocated ideal, not a fully assumable identity.

Given Culture:
Rethinking Cosmopolitical Freedom in Transnationalism

Pheng Cheah

It is now commonplace in contemporary cultural criticism to say that we live in a postcolonial world. The celebration of cultural differences and the anti-Eurocentrism that characterizes "postcolonial" cultural studies, however, belong to a broader intellectual milieu. In the humanities and the "soft" social sciences, the fact of decolonization has been made into another occasion for the ongoing debate between relativists and universalists on the possibility of knowledge that transcends cultural boundaries.[1] It is in this spirit that Jean-François Lyotard links the *défaillance* of modernity to "resistance . . . on the part of the insurmountable diversity of cultures."[2] The shift from universal culture to cultures in the plural, from cosmopolitical freedom to local autonomy is, however, accompanied by a turn toward a primitivist construction of cultural others along quasi-anthropological lines.[3] This tendency can be politically dangerous, because freedom has not come with independence from territorial imperialism. A metropolitan cultural politics that espouses a hands-off approach to a museumized cultural other leaves the neocolonial staging of that other—fundamentalism, ethnicism, patriarchal nationalism—untouched. Yet, if we intervene in those other spaces as the self-proclaimed didacts of freedom,[4] we forget that we, too, are part of the crisis, because the problems of unequal development and the postindustrial feudalization of the periphery are fundamental structures of the global staging of *our* everyday.

In the face of this historical impasse, where neither post-Enlightenment universalism nor nationalist communitarianism is a viable ideologico-institutional vehicle for freedom, cosmopolitanism as a philosophical ideal is up for modest reinvention. On the one hand, a cosmopolitical frame of analysis is a necessary response to our continuing integration into a global system at various levels: economic, political, social, and cultural. On the other hand, any contemporary revival of "cosmopolitanism" must take a critical distance from the older-style cosmopolitanism of philosophical modernity.

This ancestor cosmopolitanism is best represented by Immanuel Kant's project for perpetual peace. Kant argued that international commerce was a form of sociability between states, paving the way for a cosmopolis or world federation in which a cosmopolitan culture would flourish.[5] Such a culture is cosmopolitical in two senses. First, it can attain its fullest development only in the state of peace that world federation brings.[6] Second, the ideational and affective content of this culture transcends ethnic or racial boundaries because it fosters universally communicable values and pleasures that promote sociability, the constitutive feature of our humanity.[7] Mutually enhancing each other, the objective historical tendency of international commerce toward world federation and the humanizing processes of self-cultivation would bring about the empirical unity of humanity as a whole. Indeed, for Kant, cosmopolitical culture is a universally normative ideal because it is an asymptotic historical approximation of the universal moral community, the noumenal realm of human freedom that is no longer bound by deterministic laws of nature.

No revival of "cosmopolitanism" in contemporary neocolonial globalization can in good faith return fully to this robust sense of cosmopolitical culture. Few are now convinced of its rational-universalist grounding. The history of colonialism has disproven Kant's benign view of the unifying power of international commerce and discredited the moral and civilizing claims of cosmopolitical culture. Furthermore, although contemporary globalization has complicated the nation-state form, it has not rendered it obsolete as a form of political organization. However, given that globalization requires a cosmopolitical frame of analysis, the question is whether we can speak of the emergence of a new "cosmopolitanism"—that is, a critical or emancipatory project of a global consciousness—and, if so, what practical-logical forms this new "cosmopolitanism" has taken or ought to take.

In the course of this chapter, I will try to answer these broader questions about cosmopolitanism in the current conjuncture. However, the immediate focus of my essay is why the peculiar revival of postcolonial nationalism in neocolonial globalization—a phenomenon that I will call *given culture*—requires us to question the dominant concept of culture in postcolonial studies today. This detour is instructive because postcolonial cultural studies grew out of a critique of cosmopolitical culture but is currently reclaiming the term *cosmopolitanism*. Broadly speaking, contemporary postcolonial studies has modulated from antiuniversalist/anticosmopolitan discourses of cultural diversity to discourses of cultural hybridity that criticize the neo-Orientalist organicist presuppositions of the former. James Clifford and Homi Bhabha are the most influential theorists of hybridity. More recently, as exemplified by Clifford's term "discrepant cosmopolitanisms," both theorists have suggested that globalization inevitably leads to the formation of hybrid, radical cosmopolitanisms that attest to the ethico-political inefficacy of the nation-state. This makes hybridity theory a useful test case in assessing new articulations of cosmopolitanism in cultural studies.

In this essay, I argue that the accounts of radical cosmopolitan agency offered by hybridity theory obscure the material dynamics of nationalism in neocolonial globalization. This foreclosure occurs because hybridity theorists subscribe to the same concept of normative culture as the old-style philosophical cosmopolitanism they reject: the understanding of culture as the realm of humanity's freedom from the given. I further contend that the forms of transnational activity we are witnessing today are not new cosmopolitanisms but are instead aporetic cases of nationalism as given culture in a cosmopolitical force field. I suggest that these cases of given culture deform the philosopheme of normative culture at the heart of old and new cosmopolitanisms, including Marxist cosmopolitanism, and require us to reconceptualize the relation between culture and political-economic forces in terms of our responsibility to the given rather than our freedom from the given.

Hybridity as Cultural Agency and as New Cosmopolitanism

The concept of hybrid culture is formulated in polemical opposition to both the canonical concept of culture that grounds philosophical cosmopolitanism and the anthropological concept of culture that leads to multiculturalist relativism. *Universal* or *cosmopolitical culture* refers to a process of growth regulated by human rational self-cultivation and bound to the historical progress of entire societies. This is the canonical understanding of culture in philosophical modernity as *Bildung* (Hegel) or *Kultur* (Kant), a process and state of social existence that has universal normative validity. Homi Bhabha and James Clifford reject this canonical concept of culture for its colonialist implications and also for its historical link to neocolonial developmental narratives of political and economic modernization. However, they are also suspicious of the anthropological concept of culture, which they regard as a spurious organicist and cultural relativist attempt to manage the crisis of universalism. Hence their theories of hybrid culture have a negative and a positive aspect.

In its demystificatory aspect, hybridity theory exposes the violent implications of the canonical view of culture as an organic and coherent body, a process of ordering and a bounded realm of human value determinable by, and coextensive with, human reason.[8] Clifford detects this concept of culture in the Eurocentric cosmopolitical narrative of modernization but also in the relativist celebration of local cultures, which he sees as a displacement of the former.[9] Thus, in his discussion of ethnography and exhibitions of "primitive" art, Clifford suggests that a relativist culturalism engaged in an essentialist search for authentic cultural alterity murders local cultural futures by museumizing cultural otherness. These are very pertinent criticisms. For present purposes, however, I want to focus on the positive formulation of hybridity as a more enabling theory of cultural resistance in postcolonial globality.

Unlike culturalist relativism, which emphasizes the autonomy and uniqueness of different cultures, a theory of hybrid culture acknowledges that Eurocentric cosmopolitical culture has achieved a factual universality through the imperialist project. However, Bhabha and Clifford argue that the implementation of cosmopolitical culture on other soil leads to its hybridization with native cultures, thereby subverting imperialism's cosmopolitical-cultural project. Indeed, they make the further claim that hybridization constitutes a site of resistance to the neotraditionalist, nativist cultural face of national liberation movements and postcolonial nation-states. Clifford describes the current era as syncretic and "postcultural": "The privilege given to . . . natural cultures is dissolving. . . . In a world where syncretism and parodic invention are becoming the rule, not the exception . . . it becomes increasingly difficult to attach human identity and meaning to a coherent 'culture'" (PC, 95). He celebrates a dispersed polycentric globe where cultures are hybrid, inorganic, and indeterminate because they are relational and in persistent flux.[10] Similarly, Bhabha suggests that hybrid culture is "the strategic activity of 'authorizing' agency; not the interpellation of pre-given sites of celebration or struggle."[11]

Hybridity theorists therefore break with the object theory of culture common to cosmopolitanism and traditional anthropology (culture as a self-identical and knowable entity, norm, or subject) and attempt to articulate a political theory of culture as a process or production in language. Their ethico-political rationale is that positivist accounts of culture as a pregiven empirical object have violent consequences because they are used to justify social hegemony and oppression. Hybridity theorists suggest that if we view culture as something constructed by discourse or signification, then the subject of culture becomes the site of permanent contestation. For example, Bhabha's anecdotal accounts of mimicry and ambivalence employ a vocabulary combining the enunciative split with the psychoanalytic thematic of disavowal to suggest that the moral and civilizing aspects of colonial discourse are split from its disavowed racist enunciatory conditions.[12] The disavowal is, however, expressed in the desire of colonial discourse for a subject of cultural difference that is not-quite/not-white, different but almost the same. The colonial project implements this relationship of mimicry between colonizer and colonized metaleptically to authorize its own discourse.[13] Bhabha suggests that because colonial cultural authority is constituted through the production of hybrid objects, these objects can subvert the moral truths of colonial authority by reflecting the wound of its split self-presence and reversing colonial disavowal.[14]

Bhabha's description of anticolonial subversion as the moment when the quasi-naturalistic authority of the colonial symbolic reverts back to its prior state as arbitrary sign depends on a reductive understanding of colonial rule as the establishment of *cultural* authority through the deployment of symbols (the Bible, the Law, and so on).[15] Without any argumentation, he subsequently inflates hybridity into a wellspring for the political contestation of all forms of cultural symbolization and the general articulation of marginal political identities by extending this definition of cultural authority to cover all hegemonic forms of social and cultural organization. This simplistic analogy between the contingency of signification and the contingency of sociocultural formations repeats the axiom that reality is discursively constructed. But what exactly is the political purchase in postcolonial cultural studies of this commonplace assertion that discourse produces the real? What are the ontological presuppositions behind these political claims?

Edward Said's *Orientalism* was a pathbreaking study of the discursive construction of the Orient as an object of colonial knowledge. However, in invoking the oppositional humanist intellectual as an antidote to the inequities of Orientalist discursive effects, Said had assumed the possibility of a self-reflective critical consciousness capable of grasping the limits of its own situated perspective in order to transcend provisionally the discursive formation that this consciousness inhabits. These redemptive moments of transcendence are premised on the freedom of the rational human will from discourse in the final instance. Situating themselves within a linguistic understanding of antihumanism, Clifford and Bhabha criticize Said for maintaining the exteriority of critical consciousness and the freedom of the rational will from discourse in the final instance.[16]

For Clifford, cultural identity is not something to be grasped outside discourse because it is not a matter of what was or what is but of becoming. Cultural identity is "never given but must be negotiated," "made in new political-cultural conditions of global relationality" (*PC*, 273, 275). This emphasis on the hybrid invention of culture extends the rhetorical play of self-reflective ethnographic writing into an account of agency. In postmodern ethnographic critique, cultural identity *qua* organic totality is said to be "written" in the narrow sense: it is artificially produced by the rhetorical/stylistic fiction of ethnographic authority in field notes. An awareness of the constructed nature of cultural identity, Clifford argues, enables resistance to cosmopolitanism, because instead of basing political claims on a nostalgia for an impossible authenticity, it opens up possibilities for hybrid local futures. Hence he urges us to rethink cultures "not as organically unified or traditionally continuous but rather as negotiated, present processes" (PC, 273). In Clifford's account of Mashpee identity, hybrid resistance involves reflexive symbolic self-invention, a strategic traffic with the processes of cultural meaning.[17] Indeed, he generalizes the hybrid inventiveness of Aimé Césaire's poetry into an alternative model for cultural-political agency.[18]

While Clifford's account of strategic agency does in fact presuppose an intentionalist notion of willed agency, the more important point is that despite his linguistic antihumanism or, better yet, because of it, Clifford's antinaturalist account of hybrid agency is an anthropologistic culturalism. This is because it articulates the distinctive ontological *predicament of culture*, the symbolic and fluid nature of human identity and existence, as opposed to the givenness or organicity of the natural or nonhuman. This residual anthropologistic culturalism is the fundamental ontological presupposition of theories of hybrid culture. It resurfaces as the notion of linguistic freedom in Bhabha's claim that hybrid resistance arises from the contingency of language as a system of signs. For Bhabha, "the discourse of the language-metaphor suggests that in each achieved symbol of cultural/political identity or synchronicity, there is always a repetition of the sign that represents the place of psychic ambivalence and social contingency."[19] This claim is typical of cultural analyses from literary studies that have unfailingly confined the dictum of the discursive production of reality within an anthropocentric horizon. These analyses operate on the unspoken assumption that because discourse consists of language, and language is the mark of the *anthropos*, the discursive construction of reality indicates the freedom of the human agent *qua* linguistic-social subject from the material constraints and bondage of being-in-nature. Thus, regardless of whether hybrid resistance is conceived as intentional strategic agency (Clifford) or as inhering in the enunciatory processes of symbolic forms and cultural authority (Bhabha), the imminence of subversion is perpetually present in the rifts between nature and culture, the Real and its representation/signification, matter and language/form, necessity and freedom.

For present purposes, my question is whether these theories of hybrid cultural agency, as they have developed into accounts of new radical cosmopolitanisms, are feasible accounts of political transformation in neocolonial globalization. This is indeed the claim made by Bhabha and Clifford, who invoke the terms *transnationalism* and *cosmopolitanism* to assert the importance of hybridity to an understanding of cultural contestation and political transformation in contemporary globalization. Like his account of hybridity, Clifford's reevaluation of cosmopolitanism in his much-cited essay "Traveling Cultures" is also a polemic against dominant epistemological practices within cultural anthropology that privilege relations of dwelling.[20] For Clifford, such localizing moves elide "the wider global world of intercultural import-export in which the ethnographic encounter is always enmeshed" (TC, 100). As an antidote, he suggests that we should "focus on hybrid, cosmopolitan experiences" (TC, 101), on how culture is produced through travel relations and local/global historical encounters. Within its polemical limits, this is a valuable critique of the organic, naturalizing bias of cultural anthropology. However, just as Clifford's critical use of hybridity had modulated into a positive account of hybrid cultural agency, this critical deployment of cosmopolitanism as traveling culture also gradually becomes a positive account of practical agency.

In his use of the term, Clifford tries to dissociate cosmopolitanism from the mobility of the privileged by focusing on "the ways people leave home and return [as the] enacting [of] differently centered worlds, interconnected cosmopolitanisms" (TC, 103). He describes non-European servants, helpers, companions, guides, and translators of European travelers as bearers of "cosmopolitan" viewpoints and characterizes working-class traveling culture as "a cosmopolitan, radical, political culture" (TC, 107). However, when Clifford champions a comparative study of cosmopolitanism that accounts for the fact that, in certain cases, "mobility is coerced, organized within regimes of dependent, highly disciplined labor" (TC, 107), he begins to endow cosmopolitan mobility with a normative dimension, claiming for it an important role in cultural and political transformation. For even as he acknowledges that materially oppressed travelers move under strong cultural, political, and economic compulsions, he also argues that "even the harshest conditions of travel, the most exploitative regimes, do not entirely quell resistance or the emergence of diasporic migrant cultures" (TC, 108). These cosmopolitan movements are presented as exemplary instances of active resistance to localism and cultural homogenization under global capitalism: "Such cultures of displacement and transplantation are inseparable from specific, often violent, histories of economic, political and cultural interaction, histories that generate . . . *discrepant cosmopolitanisms*. In this emphasis, we avoid at least, the excessive localism of particularist relativism, as well as the overly global vision of a capitalist or technocratic monoculture" (TC, 108).

We see from this that in Clifford's understanding, emancipatory cultural agency involves the outstripping of oppressive economic and political forces by cultural flux and activity. He implies that cultural stasis is a regressive product of oppressive forces, whereas physical mobility is the basis of eman- cipatory practice because it generates stasis-disrupting forms of cultural dis- placement. In Bhabha's hands, this physical mobility is raised to the higher level of linguistic freedom from naturalized culture. Bhabha suggests that since "the transnational dimension of cultural transformation—migration, diaspora, displacement, relocation" involves a translational sense of culture, the formation of the transnational postcolonial subject ought to be seen as one of "the historical traditions of cultural contingency and textual indeter- minacy (as forces of social discourse)."[21] Consequently, it appears that analyses of postcolonial, postmodern transnationalism *ought* to deploy Bhabha's vocabulary of hybridity, now hyperambitiously characterized as the project of a postcolonial countermodernity:[22]

> The postcolonial prerogative seeks to affirm and extend a new collaborative dimension, both within the margins of the nation-space and across bound- aries between nations and peoples. My use of poststructuralist theory emerges from this postcolonial contramodernity. . . . It is as if [concepts such as] the arbitrariness of the sign, the indeterminacy of writing, the splitting of the subject of enunciation . . . produce the most useful descriptions of the formation of "postmodern" cultural subjects. (*LC*, 175–76)

The corollary to this translational understanding of transnationalism is a linguistic antinationalism. Bhabha suggests that it is politically reactionary and debilitating to view the nation as an empirical sociological category (for instance, the modernist theories of Gellner and Anderson) or as a holistic cultural entity (organic theories of the nation) because organic theories de- fine national identity in totalizing ways, whereas sociological theories suppress possibilities of resistance to the nation.[23] He suggests that if we denaturalize the nation and understand national identity as "a form of social and textual affiliation" (*LC*, 140), an "ambivalent signifying system" (*LC*, 146), and a narrative process ridden with contestation, then we become more alert to the constitutive ambivalence within the nation that leads to its undermining.

The hybrid revival of cosmopolitanism therefore has two steps: an anti- localist/antinationalist argument and an argument that new radical cosmo- politanisms already exist. In the second argument, globalization is reduced to cultural hybridization in transnational mobility and transnational migrant cultures are characterized as existing radical cosmopolitanisms that subvert national culture (Bhabha) or localism (Clifford). Now, these moves to "re- cosmopolitanize" postcolonial cultural studies are not entirely surprising.

First, insofar as hybridity theory was initially a critique of the cosmopolitical and anthropological concepts of culture deployed by the imperialist civilizing mission and colonialist disciplines such as ethnography, the original type case of hybridization is the colonial cross-cultural encounter. Because colonialism is a historical precondition of contemporary transnationalism, the topos of cultural hybridization is easily extended to describe "alternative cosmopolitanisms from below." Second, both Clifford and Bhabha criticize organic theories of local culture for their continuity with nationalist ideology. Hence, especially in Bhabha's case, the suggestion that contemporary cultural hybridization gives rise to new cosmopolitanisms merely develops this implicit theoretical antinationalism into speculations about the imminent ethico-political inefficacy of the nation-state.

There are, however, more fundamental theoretical explanations for why hybridity theory develops into a new cosmopolitanism: its predication of culture as the human realm of flux and freedom from the bondage of being-in-nature, and its understanding of national culture as an ideological or naturalized constraint to be overcome. Indeed, it is not excessive to say that hybridity theorists are especially attracted to historical cases of migration and diasporic mobility because they see such cases as empirical instances of the flux they regard as the ontological essence of culture.

These attempts to erect actually existing radical cosmopolitanisms on the back of anthropologistic culturalism or linguistic freedom, however, rely on a cultural-reductionist argument. The suggestion that hybrid cultural practices constitute the birth of cosmopolitan consciousness and indicate the impending obsolescence of national identity and the nation-state makes sense only if we reduce the complexity of contemporary neocolonial globalization to one of its strands: cultural hybridization. Many have pointed out ad nauseam that hybridity theories are culturalisms that notoriously sidestep the constraints and tendencies of politico-economic processes by reducing them to cultural-significatory practices. I am making a more specific point. Although they are subsequently generalized into accounts of historical agency, the ideas of linguistic freedom and cultural flux actually originate from two very limited areas of analysis: the undermining of colonial authority and the ethnographic gaze in academic critique. Their alleged pertinence is limited to their demystificatory power. Any extrapolation from this negative use of hybridity to articulate a general theory of transformative agency inevitably exaggerates the role of signification and cultural representation in the functioning of sociopolitical life and its institutions.[24]

It is not to deny the importance of cultural legitimation in the formation of sociopolitical institutions and collective identities if I suggest that social consensus is not secured by ideological means alone. The social is not coextensive with, or exhausted by, its symbolic dimensions. Over and above identification with a naturalized cultural unity or linguistic interpellation into a national ideal, the formation and deformation of group loyalty also involves political-organizational and economic factors such as law enforcement, the provision of welfare and other services by the state, and the establishment of a framework for the distribution and regulation of economic resources and capabilities to satisfy human needs. Social transformation is not achieved simply by "relocating alternative hybrid sites of cultural negotiation" (LC, 178), because to be materially effective, emancipatory consciousness cannot subsist on linguistic dynamism or cultural-symbolic flux alone. The subversion that linguistic freedom makes possible, however, operates on a purely ideational level, where the capacity and potential for transformation is the freedom from the merely given inhering in the anthropologistic realm of culture. Thus, even as hybridity theorists evacuate the human agent *qua* intentional consciousness, its role is surreptitiously filled by language or culture, a nonnatural sign system or a process *sans* subject that is a relay of human freedom. This closet idealism is especially clear in Bhabha's anecdotes of historical resistance: Algerian liberation fighters are agents of interpretation who "destroy . . . the nationalist tradition" and are "free to negotiate and translate their cultural identities in a discontinuous intertextual temporality of cultural difference" (LC, 38). For Bhabha, the resistant subaltern is a reader who, in grasping modernity's discrepant moral truths, introduces an indeterminacy or "time-lag" that short-circuits the enunciative present of modernity.[25]

These linguistic culturalisms elide the point that even though culture is not reducible to empirical determinations such as politics and economics, it is not entirely autonomous or free from the taint of such determinations because it emerges from its relationships with these forces. These sociological and empirico-material constraints constitute and bind culture. They are part of the process by which culture is given, the material conditions of its effectivity as a historical force. To claim otherwise is to commit the most absurd of idealisms: it is to deprive culture of any effectivity by dematerializing it. Hence, when Bhabha tries to referentialize or historicize the subject of hybrid culture, as indeed he must in order to claim that it has historical effectivity, "social experience" becomes a mere place holder for linguistic indeterminacy, now abstractly renamed as "the contingency of history—the indeterminacy that makes subversion and revision possible" (LC, 179).

The shortcomings of unmooring cultural agency from the field of empirico-material forces that overdetermine it are especially pronounced in hybrid revivals of cosmopolitanism. These new cosmopolitanisms cannot explain why globalization has paradoxically led to the intensification of nationalism in the postcolonial South without resorting to the knee-jerk dismissal of the national/local as an ideological form. As we have seen, for Bhabha, hybridity's denaturalizing power is also an antinationalism: for him, the postcolonial nation is a naturalized ethnonational culture imposed from above, and its internal identification is plagued by the indeterminacies of signification. Because his focus on the internal destabilization of national cohesion extracts the nation from its geopolitical context, Bhabha ignores the fact that national consciousness can be formed through negative identification, induced by political-economic factors such as interstate relations within a neocolonial capitalist world economy (see *LC*, 147–48). Although Clifford's position is not explicitly antinationalist, his chronotope of traveling culture does not give equal time to the tenacity of national dwelling. Neither can explain the persistence of the postcolonial nation-state in contemporary globalization, for their heady celebration of the subversive possibilities of global flows prevents them from grasping that, in the absence of a world-state capable of ensuring an equitable international political and economic order, *the unevenness of political and economic globalization* makes the nation-state necessary as a political agent for defending the peoples of the South from the shortfalls of neocolonial capitalist global restructuring. Contra Bhabha, it is the defense against *neocolonial* globalization that makes national formation through negative identification both historically unavoidable and ethically imperative.

But perhaps it is asking too much from these hybrid cosmopolitanisms to expect them to respond to the precarious necessity of postcolonial nationalism in neocolonial globalization. For is it not obvious, from the start, that the paradigm for these radical cosmopolitanisms is not really decolonized space but the metropolitan scenario of migrancy and mobility? Notwithstanding Bhabha's copious sermonizing about postcoloniality, the occluded model for hybridity turns out to be the migrant "minority" subject who subverts *metropolitan* national space: "colonials, postcolonials, migrants, minorities—wandering peoples who will not be contained within the *Heim* of the national culture . . . but *are themselves* the marks of the shifting boundary that alienates the frontiers of the modern nation" (*LC*, 164; emphasis added). I should not, of course, be understood as dismissing the pain and suffering of migrants, political refugees, and exiles. However, my point is that they do not represent the whole picture of contemporary globalization. For even when Bhabha makes the rare reference to transnational capitalism, the focus is not on the exploitation of labor in free trade zones in the

South, but instead on migrant workers who move to wealthier territory: "Transnational capitalism and the impoverishment of the Third World certainly create the chains of circumstance that incarcerate the Salvadorean and the Filipino/a. In their cultural passage, hither and thither, as migrant workers, part of the massive economic and political diaspora of the modern world, they *embody* . . . that moment blasted out of the continuum of history" (LC, 8; emphasis added).

Indeed, we discover that in essence, hybrid cultural agency consists of physical freedom from being tied to the earth. Such freedom is the phenomenal analogue and material condition of possibility for endless hybrid self-creation and autonomy from the given: "There is a return to the performance of identity as iteration, the re-creation of the self in the world of travel" (LC, 9). This is why Bhabha is not interested in those who do not migrate, those who cannot migrate and for whom coerced economic migration would be a plus, or in the vicissitudes of uneven economic development in the postcolonial South. Indeed, he cannot even be said to be very interested in those who leave the South temporarily, in order to return, or in the repatriation of funds by migrant workers to feed their kin in the Third World. In Bhabha's world, postcoloniality *is* the hybridity of metropolitan migrancy. Everything happens as if there are no postcolonials left in decolonized space. With the onset of decolonization, all the former colonial hybrids have become postcolonials. And it seems that to keep their hybrid powers and status intact, they have had to depart for the metropolis, following on the heels of their former colonizers, to torment them and enact moral retribution by subverting their cultural identity.

It is, therefore, at least tendentious to personify linguistic freedom and hybrid cultural flux in the diasporic subject and to celebrate these forms of cosmopolitanism, at the expense of nationalism, as the most progressive form of postcolonial transformative agency in contemporary globalization. Indeed, even though Bhabha allegedly considers subalternity, his "postcolonial perspective" is devoid of any analytic specificity, because hybrid freedom is an abstract theory of marginality general enough to accommodate experiences as diverse as slavery, diaspora, ethnic/racial minority experiences in constitutional democracies, and queer sexuality, as well as subaltern resistance. This general postcolonial perspective effaces the unbridgeable divide between the migrant literary critic in the metropolis and the subaltern in decolonizing space. It elevates the time-lag-diagnosing postcolonial critic into the best resistant hybrid who is able to grasp the condition of possibility of resistance before it is realized in experience. My point here is that Bhabha's picture of contemporary globalization is virulently postnational because he pays scant attention to those postcolonials for whom postnationalism through mobility is not an alternative.

It is true that unlike Bhabha, Clifford cautions that he is not offering a nomadology: "I am not saying there are no locales or homes, that everyone is—or should be—traveling, or cosmopolitan or, deterritorialized" (TC, 108). He tries to reconsider dwelling in its dialectical relationship with traveling and gestures toward a redefinition of mobility beyond literal travel to include different modalities of inside-outside connection so that "displacement can involve forces that pass powerfully *through*—television, radio, tourists, commodities, armies" (TC, 103). Yet the primary emphasis of his analysis of discrepant cosmopolitanisms still remains with physical mobility. When generalized into an account of hybrid resistance, it is inevitably confined to the scene of metropolitan migrancy, border transactions, and those subjects who have class access to globality. Limited to the viewpoints of translators, guides, suppliers of anthropologists, and migrant labor, Clifford's "cosmopolitan, radical, political culture" from below also leaves out those subaltern subjects in decolonizing space who have no access to globality and who view coerced economic migration as a plus. The subaltern lies outside the circuit of the international division of labor and must bear the impact of global-systemic neocolonialism on food production, consumption, and superexploitation outside wage labor. Such actions of survival cannot easily be romanticized or recuperated as hybrid resistance.

My position on hybridity theory can be summed up as follows. First, as a paradigm of postcolonial agency in globalization, hybridity is a closet idealism. It is an anthropologistic culturalism, a theory of resistance that reduces the complex givenness of material reality to its symbolic dimensions and underplays the material institution of neocolonial oppression at a global-systemic level. Second, as a new internationalism or cosmopolitanism, it is feasible only to the extent that it remains confined to metropolitan migrancy and forecloses the necessity of the postcolonial nation-state as a precarious agent that defends against neocolonial global capitalist accumulation. Third, there is a fundamental link between this new cosmopolitanism and culturalism. Hybrid cosmopolitanisms can ignore the necessity of the nation-state precisely because they regard cultural agency as unmoored from, or relatively independent of, the field of material forces that engenders culture.[26] They privilege migrancy as the most radical form of transformative agency in contemporary globalization because, for them, it is the phenomenal analogue of hybrid freedom from the given. As Bhabha puts it, "The great connective narratives of capitalism and class drive the engines of social reproduction, but do not, *in themselves*, provide a fundamental framework for those modes of cultural identification and political affect that form around issues of the lifeworld of refugees or migrants" (LC, 6).

However, as purported analyses of globalization, these accounts of transformative agency and cosmopolitanism sadly miss the mark. For although the meaning and symbols of neocolonial culture are unmotivated, their materialization through economic and political institutional structures in an unequal global order means that they cannot be translated, reinscribed, and read anew in the ways suggested by theories of hybridity. For thoroughgoing global transformation to occur, some recourse to the ambivalent agency of the postcolonial nation-state and, therefore, to nationalism and national culture seems crucial even as we acknowledge that this agency is not autarchical but inscribed within a global force field. Clifford is not entirely unaware of this, since he notes that he has not gone far enough in reconceiving practices of dwelling in a transnational context (TC, 115). My point is that in the current conjuncture, such practices of dwelling, if they are to be mass based, necessarily engender a national consciousness rather than a cosmopolitanism, no matter how "discrepant." To comprehend the possibility of the national-in-the-cosmopolitical—and I use this awkward phrase to indicate a condition of globality that, in the current conjuncture, is short of a mass-based cosmopolitan consciousness—we need to understand postcolonial national culture in terms other than as an immutable organic substrate or as an ideological form imposed from above, a constraint to be transcended by the formation of an emancipatory cosmopolitan consciousness.

The Culture-Concept in Philosophical Modernity and Given Culture in Global Neocolonialism

Theories of hybridity can, however, be valuable as ironic reminders of the tenacious lineaments of the canonical concept of culture they claim to subvert. More precisely, because they see cultural resistance as a function of the freedom of human (discursive/linguistic) reality from the givenness of nature, theories of hybridity repeat the essential feature of the culture-concept in philosophical modernity even though they are painfully oblivious to the ethical stakes of that concept. For a better understanding of how neocolonial globalization necessitates a reformulation of this tenacious culture-concept that has always governed our understandings of nationalism and cosmopolitanism, a brief outline of these stakes might be useful.

Broadly speaking, the culture-concept articulates the formative power over nature that co-belongs with humanity, not only as an animal capable of rational contemplation, but as a purposive being with the ability to shape its natural self in the image of rationally prescribed ideal forms. This practical aspect of culture involves a metaphorical extension of cultivation as agrarian activity (*cultura*) into the individual-pedagogic task of the ethical and intellectual cultivation of the mind.[27] It establishes an internal link between autonomous rational effort and the shaping of some naturally given ground into cultivated form. This ability of rational endeavor to transform and improve nature implies that humanity possesses a degree of freedom from nature. Thus, in its societal dimension, culture designates the realm of human beings in general, as opposed to nature, as well as a normative ideal to grade the differences between various peoples belonging to that realm.

The important point is that culture begins to have an objective dimension. It begins to denote a reality that is opposed to nature. In its secular meaning, *Bildung* denotes the inner-directed formation of an individual in the image (*Bild*) of a personality prescribed by moral norms. By extension, "culture" in general becomes synonymous with the totality of "objectified results of human creativity by, and due to which the 'natural constitution' of human individuals—their inborn needs, drives and propensities—become modified, developed and supplemented" (C, 15–16). Better still, culture in general designates the realm where ideal forms materialize as external objects with a reality or life independent of the individual who created them. No longer just an attitude or way of life, culture in its utopian face is an objective reality opposed to and superior to nature, the realm in which humanity overcomes nature through reason. Posed in this way, the culture-concept of philosophical modernity carries the immense ethical burden of reconciling facticity and universal normativity. It articulates nothing less than our ability to structure reality according to universal norms and values that are not just given by tradition but are, instead, rationally justified through time.

For Kant, cosmopolitical culture is precisely the realm in which humanity is able to free itself from the given, understood, first, as the passions and sensuous inclinations that subject human beings to nature and, second, as the finitude of human existence. Human beings are finite moral subjects, creatures of nature who also possess moral autonomy. As natural creatures with passions and sensuous inclinations, we are, like things and animals, creatures of a world merely given to us and are bound by the same arational, mechanical laws of causality governing all natural objects. However, as moral subjects, we are self-legislating rational agents. We belong to a transcendent realm of freedom we create for ourselves, a world that encompasses all rational beings governed by universal laws we prescribe through our reason. The moral world is supersensible and infinite because it is not subject to the blind chance and meaningless contingency that characterize finite human existence.

But how can we realize this ideal world of universal moral freedom in the world that is given to us, the world of egotistical strife and unsocial sociability? Kant proposes that culture provides a bridge to the transcendent realm of freedom because it minimizes our natural bondage by enhancing the human aptitude for purposive self-determination. Initially a negative task of discipline applied by each individual on him or herself to curb his or her animal inclinations, culture liberates the human will from the despotism of natural desires and redirects human skill toward rational purposes by forming the will in accordance with a rational image (CJ, § 83, 319). Kant suggests that the *society of culture* that grows out of individual efforts is a simulacrum of the universal moral community because it promotes a sociability that is in principle cosmopolitan:

> [For we have] the fine art[s] and the sciences, which involve a universally communicable pleasure as well as elegance and refinement, and through these they make man, not indeed morally [*sittlich*] better for [life in] society, but still civilized for it: they make great headway against the tyranny of man's propensity to the senses, and so prepare him for a sovereignty in which reason alone is to dominate. (CJ, § 83, 321)

Indeed, Kant further suggests that culture is also a means of overcoming human finitude: in view of individual mortality, the moral progress of humanity can be guaranteed only through cultural products that preserve for posterity all the significant achievements of humanity as a moral species beyond the lives of individual actors.[28] Kant justifies his idea of a cosmopolitical world order by arguing that it is the only efficient means for creating this universal society of culture.

I have drawn attention to Kant's conceptualization of cosmopolitical culture as the promise of humanity's freedom from or control over the given in order to point out that this concept is not confined to idealist cosmopolitanisms. The same concept of universal normative culture is also at work in Marx's materialist cosmopolitanism. Defining the given as the changing needs of sensuous human beings to be satisfied by labor or purposive self-objectifying human activity, Marx argues that the economic realm of natural necessity formed by social intercourse can be equitably governed only by a world community of socialized laborers and producers.[29] This community was in the process of realization because loyalty to the nation and its economy, bourgeois ideological constructs obscuring the universal interests of the proletariat,[30] were being eroded by the globalization of the market and the capitalist mode of production. Universal competition and exploitation would lead to the teleological formation of the proletariat as a universal class transcending national boundaries:

> Only this will liberate the separate individuals from the various national and local barriers, bring them into practical connection with the production . . . of the whole world and make it possible for them to acquire the capacity to enjoy this all-sided production of the whole earth (the creations of man). *All-round* dependence, this primary natural form of the *world-historical* co-operation of individuals, will be transformed by this communist revolution into the control and conscious mastery of these powers, which, born of the action of men on one another, have till now overawed and ruled men as powers completely alien to them.[31]

The crucial point here is that despite Marx's strong anticulturalism, this proletarian world community is a materialist version of Kant's society of culture. Just as Kant saw cosmopolitical culture as nature's end for humanity, the proletarian world community is also the sphere in which humanity maximizes its freedom from finitude through rational-purposive self-objectifying activity (labor). This community is also formed by a combination of human action and natural teleology (in Marx's case, world commerce *and* a globalized mode of production).

Nor should we presume that a more realistic or mundane universalism necessarily takes the form of a cosmopolitanism. The same concept of universal normative culture is also operative in varieties of nationalism ranging from Hegel's civic patriotism to the different ethnolinguistic nationalisms of Fichte and Herder. The common thread that links all these cosmopolitanisms and nationalisms—Fichte's nationalism is also a cosmopolitanism— is the idea that individuals willingly bind themselves to a collective body as a rational response to human finitude because this collective entity provides a lawful substrate or medium of subsistence for their existence. The transcendence of the givenness of existence can be understood either as the better satisfaction of essential needs through a social contract or in the higher sense of the fulfillment of humanity's moral essence or the prolonging of the effects of moral endeavors beyond one's individual life. Thus, for Hegel and Fichte, individuals willingly die for a patriotic cause because it is only in and through the transindividual body of a national culture, a people, or the state that they can achieve moral freedom, transcend their facticity, and endow their actions with an ethical significance that will endure beyond their mortal life span.[32] Hence these philosophical cosmopolitanisms and nationalisms are also secular religions or humanist ontotheologies.

We glimpse the complicity between Marxist cosmopolitanism and nationalism in their offspring, Third World socialist decolonizing nationalism, which regards national culture as the source of political liberation. The following quotation from Amilcar Cabral is representative: "Whatever the conditions of subjection of a people to foreign domination and the influence of economic, political and social factors in the exercise of this domination, it is generally within the cultural factor that we find the germ of challenge which leads to the structuring and development of the liberation movement. . . . national liberation is necessarily an act of culture."[33] Despite the shift from moral freedom to political liberation, the ontotheological theme of culture as the realm of acts by which we free ourselves from the given is unmistakable in Cabral's suggestion that cultural activity precedes and lays the ground for liberation from political, economic, and social oppression.

This utopian culture-concept is, however, premised on a complex of unresolved ontological problems. On the one hand, it presupposes that ideal forms can shape the external world according to human values and norms. On the other hand, the sharp opposition between nature and culture makes this presupposition problematic. For if nature is opposed to culture, and culture is the becoming-nature of ideas, then how can ideas be realized as external objects and yet remain in accord with human purposiveness? For instance, tradition is arguably a quasi-nature of our own making, an ossification of ideational structures specific to a certain historical moment into immutable givens. The entire Marxist problematic of alienated labor and all that follows from it—commodity fetishism and the reification of social relations into a second nature that oppresses the human producer—is a variant of this question.

When culture merely designated a process of individual cultivation according to social/moral norms, this problem of culture's power over nature was posed and answered in an obfuscating manner: the causal effects of ideas on *human* nature could be explained by psychological theories of the self-reflexive action (cultural discipline) of human beings as mind-body complexes. However, the emergence of an objective dimension to culture means that the causality of ideas needs to be extended over nonhuman nature. Crudely put, philosophical modernity resolves this problem by reconciling the nature/culture opposition in a natural-teleological account of culture as nature's final end for humanity. The success of culture as a utopian project depends on an anthropocentric conception of nature as a totality in harmony or accord with human normative interests: because nature is amenable to human purposes, nature itself leads humanity beyond nature. Put another way, the nature of the *anthropos* is to be free of nature. This is the logic behind Kantian and Marxist cosmopolitanism as well as various philosophical nationalisms.

But this reconciliation of nature and culture in humanity remains unconvincing. Insofar as human beings are irreducibly objects of nature and subject to its laws, it is unclear what our cultural activity can effect in us. Put another way, what can we hope to achieve in ourselves through our own makings insofar as we are finite beings, creatures who are given and who come and cease to exist not by our own making? I propose to call this ensemble of problems the *aporia of given culture*. The aporia is as follows. Culture is supposed to be the realm of human freedom from the given. However, because human beings are finite natural creatures, the becoming-objective of culture as the realm of human purposiveness and freedom depends on forces that are radically other and beyond human control. Culture is given out of these forces. Thus, at the same time that culture embodies human freedom from the given, it is also merely given because its power over nature is premised on this gift of the radically other.

The aporia of given culture implies a vulnerability that we have not learned to accept. We have seen that philosophical modernity smothers this aporia by recourse to the dogmatic idea that culture is nature's highest end for humanity, an end that has been variously characterized as a cosmopolitical order (Kant and Marx), a national culture (Fichte and Herder), and the ideal state (Hegel). The accounts of linguistic freedom and cultural flux grounding new hybrid cosmopolitanisms are relays of this dogmatic faith. Although hybridity theorists do not reconcile the opposition between nature/culture by means of a natural teleology because of their profound anti-naturalism, they rely on the same anthropologistic opposition between nature and culture/language insofar as they regard indeterminism as the exclusive feature of social or discursive formations.

Indeed, the canonical culture-concept of philosophical modernity takes many other protean shapes in postcolonial cultural studies. The cultural face of national liberation movements is characterized by political claims for local autonomy that are logically similar to the discourse of cultural difference. Because these discourses rely on anthropological definitions of culture, they are often seen as critiques of a universalist concept of culture. In fact, these affirmations of difference do not seek to retrieve a lost authentic tradition oppressed by universalism. In rejecting the false universalism of cosmopolitical culture, these discourses already desire access to a true universal. The argument for the autonomy of the local presupposes the universal value of autonomy and proposes to apply it to every particular group or collective unit. This desire for a polymorphic universal capable of respecting the particularities of its constituent units sublates the oppositions between the universal and the particular, modernity and tradition. As Thomas McCarthy notes, because cultural relativism derives its moral force from a quasi-Kantian universal imperative to respect the autonomy of others, the truth of cultural relativism is multiculturalist universalism.[34] Consequently, political claims for cultural specificity posit the autonomy of cultural identity either in an original state of independence or as an ideal-normative goal: all cultural groups should have equal access to the social, economic, and political forces that constitute the world-system and the freedom to direct these forces according to their own interests. They are deemed to possess this freedom from external determinations in the final instance because they are variations of *Kultur*, humanity's vocation to lead itself beyond the merely given. Political revisions of anthropology that criticize the organicism of the anthropological notion of culture also subscribe to this anthropocentric paradigm of agency:

> My anger increases to apoplexy when I hear culture magnified and reified as *"the* culture of*"* a people. If we are the agents and substantiators of our cultures, rather than their creatures, we must resist the temptation to depict culture as the monolithic determinant of our behaviour. . . . Culture is a matter less for documentation than for interpretation; it is more faithfully and sensitively depicted in metaphor than in museums. Its intellectual fascination lies in its extraordinary versatility, which is precisely what makes it such an eloquent representation of identity.[35]

To phrase my criticism of hybridity theory in terms that will cover all these cases of anthropologistic culturalism, how plausible is the hope we place in culture's freedom over nature, the primacy of culture's form in the altering of the matter that nature gives us, if culture itself becomes a quasi-nature devoid of the trait of anthropocentric freedom? Cultural studies emphasizes the power of culture in shaping politics, power, and economic systems. Yet, writing on the precarious relationship between feminism and postcolonial cultural reassertions in the contemporary world order, Valentine Moghadam observes that although "culture may have been originally introduced to overcome some of the heavy determinism associated with social and economic analysis, . . . since the latter half of the 1980s it has taken on a weight of its own, reified, even sacralized."[36] This astute remark echoes Samir Amin's point that the fundamentalist reassertion of cultural identity is the inevitable product of neocolonial globalization rather than a solution to it.[37] Taking my cue from these observations, I want to suggest that the formation of postcolonial national culture in the late twentieth century reopens the aporia of given culture and deforms the culture-concept underwriting the nationalisms and cosmopolitanisms of philosophical modernity and the hybrid cosmopolitanisms and assertions of cultural difference in postcolonial cultural studies, because it performs the impossibility of either celebrating national culture as the vehicle for freedom from the given or rejecting it as a means of resisting neocolonial globalization.

In macrosociological terms, postcolonial national identity formation is in part a response to neocolonial economic globalization.[38] The uneven accumulation of capital and distribution of wealth and resources on a global scale exacerbates the unequal distribution of political power and economic resources within decolonised countries. At the same time, globalization is accompanied by the spread of a political culture that historically emerged in the West: human rights, women's rights, equality, democratization, and so on. This intersection of cultural change and economic decline leads to resentment and resistance on the part of disadvantaged groups who may use "cultural resources to mobilize and organize opposition . . . even though a motivation and cause of opposition is economic and social disadvantage" (*IP,* 8). Political elites may also draw on "tradition" or "intrinsic cultural values" to justify their actions and maintain hegemony, sometimes overemphasizing cultural issues such as religion, morality, cultural imperialism, and women's appearance to divert attention from economic failures and social inequality. As Moghadam notes with regard to Islamic reassertions: "Culture, religion, and identity are thus both defense mechanisms and the means by which the new order is to be shaped. Islamist movements appear to be archaic but in fact combine modern and premodern discourses, means of communication and even political institutions[, and] . . . must therefore be seen as both reactive and proactive" (*IP,* 11).

It would be precipitous to dismiss all postcolonial national-cultural reassertions as fanaticist pathologies or statist ideologies. In the first place, they are not necessarily religious or confined to Islamic Middle Eastern states with economies weakened by the falling price of oil. Reassertions of national-cultural identity occur in most postcolonial states, ranging from weak neocolonial African states to the high-performing newly industrializing economies of East and Southeast Asia. The seemingly undivided stand by Asian governments in rejecting intervention by Northern states over human rights issues at the Vienna Convention on the basis of cultural differences is in small part a collective assertion of postcolonial national sovereignty in response to the history of colonialism and the inequality of contemporary North-South relations.[39] Hence Islamic fundamentalist nationalism ought to be analyzed alongside the Confucian chauvinism championed by the Singaporean government as the basis of the East Asian path of global capitalist development as cases of postcolonial nationalism in the New World Order.[40] Moreover, these cultural reassertions are not necessarily ideological constructions of state elites, because they also express the needs of disadvantaged social groups in changing economic conditions. Although nongovernmental organizations from the South concerned with human rights have rejected the position of Asian states on human rights, they have also been careful to distinguish their criticisms of their own governments from the position of Northern governments by asserting the need to respect cultural differences and the urgency of establishing an equitable international economic order and interstate system.

The resistance to global forces promised by contemporary rearticulations of postcolonial national culture is, however, severely curtailed by the fact that they arise in response to economic processes and can be manipulated by state elites in the indirect service of post-Fordist global capital. We know that, in part, decolonization failed because it involved the devolution of state power to local and regional actors who used this power to attract investment and expand production within a transnational economic system of surplus extraction. Similarly, much contemporary official postcolonial nationalist ideology is aimed at fostering social cohesion to attract foreign direct investment and providing cheap female labor for multinational-owned industries in free trade zones.

Furthermore, all postcolonial nationalisms, even popular nationalisms, run the permanent risk of majoritarian and patriarchal oppression because these national identities are the dubious gifts of colonial cartography.[41] Marie-Aimée Hélie-Lucas, an Algerian feminist, gives us a sense of the difficult double bind of a cultural identity twice given for women in decolonization—given once by colonialism and given yet again by indigenous patriarchy in an aporetic embrace with global capitalism:

> It would have been mean to question the priority of liberating the country, since independence would surely bring an end to discrimination against women. What makes me angrier in retrospect is . . . the brainwashing that did not allow us young women even to think of questioning. . . . It angers me to see women covering the misbehavior of their fellow men and hiding, in the name of national solidarity and identity, crimes which will be perpetuated after independence.
>
> This is the real harm which comes from liberation struggles. The overall task of women during liberation is seen as symbolic. Faced with colonization

the people have to build a national identity based on their own values, traditions, religion, language and culture. Women bear the heavy burden of safeguarding this threatened identity. And this burden exacts its price.[42]

The aporia, however, is that in the current conjuncture, nationalism cannot be transcended by cosmopolitan forms of solidarity no matter how pathological it may appear in its ineradicably oppressive moments. First, transnational networks are, in and of themselves, neither mass based nor firmly politically institutionalized. Proponents of a global civil society or an international public sphere that already exists independent of nation-states must gloss over the fact that we inhabit a decentralized political system in which global loyalty is thin, an ideal vision largely confined to activists and intellectuals.[43] This means that in order to be effective at the level of political institutions or the popular masses, transnational networks have to work with and through the nation-state in order to transform it. They have to negotiate directly with the state in the hope of influencing its political morality and/or mobilize local support into popular *national* movements that press against the state. As Alexander Colás observes, the nation-state is both a constraining factor and an emancipatory potential in its relation to global networks. Global networks are subject to the same constraining social and historical forces that shape other social actors, but "the nation-state is not necessarily at odds with the emancipatory aspirations of cosmopolitanism . . . [and] cosmopolitan political action would actually involve the defense of social and political rights *via* the democratic nation-state."[44]

Second, the necessity of the nation-state as a terminal that progressive global-local networks must pass through is especially salient in the postcolonial South, where economic poverty is the root cause of economic, social, and political oppression. Although foreign capital-led market growth and development may alleviate poverty when actively regulated by strong host governments to serve official national interests, such as in high-growth Southeast Asia, high economic growth cannot lead to social development or gender equity unless the existing inequitable sociopolitical-economic structures within these nation-states are overhauled. Indeed, high growth may provide greater legitimation to authoritarian regimes, as in the case of Singapore. In the worst-case scenario, as in some African nations, we have the development of underdevelopment that produces the Fourth World. The point is that in the absence of a world-state capable of ensuring an equitable international political and economic order, economic globalization is uneven. Instead of engendering an emancipatory cosmopolitan consciousness, globalization produces a polarized world in which bourgeois national development and industrialization in the periphery are necessarily frustrated by state adjustment to the dictates of transnational capital.[45] To alleviate the shortfalls of global restructuring in the South, the state needs to be an autonomous agent of economic accumulation. But the state can resist capitulation to transnational forces only if it is transformed from a comprador regime into a popular national-state. This is why popular rearticulations of postcolonial national identity are ethically imperative and cannot be dismissed per se as statist ideologies that hinder the rise of a more equitable cosmopolitan consciousness, even though the exclusionary dimension of popular nationalism can always be manipulated by state elites and captured by official nationalism.

Contemporary revivals of postcolonial nationalism that are primarily instances of negative identification in defense against neocolonial globalization should therefore be seen as weak repetitions of the earlier phase of negative identification in decolonization that initially united the people into a nation. This ambivalent necessity of postcolonial nationalism deforms the concept of cultural agency at the heart of old and new cosmopolitanisms. In Marx's version of the culture-concept of philosophical modernity, economic forces of production constitute an autotelic realm of necessity that points beyond itself to a realm of human freedom from the given—the proletarian world community—based on, but sublating, the realm of necessity. The urgency of postcolonial nationalism in contemporary globalization, however, refutes Marx's economistic assumption that transnational forces of production necessarily lead to transnational movements that engender mass-based loyalty to a transnational body or a popular global consciousness.

In his critique of orthodox Marxist cosmopolitanism, Samir Amin points out that peripheralization and the North-South conflict are the two truths of really existing capitalism. He argues that socialist revolution is not possible in the current conjuncture because "the expansion of capitalism in the periphery . . . ruins the chances of national crystallization and accentuates the fragmentation and atomization of society."[46] Consequently, he suggests that there is "no real alternative to popular national transformation in the societies of the periphery" (SM, 124) and that African and Asian popular nationalist-socialism are inheritors of the true vocation of Marxism.[47] In his vision of a polycentric world, Amin rejects the orthodox Marxist-cosmopolitanist idea of the withering away of the state because strong postcolonial states, and hence popular nationalism, are crucial to resist recompradorization (SM, 127).

Put another way, postcolonial nationalism is the irreducible stuttering that the permanent threat of peripheralization introduces into the dialectic of global socialism. Therefore, contrary to neo-Marxist critiques of postcolonial nationalism such as Partha Chatterjee's and Ranajit Guha's, postcolonial nationalism is not necessarily an ideology imposed from above, a "forced resolution . . . of the contradiction between capital and the people-nation."[48] Postcolonial nationalism is not a contradiction that we can and ought to transcend in the name of a cosmopolitanism, because it does not obey the logic of dialectical contradiction. Both medicine and poison, postcolonial nationalism is a double-edged stricture that, instead of being transcended, is made necessary by neocolonial globalization. By pulling us back from a cosmopolitical realm of freedom into nationalism as given culture, globalization problematizes the Marxist understanding of the given as something we can transcend through normative human action.

Similarly, postcolonial nationalism also reveals the limits of hybridity theory as a new cosmopolitanism. I noted earlier that although Bhabha and Clifford claim that their new cosmopolitanisms are analyses of postcolonial agency in contemporary globalization, their focus is actually transnational mobility *qua* phenomenal analogue for cultural flux and linguistic freedom. For the majority who remain in peripheral space by choice or by necessity, however, the nation-state, whatever its inconveniences, is a necessity, because postnationalism through migration is not an alternative. But more important, because these rearticulations of national culture are induced by and given from within a global field of economic and political forces, they are clearly not instances of a cultural agency that is unmoored or relatively independent from material forces. They cannot be explained in terms of symbolic flux and linguistic freedom from the given. Instead, the peculiar dynamism of given culture has to be thought from within stasis, in terms of its miredness in a material force field.

The failure of both Marxist and hybrid cosmopolitanisms to account for postcolonial nationalism as given culture should therefore be referred back to their common theoretical source: the modern philosophical concept of culture as the realm of freedom from the given. Indeed, Clifford's and Bhabha's privileging of migrant mobility in globalization as the type case of hybrid dynamism also repeats Marx's teleological view of economic development. Like Marx, they also regard global economic processes as the positive material condition for disrupting the givenness of naturalized national or local ties. The difference between new hybrid and old Marxist cosmopolitanisms is merely that the former is organized around the idea of cultural dispersal because it does not regard globalization as leading to a unified world order. Both cosmopolitanisms are premised on the transcendence of the given.

The nontranscendable finitude of postcolonial nationalism in neocolonial globalization, however, implies that a contemporary revival of "cosmopolitanism" cannot feasibly take the form of an "-ism," the project of a mass-based global emancipatory consciousness, no matter how strategic or compromised. Simply put, "discrepant cosmopolitanisms" do not cover the whole picture of what is happening in neocolonial globalization. This is not just because transnational migrancy is not identical to postcoloniality. More to the point, although globalization creates a greater sense of belonging-to-a-world insofar as it makes individual lives globally interdependent, it has not, thus far, resulted in a significant sense of political allegiance or loyalty to the world. Unlike nationalism, which is notoriously nonphilosophical or under-intellectualized, cosmopolitanism lacks a mass base. Bodies like Amnesty International and international human-rights NGOs are creatures of intellectuals aimed at promoting a wider consciousness of humanity as a whole through the power of rational or affective persuasion. They attract allegiance by working at a different level from nationalism. As I pointed out earlier, in order to reach a wider base or to be effective at the level of state policy, these transnational bodies usually have to work through the political morality of the state and through popular nationalism. Especially with regard to the postcolonial nation-state in the current neocolonial conjuncture, it is not likely that they can displace the nation, however imperfect it is, as the object of mass-based loyalty. In part, this may be because some of these transnational bodies are located in and/or depend on the hegemonic North for funding and can be unwittingly used in various ways to bypass the already beleaguered Southern nation-state and undermine its legitimacy.

But then, as given culture, postcolonial nationalism also deforms the argument of philosophical nationalisms that the nation is a better embodiment of human freedom than a world order. Because it neither respects nor is able to reconcile the divide between nature and culture, stasis and activity, necessity and freedom, the postcolonial nation is not the grasping of the *an sich* as the *für sich* through autonomous social action. On the one hand, this national identity is given, a quasi-nature incarnated in lived bodies through fiscal and technological flows and shifting linkages that are not amenable to anthropocentric self-determination. On the other hand, the postcolonial nation also cannot be regarded deterministically as an immutable epiphenomenon of these global forces, precisely because it is induced from a *heteronomous* force field. Although contemporary articulations of postcolonial national identity are responses to economic globalization, they are not *entirely* reducible to the interests of state elites indirectly serving global capital. Like a compound formed in a chemical reaction that is not reducible to its different reactants, the postcolonial nation is the volatile product of an unstable gathering together of economic, cultural, and political factors.

The crucial point here is that the body of the postcolonial nation-state is heterogeneous, and globalization can intensify this heterogeneity in positive and negative ways. For although transnational forces are inadequate to engender a mass-based global consciousness, although global capitalism produces weak neocolonial comprador states and authoritarian capitalist regimes in the South, globalization also creates new political opportunities and greater resources for popular national mobilization. The national body is the volatile substrate for a tug-of-war between elites and the people. The opportunities and resources offered by transnational networks loosen the hyphen that tethers the nation to the state without actually cutting it. They can weaken the stranglehold of state elites on the nation even as they allow the not-quite deterritorialized, popularly rearticulated nation to press against and transform the state. It might therefore be more appropriate to characterize contemporary transnational activity aimed at postcolonial transformation as aporetic cases of postcolonial nationalism in a cosmopolitical force field. It follows from this that postcolonial national culture is a double agent that grows out of, resists, and can also be pulled back into the processes of neocolonial globalization. In the concluding section, I suggest that this nationalist awareness of the cosmopolitical, this risky agency of the national-in-the-cosmopolitical, entails a certain responsibility to the given.

The Global Sheaf of the Postcolonial National Body: Responsibility to the Given

To be more concrete about how the hyphen between postcolonial nation and state is rearticulated in and by globalization, we need to ask, What position does the postcolonial state assume in relation to the fiscalization of the globe? Samir Amin notes that "in the Third World as a whole, the food crisis, the external debt crisis, and the impasses of imported technology have led to capitulation after capitulation before the *diktat* of transnational capital reorganized around the International Monetary Fund and World Bank and the consortia of big Western banks" (SM, 114). Despite the general validity of this statement, postcolonial states are not entirely passive. Contrary to appearances, multinational-led foreign direct investment is not an economic form of extraterritoriality because there is state agency on both sides. For host countries and multinational investors alike, the motivation behind foreign direct investment is to maximize fiscal inflow (profits in the case of multinationals; foreign currency in the case of host countries) and to minimize outflow (investment capital in the case of multinationals; foreign reserves in the case of host countries). For instance, the host state can impose regulations to ensure that foreign-owned production is export oriented. The closing of domestic markets would prevent the outflow of foreign reserves. The multinational will agree to these conditions only if it can sell profitably to its country of origin or to a third country. Multinationals can also enlist the states of their countries of origin to pressure postcolonial states in the South to improve conditions for foreign investment.

Obviously, it is impossible for both sides to maximize overall inflow and minimize outflow. This is why the globalization of trade and production cannot lead to the formation of a world federation of the Kantian type. The implicit hydraulic model indicates the barely visible national limits of multinationals: where profits are *repatriated* to in the final instance, and which territorial national economy benefits more from the global flow of money. In times of economic stress, one sees quite clearly that capital flows anaclitically trace the lines of state trade policies. Capital flows as trade barriers are raised and lowered depending on the economic health of the states involved. Once again, the postcolonial state is not always passive. For instance, when the United States closed its market to labor-intensive goods in the mid-1970s because its economic health was increasingly threatened, the Singaporean state responded to the drop in capital investment in these industries by restructuring its economy. It changed its labor composition and moved into high-tech manufacture to attract new forms of capital.

The active implementation of such fundamental changes of state economic policy necessarily involves a corresponding official project to transform the national body. If this official nationalism is met by a popular counternationalism, then this may lead to a rearticulation of the hyphen between nation and state. As Noeleen Heyzer observes with regard to Singapore:

> The internationalisation of the economy . . . has to be explained not only by the structural response of foreign capital, but also by the active official policy. The PAP government had always intended that multinationals should form the base of the Singaporean economy. It was hoped that the internationalisation of the economy, foreign expertise and resources would be harnessed to serve Singapore's national interest. . . . In contemporary Singapore society, the changing social formation results not only from external economic factors but also from the dialectical interplay of factors emanating from the top (i.e. the State) and from factors pushing from below (i.e. worker's participation) with factors at the top tending to dominate increasingly. *Essentially, the issue here is how the State controls, decides, arbitrates, dominates and how this affects people at the ordinary level. At the same time,*

people are seldom totally passive, and certain sectors, at least, provide challenges to the State-defined reality.[49]

For those who do not have the option of postnationalism through transnational migrancy, the postcolonial state is not so easily dismissable. Heyzer suggests that in its aporetic embrace with global capital, the postcolonial Singaporean state is at once liberator and oppressor.[50] On the one hand, this embrace generates economic growth and national prosperity with all its trappings—higher standards of living, upward mobility, and consumerism. But in its project of making the nation attractive to multinational investment, the Singaporean state also represses challenges to its official picture of what constitutes the good life, especially meaningful political life. This official nationalizing project computes well-being in terms of increasing the economic wealth of individuals. The widespread inculcation of this idea curbs popular counternationalizing sentiments by producing a depoliticized population that identifies the nation's well-being with the state's well-being.

The inherent danger of any rearticulation of the loosened hyphen between the postcolonial nation and its state in economic globalization is that instead of being transformed in the image of the nation-people, the state may gain greater control over the nation-people. The Singaporean administrative state has enjoyed an immense degree of legitimacy because of its high level of economic prosperity. Together with other comparable cases of rapid industrialization in high-growth East and Southeast Asia, the Singaporean economic miracle is often adduced as evidence to refute the theory of the development of underdevelopment. It is, however, crucial to remember that such miracles occur within the framework of uneven global capitalism. In the Singaporean case, the burden and costs of this apparently jointless soldering of nation to state in globalization are borne by migrant workers who are periodically abjected from the proper boundaries of the nation-state or whose assimilation is tightly controlled, even as they are crucial to the daily functioning of the nation-state. As Heyzer points out, although foreign workers are an indispensable stopgap to national-industrial labor shortages, they are seldom admitted into the body of the official Singaporean nation, especially if they are only semiskilled: "Foreign workers earning below a certain income level are not allowed to marry Singaporeans under current marriage laws."[51] Conversely, the emergent possibility of a popular counternationalism that seeks to reclaim the state is displaced from the economically strong Singaporean nation-state to those weaker neighbors from which it imports its labor. Witness the ripple effects in the Philippines of the hanging of Flor Contemplacion.

This risky agency of the national-in-the-cosmopolitical becomes more pronounced if we consider the precariousness of feminism in weaker neo-colonial Southern states. If the intensified reassertion of national cultural identity in the periphery is supposed to introduce a degree of freedom from global-system imperatives in the shaping of the destiny of nations, it is generally the case that the burden of this illusory autonomy is borne by women, because of a corresponding politicization of gender and the family. This link between women and national culture has a prehistory in the symbolic role of woman in national liberation movements, and, generally speaking, post-colonial feminist consciousness grows out of nationalist sentiments that can either conflict with or remain an integral part of the goals and aims of feminism.[52] Women and the family unit have integral functions in the formation of decolonizing national culture and are also essential links in the post-colonial project of patriarchal ethnocultural fundamentalism, which "seeks to meet the needs of international capital with its liberal window dressing ('a modern look') without being culturally imperialized."[53]

This uneasy fit between the various subject positions of women in the postcolonial nation-state imposes an interminable responsibility to given culture on postcolonial feminisms. Cherifa Bouatta and Doria Cherifati-Meratine observe that Algerian women who espouse women's rights are denigrated for abandoning their own natural and sacred tasks: "They are soulless bodies and souls whose bodies give course to baseness. They are the offspring of France. They want to transgress what is sacred and based in nature and culture."[54] This cultural identity is, of course, not quite natural, because it is induced from within a global force field. Nawal el-Saadawi writes that in the Arab world, "religious and moral appeals and claims" about women's cultural identity conceal "the links between imperialism and conservative religious forces and the economic reasons for expelling women from the wage-labour market and from public life"—"international struggles over petrol and Arab wealth, Israel's occupation of Palestine, the employment of petrol revenue against the interests of the Arab peoples, spurious dependency projects, more external debt, more unemployment, rising prices and inflation."[55]

Yet, in the chance and necessity of the current neocolonial conjuncture where national identity is given culture, a feminist also cannot dismiss the postcolonial nation-state even if she has to criticize it. Hélie-Lucas notes that in Islamic countries,

> women's organizations range from participating in the fundamentalist movement, to working for reform within the framework of Islam, and to fighting

for a secular state and secular laws. In spite of this wide range of tendencies and strategies, all of them have internalized some of the concepts developed and used by fundamentalists. In particular, they have internalized the notion of an external monolithic enemy, and the fear of betraying their identity—defined as group identity, rather than gender identity in the group.[56]

In the face of the mutual exclusivity of being a feminist and being a nationalist in these cases, a gender activism has arisen in Egypt that is not political in a highly organized, self-conscious sense, but is instead a form of low-profile pragmatic activism within the milieu of the popular-religious-national everyday. Margot Badran observes that "today's feminists in Egypt are women with layered identities, only one of which is feminist. By publicly asserting one identity they might be seen as giving priority to that identity over others, and this they are most unwilling to do."[57]

Listen now to Hélie-Lucas speaking of the haunting hold of the nation as given culture over her activity as a feminist in international public space:

> I personally believe in internationalism, also among women's groups, but I am not representative of the opinion of Algerian and Third World women in general. . . . accusing the West, and imperialism is fine, but I don't see how we can get any solution except by identifying with the Left forces, *however limited their awareness is of our situation*, of the evils of international capitalism. . . . But believing in *this kind of internationalism*, acknowledging all the differences of interest and in wealth and class, and whatever . . . this I don't deny, and I think we have to work on it. . . . I haven't always been like this, either—I have been very *blindly nationalist* in the past.[58]

But then to be "this kind of an internationalist" is not to be a postnationalist. It is about being an *unblind* nationalist at the same time, however difficult that may be. Speaking about Muslim feminist internationalists who fight for the legal reform of Muslim personal codes, Hélie-Lucas observes that "internationalism in their view *does not transcend or erase their belonging to a cultural-religious compound in which they still want to grow their roots*; nor does it come into conflict with forms of nationalism drawn from the full consciousness of imperialism and memories of the time of colonization" (*IP*, 402; emphasis added). In the face of the persistent threat of peripheralization in neocolonial globalization, these feminist activists must lovingly inhabit the postcolonial nation-state even as they resist being crushed by the official renationalizing project of the patriarchal state weakened by its aporetic embrace with global capitalism. Conversely, these feminists can remake the state in the image of a popular-feminist counternationalism only by linking up with a larger global network, all the while remaining aware that these persistently shifting global alignments can also undermine the post-colonial state that they are trying to save from neocolonialism. This is an-other manifestation of the aporia of given culture: that the recathexis of the postcolonial state by popular nationalism must occur both with and against the state, through the cosmopolitical that can always work in the service of neocolonialism. It involves a risky self-inoculation where the vaccine could also be poisonous.

This responsibility to given culture becomes even more onerous and fraught with danger if we remember that these feminists are not women "at the bottom," women in poverty or subaltern women. Let us turn to a development-oriented example where the responsibility of feminist activists to women "at the bottom" must occur through the class-divided nation-state: the attempt to translate growth and poverty alleviation into social de-velopment through people's participation and state regulation. Commenting on the need for advocacy in making the voices of poor women heard and ad-dressed by the market and the postcolonial state, Gita Sen notes:

> In general, the non-governmental sector has been particularly active in South Asia and the Philippines as well as in parts of the Pacific. It has under-stood the need to empower women and has acted as a vital catalyst that has been able to experiment, innovate, and respond flexibly to needs on the ground, providing governments with invaluable inputs when the latter have been able and willing to recognise them.[59]

What is broached here is a progressive rearticulation of the hyphen between nation and state through normative publicness (*Öffentlichkeit*) in order to achieve social cohesion and change fundamental social, political, and legal structures. Likewise, Heyzer observes:

> The types of state-led development that can have a positive effect on gender equity are those that have invested in social development; . . . [those that have] provided . . . the legal and institutional framework for the regulation of the market so that the entitlements of the poor may be strengthened through better access and protection; those that recognize poor women's productive and reproductive roles; those that recognize women as citizens in their own right and not merely as "dependents", "target groups", or "instru-ments of development".

For women to hold the market and the state accountable, there must first be a strengthening of poor women's rights . . . to active participation in the public sphere of market and state. In this regard the potential role of education, non-governmental organizations and women's groups in developing the capacity of poor women to define, defend and extend their rights through the empowerment process cannot be understated.[60]

But this effort cannot afford to limit itself to resources from within the nation-state. As Heyzer points out, "The state can intervene to bring about social equity. However, the state itself reflects the interest of powerful organized groups and is subject to pressures by multilateral donor agencies."[61] The danger is that the state can capture these NGOs and turn them into its de facto agencies for service delivery, devolve responsibility to them, and filter (elite) state interests through them, thereby perverting their ideal function of making the state accountable to the nation-people. Thus the state must be made to recognize the claims of poor women and cultural minorities through pressure from emerging nonelite women's and human-rights groups that try to link up with international networks and seek immediate support from international aid donors. Yet such multilateral donor agencies may preach the same policies of world trade liberalization that aim to re-compradorize the postcolonial state, thereby exacerbating existing gender hierarchies and discrimination along lines of culture and religion. Here, where every political decision is a response to the undecidability of its eventual effect, agency is not an assertion of freedom from givenness. Instead, it involves a rigorous responsibility to a condition of miredness within the shifting cosmopolitical linkages that give the postcolonial nation-state and enable the hyphen between nation and state to be rearticulated.

In neocolonial globalization, a metropolitan cultural politics that desires (or demands) the subaltern to speak so that *we can teach her our* ethical and political theories of freedom and clean our hands in the process seems somewhat absurd.[62] If, however, we want to learn how to respond to the subaltern woman in neocolonialism, we might reverse the charge and see Hélie-Lucas, Heyzer, et al. as teaching us the lesson that our response to the subaltern works through an interminable responsibility to the postcolonial nation-state as given culture within a cosmopolitical force field. This responsibility to given culture is (a) prior(i) to all forms of cultural agency that are based on the axiom of humanity's freedom from the given. It is a practical awareness of our structured co-implication with the world, everything that we take for granted when we begin from the claim of an existent condition of freedom that transcends the given. Yet we must presuppose this co-implication in order for our actions to be effective.

What is broached here is the radical vulnerability of politics to finitude that previous philosophical nationalisms and old and new cosmopolitanisms have always foreclosed. The culture-concept of philosophical modernity that became articulated into these different secular religions promised humanity a vocation that would lead it beyond the meaningless anonymity and permanent death of the merely given, the promise of a certain life beyond death through the nation, the ideal state, cosmopolitical culture, cultural hybridization, and so on. This foreclosure of the fact that it is in finitude that human beings *qua* finite corporeal creatures are given life informs the culturalism and economism of old cosmopolitanisms and their new hybrid successors in postcolonial cultural studies. Marxist economism suggests that political, social, and cultural forces are embedded in, grow out of, and reflect a material infrastructure. But it also suggests that the contradictions between base and superstructure are resolved by a teleological development of the material base that will point beyond necessity to a realm of cosmopolitical freedom. By contrast, culturalism grants autonomy to cultural forces. Autonomous culture can be regarded either as a unified realm that regulates, controls, or transcends material forces (idealist cosmopolitanism and nationalism) or as a force that outstrips and subverts the tendencies of material forces (varieties of nihilism and aestheticism relying on negative dialectics, of which hybridity theory is an unreflective example). Economism and culturalism are complicit because, regardless of whether they reconcile material and cultural forces or assert the freedom of the latter over the former, both regard the vocation of humanity as the transcendence of the given.

The theoretical significance of postcolonial nationalism—the work that it does in the house of theory—is that as given culture in neocolonial globalization, it is a historical case of the gift of life in finitude. We are speaking here of a life-giving death, a death that gives life. Not a certain life beyond death, but life in a certain kind of death. A spectral life—life perpetually haunted by the spectrality from within that constitutes it. For the processes of globalization are not antipathetic to the postcolonial nation-state even though they threaten to recompradorize it. Because the postcolonial nation-state remains a necessary terminal for these processes, they are its condition of (im)possibility. They make up the cosmopolitical sheaf of the postcolonial national body. Both noun and verb, the word *sheaf* can denote a cluster of disparate strands as well as the process of gathering. The global sheaf of the postcolonial national body is the shifting field within which the nation-state finds itself both dislocated and rearticulated. This field is not the cosmopolis as an ideal horizon of the Kantian type. Nor is it the global capitalist system as a factual totality awaiting to be sublated into a global proletarian consciousness. It is definitely not a transnational realm of cultural hybridization unmoored and exhibiting a subversive freedom from the weighty constraints of political and economic determinations. It is a nontranscendable moving ground extending across the globe in which political, cultural, and economic forces are brought into relation. These forces constrain, alter, and bleed into each other without return to form and deform the postcolonial nation-state. Because no single force is thereby able to assert itself as the final determinant that overarches the entire field, the postcolonial nation-state finds itself persistently modulating from being an agent for resisting international capital to being a collaborator of global economic restructuring.

No account of postcolonial political transformation in neocolonial globalization can in good faith suggest that the postcolonial nation-state has been or can be transcended in the name of a cosmopolitanism or postnationalism. But neither can any popular nationalism seeking to reclaim the postcolonial state choose not to respond to and tap the motility of the cosmopolitical sheaf that gives it body. This means that the postcolonial nation-state is always under negotiation in response to a changing globality, and that we cannot calculate absolutely the value of these globalizing processes for the realization of freedom. The most rigorous sense of responsibility to the given is imperative here.

Notes

An earlier version of this essay was presented at "Rethinking the Political," the inaugural conference of the Institute of Critical and Cultural Studies, Monash University, July 1993. This essay is dedicated to Elizabeth Grosz, for teaching me the complexity of the nature/culture problem; to György Markus, who took my questions on cultural modernity seriously; to Jonathan Culler, for his kind encouragement; and to Benedict Anderson, for his generosity and his brilliant work, which taught me to inflect the nature/culture problem through the nation form. I would also like to thank Beth Povinelli, Jim Siegel, Khachig Tölölyan, and Ellen Rooney for their criticisms and suggestions.

1. See, for instance, Fred Dallmayr's discussion of figures like Habermas, Rorty, Lyotard, and Merleau-Ponty in "Polis and Cosmopolis," *Margins of Political Discourse* (Albany: State University of New York Press, 1989), 1–21.
2. Jean-François Lyotard, "Universal History and Cultural Differences," in *The Lyotard Reader*, ed. Andrew Benjamin (Cambridge: Basil Blackwell, 1989), 319.
3. In his case for paralogical/local legitimation by way of the *petit récit*, Lyotard invokes the Casinahua as a primitive model that precedes the violent imposition of a universal/cosmopolitical narrative. See Jean-François Lyotard, *The Differend: Phrases in Dispute* (Minneapolis: University of Minnesota Press, 1988), 152–61.
4. For instance, in the pious lament that the problems of constitutionalism in decolonization arise because decolonized space is inadequate to the world historical ideal of con-

stitutionalism as realized in the West. For some of the arguments in this debate, see R. N. Spann, ed., *Constitutionalism in Asia* (New York: Asia, 1963); "Constitutionalism" (special issue), *Nomos* 20 (1979); Lawrence Beer, ed., *Constitutionalism in Asia: Asian Views of the American Influence* (Berkeley: University of California Press, 1979); Louis Henkin and Albert Rosenthal, eds., *Constitutionalism and Rights* (New York: Columbia University Press, 1990).

5. See Immanuel Kant, "Perpetual Peace: A Philosophical Sketch," in *Political Writings*, ed. Hans Reiss (Cambridge: Cambridge University Press, 1991), 114.

6. Immanuel Kant, "Idea for a Universal History with a Cosmopolitan Purpose," in *Political Writings*, ed. Hans Reiss (Cambridge: Cambridge University Press, 1991), 48.

7. Immanuel Kant, *Critique of Judgment*, trans. Werner Pluhar (Indianapolis: Hackett, 1987): "*Humanity [Humanität]* means both the universal *feeling of sympathy*, and the ability to engage universally in very intimate *communication*. When these two qualities are combined, they constitute the sociability that befits [our] humanity *[Menscheit]* and distinguishes it from the limitation [characteristic] of animals" (§ 60, 231). Hereafter cited as *CJ*; page numbers for further references to this work appear in text.

8. James Clifford, *The Predicament of Culture: Twentieth-Century Ethnography, Literature, and Art* (Cambridge: Harvard University Press, 1988), 95. Hereafter cited as *PC*; page numbers for further references to this work appear in text.

9. In his genealogy of culture, Clifford points to a strong continuity between the concept of high culture as the elevated domain of human value and the anthropological definition of culture: "Much of the vision embodied in *Culture and Anarchy* has been transferred directly into relativist anthropology. A powerful structure of feeling continues to see culture, wherever it is found, as a coherent body that lives and dies. Culture is enduring, traditional, structural." *PC*, 235.

10. See ibid., 15, 246, 250, 274.

11. "The Postcolonial Critic: Homi Bhabha interviewed by David Bennett and Terry Collits," *Arena* 96 (1991): 50–51.

12. The subject of a proposition (*énoncé*) is a psychic unity constituted in language on the uttering of the pronoun *I*. It is an empty and assignable slot that presupposes a material paralinguistic speaker (the subject of enunciation) from which it is split. See Emile Benveniste, *Problems in General Linguistics* (Bloomington: Indiana University Press, 1961), 224–26; Michel Foucault, *The Archaeology of Knowledge* (New York: Pantheon, 1972), 102–5.

13. Homi Bhabha, "Of Mimicry and Man: The Ambivalence of Colonial Discourse," in *The Location of Culture* (New York: Routledge, 1994), 86. Hereafter cited as *LC*; page numbers for further references to this work appear in text.

14. See Homi Bhabha, "Signs Taken for Wonders," in *LC*: "Hybridity is the revaluation of the assumption of colonial identity through the repetition of discriminatory identity effects. . . . The ambivalence at the source of traditional discourses on authority enables a form of subversion, founded on the undecidability that turns the discursive conditions of dominance into the grounds of intervention" (112).

15. "The displacement of symbol to sign creates a crisis for any concept of authority based on a system of recognition. . . . Hybridity [enables] . . . other 'denied' knowledges [to] enter the dominant discourse and estrange the basis of its authority" (*LC*, 114).

16. Edward Said, *Orientalism* (New York: Random House, 1979). Compare Homi Bhabha, "The Other Question: Stereotype, Discrimination and the Discourse of Colonialism," in *LC*: "[Said] rightly rejects a notion of Orientalism as the misrepresentation of an Oriental essence. However, having introduced the concept of 'discourse' he does not face up to the problems it creates for an instrumentalist notion of power/knowledge that he seems to require" (72); and James Clifford, "On Oriental-

ism," in *PC*: "Said's humanist perspectives do not harmonize with his use of methods derived from Foucault, who is of course a radical critic of humanism" (264).

17. James Clifford, "Identity in Mashpee," in *PC*: "Mashpee's semi-autonomous plantation, a specific mix of individual citizenship and collective entailment, now appeared as a precursor of reinvented tribalism. No return to a pure Wampanoag tradition was at issue, but rather a reinterpretation of Mashpee's contested history in order to act— with other Indian groups—powerfully, in an impure present-becoming-future" (344).

18. Clifford suggests that Césaire's antiessentialist negritude is a reflexive model of rebellion, a "New World Poetics of continuous transgression and cooperative cultural activity" (*PC*, 181).

19. Homi Bhabha, "Postcolonial Authority and Postmodern Guilt," in *Cultural Studies*, ed. Lawrence Grossberg, Cary Nelson, and Paula A. Treichler (New York: Routledge, 1992), 59. Hereafter cited as PA.

20. James Clifford, "Traveling Cultures," in *Cultural Studies*, ed. Lawrence Grossberg, Cary Nelson, and Paula A. Treichler (New York: Routledge, 1992), 107–8. Hereafter cited as TC; page numbers for further references to this work appear in text.

21. Homi Bhabha, "The Postcolonial and the Postmodern: The Question of Agency," in *LC*, 172, 173.

22. This is nothing less than "a general intervention within the field of modernity . . . both as an epistemological and political project." See "The Postcolonial Critic," 49.

23. See Homi Bhabha, "DissemiNation: Time, Narrative and the Margins of the Modern Nation," in *LC*, 139–70.

24. Suffice it to say that in his account of colonial ambivalence, Bhabha's attribution of subversive powers to the vicissitudes of colonial representation relies on too narrow an understanding of the historical project of colonialism, which involves more than the establishment of civility and cultural authority through the deployment of colonial symbols.

25. See PA, 59; and Homi Bhabha, "'Race,' Time and the Revision of Modernity," in *LC*, 245. This closet idealism is appropriately disguised as the self-proximate ipseity of the ever-changing human body (Clifford) or as the subaltern's "affective inscription at the point of human enunciation" (Bhabha, PA, 59), but in both instances, the hybridized body is a cultural sign in free flux, the site of autonomous dispersal and reinvention, and the ultimate act of human freedom.

26. In his response to the contributions to this volume, Clifford distinguishes his position from Homi Bhabha's. He suggests that I have misconstrued his focus on cultural invention as an unmooring of cultural hybridization from politics and economics and mistakenly conflated hybrid agency with Marxist *Aufhebung*. Taking issue with my account of nationalism as given culture, he suggests that the nation-state is not the only thing given by history and that broadly defined democratic socialist alliances should rely on cosmopolitan competences. In response, I wish to point out that my comments about Clifford's reliance on an ontology of flux and cultural freedom are a critical development of his own worries: "Perhaps this book goes too far in its concern for ethnographic presents-becoming-futures. Its utopian, persistent hope for the reinvention of difference risks downplaying the destructive, homogenizing effects of global economic and cultural centralization" (*PC*, 15). Whereas I agree that hybrid agency is not identical with Marxist dialectics (my argument is that they are variations of the same culture-concept), it is unclear how much the pragmatic rationality and cultural inventiveness of hybrid agency depart from the anthropocentric freedom of the canonical culture-concept. "Working between given historical powers" seems to be a local and more strategic variation of Hegel's "work of the concept" or Marx's material labor, and not a radical responsibility to finitude. At any rate, Clifford does not discuss the predica-

ment of *nature*. It should be apparent from my later remarks on the global sheaf of the national body that I do not dismiss the importance of transnational forces. But in the periphery, where the democratic socialist alliances to which Clifford refers are impossible because of the truncation of democratic projects by economic globalization, the nation-state is the starting point of political transformation and celebrations of transnational solidarity run the perpetual risk of serving global capital.

27. The next few paragraphs rely heavily on the scholarly work of the Budapest school philosopher György Markus. See Markus, "Culture: The Making and the Make-up of a Concept (An Essay in Historical Semantics)," *Dialectical Anthropology* 18 (1993): 3–29. Hereafter cited as C; page numbers for references to this work appear in text.

28. Immanuel Kant, "Conjectures on the Beginning of Human History," in *Political Writings*, ed. Hans Reiss (Cambridge: Cambridge University Press, 1991), 228.

29. Karl Marx, "The Trinity Formula," in *Capital: A Critique of Political Economy*, vol. 3, trans. David Fernbach (Harmondsworth: Penguin, 1991): "Freedom, in this sphere [of natural necessity], can consist only in this, that socialized man, the associated producers, govern the human metabolism with nature in a rational way, bringing it under their collective control instead of being dominated by it like a blind power" (959).

30. See Karl Marx, "Draft of an Article on Friedrich List's Book, *Das nationale System der politischen Ökonomie*," in Karl Marx and Friedrich Engels, *Collected Works*, vol. 4 (New York: International, 1975), 265–93.

31. Karl Marx and Friedrich Engels, *The German Ideology* (Moscow: Progress, 1976), 59.

32. Compare Johann Gottlieb Fichte, "What Is a People in the Higher Meaning of the Word, and What Is Love of Fatherland?" Eighth Address, in *Addresses to the German Nation* (New York: Harper & Row, 1968); and G. W. F. Hegel, *The Philosophy of Right*, trans. T. M. Knox (Oxford: Oxford University Press, 1967), §§ 325–28.

33. Amilcar Cabral, "National Liberation and Culture," in *Unity and Struggle: Speeches and Writings*, trans. Michael Wolfers (New York: Monthly Review Press, 1979), 143.

34. Thomas McCarthy, "Doing the Right Thing in Cross-Cultural Representation," *Ethics* 102 (April 1992): 644.

35. Anthony P. Cohen, "Culture as Identity: An Anthropologists's View," *New Literary History* 24 (1993): 209.

36. Valentine M. Moghadam, "Introduction: Women and Identity Politics in Theoretical and Comparative Perspective," in *Identity Politics and Women: Cultural Reassertions and Feminisms in International Perspective*, ed. Valentine M. Moghadam (Boulder, Colo.: Westview, 1994), 6. Hereafter cited as *IP*.

37. Samir Amin, *Eurocentrism* (London: Zed, 1988), xi, 124, 134, 135.

38. For a more detailed elaboration from which my sketch is drawn, see Moghadam, "Introduction," 6–11.

39. More recently, the Malaysian prime minister, Dr. Mahathir Mohamad, has suggested that in order to rid itself of its "colonialized" mentality in its dealings with Western countries over social issues such as human rights abuses and corruption, Malaysia should "set up a body like Europe Watch to monitor the Europeans' index on racial discrimination, immorality and corruption." See "PM: We Can Also Tell Off the West," *Star*, June 5, 1996.

40. See, most recently, Lee Kuan Yew's lecture on June 17, 1996, at the Ludwig-Maximilians University, Munich, "Asia: How It Became a Dynamo of World Economies," reprinted in the *Straits Times*, June 18, 1996; see also Pang Gek Choo, "East Asian Growth Depends on Its Keeping Culture of Hard Work: SM," *Straits Times*, June 18, 1996.

41. See Benedict Anderson, "Census, Map, Museum," in *Imagined Communities: Reflections on the Origin and Spread of Nationalism*, rev. ed. (New York: Verso, 1991), 163–85.

42. Marie-Aimée Hélie-Lucas, "Women, Nationalism and Religion in the Algerian Libera-tion Struggle," in *Opening the Gates: A Century of Arab Feminist Writing*, ed. Margot Badran and Miriam Cooke (Bloomington: Indiana University Press, 1990), 107.

43. See M. J. Peterson, "Transnational Activity, International Society and World Politics," *Millennium: Journal of International Studies* 21, no. 3 (1992): 371–377.

44. Alexander Colás, "Putting Cosmopolitanism into Practice: The Case of Socialist Inter-nationalism," *Millennium: Journal of International Studies* 23, no. 3 (1994): 533.

45. See Samir Amin, *Empire of Chaos* (New York: Monthly Review Press, 1992), 38–44.

46. Samir Amin, "The Social Movements in the Periphery: An End to National Libera-tion?" in *Transforming the Revolution: Social Movements and the World-System*, ed. Samir Amin, Giovanni Arrighi, Andre Gunder Frank, and Immanuel Wallerstein (New York: Monthly Review Press, 1990), 124. Hereafter cited as SM; page numbers for further references to this work appear in text.

47. See especially Samir Amin, "The Asian and African Vocation of Marxism," in *Delink-ing: Towards a Polycentric World* (London: Zed, 1990).

48. Partha Chatterjee, *Nationalist Thought and the Colonial World: A Derivative Dis-course?* (London: Zed, 1986), 169.

49. Noeleen Heyzer and Yao Souchou, "The State, Industrialization and Women in Singa-pore," in *Transnationals and Special Economic Zones: The Experience of China and Se-lected ASEAN Countries*, ed. Theresa Cariño (Manila: De la Salle University Press, 1989), 69–70; emphasis added.

50. Ibid., 70.

51. Ibid., 79.

52. See Kumari Jayawardena, *Feminism and Nationalism in the Third World* (London: Zed, 1986).

53. Sondra Hale, "Gender, Religious Identity and Political Mobilization in Sudan," in *IP*, 147.

54. Cherifa Bouatta and Doria Cherifati-Meratine, "The Social Representation of Women in Algeria's Islamist Movement," in *IP*, 195.

55. Nawal el-Saadawi, "The Political Challenges Facing Arab Women at the End of the Twentieth Century," in *Women of the Arab World: The Coming Challenge*, ed. Nahid Toubia (London: Zed, 1988), 19.

56. Marie-Aimée Hélie-Lucas, "The Preferential Symbol for Islamic Identity: Women in Muslim Personal Laws," in *IP*, 398.

57. Margot Badran, "Gender Activism: Feminists and Islamists in Egypt," in *IP*, 203.

58. Marie-Aimée Hélie-Lucas, "Bound and Gagged by the Family Code," in *Third World—Second Sex*, vol. 2, ed. Miranda Davies (London: Zed, 1987), 11; emphasis added.

59. Gita Sen, "Poverty, Economic Growth and Gender Equity: The Asian and Pacific Ex-perience," in *Gender, Economic Growth and Poverty: Market Growth and State Plan-ning in Asia and the Pacific*, ed. Noeleen Heyzer and Gita Sen (Kuala Lumpur: Asian and Pacific Development Centre, 1994), 50.

60. Noeleen Heyzer, "Introduction: Market, State and Gender Equity," in *Gender, Eco-nomic Growth and Poverty: Market Growth and State Planning in Asia and the Pacific*, ed. Noeleen Heyzer and Gita Sen (Kuala Lumpur: Asian and Pacific Development Centre, 1994), 25.

61. Ibid., 24.

62. See Gayatri Chakravorty Spivak, "Can the Subaltern Speak?" in *Marxism and the In-terpretation of Culture*, ed. Lawrence Grossberg and Cary Nelson (Urbana: University of Illinois Press, 1986), 271–313.

Cultural Talks in the Hot Peace:
Revisiting the "Global Village"

Gayatri Chakravorty Spivak

The "globe" is counterintuitive. You walk from one end of the earth to the other and it remains flat. It is a scientific abstraction inaccessible to experience. No one lives in the *global* village. The only relationship accessible to the globe so far is that of the gaze. Both the Greek and the Sanskrit words for transcendental knowledge or theory—*theoria* and *darsana*—relate to seeing. Culture at work or at play, on the other hand, is not a problem of knowledge, but a regulator of relations. My question, therefore: In what interest, to regulate what sort of relationships, is the globe evoked?

"Culture" is also a regulator of how one knows: Foucault's famous capacity-to-know doublet, *pouvoir/savoir* as the ability to know is "culture" at ground level. (Of course, Foucault uses other words, most noticeably *discourse*.) From this point of view, taxonomies of culture are possible and useful. But any "culture" at work is a play of differences (if you can separate work and play) from these taxonomies. This is not a poststructuralist pronouncement. Simply put, it is how language use is a play of differences from dictionaries. Yet dictionaries are possible and useful. No *langue/parole* or system/process distinction can catch this play, culture at work. Culture alive is always on the run, always changeful. There is no reason to throw up one's hands over this. We do our work with this limit to the power of vanguardism of theory in view.

I am therefore a student of cultural politics. In what interest are differences defined? When the process people correct the systems people, what may be the agenda? As I work at this, I am of course open to your view. You will judge my agenda in the process.

In January 1993, my attention was particularly focused on the failure of nationhood in India that was symbolized by the destruction of a mosque in Ayodhya a month earlier, rather than on an investigation of globality. In the interest of academic responsibility, I adjusted my focus to the theme of the conference.

I pointed out that it was not only the political power brokers in the nation who mobilized the forces of fundamentalism in the name of historically authoritative national identity; there is an isolationist counternationalism among the ideologues of the left as well. Indeed, although I am a professed antinationalist, my passionate stand against religious nationalism in the country of my citizenship betrayed the power of the reactive nationalism of the expatriate. Nationalism, like culture, is a moving base—a *socle mouvant* (to quote Foucault again)—of differences, as dangerous as it is powerful, always ahead or deferred by definitions, pro or contra, upon which it relies.[1] Against this, globality or postnationalist talk is a representation—both as *Darstellung* or theater and as *Vertretung* or delegation as functionary—of the financialization of the globe, or globalization.[2] Fundamentalist nationalism arises in the loosened hyphen between nation and state as the latter is mortgaged further and further by the forces of financialization, although the determinations are never clear.[3] Therefore I will propose yet another way of conjuring with nationalism later in this essay, in the name not of the globe but of a global girdling.

McLuhan and Lyotard

Globality is invoked in the interest of the financialization of the globe, or globalization. To think globality is to think the politics of thinking globality. In support of this intuition, I looked at two books. The conference had invoked Marshall McLuhan's *The Global Village*.[4] I dragged the line forward to Jean-François Lyotard's *The Postmodern Condition*.[5] Although McLuhan belongs to the mad scientist phase of the 1960s, and Lyotard leans on the critique of the paradigms of modernist science produced by philosophers of science such as Kuhn, Feyerabend, Roy Bhaskar, and Nancy Cartwright,[6] the two share a common and stated presupposition: that the advances in electronic technology have made it possible for "the West" (McLuhan) or "telematic society" (Lyotard) to go back to the possibility of precapitalist spiritual riches without their attendant discomforts. McLuhan launches the argument in terms of the activities of the left brain—rational and visual—in which the West has so far been engaged—over against the activities of the right brain—holistic and acoustic—to which the West is graduating, thanks to electronic technology. To prove this he proposes to rewrite the history of scientific discoveries through the rationalist model of the tetrad, which he passes off as a metaphor.[7]

According to McLuhan, although the Third World has so far operated through the holistic right brain, it is now coming more and more toward the left side. How McLuhan manages to draw this absurd conclusion from the hegemonic Moorish, Arabic, Persian, Indian, Korean, Chinese, and Japanese traditions is, alas, only too easily explained, but would involve analytic polemics that have no place here. The point is that certainly by the turn of the century, the Third World will implode upon it-self for different reasons: too many people and too little food . . . the tetrad of the cancer cell reveals, in small, the immediate hereafter of the world: cancer enhances cell reproduction, retrieves primitive cell evolution, and transforms itself into self-consumption. . . . The new technologic man . . . must become his brother's keeper, in spite of himself. (M 100)

Ecology shifts the "White Man's Burden" on to the shoulders of the "Man-in-the-Street." (M 93)

Here we see the general justification for "Development," the civilizing mis-sion (*la mission civilisatrice*) of the new imperialism. (I will resume discus-sion of the use of women in the next section.) We are now the New World, we must take the old New World upon our shoulders. And what is going to be the model?

"EFTS (Electronic Funds Transfer System) . . . may be considered the working prototype of all . . . planetary data bases" (M 108). "When an orga-nization becomes the largest economic grouping in the nation, it *is* the social structure" (M 124). And, we might add, such financialization *is* the secret of globalization. The rest of the book is an impassioned song of praise for the Bell Telephone System and AT&T. We are not surprised that the book ends on a particular nationalist/imperialist note: "Canadians and Americans share something very precious: a sense of the last frontier. The Canadian North has replaced the American West" (M 147).

Of course Lyotard doesn't mess with theories of right-brain conscious-ness. The entire argument is muted in his book. He advances the idea that each "condition" offers or is produced by—one can't be sure—language games used for legitimation. He suggests that in the telematic or electronic world, neither the narrative of social justice (Marx) nor the narrative of de-velopment (capital) provides legitimation. *Now* legitimacy is offered accord-ing to a model that generates forms—otherwise identified as short tales—without an end in view: morphogenetic, innovative, but nonteleological. Although there is no unsophisticated faith in a raised consciousness here, the acquisition of a new language game to match the telematic or electronic con-dition shows a naive faith (that many share) that minds change collectively at the same speed as world structures.

Lyotard gets his model of legitimation by short tale from the oral formu-laic epic tradition. The argument is itself a hidden great narrative that might go like this: under the pressure of the slow historical movement that finally led to modernity, the great oral epics, such as the *Iliad*, the *Odyssey*, the

Mahābhārata, the *Rāmāyana*, and, of course, the epics of the Nordic tradition, received narrative closure. They became long stories with beginnings, middles, and ends. When the premodern singer of tales actually performed the epics, however, *his* legitimation came from how many new episodes or tales he could spin, through his memory of the oral formula. We fully telematic societies, with our vast impersonal "virtual" memories, are supposed to have acceded to the premodern, precapitalist condition, with none of its problems, and we can proceed like the old singer of tales. Lyotard's model is the singer of tales from the Native American tribe Kashinahua. Incidentally, this particular tradition, through long historical transmogrification, is alive and well in counterglobal revolutionary theater (indeed, the theater for political mobilization is the most stylized end of all politics of counterdiscourse), not necessarily in the hegemonic language, owing little or nothing to the European novelistic tradition, about which Benedict Anderson et al. go on endlessly.[8] This phenomenon falls out of benevolent definitions of world literature, produced in the North. Cultural politics.

It is not surprising that both Lyotard and McLuhan end on the pious note that "what knowledge there is will [McLuhan] or should [Lyotard] be available to all." Hail to thee, *pax electronica.*[9]

It is also no surprise that, in the hot peace following the Cold War, it is in fact the great U.N. conferences that legitimate themselves, mostly in the name of woman, innovatively and morphogenetically, proliferating bureaucratic forms that seem international activism to women who will forever remain protected from subaltern *pouvoir/savoir*. But Lyotard may be wrong also in estimating that the ancient singer of tales legitimated himself by a simple and acknowledged absence of the teleologic. The binary opposition between "linear" and "layered" or "cyclical" time is peculiarly "modern." Another version of that same uncritical assumption: that the collective subject is isomorphic with social structures of cultural explanation.[10] These self-legitimating modern(ization) conferences are in fact nonteleological only in terms of the telos that they so abundantly proclaim: the End of Woman as the End of Man.

The great narrative of Development is not dead. The cultural politics, of books like the two I've discussed and of the completely well-meaning speech upon the global electronic future that we heard at the conference, is precisely to provide the narrative of development an alibi. My generation in India, born before independence, realizes only too well that many of the functionaries of the civilizing mission of imperialism were well-meaning.[11] The point here is not personal accusations. And in fact what these functionaries gave was often what I call an enabling violation—a rape that produces a healthy child, whose existence cannot be advanced as a justification for the rape. Imperialism cannot be justified by the fact that India has railways and I speak English well. Many of the functionaries of the civilizing mission were well-meaning; but alas, you can do good with contempt or paternal-maternal-sororal benevolence in your heart. And today, you can knife the poor nation in the back and offer Band-Aids for a photo opportunity, even as you declare an end to all varieties of nationalism in the metropolis.

Yet a crude theory of national identity—we were asked by Indians, we were asked by the Somalis, we were asked by Africans—is used to legitimate this narrative and silence opposition.[12] Alternative development collectives, national-local health care, ecology, and literacy collectives have been in place for a long time, and play a critical role at the grassroots level. Why are they seldom heard? These oppositional structures are indigenous NGOs, or non-governmental organizations. The governments of developing nations are, with the disappearance of the possibility of nonalignment in the post-Soviet world, heavily mortgaged to international Development organizations. The relationship between the government and the spectrum of indigenous non-governmental organizations is at least as ambiguous and complex as the glibly invoked "identity of the nation."[13] The NGOs that surface at the "NGO Forums" of the U.N. conferences have been so thoroughly vetted by the donor countries, and the content of their presentations so organized by categories furnished by the United Nations, that neither subject nor object bears much resemblance to the "real thing," if you will pardon the expression.

The main funding and coordinating agency of the great narrative of development is the World Bank. The phrase *sustainable development* has entered the discourse of all the bodies that manage globality. Development to sustain what? The general ideology of global Development is racist paternalism (and alas, increasingly, sororalism); its general economics capital-intensive investment; its broad politics the silencing of resistance and of the subaltern as the rhetoric of their protest is constantly appropriated.

Sweden and India

Sweden, as it happens, is a generally "enlightened" donor country, responsible in the context of globality. In the late 1970s and the 1980s, when liberals of the right brought up Cuba, many brought up Sweden—the last holdout of the Socialist International—as a model for the Sandinista. It was therefore peculiarly troubling that in its domestic treatment of the great waves of migration generated by the so-called end of the Cold War the enlightened practices of the Swedish welfare state began to crumble. This piece, like all my current work, forages in the crease between global postcoloniality and post-colonial migrancy. Thus it was important to me, speaking in Sweden, that, whatever its image in the field of global aid, the Swedish state was closing off welfare for the detritus of globality. It seemed to be the final demise of Second International socialism. I say final because we used to think it died in 1914 when the German Social Democrats voted in war credits. As Immanuel Wallerstein and others have pointed out, the benefits of the Second International can, however, be felt in the state structures of Northwestern European countries. It was these benefits that were being regulated and withdrawn by way of a 1976 amendment to the Aliens Act that introduced "special reasons for denial." Under pressure of economic restructuring and the New World Order, socialism in one country was crumbling in the North as well.

I will often sound the note that, in the New World Order—or hot peace—the hyphen between nation and state has come looser than usual; that in that gap fundamentalisms fester.[14] It is curious that, in the context that I was then inhabiting, Sweden, of all places, could offer me the first example. I quote some words I uttered at the conference, at the very end of a rather long section on Hindu nationalism that I have suppressed for this version:

> India too used to be a "socialist country with a mixed economy." We have our King Rāma (the mythic Hindu king who is the hero of the Hindu nationalists), and you your Karl XII.[15] I know Swedish protest against the outrage of November 30, 1992 (when a group of young Swedish racists marched under the banner of the King), was strong. Yet, unless you believe (and many do) that faith in human equality is simply a natural characteristic of the Swedish nation, I am obliged to remind you that we nonsectarian Hindus had thought, until the massacre of December 6, 1992, "It can't happen here."

Although we must work to elect public officials who must soldier to shore up the benefits of the welfare state, that alone is not the kingpin of the global future.

Let us now place cultural studies at the academic end of a spectrum that, traversing the political, vanishes at last into the necessary impossibility of the ethical.[16] Thus: cultural studies, "radical" art, mainstreaming, globe-girdling movements. I explain each of the first three by way of somewhat singular cases in order to get to the last. Perhaps this is not just due to the idiosyncrasy of the lecture circuit. Perhaps this is the problem with all radical interventions within firmly established conventions—academy or art—

insufficiently canny not only about globality but about their own unwitting place and role in globalization. Part of what I include in the next few pages is an extract from a speech addressed to Indian cultural studies academics a week before the conference in Sweden.[17]

The initial attempt in the Bandung conference (1955), to establish a third way, within neither the Eastern nor the Western bloc in the world-system, in response to the seemingly New World Order established after the Second World War, was not accompanied by commensurate intellectual effort. The only idioms deployed for the nurturing of that nascent Third World in the cultural field belonged to positions emerging from resistance within the supposedly Old World Order, anti-imperialism and/or national-ism. The idioms that are coming in to fill that space in this New World Order ascertain perhaps that the cultural lobby be once again of no help in producing a transnationally literate appropriate subject.[18] They are national origin, subnationalism, nationalism, cultural-nativism or relativism, religion, and/or—in Northern radical chic—hybridism, postnationalism. It is this last group that produces most of the cultural studies talk. Speaking to this In-dian audience, full of many people who are finished in the United States as in a finishing school, I quoted Antonio Gramsci. Necessarily without a de-tailed awareness of the rich history of the African American struggle, Gram-sci was somewhat off the mark when he presented the hypothesis that American expansionism would use African Americans to conquer the African market and the extension of American civilization (although the case of South Africa and the use of African Americans in U.S. military aggression seem to support Gramsci).[19] But if his hypothesis is applied to the New Im-migrant intellectuals and their countries of national origin, it seems particu-larly apposite today.[20] The partners are of course, cultural studies, liberal multiculturalism, post-Fordist transnational capitalism in aid of export-based foreign capital investment, and so-called free trade. Globalization de-constructs the difference between this set and Development as such.

Perhaps because of this, the same students in the United States spend much time and money (fellowships abroad, recommendation letters, and so on) to get hegemonic languages just right to catch Lacan or Negri—not to mention Heidegger or Marx—but think a proposal to learn the language of a migrant group elitist. Whereas international affairs, development econom-ics, and business administration merrily traffic in transnationality, cultural studies—talking interdisciplinary, even postdisciplinary talk, will not walk the walk for transnational *literacy* (not expertise); too intimidating![21] Against such a tough group, what I say below may seem peculiarly fragile. But, although every victory is a warning, we cannot afford to forget that the people did push the World Bank out of the Narmada Valley in India in March 1993.

To repeat, then: unexamined cultural studies export/import between a "developing" country and its migrant group in the United States, emphasizing hybridity, can provide crucial ideological support for the crude cultural relativism of the received narrative of Development. Some time ago, I was involved in a site-specific art show on a migrant community in London. When I proposed that we show evidence of the fact that ethnic entrepreneurs were pimping for the transnationals and selling their women into sweated labor (lowering wages without legal control), my collaborating artist's response was that he did not want to show sexist exploitation within the community. He wanted to show just white racism. Cultural politics. Abdication of responsibility. The migrant is all good. The whites are all bad. Legitimation by reversal. Reverse racism.

What I was trying to make visible to the viewing public rather than activists in the field was precisely the keeping apart of migrancy and development—that thousands of unskilled female Bangladeshi homeworkers in London's East End were being set in unwitting competition with thousands of unskilled female workers in the export-based garment industry in Bangladesh proper. The latter are "winning," because they cost five hundred pounds less per head a year, and can bear witness to "women in development." Ethnicization of female superexploitation is a global story, an episode in the same large-scale story that generates our demand for cross-culturalism; successful pimping requires it. In the end, the ignorance of artist and journalist was written up in the pages of the *Guardian* as deconstruction waylaying political art, because I had used the word *invisible* for women's sweated labor.[22]

This kind of competition is part of the broad competition between Northern and Southern trade unions as well as Northern and Southern industry in the New World Order that is an obstacle to any nonhyphenated international solidarity, cultural or economic, indeed on any front. Here is an example, but this can be indefinitely multiplied, on diverse and discontinuous levels:

> In applying preferential liberalizing measures to Bangladesh, Canada may have to extend similar facilities to all other LDCs [least developed countries], including Vietnam and Haiti. Vietnam in particular is a potentially serious threat to Bangladesh, though currently its privileges are restrained by the on-going trade embargo, thereby giving Bangladesh a short head-start in rationalizing its garment export activities.[23]

This is what is usually described as "the free market." The World Bank and the World Trade Organization are major manipulators of such competition.[24] And you cannot work to undo the aporia between migrancy-in-racism and Development with a capital D if you are not transnationally literate, if you do not take forced competition into account. It seems interesting that the same artist now has a show called "a cemetery of images" on Rwanda (where he spent twelve days recently), which celebrates international NGOs as the only correct access route to the images of Rwandan suffering. I do not doubt the seriousness of his shock, or the sophistication of his innovations within modernist aesthetic conventions. But history is larger than personal good-will, and we must learn to be responsible as we must study to be political. "The world has abandoned Africa," the artist said to a writer from the *Chicago Tribune*.[25] Such would not have been his feeling if he had attended one of the seminars at my university, or read the regular World Bank bulletins, on "emergent" stock markets. In the absence of global analysis, sensationalism ostentatiously withheld—his photographs were in sealed boxes, a technique I have already seen copied—repeats the tongue-clucking horror of sensationalism abundantly purveyed.

From our academic or "cultural work" niches, we can supplement the globe-girdling movements with "mainstreaming," somewhere between moonlighting and educating public opinion. My example is an economics professor, so the intervention might seem too cut-and-dried. It is not without significance, I think, that a literary or artistic example of *global* mainstreaming (neither romantic anticapitalism nor grandiose anti-imperialism) is hard to find. Aesthetics and politics? Think it through. My example for the moment is Amartya Sen, whose defense of support for higher education in the South, in the face of the World Bank's insistence that higher education in the developing countries should be de-emphasized because it is unproductive, is a case in point.[26] At the same time, my own university has won a competition, and opened a program funded by the World Bank, where the eligible students are middle-level bureaucrats from developing countries. High-level indoctrination in Columbia University, but no higher education in Dhaka or Delhi.

Local and Global

In the contemporary context, when the world is broadly divided simply into North and South, the World Bank and other international agencies can divide the world into maps that make visible the irreducibly abstract quality of geography. One of the guiding principles of geo-graphy—"nation"—being inextricably tangled with the mysterious phenomena of language (synthesis with the absolute other) and birth (susceptible to both species-life [gestation] and species-being [Law])—both discloses and effaces this abstract character.[27] But the boundaries crosshatching these new maps or "information systems" are hardly ever national or "natural." They are investment boundaries that change constantly because the dynamics of international capital are fast moving. One of the not inconsiderable motive forces in the drawing up of these maps is the appropriation of the Fourth World's ecosystems in the name of Development.

A kinship in exploitation may be mobilized through the land-grabbing and reforestation practiced against the First Nations of the Americas; the destruction of the reindeer forests of the Suomis of Scandinavia, Finland, and Russia; the tree-felling and eucalyptus plantations against the original nations in India; and the so-called Flood Action Plan against the fisher folk and landless peasants of Bangladesh, honorary Fourth Worlders. Indeed, such a kinship exists potentially among all the early civilizations that have been pushed back and away to make way for more traditional geographic elements of the map and the world today.

Upon the body of this North/South world, and to maintain the fantastic cartography of the World Bank map, yet another kind of unification is being practiced. As the barriers between fragile national economies and international capital are being removed, the possibility of social redistribution in the so-called developing states, uncertain at best, is disappearing even further. What we have to notice here is that the developing national states are not only linked by the common thread of profound ecological loss, the loss of forest and river as foundation of life, but also plagued by the complicity, however apparently remote, of the power lines of local developers with the forces of global capital. That this complicity is, at best, unknown to the glib theorists of globality talk or those who still whinge on about old-style imperialism is no secret to the initiative for a global movement for non-Eurocentric ecological justice.

Why non-Eurocentric? Theorists who used to define New Social Movements as antisystemic now say that the future lies with these movements. But they are skeptical because, taking the European Economic Community as model, they see these movements as still having to solve the problem of state power.[28] If, however, the focus is shifted from the EEC, the predicament of the developing state, in spite of the fact that it negotiates with nationalism and is still the site of justice and redistribution, is such that it is no longer the main theater for these movements that must aspire to global reach. They have to stand behind the state, plagued as it is from the inside by the forces of internal colonization and the local bourgeoisie and plagued from the outside by these increasingly orthodox economic constraints under global economic restructuring. Therefore, there is no interest in grabbing state power as a main program in the non-Eurocentric global movement for ecological justice. These matters certainly seem arcane to the benevolent study of "other cultures" in the North, although, given that the agents of transnational financialization are attempting to appropriate so-called non-governmental organizations by much publicized participation in the U.N. conferences, and naming the collectivity of collaborative NGOs an "international civil society," precisely bypassing the individual states, this point seems hardly worth making today.

And here a strong connection, indeed a complicity between the bourgeoisie of the Third World and migrants in the First cannot be ignored. It is important to acknowledge the affective subspace in which migrants, especially the underclass, must endure racism. Yet, *if* we are talking globality, it is one of the painful imperatives of the impossible within the ethical situation that we have to admit that the interest of the migrant, however remote, is in dominant global capital. The migrant is in First World space. I am not saying anything against migrant activist movements, but we are talking globality here. There are some severe lessons that one must learn. We have to keep this particularly in mind because this is also the export/import line from religious national parties in the South to cultural studies folk in the North.[29] (The division is further exacerbated by the trade union movement in the North being asked to circumvent even the General Agreement on Tariffs and Trade by invoking "human rights violations" at the same time as, as part of economic restructuring, the World Bank demands privatization and the decimation of trade unions in the South—unions that can otherwise agitate for more humane labor laws.)

Having seen the powerful and risky role played by Christian liberation theology, some of us have dreamed of animist liberation theologies to girdle the perhaps impossible vision of an ecologically just world.[30] Indeed, the name theology is alien to this thinking. Nature is also supernature in this way of thinking and knowing. (Please be sure that I am not positing some generalized tribal mind.) Even super, as in supernatural, is out of the way. For nature, the sacred other of the human community, is in this thinking also bound by the structure of ethical responsibility. No individual transcendence theology, of being just in this world in view of the next, however the next is underplayed, can bring us to this.

It is my conviction that the internationality of ecological justice in that impossible, undivided world of which one must dream, in view of the impossibility of which one must work, obsessively, cannot be reached by invoking any of the so-called great religions of the world because the history of their greatness is too deeply imbricated in the narrative of the ebb and flow of power. In the case of Hindu India, a phrase as terrifying to us as "Christian Europe," no amount of reinventing the nature poetry of the *Rgveda* will in this view suffice to undo that history. I have no doubt that we must learn to learn from the original practical ecological philosophies of the world. Again, I am not romanticizing; liberation theology does not romanticize every Christian. We are talking about using the strongest mobilizing discourse in the world in a certain way, for the globe, not merely for Fourth World uplift. I say this again because it is so easy to dismiss this as quixotic moralism. This learning can only be attempted, through the supplementation of collective effort by love. What deserves the name of love is an effort—over which one has no control yet at which one must not strain—that is slow, attentive on both sides (How does one win the attention of the subaltern without coercion or crisis?), mind changing on both sides, at the possibility of an unascertainable ethical singularity that is not ever a sustainable condition. The necessary collective efforts are to change laws, relations of production, systems of education, and health care. But without the mind-changing one-on-one responsible contact, nothing will stick.[31]

One word on ethical singularity, not a fancy name for mass contact, or for engagement with the common sense of the people. It is something that may be described by way of the following situation, as long as we keep in mind that we are (a) phenomenalizing figures and (b) *not* speaking of radical alterity.

We all know that when we engage profoundly with *one* person, the responses—the answers—come from both sides. Let us call this responsibility. And "answer"ability or accountability. We also know, and if we don't we have been unfortunate, that in such engagements, we want to reveal and reveal, conceal nothing. Yet on both sides, there is always a sense that something has not gone across. This is what we call the secret, not something that one wants to conceal, but something that one wants desperately to reveal in this relationship of singularity and responsibility and accountability. (It would be more philosophical to say that "secret" is the name lent to the fact or possibility that everything does not go across. Never mind.) In this sense, ethical singularity can be called a secret encounter. (Please note that I am not talking about meeting in secret.)[32] Ethical singularity is approached when responses flow from both sides. Otherwise, the idea that if the person I am doing good to resembles me and has my rights, he or she will be better off, does not begin to approach an ethical relation (nor, of course, does an attitude of unqualified admiration for the person as an example of his or her culture).

Among Indian Aboriginals, I know a very small percentage of a small percentage that was "denotified" in 1955. These forest-dwelling tribals had been earlier defined as "criminal tribes," and therefore had been left alone not just by the British, but also by the Hindu and Muslim civilizations of India. They are not "radicals." But because they (unlike the larger tribes) were left alone, they conform to certain cultural norms, thinking, like us, that culture is nature, and instantiate certain attitudes that can be extremely useful for us, who have lost them, in our global predicament.

If I may bring us back to my opening remarks, I would remind ourselves that their living culture is as much on the run, as ungraspable, as anyone else's. We are not proposing to catch their culture, but using some residues to fight the dominant, which have irreducibly changed us. They are themselves interested in changing their life pattern, and, as far as we can, we too should be interested in following into this desire. But must that part of their cultural habit that internalizes the techniques of ecological sanity be irretrievably lost in the urgently needed process of integration, as a minority, into the modern state?

If the non-Eurocentric ecological movement offers us one vision of an undivided world, the women's movement against population control and reproductive engineering offers us another. Here too, the role of the state is interpretable. Mortgaged as it is to the forces of the New World Economic Order, it bows to the dictates of international population control. When McLuhan writes that "ecology shifts the 'White Man's Burden' on to the shoulders of the 'Man-in-the street'" (M 93), he anticipates the kettle logic of today's international population control policies exactly. The blame for the exhaustion of the world's resources is placed on Southern population explosion, and hence upon the poorest women of the South. This in turn— making women an issue—is taken as a justification for so-called aid, and deflects attention from Northern overconsumption: the two faces of globalization. McLuhan himself, did not, of course, think of women at all. But today, in the post-Soviet world, when globalization is the name of the game, a much older topos is activated. I put it this way some years ago: "To mark the moment when not only a civil but a good society is born out of domestic confusion, singular events that break the letter of the law to instill its spirit are often invoked. The protection of women by men often provides such an event."[33] In this phase of capitalism/feminism, it is capitalist women saving the female subaltern. Women in Development (WID) is a subsidiary of USAID, and the Women in Environment and Development Organization

(WEDO) is a generally North-controlled international nongovernmental organization with illustrious Southern spokeswomen. This matronizing and sororizing of women in development is also a way of silencing the subaltern.[34] As for the metaphor of cancer, some think that mistaking so-called economic growth for health links that metaphor much more strongly to the so-called self-determination of capital.[35]

The globe girdlers have neither time nor money for fanfare. "Links between individual women, *critical* grassroots investigation"—these unemphatic phrases in the publicity leaflet of FINRAAGE (Feminist International Network of Resistance to Reproductive and Genetic Engineering), when seen in action, are signposts to that two-way road, with the compromised other as teacher when needed.

If in globe-girdling ecology one confronts the World Bank on one side and on the other side learns to earn a secret encounter, in this sort of feminist initiative against population control and genetic engineering, the movement faces the multinational pharmaceutical on one side, but on the other side there is, again, that slow supplementing tempo of the secret encounter. Otherwise, the metropolitan feminist too often asks all women to become like herself: citizen of a dead-end world. The recoding of the *pouvoir/savoir* of women in globality is an immense field of study. Abortion as right or murder, queerness as preference or sin, surrogacy as fulfillment or trade are only three items within it. A consideration of this epistemic upheaval cannot be launched here.

Yet another item in this necessary and impossible task of globe girdling is resistance to Development as a strategy of alternative development: organizing homeworkers—women who work at home under conditions of "sweating" (piece-wage indefinitely lowered if necessary). This type of woman's labor dates from before capitalism, but under international subcontracting and now post-Fordist capitalism it extends from Aran Islands sweaters to high-tech computer terminal work at home. Now women all over the world are absorbing many of the costs of management, of health care, of workplace safety and the like by working at home. We must therefore learn not to treat homeworking as a peripheral phenomenon, as if it is no more than a continuation of unpaid service in the home. We must keep trying to deconstruct the breach between home and work in the ideology of our global struggle to reach this female bottom layer that holds up contemporary global capital.[36] We have to face this difficult truth: that internalized gendering by women, perceived as ethical choice, accepts exploitation as it accepts sexism in the name of a willing conviction that this is how one is good as a woman, even ethical as a woman. We must fight to pass laws, and be vigilant that they are implemented. But the real force of the struggle comes from the actual players' contemplating the possibility that to organize against homeworking is not to stop being a good woman, a responsible woman, a real woman (therefore with husband and home), a woman, and only then walk with us in a two-way response structure toward the possibility of a presupposition that is more than a task merely of thinking on both sides: that there are more ways than one of being a good woman.[37]

Although no account of contemporary globe-girdling movements is complete without mention of the struggle for justice for homeworkers, homeworking is, strictly speaking, largely an urban phenomenon. It relates to the "global village" insofar as that expression carries the tenor of the McLuhan-Lyotard claim to the appropriations of the rural. It is the exacerbation, in globality, of a residual phenomenon already accompanying industrial capitalism.[38] In the movements for ecological, environmental, and reproductive justice, the rural-local directly fronts the global, and the "village" is a concept-metaphor contaminated by the empirical.

It is this new village form that must teach us to make the globe a world. We must learn to learn. Cultural studies is otherwise only a symptom. Electronification of biodiversity is colonialism's newest trick. When we move from learning to learn ecological sanity from "primitive communism" in the secret encounter to the computerized database, we have moved so far in degree that we have moved in kind. From the infinite care and passion of learning we have bypassed knowledge (which is obsolete now) into the telematic postmodern terrain of information command.[39]

Notes

This essay is an edited version of a speech given in 1993 in Lund, Sweden, under the auspices of a municipal art gallery. The concern of the occasion was a reexamination of Marshall McLuhan's *The Global Village*. I thank Brent Edwards for a speedy and much-needed hatchet job on this piece.

1. Cited in Gayatri Chakravorty Spivak, "More on Power/Knowledge," in *Outside in the Teaching Machine* (New York: Routledge, 1993), 2.

2. See, for example, Arjun Appadurai, "Patriotism and Its Futures," *Public Culture* 5, no. 3 (1993): 411–29.

3. Information on this progressive mortgaging is ceaselessly proliferating on all fronts. For a brief introduction to the principle, see Cheryl Payer, *Lent and Lost: Foreign Credit and Third World Development* (London: Zed, 1991).

4. Marshall McLuhan, *The Global Village: Transformations in World Life and Media in the 21st Century* (New York: Oxford University Press, 1989). Hereafter cited in text as M, with page references following.

5. Jean-François Lyotard, *The Postmodern Condition: A Report on Knowledge*, trans. Geoff Bennington and Brian Massumi (Minneapolis: University of Minnesota Press, 1984).

6. Thomas S. Kuhn, *The Structure of Scientific Revolutions* (Chicago: University of Chicago Press, 1970); Paul K. Feyerabend, *Against Method: Outline of an Anarchistic Theory of Knowledge* (New York: Schocken, 1978); Roy Bhaskar, *A Realist Theory of Science* (Hassocks, Sussex: Harvester, 1978); Nancy Cartwright, *How the Laws of Physics Lie* (Oxford: Clarendon, 1983).

7. To read this move would involve us in the history of the interested differentiation between concept and metaphor, for which there is no time. I refer you to Derrida's essays "White Mythology"—white does also mean "white people" in the essay, White Mythology being reason—and "The *Retrait* of the Metaphor." Jacques Derrida, "White Mythology: Metaphor in the Text of Philosophy," in *Margins of Philosophy*, trans. Alan Bass (Chicago: University of Chicago Press, 1982): 207–71; "The *Retrait* of Metaphor," *Enclitic* 2, no. 2 (1978): 5–33. McLuhan's initiative is also a profound denial of language, which, assuming this model of the brain to be correct (an assumption by no means unquestioned), negotiates the gap between the so-called two sides of the brain in diversified ways that might as well be called "cultural."

8. Benedict Anderson, *Imagined Communities: Reflections on the Origin and Spread of Nationalism* (London: Verso, 1983), 28–40. The conservative and liberal, literary and political, influence of this received idea is vast in its range and scope and long predates Anderson. Margaret Doody's compendious effort at breaking modernist parochialism in *The True Story of the Novel* (New Brunswick, N.J.: Rutgers University Press, 1996) gives hope that similar research can be undertaken for other great ancient traditions. There are disciplinary-historical, indeed disciplinary-historiographical, reasons why such research has not been forthcoming. In the absence of sufficient consideration of counterexamples, there is surely rather a degree of question begging in the transformation into scholarly premise of what is otherwise a cliché. It must, however, be added that such scholarly investigation may soon be dismissed as "nationalist" or "parochial." In the Indian case, a recent "Indian" issue of the *New Yorker* (June 23–30, 1997), firmly founded on what I have long called "sanctioned ignorance," has dismissed all Indian regional literatures, some with millennial histories and active contemporary scenes—Jacques Derrida opened the 1997 Calcutta Book Fair, where most of the books presented were in Bengali and other Indian languages—as a mere curiosity. I understand that *The Vintage Book of Indian Writing*, edited by Salman Rushdie, devotes itself entirely to Indian writing in English. It is sadly evident that, in the global village, the same system of (linguistic) exchange must operate; it must complete the work of imperialism. The well-known words bear repeating: "I have no knowledge of either Sanscrit or Arabic. . . . I have never found one among them [the Orientalists] who could deny that a single shelf of a good European library was worth the whole native literature of India and Arabia. . . . In India, English is the language spoken by the ruling class. It is spoken by the higher class of natives at the seats of Government. It is likely to become the language of commerce throughout the seas of the East. It is the language of two great European communities which are rising, the one in the south of Africa, the other in Australasia. . . . We must at present do our best to form a class who may be interpreters between us and the millions whom we govern; a class of persons, Indian in blood and colour, but English in taste, in opinions, in morals, and in intellect." Thomas Babington Macaulay, "Minute on Indian Education," in *Selected Writings*, ed. John Clive and Thomas Pinney (Chicago: University of Chicago Press, 1972), 241, 242, 249. This regrettable politics of the production of dominant "history," dominant "knowledge," is matched by the *Encyclopedia of Life Support Systems* projected by UNESCO, which "defines" the Aboriginal period of human history as the

"timescale of the *far past* . . . associated with *inactive* approaches in which there is no concern for environmental degradation and sustainability." *EOLSS: Encyclopedia of Life Support Systems: Conceptual Framework* (Whitstable, 1997), 13. It was of course as impossible for the Aboriginal to think sustainability as it was for Aristotle to "decipher . . . the secret of the expression of value," because of "the historical limitation inherent in the society in which [they] lived." Karl Marx, *Capital: A Critique of Political Economy*, vol. 1, trans. Ben Fowkes (New York: Vintage, 1976), 152. Yet the practical philosophy of living in the rhythm of the ecobiome is hardly to be dismissed as "no concern"!

9. I recently discussed the alarming developments of this piety at the Global Knowledge '97 Conference, held, interestingly, in Toronto, Canada. See also Gayatri Chakravorty Spivak, "Claiming Transformations," in *Proceedings of the "Thinking through Feminism" Conference, University of Lancaster, July 17–19, 1997* (forthcoming).

10. "What if there was no other concept of time than the one that Heidegger calls 'vulgar'?" asks the Derrida from whom I learn. However peoples theorized time, the idea that the theory reflected a naturalized mind-set may be a modernist mistake. As much as it is for us, for them too, a theory of time may have been a site of conflict with the vulgar experience of time. "What if the exoteric aporia therefore remained in a certain way irreducible, calling for an endurance, or shall we rather say an *experience* other than that consisting in opposing, from both sides of an indivisible line, an other concept, a nonvulgar concept, to the so-called vulgar concept?" Jacques Derrida, *Aporias*, trans. Thomas Dutoit (Stanford, Calif.: Stanford University Press, 1993), 14.

11. "The hearts of innumerable men and women responded with idealistic fervor to [Cecil Rhodes's] clarion, because it went without saying that it would be good for Africa, or for anywhere else, to be made British. At this point it might be useful to wonder which of the idealisms that make our hearts beat faster will seem wrong-headed to people a hundred years from now." Doris Lessing, *African Laughter: Four Visits to Zimbabwe* (New York: Harper, 1992), 3. For a less nuanced but more detailed account, see Ranajit Guha, "Dominance without Hegemony and Its Historiography," in *Subaltern Studies* (Delhi: Oxford University Press, 1989): 204–5.

12. This monolithic notion of identity quite ignores the critical diversity within a country. I will tax your patience with a single and random example: the "Telecom Revolution" issue of *Seminar* 404 (April 1993), a Delhi-based journal. The editorial politics of the journal are critical of "Development." Yet in this issue, as in others, the journal allows all sides to speak around a topic. The industry-affiliated and management-affiliated "Indians" are of course in favor of versions of the "Development" perspective. One writer, arguing for gradual privatization, asserts: "One aspect of the socialistic pattern ethos was the tendency to make a sacred cow of distributive justice and the needs of the poor rural populace. . . . Even when sincere, it was the wrong priority. The rural and urban poor need food, shelter, drinking water, literacy, health care and many other basic things before they need a telephone"; M. B. Athreya, "Managing Telecoms," 35. Another invokes the "global village" and recommends out-and-out "foreign . . . direct . . . large-scale investment" on the model of Indonesia; N. Vittal, "Shaping a New Future," 39. One sole voice, from applied electronics research at the Indian Institute of Technology, points to the rise of paper consumption (contrary to all predictions), to info-glut, to the fact that "the market by itself is likely to worsen rather than improve certain grievous distortions in our economy," and diagnoses "the real worry today" to be "the distortion caused by the large rent-seeking opportunities offered by technology imports"; P. K. Indiresan, "Social and Economic Implications," 14, 17. Will the "real Indian" please stand up? He will be called a "consensus breaker."

13. Feminists know that every generalization is set askew if you bring in the question of

women. Think of this twist: there is a comparatively innocent pastime in a poor country of wrenching a salary structure from international funds. Even in such cases, there is a difference between the men in, say, the large village or small town, who actually put together this local NGO, and the far less well paid selfless rural woman workers, who use this structure to break out of family restriction and work in the countryside.

14. Here my insistence supplements Etienne Balibar's justly influential work on nationalism, which precomprehends migrancy and proceeds to nationalism by back-formation. Etienne Balibar and Immanuel Wallerstein, *Race, Nation, Class: Ambiguous Identities*, trans. (of Balibar) Chris Turner (New York: Norton, 1991).

15. A note for non-Swedish readers: Karl XII (1682–1718) is the national hero for romantic Swedish nationalists. The last of the absolutist kings, this young militarist, masculist, charismatic monarch fought for eighteen years valiantly, tragically, and in vain—to hold together the extensive Swedish empire. Defeated and bereft, he rode back with one companion over a thousand miles in three days to continue fighting on the home front and was mysteriously shot while inspecting the military situation from the ramparts. It may seem surprising that the man who lost the empire should be a national hero. But identity politics often attempts to renegotiate the state in the name of the nation by way of a promise of the return of the glorious repressed of history. For such "wild" psychoanalyses of the "discontent" of a "nation," an object lost can produce much more politico-ideological momentum. It should perhaps be recalled that in the narrativization of the career of King Rāma in the epic *Rāmāyana*, it is his filial, martial, and racist heroism in unjust banishment that feeds the "national" imaginary; his actual reign is not foregrounded. Indeed, the Sanskrit denomination for India chosen for "contemporary" designation is *Bhārata*, the kingdom of Bharata, Rāma's younger stepbrother, who governed "in his name." "Carrying on Charles XII's task," or "reestablishing a nation to govern in Rāma's name,"are better projects for psychological mobilization.

16. I have written at length of the ethical moment and the secret encounter in the "Afterword" to Mahasweta Devi, *Imaginary Maps*, trans. Gayatri Chakravorty Spivak (New York: Routledge, 1995), 197–205. Friends have asked me what I meant by writing: "'Culture' is an alibi for 'Development,' which is an alibi for the financialization of the globe. The new subject of 'culture' is the witting or unwitting spokesperson for economic restructuring." "Cultural Studies Questionnaire," *Travesia* 3, nos. 1–2 (1994): 286. I suppose this section is an indirect amplification of that idea.

17. This is included in my "Translator's Preface" to Devi, *Imaginary Maps*, xxiii–xxxi.

18. A subject is never, of course, appropriate to a historical occasion. We are able to read the world historical subject as an absolutely necessary theoretical fiction. Within these constraints, one can think of the mechanics by which groups of subjects as agents are centered. I could even say that I use the word *subject* in the text because *agent* would have been awkward.

19. Antonio Gramsci, "The Intellectuals," in *Selections from the Prison Notebooks*, trans. Quintin Hoare and Geoffrey Nowell Smith (New York: International, 1971), 21.

20. I use the term *New Immigrants* to denote the "massive brain drain from developing countries and [the] 500 per cent increase [in] Asian immigration" after "the Immigration and Nationality Act of October 1, 1965." Maldwyn Allen Jones, *American Immigration* (Chicago: University of Chicago Press, 1992), 266–67.

21. For pedagogic suggestions, see Gayatri Chakravorty Spivak, "Teaching for the Times," in *Decolonizing the Imagination*, ed. Jan Nederveen Pieterse (London: Zed, 1995), 177–202.

22. Bits of this paragraph will appear in my "'India,' Echo and Two Postscripts," in *Echoes from Elsewhere*, ed. David Wills (Baton Rouge: Louisana University Press, forthcoming).

23. Econolynx International, Ltd, "Impact Study of the Multi-Fibre Arrangement (MFA) on Bangladesh," unpublished document, Nepean, Ontario, 1992), i.

24. For a fascinating prehistory of this conflict, see Colleen Lye, "Model Modernity: Writing the Far East," Ph.D. diss. in progress, Columbia University.

25. Abigail Foerstner, "Africa's Holocaust: Alfredo Jaar Creates a Photo Memorial to Rwanda," *Chicago Tribune*, February 19, 1995, "Arts," 26.

26. For the defense, see Amartya Sen, *Education and Training in the 1990s: Developing Countries' Needs and Strategies* (New York: U.N. Development Program, 1989). For the World Bank argument, see George Psacharopoulos, *Higher Education in Developing Countries: A Cost-Benefit Analysis*, World Bank Staff Working Paper no. 440 (Washington, D.C.: World Bank, 1980); and George Psacharopoulos, *Education for Development: An Analysis of Investment Choices* (New York: Oxford University Press for the World Bank, 1985).

27. See Gayatri Chakravorty Spivak, *Outside in the Teaching Machine* (New York: Routledge, 1993), 69.

28. Immanuel Wallerstein's position in "Post-America and the Collapse of Leninism," *Rethinking Marxism* 5, no. 1 (1992): 99–100, remains representative.

29. I. K. Shukla, "'Fear the Hindu' Award," *Frontiers* 271, no. 49 (July 15, 1995): 5–7, a scathing critique of the Indian diasporic in the United States, may be hard for us to stomach, but it is closer to the global text. Contrast Roger Cohen, "A War in the Family," *New York Times Magazine*, August 6, 1995, 32–60, which is basically a celebration of the birth of the first Bosnian American in a Bosnian family divided by the war. But the sentimentality of the piece can only exacerbate divisive feeling in the migrant, which, in the telematic age, can quickly lead to the kind of support for violence through the cultural import-export line that I am describing here.

30. For a critique of the risks of Latin American liberation theologies, see Ofelia Schutte, *Cultural Identity and Social Liberation in Latin American Thought* (Albany: State University of New York Press, 1993), 175–205.

31. After I spoke of the destruction of a centuries-old ecological culture in Bangladesh through the transformation of common property and the substitution of learning by information command and the subsequent transformation of the country into the raw material for maps of investment, Andrew Steer, the deputy director of the Department of Environment at the World Bank, remarked that I had been "giving a sermon" (European Parliament, April 28, 1993). And yet, under the new intellectual capital agreements of the GATT, it is precisely the traditional knowledge of indigenous and rural peoples of the South that is being appropriated, patented, and "sold" back to them by the South, without any attempt at learning the attendant biorhythms that persistently deconstruct the opposition between human and natural. I am not "responsible" enough in a sacrificial tradition to be able to guess, without anthropologistic contamination, how this transfers to human/animal. It is because Derrida is not "responsible" on this terrain that his "New International" is so pretentious and feeble (for extended discussion, see Gayatri Chakravorty Spivak, "Ghostwriting," *Diacritics* 25, no. 2 [1995]: 65–84). U.N. conferences provide alibis for derailing these efforts in the interest of capital rather than the social in the name of an ethics about the achievement of which they know little. The worst offenders, precisely because they dare to witness, are so-called U.S. feminists whose "activism" is merely organizing these conferences with a ferocious leadership complex and an insatiable hunger for publicity. I use these violent adjectives advisedly, to warn against every achievement-of-solidarity claim coming from these quarters, to "work at the screen" of the production of the attendant images.

32. This discussion is indebted to Derrida's scattered writings on responsibility, my understanding of which I have tried to set to work in "Responsibility," *boundary 2* 21, no. 3

(1994): 19–64. The theme of the secret is my vulgarization of a moment in Derrida, "Passions," in *Derrida: A Critical Reader*, ed. David Wood (Cambridge: Blackwell, 1992).

33. Gayatri Chakravorty Spivak, "Can the Subaltern Speak?" in *Marxism and the Interpretation of Culture*, ed. Cary Nelson and Lawrence Grossberg (Urbana: University of Illinois Press, 1988), 298.

34. I have discussed this in "Who Claims Sexuality in the New World Order?" keynote lecture delivered at the Culture, Sex, Economy Conference, University of Melbourne, December 1994.

35. For a more detailed position paper on international population control, see Gayatri Chakravorty Spivak, "A Reply to Gro Harlem Bruntland," *Environment* 37, no. 1 (1995): 2–3. There is a precipitate response to this by Rayah Feldman ("Reply to Gayatri Chakravorty Spivak," *WAF Journal* [Spring 1996]: 5–7), which concludes that "the most important claim in Gayatri Spivak's article is that abortion is not an issue for poor women." My piece remarks that "*where* . . . children mean social security the *right* to abortion may be immaterial" (emphasis added). In such places, women's access to rights in the books is also a prior issue, which could not be spelled out in my brief response. At any rate, my piece does not question the need for access to safe and legal abortion. It simply refuses to give it unquestioned first place everywhere. I quote Feldman's unfortunately divisive document because it is typical of the way in which the critical voice of the South is silenced by conflating it with the forces of cultural conservatism. Feldman cites Madhu Kishwar, who is certainly an eminent feminist urban radical nation-focused international journalist in India; no population control activist, which in no way detracts from her deserved reputation.

36. See Swasti Mitter, *Common Fate, Common Bond* (London: Pluto, 1986); Carol Wolkowitz and Sheila Allen, *Homeworking: Myth and Reality* (London: Macmillan, 1987).

37. "The solution is not in the courts but in an awake, aware people." Mumia Abu-Jamal, *Live from Death Row* (Reading, Mass.: Addison-Wesley, 1995), 102.

38. "Residual" comes from Raymond Williams, "Base and Superstructure in Marxist Cultural Theory," in *Problems in Materialism and Culture* (London: Verso, 1980), 40–42; and *Marxism and Literature* (Oxford: Oxford University Press, 1977), 122ff.

39. What does it mean to say: "Based on this publication, UNDP will begin a process of consultations with indigenous people's organizations in Latin and Central America, Asia and the Pacific and, possibly, Africa. What we will seek is their view of the most appropriate strategies for preserving traditional knowledge and garnering acknowledgment for their innovations and contributions"? Sarah L. Timpson and Luis Gomez-Echeverri, "Foreword," in *Conserving Indigenous Knowledge: Integrating Two Systems of Innovation* (n.p.: UNDP, n.d.), iv. You do not learn mind-sets, "epistemes" if you can think υποκειμενα, by "consulting organizations." For better or for worse, by the time these people have formed organizations to consult with a U.N. body, the discursive formation has already been ruptured. The words *conserving* and *integrating* in the title of the pamphlet tell their own tale. For better or for worse, we are confronting an aporia here. When the work of the rupture is more or less complete—colonization through privatization securely in place—then these conservative integrations will acquire a high degree of convenience. This is the mechanism by which they will have stood the test of time. It is predicated upon the success of imperialist social transformation. This is not a Luddite position, but rather the opposite. I accept the consequences of the technicity of so-called natural intelligence. It cannot be upgraded as so-called artificial intelligence can. Prosthetic arguments for computer-aided education and theories of virtual reality seem by comparison naive.

Part IV ▸ **Responses**

A New Cosmopolitanism Is in the Air:
Some Dialectical Twists and Turns

Rob Wilson

A new cosmopolitanism is in the air, heady with postmodern fusions of cultures and cuisines, mobile with dynamics of capital and consumption, situated within the very public heart of transnational capitalism, and, as the contributions to this collection point out, all too eagerly embracing the post of *postnational* as promissory of some egress from xenophobias of nationalism and traumas of identity politics that have wrought havoc within the twentieth century. This lyric promise of a postnational culture is captured in the first issue of *Public Culture* in 1988, at the threshold of the globalizing era, as Arjun Appadurai and Carol Breckenridge answer the transcultural/transnational question "Why public culture?" with "It's a cosmopolitan world" evocations like the following: "The world of the late twentieth century is increasingly a cosmopolitan world. More people are widely traveled, are catholic in their tastes, are more inclusive in the range of cuisines they consume, are attentive to global media-covered events and are influenced by universal trends in fashion."[1]

Such transnational practices, here figured in the postcolonial shopping-mall sensibility of those who have, and can rise and choose rather than from those more shadowy corridors of the "global assembly line," Euro-trash, or the trickle-down fashion choices of the street people, do seemingly call out for a renewed cosmopolitan framework of understanding, a way of coming to sharper global/local terms with the geopolitical horizon that Pheng Cheah calls "the cosmopolitical." As in some carnivalesque profusion of ethnic mixture, we may see video nights in Kathmandu and Indian dinners in Chicago, a disjunctive, win-win brew for some sites and ecumenical subjects. Unevenly, to be sure, the global has already flowed across national and local borders. Margins and centers collide and interact. We do face a more cosmopolitan situation in which (as Benedict Anderson remarks in his essay on rather anachronistic forms of census-style identification and boundedness) "revolutions in communications and transportation of the post-World War II era have combined with postindustrial world capitalism to produce cross-national migrations on a historically unprecedented scale." Anthologizing the diasporic literary results for a multiculture-hungry yet immigrant-paranoid American market, Garrett Hongo asks of his Asian/Pacific enriched "open boat" of "Asian American" poets, "But can it be fairly judged who is the cosmopolitan and who the provincial?" For "We [Asian Americans as representative Americans] are of the diaspora."[2]

It may paradoxically remain the case that, as Pheng Cheah suggests in his introduction, "nationalism is not antithetical to the cosmopolitanism" we now desire and need, the movement toward a *progressive cosmopolitanism* that he evokes as "socialist cosmopolitanism" and links to the threatened, still-emergent popular nationalisms in the periphery. Citing Samir Amin's vision of uneven and unjust capitalist development of labor in *Re-reading the Postwar Period* (1994), Cheah would counter what he calls a "false imperializing cosmopolitanism" with the more "genuine cosmopolitanism" of something liberating and justice inducing on an international scale and now seen as working through (rather than blithely *posting* at the core of the superstate) such nation-states and spaces of surplus labor on the periphery. Wary of dislocation, this new internationalism is something this collection helps to unpack, as capital itself goes on (to echo John Stuart Mill and the OED) "becoming more and more cosmopolitan."

Almost any use of "cosmopolitan" implies, I think, some embedded geopolitical allegory, a world mapping of contradictory locations and multiple flights from and/or toward the territory/positioning of the local (nation) and world-cultural center (cosmos). The term packs into itself not only the voluntary adventures of liberal self-invention and global travel, but also those less benignly configured mixtures of migration, nomadism, diaspora, tourism, and refugee flight. Hence one must be wary by now of some "multicultural cosmopolitanism" trope packing into its amnesiac postmodern mix the splendors and traumas of the "the immigrant as global cosmopolitan," carrier of some liberal and liberated hybridity, which of course the United States of America represents to the world as capitalist vanguard.[3]

Postmodern cosmopolitanism may itself reflect one *uneven* effect of a "disorganized capitalism" in which conditions of heightened risk, post-Fordist restructuring, cultural loosening, and transnational mobility have made for an aggravated "reflexivity" about physical and social environments as well as about the terms of cultural/national identity and belonging as such.[4] Tracking global/local dialectics, Ulf Hannerz has called attention to (if not endorsed) the rise of a "new class" of transnational cosmopolitans. Armed with free-floating credentials and go-between talents and serving as protean embodiments of important symbolic/economic resources of code switching and "decontextualized cultural capital," they can relocate across "world culture."[5] The scattered location of such cosmopolitan culture is everywhere and nowhere, high, middlebrow and low, and the image of "the indigenous photographer as a kind of bush cosmopolitan" still shocks and amazes the makers of metropolitan culture.[6] Yet such transnational-class cosmopolitans and diasporic opportunists, as Masao Miyoshi contends, "now have and will continue to have disproportionate income and freedom with which to master the new global spatiality."[7]

What I am getting at is that any dialectical unpacking of *cosmopolitan* as sign of geopolitical location will still reveal a storehouse of uneven contradictions, regressive and progressive twists and turns in its historical deployment from the eras of Kant, Goethe, and Marx onward into these postmodern new times. On the one hand, the cosmopolitan can be invoked as a figure for rootless and mobile, avowedly universal, uncommitted, and detached positions (as when Karl Marx castigates a surplus-driven cosmopolitanism that reeks of the mobility of international capital). Jonathan Friedman warns, in his portrait of "disillusioned cosmopolitanism" as a modern fate of ironic self-consciousness toward merely local identity, "[The] Cosmopolitan is, in identity terms, betwixt and between, without being liminal," and as such reflects "the position and identity of an intellectual self situated outside of the local arenas in which he or she moves."[8] Conjunctural of universal and particular if not place and system, the cosmopolitan still reeks of a certain weightlessness and an unwillingness to settle down and commit. For example, cosmopolitan citizens can become contemporary globalists like those "transnational astronaut fathers" shuttling between Hong Kong and Vancouver, for whom (as Aihwa Ong portrays in her essay), "bravado constructs a bearable lightness of being that capital buoyancy can bring."

On the other hand, to speak affirmatively, cosmopolitan can prefigure some "world citizen" at once more enlightened and mobile, all but freed from particularized prejudices, fixed ties, and narrow local/national boundaries. This happens when Karl Marx, in the very same passage (echoed by me above) from the *Communist Manifesto* on how the "bourgeoisie has through its exploitation of the world market given a cosmopolitan character to production and consumption in every country," goes on to show how this cosmopolitan framework liberates liberal-capitalist subjects from "the old local and national seclusion and self-sufficiency" to the point that we can increasingly move beyond narrow-minded local and national frames toward the freer creation of a "world literature" and international forms reflecting this interaction.[9] Taking up the current transnational situation, Paul Bové rephrases this affirmative cosmopolitan sense toward globalization in these scaled-down terms of intervention: "Expertise suggests," he writes with Spinozan wariness toward the being of the market, "that the hybrid intellectual can acquire something like a 'cosmopolitan' as opposed to a global persona or function; the 'cosmopolitan' [as in the cultural criticism of Edward

Said or Gayatri Spivak] can take up the perspectives and knowledge needed to acquire a point of view on the global whether imagined as total or seen in struggle with the local."[10]

The value of this far-reaching collection, then, is to help us to unpack these devious twists and turns of ideology and sentiment, these complex rootings and reroutings of the "cosmopolitan" stance in transnational culture today, when the very dynamics of international production and high finance that Marx dialectically outlined, in affirmative and critical senses, have only intensified. State borders and national formations of eligible citizenship, as Etienne Balibar tracks in his essay (and Bonnie Honig theorizes and laments in another national-imperial context), are more porous and yet have also become more exclusionary, paranoid, re-racialized, and policed by neofundamentalisms. We must begin to conceptualize culture, place, sovereignty, and subjectivity in disorganizing formations and unstable frameworks that can render so-called postnational defenses (and, no less so, the border-crossing "culture of postmodernity") ambiguous and glib, in ways Pheng Cheah is cautionary about in his introduction.

We have only begun to theorize social transformation and globality in a world of transnational and postcolonial interaction where, as Gayatri Chakravorty Spivak quips of "the left multicultural imaginary," it is now Sweden that has become "the last holdout of the Socialist International," and culture itself (as in the cultural studies boom under way) may have already become the unwitting vocabulary (if not unconscious allegory) by which to bespeak the current economic restructuring she calls "the financialization of the globe, or globalization as telematic development." The goal for a certain, soft version of left cosmopolitanism (as in Jean-François Lyotard's global village of postmodern little stories along with an overextended incredulity toward master narratives of capital), as Spivak warns, is "to go back to precapitalist spiritual riches without their attendant [imperialist] discomforts."

Canonical heritages of "the local" and "the national," not to mention such fixities of imperial identity as "Europe," "China," "Japan," and "America," have been set in comparativist motion by the reign of this global market and the impact of new media, offshore finance, and alien inputs. Bruce Robbins captures this *necessary* sense of thinking/feeling our geopolitical situation (if not totality) and the push toward a more trenchantly cosmopolitan understanding of global and local transformations of cultural identity when he urges (in his essay "Comparative Cosmopolitanisms") the following:

> When we speak today of world literature or global culture, we are not naming an optional extension of the canon. We are speaking of a new framing of

the whole that revalues both unfamiliar and long-accepted genres, that produces new concepts and criteria of judgment, and that affects even those critics who never 'do' world literature or colonial discourse at all—that affects all critics, that is, by shifting criticism's whole sense of intellectual enterprise.

For, at best, globalization is generating new forms of reflexivity, altered terms of citizenship, amplified melanges and ties to transnational culture, and thus provoking *an aesthetic of openness* toward otherness that is not just the chance for commodification, spectatorship, and colonization. As Scott Lash and John Urry describe this geopolitical situation in *Economies of Signs and Space,* "Such a cosmopolitanism presupposes extensive patterns of mobility, a stance of openness to others and a willingness to take risks, and an ability to reflect upon and judge aesthetically between different natures, places and societies, both now and in the past."[11]

On the other side of liberal modernity, and speaking from within its mobile terms, Kwame Anthony Appiah puts an autobiographical spin upon the contradictory dialectics of "cosmopolitan" when he theorizes the complicated postcolonial makings of a "rooted cosmopolitanism" and, conversely, "cosmopolitan patriotism" in his own trajectory from Ghana and Africa to England and the United States. Affirmatively aesthetic, Appiah's representative embrace of liberal self-invention ("the tool kit of self-creation") and global mobility ("take your roots with you"), organized around "the cultural variability that cosmopolitanism celebrates," is predicated upon a free market abundance of upward circulation where postmodern heterogeneity will overwhelm ancient domination patterns.

Such an American-centered vision of cosmopolitanism affirms, I would suggest, some mutual space of globality/locality, where the liberal state supports freedom and the nation promotes sentiments of group belonging; in effect, the transnational market is all but etherialized into the space of autonomy and private realization. We stand renewed as free-thinking patriots, as in some American Dream of the Whitmanic Cosmos materialized on a new global scale of imperial disavowal—a figure that, by the way, Americanists themselves are finding it harder to believe in, at home or abroad, when spectacles of uneven development are factored into the cultural equation.[12]

It is exactly such American-based "global asymmetries" that are unmasked by Louisa Schein in her global-local ethnography of the International Symposium on Hmong People held in St. Paul, Minnesota, in 1995 to forge some flexible and pragmatic vision of horizontal solidarity between the Chinese "Miao" and the Hmong overseas as coethnics and business partners in what one of the planners called "a world spread nation." But rather than a free staging of "nonelite cosmopolitanism," what emerged was this: "At the level of structure, then," Schein writes, "the symposium produced a startlingly close replication of an American vision of a global order in which non-Western others supplied exotic culture and raw material for core desires." Aihwa Ong presents a no less wary, complicated, multisituated portrait of "overseas Chinese [who] are key players in the booming economies of the Asia-Pacific," living with the postmodern pressures of capital mobility. As she remarks of the "flexible citizenship" (cum "flexible accumulation") required of such transnational Pacific Rim players, she relocates the *American dream*, as it were, offshore on the Pacific shuttle somewhere between Los Angeles and Hong Kong: "Thus for Hong Kong Chinese," Ong observes, "for whom the meanings of motherland, country, and family have long been discontinuous and even contradictory, legal citizenship is sought not necessarily in the sites where one conducts one's livelihood, but in places where one's family can pursue the 'American dream.'" Ong rightly warns that "a different kind of cosmopolitical right is at play," as in her figuration of border-running executives with no state loyalty but flexible citizenships and cultural identities in the service of maximal profit to family and self.

If haunted by some post-Kantian dream of liberal self-invention and perpetual peace, if not some imaginary figuration of international socialism awakened from within the seeming closures of transnational capitalism as world-system, the scaled-down measure of what James Clifford has called "discrepant cosmopolitanisms" must be taken in both local and global senses, in official and vernacular contexts that deform and bewilder easy semantic practice or indictment of the cosmopolitical: "In this emphasis we avoid, at least, the excessive localism of particularist cultural relativism, as well as the overly global vision of a capitalist or technocratic monoculture."[13] Forging a fluid poetics of multiple diasporas emerging in between the tired binary of McWorld and jihad, Clifford evokes not so much a postnational as a "postcultural" condition of contemporary globalism in which centers and peripheries are mutually entangled, local frontiers dissolve, and borders have become entry points for uncanny mixes, amazed mirrorings, and creolized representations. Cosmopolitan hybridity as such has seemingly become some normative postmodern condition in the city and bush. And yet, "like nations," as Bruce Robbins puts it in his introduction (and exemplifies in his far-reaching essay on this new sensibility), these discrepant "cosmopolitanisms are now plural and particular," hence need to be situated, conjoined, compared, and unpacked in all their contextual ambiguity, material embodiment, and idealist promise. Tracking the spread of the "new cosmopolitan"

vocabulary across various genres as a hunger for reflexively situated universals, Amanda Anderson notes that the topos of "cosmopolitanism has repeatedly emerged at times [from Seneca to Julia Kristeva] when the world
has suddenly seemed to expand in unassimilable ways" and the tired discourse of "universalism needs the rhetoric of worldliness that cosmopolitanism provides."

Still, the question remains, amid such post-Kantian heteroglossia of context and ambiguity of usage, such "universal abandon" as portrayed in the
thick-and-thin conceptualizations of morality, loyalty, and reason by Richard
Rorty in his essay here, how can cosmopolitanism be invoked in any kind of
critical or normative sense, as Robbins and others would want to use it ("essays in this collection take the risk of trying to locate or embody cosmopolitanism without renouncing its critical, normative power"). Given its free-
floating mobility, its heritage of privilege, detachment, and ethnographic
gaze, how can cosmopolitanism be used to imply some kind of coherent
geopolitical allegory or progressive narrative of cultural-political vision? The
push toward cosmopolitan globality, if necessary, is ambiguous in its tactics
and goals.

What indeed would the imperatives, norms, and tactics of a "global
moral community" be when, as Rorty advises postmodern philosophers of
liberal reason and enlightenment loyalties, "the rhetoric that we Westerners
use in trying to get everybody to be more like us would be improved if we
were more frankly ethnocentric and less professedly universalist"? The cosmopolitanism of the Enlightenment project, which viewed "perpetual
peace" as the fulfillment of some historical vocation on a global (or at least
European) scale, is, as Allen W. Wood reminds us in his analysis of Kant, "rejected equally by communitarians and cultural relativists," even if what the
international system still needs is a vision of "peaceful cosmopolitan federation" that is not just that of the World Bank or IMF. But if, at a more radical
extreme of Western social vision, the old internationalism is dead (or at least
moribund) at century's end, new social movements of women, ecology,
peace, human rights, and regional organization (as Peter Waterman et al. remind us) take energy, strategy, and direction from linking the grassroots
(local) to the international (global) in ways that can only be affirmed as "critical cosmopolitanism."[14] In the wake of certain forms of state socialism and
the triumphs of capital on a new scale, the assessment of Allen W. Wood
that "the twentieth century has not been the century of enlightenment, but
the century of disillusionment" should give us pause and stimulate critique,
at multiple—global, national, and local—levels of commitment.

If many of the essays in this volume can be seen as rejecting a certain kind of "romantic localism" as the foundational basis of social solidarity, horizontal fraternity, and primary loyalty, the danger at times in this collection is a dialectically related one: cosmopolitanism generated as a discourse of romanticized globalism, as I have been suggesting, at once reflecting a U.S.-centered ideal of multiple belonging and international community (what Robbins affirms as "some transnational sort of fellowship") and thus all too blithely at times bespeaking a border-crossing postcolonial expansiveness that somehow will spell freedom, equality, and justice on a new scale of human solidarity. This win-win linking of the national/local to cosmopolitan forms of the global dynamic is something Stuart Hall had warned against in his cautionary mapping of "postmodern" global/local dynamics as implicitly serving dominant interests and the consumer-culture hegemony of American capital.[15]

Earlier, in the more "Fordist" moment of U.S. internationalization, Antonio Gramsci had critiqued a certain kind of "vague 'cosmopolitanism'" of the cultural critic as an imperialist legacy of mobility coming down from Catholicism and the Latinate culture of the Roman Empire to internationalize—and, in effect, delink—the formation of Italian intellectuals from their regional, "organic," and national struggles. Later, in postcolonial contexts, Frantz Fanon and others (in a criticism echoed by Rob Nixon against V. S. Naipaul, and Tim Brennan against Salman Rushdie) dismantled a certain kind of free-floating comprador cosmopolitanism as undermining the will to "national vocation" and Third World struggles to decolonize.[16] These critiques must, given this globalizing moment of postnationality/postmodernity reaching out from the U.S. and European core, give us critical pause. Several essays here reflect upon such warnings. For such "cosmopolitan" stances may effectively be tied, in contemporary U.S. stratifications, to a residual professional idealism and cheery-pluralist politics of liberal-market selfhood (at times more Emersonian than Kantian in its pragmatic applications as literature, cultural criticism, and philosophy) that still deforms the political economy in its "postnational" reach outward, from superpower centers, toward generating what Ulf Hannerz has called the "context-free cultural capital" and semiotic reflexivity—toward national identity, commitment, and location—of these emerging transnational intellectuals.

Still, it does not do to make cosmopolitanism as such simply into another apology for, and mere reflex of, the hybrid dynamics of global capital in its transnational reach across state borders and upon the imagined communities/belated ideologies of the nation.[17] Economic advantage and military might make it all the more imperative for American cultural critics, as Bruce Robbins concludes in his introduction to this volume, to measure not just the pride but the shame and trauma of the superpower nation, the damages that can be wrought in distant places and upon diverse citizens and races in the world within which our economy is so deeply imbricated. A new—nonimperial—cosmopolitanism, as Scott L. Malcomson suggests and gestures toward in his essay here, represents a strategic bargain with globality and enacts a multisituated struggle toward securing universal human rights and distant impacts, given a world order where "capital must become more heterogeneous, or multicultural, in order to find new markets and so continue expansion."

As modernist visions of cosmopolitan belonging have "yielded ground to the prejudices of identity and internationality" (meaning the political system of nation-states that developed under capitalism), Jonathan Rée can only wonder (after tracking down various national delusions of origin, territory, language, and culture as self-evident wholes), "Is it possible to hope for a new cosmopolitanism, after internationality?" All but posting the national and the local as sites of peculiar, bounded, and prejudicial belonging that go on aggravating political differences, Rée turns at the end of his end-of-millennium essay to invoke the cosmopolitical as some vision of a utopic transnational community—"a postnational and postinternational world, which would no longer make a fetish of political form; a new cosmopolitan world, which could put the illusions of internationality [and the nation system] behind it, for good." Needless to say, the gesture is a desperate one, filled with historical pathos and imaginative longing, and challenged by other findings in this collection itself, not to mention struggles for recuperated nationhood from Hawaii to Palestine to Ireland.

At century's end, perhaps these new forces of globalization can now make possible, as Lash and Urry et al. suggest, the formation of a growing cosmopolitanism in which we are able "to extend reflexive critique beyond the 'neo-tribes,' a chance for translation between speech communities" to take place in nondomineering ways, across geopolitical situations, and in multiple media.[18] It would be a material cosmopolitanism that dreams not of eternal traveling or of textualizing "hybridization as the undoing of the imperialist or cosmopolitical-cultural project" (see Pheng Cheah's critique of postcoloniality discourse as "closet idealism"). It would be a material cosmopolitanism that builds outward from nation-state grounding in place toward imagined forms of global civil society and interconnected public spheres. "Thinking and feeling beyond the nation," as Cheah and Robbins suggest in this thick-descriptive, multiple-genre collection, we can arrive at the end-of-millennium condition of a spiritual cosmopolitanism disgusted with legacies of imperialism and delusions of free-floating irony. Still, this collection wagers, the global terrain of the cosmopolitical does not belong only to transnational capital, imperial power, and jeremiad despair, but to new cultures of global/local mixture whose hope-generating resources can be marshaled to serve better ends than the xenophobic hegemony of mononations, monoraces, and monocreeds.

Notes

1. Arjun Appadurai and Carol A. Breckenridge, "Why Public Culture?" *Public Culture* 1, no. 1 (1988): 5.
2. Garrett Hongo, "Introduction," in *The Open Boat: Poems from Asian America*, ed. Garrett Hongo (New York: Anchor, 1993), xx.
3. See Frederick Buell's free-floating vision of postmodern hybridity and immigrant visions in *National Culture and the New Global System* (Baltimore: Johns Hopkins University Press, 1994), 205. Affirmative of the cosmopolitan carnival driven by American consumer culture, Buell's view on such matters remains close to Pico Iyer's in *Video Night in Kathmandu* (1988): "He celebrates the vitality of the cultural heterogeneity produced when a postmodernizing globalization of American commercial popular culture incites cultures and communities worldwide to produce a carnivalesque profusion of hybrid forms" (11). On the "indifferent" cosmopolitan hybridity of Bharati Mukherjee's American immigrants, see Fred Pfeil's critique, "No Basta Teorizar: In-Difference to Solidarity in Contemporary Fiction, Theory, and Practice," in *Scattered Hegemonies: Postmodernity and Transnational Feminist Practices*, ed. Inderpal Grewal and Caren Kaplan (Minneapolis: University of Minnesota Press, 1994), 197–230.
4. See Scott Lash and John Urry, *Economies of Signs and Space* (London: Sage, 1994), chap. 10.
5. Ulf Hannerz, "Cosmopolitans and Locals in World Culture," *Theory, Culture & Society* 7 (1990): 237–52.
6. See Faye Ginsburg, "Aboriginal Media and the Australian Imaginary," *Public Culture* 5 (1993): 557–78.
7. Masao Miyoshi, "Sites of Resistance in the Global System," *boundary* 2 22 (1995): 70.
8. Jonathan Friedman, "Global System, Globalization, and the Parameters of Modernity," in *Global Modernities*, ed. Mike Featherstone, Scott Lash, and Roland Robertson (London: Sage, 1995), 78.
9. Karl Marx, "Manifesto of the Communist Party," in *The Revolutions of 1848: Political Writings*, vol. 1 (Harmondsworth: Penguin, 1973), 70–71.
10. Paul Bové, "Afterword: Memory and Thought," in *Global/Local: Cultural Production and the Transnational Imaginary*, ed. Rob Wilson and Wimal Dissanayake (Durham, N.C.: Duke University Press, 1996), 378.
11. Lash and Urry, *Economies of Signs and Space*, 256.
12. See the array of critical essays gathered in Amy Kaplan and Donald E. Pease, eds., *Cultures of United States Imperialism* (Durham, N.C.: Duke University Press, 1993), for example, "'Make My Day!': Spectacle as Amnesia in Imperial Politics and the Sequel" by Michael Rogin (499–534).
13. James Clifford, "Traveling Cultures," in *Cultural Studies*, ed. Lawrence Grossberg, Cary Nelson, and Paula A. Treichler (New York: Routledge, 1992), 98.
14. Peter Waterman, "Internationalism Is Dead! Long Live Global Solidarity," in *Global*

Visions: Beyond the New World Order, ed. Jeremy Brecher, John Brown Childs, and Jill Cutler (Boston: South End, 1993), 257–61.

15. Stuart Hall, "The Local and the Global: Globalization and Ethnicity," in *Culture, Globalization, and the World-System*, ed. Anthony King (Binghamton: State University of New York at Binghamton, 1991), 19–40.

16. Antonio Gramsci, *Selections from the Prison Notebooks*, ed. and trans. Quintin Hoare and Geoffrey Nowell Smith (New York: International, 1971), 17. For related concerns in the contemporary moment of postmodern celebrity and image engineering, see Paul Bové on the cautionary work of Régis Debray, "Celebrity and Betrayal: The High Intellectuals of Postmodern Culture," in *In the Wake of Theory* (Hanover, N.H.: Wesleyan University Press, 1992), 98–121.

17. Refusing center-periphery and global-local models as residually colonial and Marxist-modernist, a collection like *Scattered Hegemonies* ends up using the term *transnational* in an affirmative but rather empty sense, as in the de-differentiated longing for "transnational feminist solidarity" across racial, class, nation, and gender lines. Inderpal Grewal and Caren Kaplan, "Introduction: Transnational Feminist Practices and Questions of Postmodernity," in *Scattered Hegemonies: Postmodernity and Transnational Feminist Practices*, ed. Inderpal Grewal and Caren Kaplan (Minneapolis: University of Minnesota Press, 1994), 9–15.

18. Lash and Urry, *Economies of Signs and Space*, 143.

Mixed Feelings

James Clifford

Cosmopolitanism evokes mixed feelings. This, at least, emerges with clarity from the essays collected here. Considered as a range of cultural practices in the contemporary world of nations and global capital, cosmopolitanism points in ambiguous political directions. Nor is it even certain that the term, used in the plural here, names a coherent cluster of experiences. Yet it recognizes something important: worldly, productive sites of crossing; complex, unfinished paths between local and global attachments. Cosmopolitanism, viewed without universalist nostalgia, seems to hold a promise. Of what?

Kwame Anthony Appiah offers a moving vision, bringing to his discussions of U.S. political culture a perspective with braided Western and non-Western roots. His personal history of "cosmopolitan patriotism" actively resists the idea that national cultural belonging is an all-or-nothing proposition. Exiles, immigrants, diasporic dwellers "take their roots with them." This at least is his hope, an ideal that resonates with other recent attempts to articulate forms of "cultural citizenship." Appiah draws on, and complicates, a specific cosmopolitan tradition: several centuries of "Pan-African" thought, desire, and action. This tradition has sustained ways to live and contribute to one part of the word while keeping meaningful attachments with another. Appiah's "American" remix of his father's British/Ghanaian mix confirms the tradition while challenging its more reductive Afrocentric versions.

One wonders whether a transatlantic democratic political tradition of this kind could be part of the edifying "story" Richard Rorty, in his final pages, imagines "the West" telling "the non-West." Is Rorty's rigorous embrace of "ethnocentrism" a way of affirming roots in order to reach beyond them more honestly? Should we think of his imagined choice between cultural/political traditions as an invitation to discussion and translation? Or is it a take-it-or-leave-it proposition? Hard to tell. And is Rorty's way of being "a loyal Westerner" much like Appiah's father's syncretic way of being a loyal African? Probably not. In any event, the contrast between Rorty's rootedness and Appiah's routedness brings us directly into the ambivalent force field that Bruce Robbins and Pheng Cheah aptly term the "cosmopolitical."

Aihwa Ong's unblinking account of "flexible citizenship" among Chinese business families tracks loyalties that are governed by rigid kinship structures, reinstating "premodern forms of children, gender, and class oppressions." Moreover, to the extent that these relatively affluent groups "spin human relations across space," they do it in search of "ever new niches to exploit." Their cosmopolitan practices amount, finally, to "a postmodern habitus that is finely tuned to the turbulence of late capitalism." Whatever diverse paths this "turbulence" allows, there is nothing automatically democratic about crossing borders or living in diaspora.

Overseas Chinese investors meddle in mainland development. Diasporic Hindu nationalists bankroll and vicariously participate in risk-free ethnic chauvinism on the subcontinent. Benedict Anderson sees a manipulated and manipulative "long-distance nationalism" in these, and indeed in most experiences of diaspora. There are certainly quite a few examples to support his view. But the growing literature on diasporas, immigration cycles, remittance economies, and regional (translocal, not global) borderlands suggests a rather more complex range of experiences.[1] Moreover, this panoply of hybrid cultures and flexible citizenships is not merely the result, as one sometimes hears, of a single "postcolonial" experience, or of a managed "postmodernism." Caution and attentiveness are in order.

Any array of comparative cosmopolitanisms must cobble together quite disparate histories. The term *cosmopolitan*, separated from its (European) universalist moorings, quickly becomes a traveling signifier, a term always in danger of breaking up into partial equivalences: exile, immigration, migrancy, diaspora, border crossing, pilgrimage, tourism. Thus, before we even begin to speak of "cosmopolitanisms" we are caught up in the unmanageable, risky work of translation. Amanda Anderson, Bonnie Honig, and Gayatri Spivak keep this predicament clearly in sight.

Louisa Schein's complex ethnographic account of a Hmong symposium in St. Paul, Minnesota, is particularly revealing. She effectively warns against any tendency to romanticize nonelite cosmopolitanisms, and she insists, like others in the book, that transnational and national cultural forms are mutually constitutive. Her account shows diasporic Hmong in the midst of becoming U.S. "minorities," their ongoing transpacific connections foreshortened by this project. One wonders, however, whether the symposium she portrays as affirming the global centrality of the United States would have been somewhat different at a less strained political moment, when China might have allowed more delegates to attend. Moreover, the "homeland nostalgia" she glosses as superficial and standardized is surely worth deeper ethnographic probing. (Here Honig's rich conception of "mourning" could be relevant.) Schein's account draws primarily from the structure of the event rather than from its reception(s).

With this limitation, she shows effectively how nation-states inflect subaltern transnational "identities." And, importantly, her argument is not directed toward reasserting a view of immigration as assimilation. Nor is it a matter of saying that the involvement of "the state" in the articulation of specific cosmopolitanisms is a matter of manipulative agency or top-down control. Rather, in her final example of Hmong Boy Scout activities, she argues that national orders are, in practice, hybrid processes of reconstitution, not paths to a continuous national culture. Her good news/bad news is that national orders are more flexible and creative, less rigid and monolithic than often assumed by both their champions and their critics. Nonelite cosmopolitanisms contribute to the normal remaking of national multicultures and render them less fixed.

In Louisa Schein's contribution, and in Benedict Anderson's advocacy of the "unbound seriality" of national allegiances and visions, the nation ceases to function as cosmopolitanism's "other." Anderson effectively stresses that national movements open people to wider solidarities and new senses of self and possibility. His story of a Javanese girl's liberation through access to the new international status of "typist" is almost worth the price of admission. There is a price. For of course national orders *also* close down frontiers, reject threatening "others," police identities, and generally behave like the "bound" ethnic movements Anderson expels to a separate category. I remain skeptical whether clear distinctions such as nation/ethnicity, nation/state, progressive/bourgeois, "bound"/ "unbound" can be sustained for very long. The last-named pair, as used by Anderson, is a heuristic device that organizes rich historic material around a *tension* inherent in the forces unleashed by national/international formations. But by the end of his essay the tension freezes into a moralized *binary*. The "bound"/"unbound" opposition becomes, finally, a club wielded against an ethnic politics reductively portrayed as the simple product of state censuses.

Distinguishing good and bad, progressive and regressive nationalisms is a risky undertaking. We are always dealing with a double-edged sword. The problem is particularly troublesome for the "popular nationalist" hope sustained by theorists such as Samir Amin and, with significant reservations, by Pheng Cheah in his theoretically sophisticated contributions to the volume. Any Leninist notion that democratic nationalisms can be stages on the path to socialist internationalism should by now evoke immediate skepticism. For it is hard to persuade oneself that there is any reliable way to make safe for progressive democracy certain *aspects* of nationalism (or perhaps it would be better to say *moments*: the early, Mazzinian mobilization, or the moment of anticolonial resistance in the periphery) while relegating to the bourgeois, capitalist, ethnic, comprador state those aspects or moments that prove oppressive or xenophobic. The hope that "popular" nationalisms will ultimately be different from other nationalisms is surely utopian.

Pheng Cheah accepts Amin's notion that "popular national" struggles are the only site for serious transformative politics, but he rejects any notion that these struggles can revolutionize or transcend the horizons of contemporary nation-states in a neocolonial political economy. All they can do is "loosen the hyphen" between nation and state. "Cosmopolitical" experiences, in this perspective, can never be redemptive or transcendent. Pheng Cheah's conclusion is grimly rigorous. And although I share his sense of historical predicament, I would nonetheless urge recognition for a broader range of cosmopolitical formations than those subsumed (teleologically?) under the formula "nationalism as given culture in neocolonial globilization." Discrepant cosmopolitanisms such as "Fourth World" tribal movements may work within and against national structures, but they cannot, I think, be said to work "through" them. The colonial or postcolonial nation is only one of their horizons. The same can be said of cosmopolitanisms articulated in terms of world religions, or those expressed in persistent cultural forms such as oral tradition or music. We need to distinguish different degrees of entanglement in national/transnational orders.

Whatever the ultimate value of the term *cosmopolitan*, pluralized to account for a range of uneven affiliations, it points, at least, toward alternative notions of "cultural" identity. It undermines the "naturalness" of ethnic absolutisms, whether articulated at the nation-state, tribal, or minority level. Discrepant cosmopolitanisms begin and end with historical interconnection and often violent attachment. Cultural separation and claims for ethnic purity appear as strategies within this historical context, moments not ends. Such a perspective opens up a more complex, humane understanding of hybrid realities. For example, it makes room for immigration policies that do not presume all-or-nothing assimilation. "English only" legislation, in this view, appears not as a reestablishment of something normal or natural but rather as a violent, probably futile, attempt to create and police an area of cultural homogeneity.

A focus on *discrepant* cosmopolitanisms also allows us to hold on to the idea that whereas something like economic and political equality are crucial political goals, something like cultural similarity is not. It gives us a way of perceiving, and valuing, different forms of encounter, negotiation, and multiple affiliation rather than simply different "cultures" or "identities." And surely any move beyond what Bernice Johnson Reagon calls the "barred room" of identity (people just like us) into the risky world of coalition politics, presupposes encounters between worldly historical actors willing to link up aspects of their complex, different experiences.[2]

Whereas separatist moments—cultural "delinking"—may be necessary

365

tactics of resistance to homogenizing pressures, the cosmopolitan agendas probed in this book all assume that local autonomy will necessarily be asserted within and against larger contexts structured by national and transnational forces. Even in the limit cases of "first nation," or "tribal," sovereignty movements, the goal is not complete separation from the global systems that descended on indigenous peoples during the past few centuries. The struggle is rather for a real degree of control over areas such as land and culture, more power in managing the ongoing interaction.

The authors of the essays collected here largely agree that any vision of an emerging "postnational" world is problematic. Global capital flows, financial institutions, commodity and labor markets unevenly challenge *and* depend on nation-states. Moreover, it is now widely understood that the capitalist world system allows/produces differences as well as commonalities.[3] Modern hybrid "cultural" forms, articulating local, national, and global relations, do not cumulate as a smooth process of "Westernization." What are we to think of the entangled, impure, stubborn collective differences that are reproduced through and against nations and capital? Are they evidence of human visions and experiences that escape, point beyond, even challenge, a flexibly hegemonic world political economy? Or are they simply areas of diversity and identity within a system that tolerates and commodifies diverse cultural forms as long as they do not fundamentally challenge politicaleconomic control? Because good arguments can, I think, be made in support of each of these positions, it behooves us not to repress our mixed feelings, to be skeptical of simple stories, utopic or dystopic projections.

In this spirit I would offer a rather different version of the "hybridity theory" Pheng Cheah attributes to me and to Homi Bhabha. It does not rely, as he asserts, on an ontology of "linguistic freedom and cultural flux." Whatever "freedom" is asserted is not inherent in discourse (on this I may differ somewhat from Bhabha), but is, rather, a pragmatic response, making the best of given (often bad) situations. The cultural inventiveness at stake is a matter of specific juxtapositions, selections, and overlays offered and imposed in limited historical conjunctures. Thus it has little to do with the "flux," the freedom from "givenness," or the "cultural" transcendence of "nature" he reads into our invocations of transgression and invention. His conflation of hybrid agency, which is all about working between given historical powers, and Marxist *Aufhebung* or revolutionary teleology seems particularly forced.[4]

If there is utopia here, it is utopia in a minor key, or, as I have argued elsewhere, a utopic/dystopic tension.[5] In this vision, colonial, postcolonial, and neocolonial histories (abetted by world wars, political repression and genocide, capital, and labor and market displacements) have produced a variety of elite and subaltern experiences of movement among cultures, polities, and economies. In these contexts people have understood their fate, negotiated with difference, preserved a dignity in confrontation, survived as cultural/political subjects through complex tactics of separatism *and* accommodation. Some have moved or been moved physically; some have stayed or been confined in a locale. You do not, of course, have to leave home to be confronted with the concrete challenges of hybrid agency. (At least since 1492, the outside world is guaranteed to find you!) In these diverse cosmopolitical encounters, specific, hybrid accommodations with national and transnational forces are worked out.

This historical vision does not place much immediate hope in the aggregation of a "socialist" or "progressive" cosmopolitan front at a scale capable of broadly resisting or bringing about a revolution in the capitalist world system. It finds some usable hope in people's resilient and inventive strategies for survival, for the maintenance of dignity and a limited, but important, autonomy. Moreover, it sees that separatism is not an option for the vast majority. An ability to sustain and rearticulate a sense of who one is by appropriating, cutting, and mixing cultural forms appears as a significant alternative to homogenizing, normalizing disciplines exercised at national and transnational levels. This view also resists the assumption that human sociopolitical belonging in the twentieth century is most naturally, or inevitably, articulated at the nation-state level. While recognizing the enormous appeal of national affiliations, it does not assume the nation-state (however loose the hyphen) to be "given" by History. At any rate, it is not the only thing given.

People have, for many centuries, constructed their sense of belonging, their notions of home, of spiritual and bodily power and freedom, along a continuum of sociospatial attachments. These extend from local valleys and neighborhoods to denser urban sites of encounter and relative anonymity, from national communities tied to a territory to affiliations across borders and oceans. In these diverse contact zones, people sustain critical, non-absolutist strategies for survival and action in a world where space is always already invaded. These competences can be redeemed under a sign of hope as "discrepant cosmopolitanisms." But it is a chastened hope associated more with survival and the ability to articulate locally meaningful, relational futures than with transformation at a systemic level.

Many critics, especially those struggling to sustain a more coherent, transformative left politics, have been quick to object that this is not enough. They are right. (I demur only when the statement "This—cultural politics—is not political *enough*" escalates to the claim "This is not *really* political," or "This is *apolitical*, thus ungrounded, reactionary, etc.") But it is easier, these days, to say what is *not* sufficient than to give a realistic account of what *is* enough. Cosmopolitan competences, the arts of crossing, translation, and hybridity do not inevitably lead in "progressive" (generally democratic and socialist) directions. Indeed, they can undermine the strategic equivalences, the identifications, needed to sustain large-scale political movements. But if cosmopolitan historical experiences, by themselves, are not enough, they do provide concrete starting points that can be hooked together—articulated (in Stuart Hall's updated Gramscian sense), not transcended—through political work.

In my view, "democratic socialism" names a hegemonic project most likely to negotiate the sometimes contradictory goals of social/economic equality and national, regional, cultural, gender, racial, and sexual diversity. Any dream of *transcending* such differences in a revolutionary synthesis has been pretty thoroughly discredited by the history of divisions on the left. The folding of different bodies and histories into one big union was never a realistic long-term goal. Thus if we must work *through and among* differences of culture and identity, it is all the more critical to recognize, and mobilize, nonuniversalist cosmopolitanisms, with their abilities to translate different histories, to cross narrow identities, to lend themselves to others' projects.

At what social and spatial "levels" should, can, the coalitional work proceed? It would be futile to prescribe too narrowly. Debates are still unresolved over "left nationalist" strategies and the degree to which socialist energies should be channeled through national legislative priorities, traditional union organizing, transnational institutions, or more regional culture- and identity-based social movements. The "cosmopolitical" perspectives developed in this book suggest at least that any strict choice between national and international sites of political/cultural action is an abstraction and a foreshortening of lived realities. We begin with the givenness of national *and* transnational forces, sometimes acting in concert, sometimes in conflict, articulated at different elite and subaltern levels. This is the messy historical material with which democratic socialist alliances must work.

An effective "cosmopolitan" politics on the left? Conceived without nostalgia? We might at least cultivate, as Bruce Robbins does in his chapter in this volume, a clear-sighted awareness of institutional entanglement and a skepticism of the purifying dodges that abound in "political" critique. In the left's current disarray, setting up high standards for radical transformative agency or narrow definitions of "real politics" will only cut off potential allies. The recent widespread recoil from so-called identity politics is a case in point. It reflects an important concern about the fragmentation of post-1960s left coalitions, particularly at the national level. But anti-identity politics often seems to argue that appeals to culture and identity are just mistakes, deviations from "progressive" agendas. Whatever excesses and blind alleys such appeals have produced, the left can hardly be too sanctimonious, given its less than triumphal recent history. In a Gramscian spirit, effective political strategy begins where people *are*, rather than where one wishes they were. For better *and* worse, claims to identity—articulations of ethnic, cultural, gender, and sexual distinction—have emerged as things people, across the globe and the social spectrum, care about. It is surely fruitless to blame this development on postmodern false consciousness or to wish it would all would go away so the left can return to enlightenment universalism, or to an idealized "progressive" past (a past that saw its share of xenophobia).

A more realistic approach would engage in a nondismissive critique of identity politics (this could also help distinguish left criticisms of multiculturalism and all the fragmenting "post-" discourses from right-wing attacks): post-identity politics rather than anti-identity politics. Such a project can, I think, find support in attempts such as the present book, to pluralize and rethink the cosmopolitan. For in cosmopolitical perspective, identity is never only about location, about shoring up a safe "home," crucial as that task may be in certain circumstances. Identity is also, inescapably, about displacement and relocation, the experience of sustaining and mediating complex affiliations, multiple attachments. The challenge is to articulate, not transcend, these aspects of identity in broadly defined democratic socialist coalitions.

Discrepant cosmopolitanisms guarantee nothing politically. They offer no release from mixed feelings, from utopic/dystopic tensions. They do, however, name and make more visible a complex range of intercultural experiences, sites of appropriation and exchange. These cosmopolitical contact zones are traversed by new social movements and global corporations, tribal activists and cultural tourists, migrant worker remittances and e-mail. Nothing is guaranteed, except contamination, messy politics and more translation.

Notes

1. For example, Paul Gilroy, *The Black Atlantic: Double Consciousness and Modernity* (Cambridge: Harvard University Press, 1993); Nestor García Canclini, *Culturas híbridas: Estrategias para entrar y salir de la modernidad* (Mexico City: Editorial Grijalbo,

1990); Sherri Grasmuck and Patricia R. Pessar, *Between Two Islands: Dominican International Migration* (Berkeley: University of California Press, 1991); Roger Rouse, "Mexican Migration and the Social Space of Postmodernism," *Diaspora* 1, no. 1 (1991): 8–23.

2. Bernice Johnson Reagon, "Coalition Politics: Turning the Century," in Barbara Smith, ed., *Home Girls: A Black Feminist Anthology* (New York: Kitchen Table, Women of Color Press, 1983), 356–68.

3. Jonathan Friedman, *Cultural Identity and Global Process* (London: Sage, 1994).

4. Pheng Cheah finds in my work an argument for the existence of (as he puts it in his penultimate paragraph) "a transnational realm of cultural hybridization unmoored and exhibiting a subversive freedom from the weighty constraints of political and economic determinations." It is true that I attach more importance to the ruses and inventions of culture-contact than he apparently does. But that is a far cry from considering them "unmoored," ontologically in "flux," or a realm of "freedom." I do not know how anyone can read, for example, my essay on the Mashpee Indians in *The Predicament of Culture* in this light. A political struggle around "culture" is foregrounded in that essay. But the historical embeddedness of Mashpee's relational cultural formations in political and economic structures is continuously shown. And if the essay holds out some guarded hope for modern tribal agency, it hardly assumes a realm of freedom or transcendence based on an ontology of cultural flux. Pheng Cheah's relentlessly symptomatic reading constructs a simplistic "culturalism" and "hybridity theory." Caveat lector. With respect to my own work at least, the summary descriptions he provides often bear a strained relation to what I have actually written. Indeed, his citations of *Predicament of Culture* tend to be one-sided or inconclusive, and sometimes they directly contradict the assertions they purportedly illustrate (the idea that I adopt a "postcultural" position, for example). Overall, I would have thought that Pheng Cheah might have found my discussions of culture as a "predicament" (that is, a historical site of struggle, not a liberation from nature, and certainly not an idea or condition that can be left behind) congenial in the light of his own trenchant antiteleology and critique of visions of transcendence. On this point I generally agree—while no doubt harboring a few too many wishy-washy humanist hopes. James Clifford, *The Predicament of Culture: Twentieth-Century Ethnography, Literature, and Art* (Cambridge: Harvard University Press, 1988).

5. James Clifford, "Diasporas," *Cultural Anthropology* 9, no. 3 (1994): 302–38.

Contributors

Amanda Anderson is an associate professor at the University of Illinois, where she holds appointments in the Department of English, the Women's Studies Program, and the Unit for Criticism and Interpretive Theory. She is the author of *Tainted Souls and Painted Faces: The Rhetoric of Fallenness in Victorian Culture* (1993) and of several articles on Victorian culture, feminist theory, and critical theory. Her contribution to this volume is drawn from her current project, tentatively titled *Forms of Detachment: Ethics, Aesthetics, and the Challenges of Modernity.*

Benedict Anderson is Aaron L. Binenkorb Professor of International Studies at Cornell University. He is primarily a specialist on the politics and history of Southeast Asia.

Kwame Anthony Appiah is professor of Afro-American studies and philosophy at Harvard University and the author of *In My Father's House: Africa in the Philosophy of Culture*, as well as of an introduction to analytic philosophy, monographs in the philosophy of language, and three novels: *Avenging Angel, Nobody Likes Letitia*, and *Another Death in Venice*. His most recent book is *Color Conscious: The Political Morality of Race*, which is coauthored with Amy Gutmann.

Etienne Balibar, born in Avallon (France), was a student at the Ecole Normale Supérieure. He is currently professor of political and moral philosophy at the University of Paris (Nanterre). He is the author of *Reading Capital* (1965), with Louis Althusser et al.; *Spinoza et la politique* (1985; English translation forthcoming); *Race, Nation, Class* (1988), with Immanuel Wallerstein; *The Philosophy of Marx* (1993); and *Masses, Classes, Ideas* (1994).

Pheng Cheah was a student at Cornell University and is currently associate professor of English at Northwestern University. He is coeditor of *Thinking through the Body of the Law* (1996) and author of articles on legal philosophy, neocolonial globalization, feminist theory, and contemporary critical theory. He is also a lawyer.

James Clifford is professor in the History of Consciousness Department, University of California, Santa Cruz. He is the author of *Person and Myth: Mau-*

rice Leenhardt in the Melanesian World (1982) and editor (with George Marcus) of *Writing Culture: The Poetics and Politics of Ethnography* (1986). His most recent books are *The Predicament of Culture* (1988) and *Routes: Travel and Translation in the Late Twentieth Century* (1997).

Bonnie Honig is professor of political science at Northwestern University. She is the author of *Political Theory and the Displacement of Politics* (1993) and the editor of *Feminist Interpretations of Hannah Arendt* (1995). She is currently completing a book titled *No Place like Home: Democracy and the Politics of Foreignness.*

Scott L. Malcomson is the author of *Empire's Edge: Travels in Southeastern Europe, Turkey, and Central Asia* (1995) and *Tuturani: A Political Journey in the Pacific Islands* (1990). His essays and reports have appeared in numerous publications, including *Transition,* the *New Yorker, London Review of Books,* the *New Republic, Lettre Internationale,* and the *Voice Literary Supplement.* He is currently writing a history of racial separatism.

Aihwa Ong is associate professor of anthropology at the University of California, Berkeley. Her books are *Spirits of Resistance and Capitalist Discipline: Factory Women in Malaysia* (1987); *Bewitching Women, Pious Men: Gender and Body Politics in Southeast Asia* (coeditor Michael Peletz; 1995); and *Ungrounded Empires: The Cultural Politics of Modern Chinese Transnationalism* (coeditor Don Nonini; 1997). She is completing a book titled *Flexible Citizenship.*

Jonathan Rée teaches philosophy at Middlesex University in London, England. His books include *Proletarian Philosophers* (1984) and *Philosophical Tales* (1987). He is currently working on two books: a historical study of the human voice and a history of philosophy and the English language.

Bruce Robbins teaches English and comparative literature at Rutgers University. He is the author of *Secular Vocations: Intellectuals, Professionalism, Culture* (1993) and editor of *Intellectuals: Aesthetics, Politics, Academics* (Minnesota, 1990) and *The Phantom Public Sphere* (Minnesota, 1993). His book *The Servant's Hand: English Fiction from Below* was reissued in paperback in 1993. He is also a coeditor of *Social Text.*

Richard Rorty is University Professor of Humanities at the University of Virginia. He previously taught at Wellesley and at Princeton. He is the author of *Philosophy and the Mirror of Nature* and *Contingency, Irony, and Solidarity,* and he is currently writing a short book on the history of the left in twentieth-century America.

Louisa Schein teaches anthropology at Rutgers University, New Brunswick, and specializes in gender, ethnicity, sexuality, and transnational processes. She has conducted rural and urban fieldwork in China since 1982 and is currently writing a book on cultural politics in China's post-Mao era. Her ongoing research includes a multisite project on the forging of transnationality among the Hmong/Miao ethnic group.

Gayatri Chakravorty Spivak is Avalon Foundation Professor in the Humanities at Columbia University. She has published critical translations of Jacques Derrida's *De la grammatologie* (1976) and Mahasweta Devi's *Imaginary Maps* (1994). Her own publications include *In Other Worlds* (1987) and *Outside in the Teaching Machine* (1993). *The Spivak Reader* was published in 1996. Her latest book is *Don't Call Me Postcolonial: From Kant to Kawakubo.*

Rob Wilson teaches in the English Department at the University of Hawaii at Manoa. He is the author of *American Sublime* (1991) and *Waking in Seoul* (1988), and coeditor of *Global/Local: Cultural Production and the Transnational Imaginary* (1996) and *Asia/Pacific as Space of Cultural Production* (1995).

Allen W. Wood received a B.A. at Reed College and a Ph.D. at Yale University. For many years he taught at Cornell University, and he is now professor of philosophy at Yale University. He has numerous publications on the history of German philosophy in the eighteenth and nineteenth centuries, chiefly the philosophies of Kant, Fichte, Hegel, and Marx, and on topics in moral and political philosophy.

Index

375